Learning Windows® 98

Margaret Brown

DDC *Publishing*

To My Husband Larry

Thank you for hanging in there.

Managing Editor
Kathy Berkemeyer
Chicago, IL

Project Manager
Cathy Vesecky
Chicago, IL

Elsa Johannesson
New York, NY

English Editor
Rebecca Fiala
Quincy, MA

Technical Editor
Candi Dickerson
Chicago, IL

Jeff Grisenthwaite
Chicago, IL

Cathy Vesecky
Chicago, IL

Carolyn Stemen
McKinleyville, CA

Design and Layout
Elsa Johannesson
New York, NY

Julie Janssen
Chicago, IL

Maria Kardasheva
New York, NY

Paul Wray
New York, NY

CD-ROM
Producer
Maryellen Hopper
New York, NY

Programmer
Ed Christensen
New York, NY

Technical Editor and Consultant
Margaret Brown
Eureka, CA

Audio Producer
Scott Kopitskie
New York, NY

Narrator
Monique Peterson
New York, NY

Published by DDC Publishing, Inc.

DDC Publishing, Inc.
275 Madison Ave.
New York, NY 10016
Phone: 1-800-528-3897
Fax: 1-800-528-3862
http:www.ddcpub.com

Cat. No. Z26
ISBN: 1-56243-487-X
UPC: 7-15829-17171-7

10 9 8 7 6 5 4 3 2 1

Printed in the United States of America.

WHAT'S NEW IN WINDOWS 98

The blending of the Internet Browser with the operating system

Access to the Web is built in... everywhere:

- the Start menu
- the desktop
- the taskbar, with its Quick Launch toolbar
- folder windows

Using features like:

- Internet Explorer icon
- Address Bar
- Links toolbar
- Favorites menu
- Go menu
- Explorer bars
- Channel bars
- Find people

The most noticeable new Windows 98 feature, if it is turned on, is the Web style folder options in which you can select objects by pointing to them and open them by clicking them... just like you do in Web browsers.

The Active Desktop is another Web feature.

Two Windows 98 browsing modes to choose from

The Folder Options dialog box offers two folder styles:

- Web style
- Classic style

  (or a customized combination of the two styles).

In the table below, affected Folder features are listed in the left column. The middle column shows the Web style option for the feature, while the right column shows the Classic style option for the feature:

Folder Option	Web style	Classic style
Active Desktop	Use the Active Desktop	Use the standard desktop
Browse folders	Open each folder in the *same* window	Open each folder in its *own* window
Web Page view	Turn on Web Page view in all folders.	Does not turn on Web Page view in folders
Click items as follows	Single-click to open an item; point to select	Double-click to open an item; single-click to select
Underline items	Underline icon titles like Internet Explorer.	Icon titles are *not* underlined

New ways to customize Windows 98 to make it more versatile and easier to use

THE START MENU:

New menu items include:

On the Start menu:

- Log Off (your name) item
- Favorites Menu
- Internet Explorer icon
- Windows Update icon

On the Settings menu:

- Folder Options
- Active Desktop
- Windows Update

On the Documents menu:

- My Documents folder

Menus remain just one panel wide:

If all the menu items don't fit on the panel, directional arrowheads at the top and/or bottom of the panel indicate that there are more menu items than you can see in the direction of the arrowhead. Simply point to the arrowhead to scroll to the other menu items.

Menu items can be rearranged:

Simply drag a menu item to the new location on the menu and drop it.

THE ACTIVE DESKTOP:

The Active Desktop adds a Web layer to the standard desktop so you can display Web items such as:

- headlines for breaking news stories
- tickers for stock quotes
- weather reports

THE TASKBAR:

- Toolbars can be added to the taskbar
- Taskbar toolbars can be dragged to the desktop
- By default, the taskbar contains the Quick Launch toolbar with icons to:
  - launch the Internet Explorer browser
  - launch Outlook Express (an e-mail program)
  - show the desktop (takes you to your desktop)
  - view Channels
- You can add program shortcuts to the Quick Launch toolbar to make it easier to open them.

FOLDER WINDOWS:

A new Internet icon at the right end of the Menu bar:

Click it to open the Web browser.

New Toolbars:

- Address Bar
- Links Bar

New menus:

The *Go menu* that contains these items:

- Back
- Forward
- Up One Level
- Home Page
- Search the Web
- Channel Guide
- Mail, News
- My Computer
- Address Book
- Internet Call

The *Favorites menu* that contains these items:

- Add to Favorites
- Organize Favorites
- Manage Subscriptions
- Update All Subscriptions
- Channels
- Links
- Software Updates
- My Documents

New items on the View menu include:

Explorer Bars:

- Search
- Favorites
- History
- Channels

Customize a folder. You can choose a background picture or create an HTML page.

View, as Web Page: displays information about the selected item, including actual thumbnail pictures of graphic items and Web items.

New items on the File Menu include:

- The name of the current folder.
- The Work Offline option that allows you to display Web pages stored on your system without connecting to the Internet.

New Standard toolbar:

- added the Back button and the Forward button
- changed Views to a single button with a drop down list

Behind the scenes improvements

Windows 98 has been updated to provide an easier to use, more reliable, and faster operating system while offering more sophisticated features. It offers performance features such as:

- faster installation
- faster shutdown
- better stability
- built-in support
- better display drivers
- accelerated Graphics Port graphics cards
- a System Information Utility program
- the Windows Tune-Up wizard
- The System File Checker program
- Windows Update

Tips

As you work through the exercises in Lessons Two through Lesson Seven, you will develop a data disk. This disk should be accurate enough to insure that the exercises in Lessons Eight, Nine, and Ten can be completed.

If necessary, you can create a data disk that is accurate to use for the Exercises in Lesson Eight, Nine, and Ten from the CD-ROM if you: open the DATA DISK 1 folder on the CD-ROM, select everything in it including the folders, and copy it to a floppy disk (See page 168 for more specific directions.). If you are inexperienced at using computers, have a friend with computer experience help you with this procedure.

You will develop a second disk for use with the practice exercises. You can also create a data disk from the CD-ROM for use with the Practice Exercises for Lessons Eight, Nine, and Ten by following the procedures above using the DATA DISK 2 folder.

The Keyboard Steps that appear in the side column are for reference for those users who need them or are interested in them. They are not a necessary part of the exercise, and you are not expected to perform the exercises using them.

The Internet section of this book, Lessons Twelve and Thirteen, directs you to access the Internet live. Although efforts have been made to create a stable environment, keep in mind that the Internet is dynamic, and Web sites redesign their Web pages, change their addresses (URL), or disappear.

Assumptions

It is assumed that:
- Windows 98 has been properly installed on your computer, or that you have installed Internet Explorer 4 on your computer which uses Windows 95.
- Your printer has been properly installed.
- You can provide four disks to use with the exercises.
- You have established a connection to the Internet through direct access, an Internet service provider, or an online service (such as AOL, CompuServe, or Microsoft Network) to complete the last two lessons in the book.

Conventions

Every action in the exercises starts with a bullet (●) and a **bold** action word.

Keys that should be pressed together have a plus (+) between them. For example, Ctrl + →.

Keys that should be pressed in succession are separated by commas. For example, Alt, F, X.

Using this book with Windows 95 and Internet Explorer 4

The exercises in this book work with Windows 95 that has Internet Explorer 4 installed. Two differences that may show up are noted below:
- The Internet icon illustrations in this book (a flag on a black background that appears on the right end of the menu bar) may not match the Internet icon in your screen.
- In Windows 98, when the Web page view feature is turned on, a warning window appears in which you must click Show Files before the Windows folder will open. This warning window may not appear in Windows 95 with Internet Explorer 4 installed.
- The bitmap icon that is associated with the Paint program may look different.

Reference Material

Learning Windows 98 can be used as a reference when you complete the book. You can look up the task you want to perform, review it as needed, and then apply the steps to your situation.

Five DDC Publishing books may be of use to you as companion books to *Learning Windows 98*.
- *Learning the Internet, 2nd Edition*
- *Visual Reference Basics for Windows 98*
- *Windows 98 Quick Reference Guide*
- *Upgrade to Windows 98 One-Day Course*
- *Windows 98 Short Course*

ABOUT THIS BOOK

Learning Windows 98 introduces you to the Windows 98 user interface with 26 Topics and 150 Exercises. The hands-on tutorial style of this book is designed to let you work at your own pace.

Topics appear at the beginning of most lessons. They teach basic Windows 98 concepts using easy-to-understand explanations and illustrations.

Exercises

Exercises are characterized by the following:

- Exercises are easy to locate; the exercise number is in the top outside corner of the page.
- The name of each exercise reflects the Windows 98 tasks to be performed.
- Each exercise is defined.
- Results of exercise steps are explained and/or illustrated where appropriate.
- Occasional notes explain concepts within the exercise steps.
- Terms appropriate to each exercise appear in the side column.
- Warnings, important comments, and notes appear in the side column when needed.
- Keyboard Steps in the side column provide the procedures to perform the exercise task.

Browsing Options

In Windows 98, you can choose between two folder browsing modes—Classic style and Web style. The Classic style (the default) is like Windows 95. You click to select objects and double-click to open them. Using the Web style browsing option, however, you point to select objects and click to open them—just as you would in a Web browser.

You are instructed to use Web style browsing when doing most of the exercises in this book. In Lesson Four, you are instructed to switch between the two browsing styles and then to leave Web style browsing in effect for the rest of the exercises.

TABLE OF CONTENTS

Lesson One
Windows Basics

Table of Contents

TOPIC 1 • Computer System, Hardware

Terms and Notes

CD-ROM (Compact Disk Read-Only Memory)
A removable, read-only optical disk that can store relatively (when compared to 3½" floppy disks) large amounts of data.

CD-ROM drive
A drive that retrieves information from *CD-ROMs*.

disk drive
A mechanical device used to transfer information back and forth between the computer's memory and a disk.

floppy disk
A removable, magnetically coated diskette on/from which information can be stored and retrieved.

hard disk
A large capacity storage area on/from which information can be quickly stored and retrieved.

hardware
The group of components that makes up the computer system. Hardware can be seen and touched.

keyboard
A device used to enter data and issue commands to the computer.

memory (RAM)
The workspace area of the computer that temporarily holds the instructions (software or programs) and information (data or commands) you give it. When you turn the computer off, everything in RAM disappears.

modem
A device that converts data so that you can transmit it over telephone lines. Also called *fax/modem*.

monitor
A screen that displays the information in the computer.

mouse
A small, hand-held device used to control the pointer on the screen and issue commands to the computer.

printer
A device that makes a hard copy of data in the computer.

processor (CPU)
The part of the computer that processes the instructions in the memory.

read-only memory (ROM)
A computer chip that holds information that cannot be changed.

speakers
Devices that play sounds which are transmitted from your computer.

The computer system is your assistant. It has its own:
- brain (**processor [CPU]** or *central processing unit*)
- workspace (**working memory [RAM]** or *random-access memory*)
- built-in instructions (**read-only memory chips [ROM]**)
- file cabinets (**disk drives**)
- storage medium (**hard disk** and **floppy disks**)

Your computer comes with a:
- **monitor** (to show you what is going on)
- **printer** (to make hard copies of documents)
- **keyboard** (to enter commands and data)
- **mouse** (to control the pointer on the screen)
- **modem** or *fax/modem* (to e-mail, chat, fax, and use the Internet)
- **CD-ROM drive** (to install large programs, etc.)
- **speakers** (to play music and sounds)

Other hardware that is becoming common with today's computer systems includes:
- **scanner** (to digitize information so the computer can understand it)
- **network interface card** (to connect to other computers)

Basic Computer System, Hardware

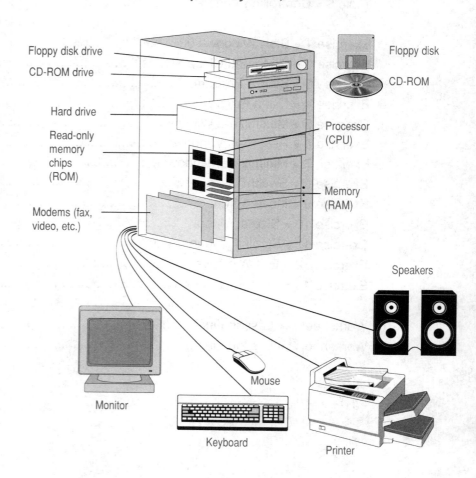

Floppy disk drive
CD-ROM drive
Hard drive
Read-only memory chips (ROM)
Modems (fax, video, etc.)
Floppy disk
CD-ROM
Processor (CPU)
Memory (RAM)
Speakers
Mouse
Monitor
Keyboard
Printer

The computer can do nothing until it is given instructions—software. **Software** is a set of instructions that tells the computer what to do. There are two main kinds of software:

- **system software** (firmware and an operating system)
- **application software** (programs)

Software is an essential part of your computer system, and the operating system is required to make your computer work. The **operating system** looks after the different parts of your computer system, linking them to each other and to you.

All software originates on CD-ROMs and floppy disks (except for **firmware** which is built into your computer). The hard drive on all computers is initially empty, but most computers come from the factory with an operating system (usually Windows) and other programs pre-installed on the hard drive. If you prefer, however, you can wipe the hard drive clean (format it) and install a different operating system and/or new programs.

Application software is copied from CD-ROMs and floppy disks onto the hard disk for convenience and speed. You then put the original software away for safe keeping—in case your hard drive crashes and you need to reinstall the software later.

Basic Computer System, Software

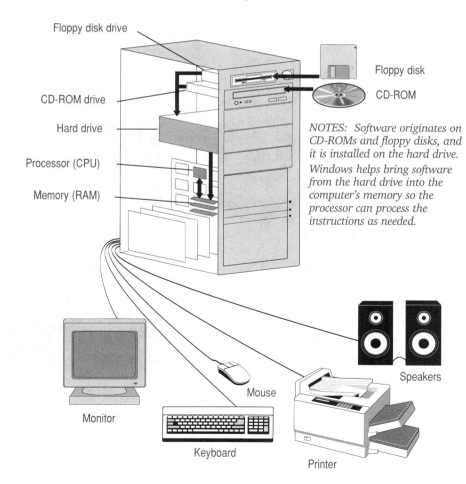

Floppy disk drive

Floppy disk

CD-ROM

CD-ROM drive

Hard drive

Processor (CPU)

Memory (RAM)

NOTES: Software originates on CD-ROMs and floppy disks, and it is installed on the hard drive. Windows helps bring software from the hard drive into the computer's memory so the processor can process the instructions as needed.

Monitor

Mouse

Keyboard

Printer

Speakers

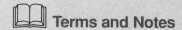 **Terms and Notes**

application software
A set of instructions that your computer follows to perform one specific task, such as word processing or creating a graphic. While the term *application* is used a lot in Windows, this book uses the term *program* more often.

computer
An electronic device that performs complex tasks at a high speed and with great accuracy. There are two main parts of a computer—the *processor* and the *memory*.

firmware
A kind of *system software*. More specifically, *firmware* is instructions that are built into the computer system on *ROM* chips.

operating system
System software that acts as a link between you, application software (i.e., programs), and hardware.

ROM (read-only memory)
A computer chip that holds information that cannot be changed.

software
Instructions that tell your computer how to perform a task. Software is stored on disks in program files. *(See Topic 14, Files and Filenames, and Topic 15, Disk Drives and Folders.)* Unlike hardware, software cannot be seen or touched. There are two main kinds of software: system software and application software.

system software
Software that runs the computer system. This includes *firmware* and your *operating system*.

TOPIC 3 • What is Windows 98?

 Terms and Notes

graphical user interface (GUI)
A phrase that is commonly used to describe *Microsoft Windows* 98 and other *operating systems* that use pictures (i.e., graphics) to help you connect to the computer system's hardware and software in an easy-to-understand, intuitive way.

Microsoft Windows 98
An *operating system* that uses a graphics environment (i.e., *graphical user interface*) to connect you to the computer system's hardware and software in an easy-to-understand, intuitive way. Microsoft Windows 98 also offers many built-in, general use programs.

operating system
System software that acts as a link between you, application software (i.e., *programs*), and hardware.

program
A set of instructions that your computer follows to perform one specific task, such as word processing or creating a graphic.

you
The operator (or user) of the computer system (its hardware and software).

Windows is an Operating System

An **operating system** links you to your programs (also called *applications* or *software*) and then links your programs to the computer system's hardware. The Windows 98 operating system is called a **graphical user interface (GUI)** because it uses pictures to help you communicate with the computer.

Windows 98 has been designed to provide you with an easy-to-use, reliable, and fast operating system. In addition, access to the Internet is built in, with the Internet Explorer 4.0 browser integrated as a central part of Windows 98.

Your Computer System

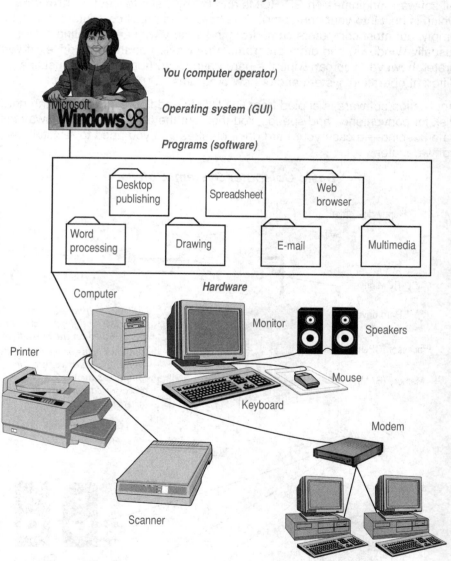

What does Windows 98 Do?

Microsoft Windows 98 does the following:

- **Provides an easy way to start programs.**
  (the Start button does this)

- **Runs more than one program at a time.**
  (called *multitasking*)

- **Provides an easy way to switch between open programs.**
  (the taskbar does this)

- **Lets you open more than one program at a time.**
  (it uses *windows* to do this)

- **Makes it easy to work with files, folders, and other objects.**
  (Windows Explorer does this)

- **Transfers information between programs.**
  (called *Object Linking and Embedding [OLE]*)

- **Provides a "Web-page" desktop and folder environment.**
  (you can change the environment back to the classic Windows 95 style if you wish, however)

- **Provides access to the Internet.**
  (Internet Explorer does this)

- **Provides access to e-mail and newsgroups.**
  (Outlook Express does this)

- **Lets you talk with others using live video and a shared whiteboard.**
  (Microsoft NetMeeting does this)

- **Provides networking support.**
  (Network Neighborhood provides easy network access)

- **Provides multimedia programs.**
  (use CD Player to play compact disks; Media Player to run multimedia files; and Sound Recorder to record, edit, and play recorded sounds)

- **Provides an HTML editor so you can design Web pages.**
  (FrontPage Express does this)

- **Provides other general-use programs.**
  (called *accessories*. For example, WordPad, Paint, Calculator, and games)

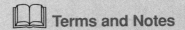 **Terms and Notes**

e-mail (electronic mail)
A global communication system for exchanging messages and attached files; this is probably the most widely used feature on the Internet. Many Web browsers include an e-mail program—Internet Explorer uses Outlook Express for e-mail.

HTML (Hypertext Markup Language)
The programming language used to create Web pages so that they can be viewed, read, and accessed by any computer running on any type of operating system.

Internet
A global collection of computers that communicate with one another using common communication protocols (e.g., HTTP).

Internet service provider (ISP)
A company (often local) that provides you with a connection to the Internet for a fee.

multimedia
The combination of many various communication methods, including text, graphics, sound, animation, and video.

multitasking
The ability of an operating system to run more than one program at a time.

network
Two or more computers that are linked together to share programs, data, and certain hardware components, for example, a printer.

newsgroup
A collection of special-interest messages posted by individuals to a news server on the Internet. You need a special program to read and respond to newsgroups.

object
One of the many things that you use when working with the computer system—items such as: files, programs, folders, shortcuts, disk drives, Control Panel tools, My Computer, Network Neighborhood, the Recycle Bin, and My Briefcase.
NOTE: As used here, object is really just another catch-all term for an item, element, thing, or what-cha-ma-call-it. The terms object and object-oriented also have a more formal computer-related meaning that is not used in this book.

Web page
A document created using HTML that can be posted on the World Wide Web.

window
A rectangle that holds a dialog box, folder, program, or document.

TOPIC 5 • The Desktop

 Terms and Notes

button
A graphic element found in dialog boxes, on toolbars, and in certain other places that, when activated, performs a specific function.

A *command button* in a dialog box is a rectangular button with the name of its function on it, such as OK, Yes, No, Cancel, Save, Open, etc.

A *toolbar button* is a square button with an *icon* that illustrates its function—you can usually display or hide text labels under toolbar buttons.

Buttons also appear on a window title bar and on the taskbar. When you point to buttons (other than command buttons), a ToolTip appears that names, or describes the action of, the button.

desktop
The opening screen in Windows 98 that contains a few *objects*, the *Start button*, and the *taskbar*. The button shown above is the Show Desktop button on the Quick Launch toolbar.

icon
A small picture that represents one of the many *objects* that you use when working with the computer system.

object
One of the many things that you use when working with the computer system—items such as: files, programs, folders, shortcuts, disk drives, Control Panel tools, My Computer, Network Neighborhood, the Recycle Bin, and My Briefcase.

Start button
The *button* located at the left end of the taskbar that is labeled *Start*. Click the Start button to open the Start menu, from which you can open other menus and launch programs.

taskbar
The bar that appears by default on the bottom of the desktop and lets you quickly start programs and switch between tasks.

The Windows Desktop

The redesigned Windows desktop is clean and straightforward. However, there is still the same obvious starting point—the Start button.

Windows 98 Web-Style Desktop

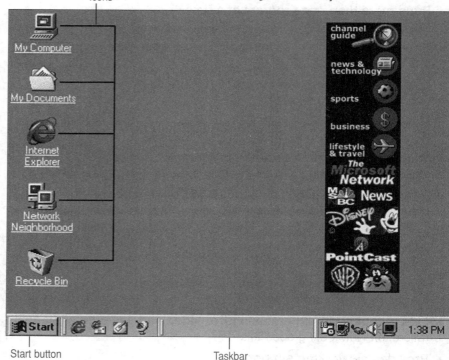

Start button   Taskbar

Windows 98 Desktop with Pop-Up Menus Displayed

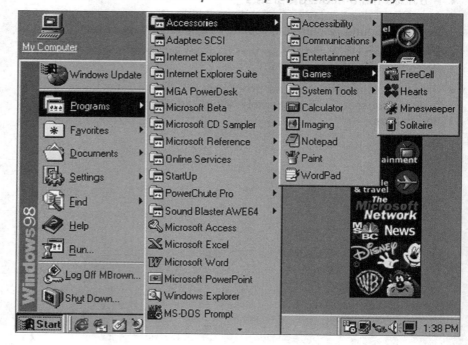

Window Elements

Most window elements activate commands.

Control menu

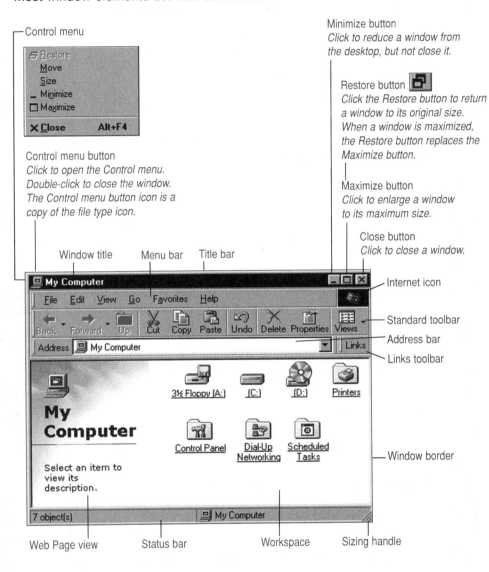

Control menu button
Click to open the Control menu.
Double-click to close the window.
The Control menu button icon is a
copy of the file type icon.

Minimize button
Click to reduce a window from
the desktop, but not close it.

Restore button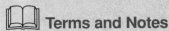
Click the Restore button to return
a window to its original size.
When a window is maximized,
the Restore button replaces the
Maximize button.

Maximize button
Click to enlarge a window
to its maximum size.

Close button
Click to close a window.

Window title   Menu bar   Title bar

Internet icon

Standard toolbar

Address bar

Links toolbar

Window border

Web Page view   Status bar   Workspace   Sizing handle

Terms and Notes

Address bar
A drop-down text box that lets you access a Web page or a location on your computer by typing or selecting an address or path.

Close button ☒
A button located at the right end of a document and/or program title bar that you click to close a window.

Control menu
A menu with items that you use to manipulate a program window (Restore, Move, Size, Minimize, Maximize, and Close). It is opened by clicking the *Control menu button* or by right-clicking the desired program's taskbar button.

Control menu button
An icon at the left side of the title bar that opens the *Control menu.* The icon for the Control menu button matches the file type icon. (For folder windows, the icon is a folder.)

Internet icon
The button at the right end of the menu bar, illustrated with a Windows flag, that accesses the Internet when clicked.

Links toolbar
The toolbar that provides quick access to commonly used Web sites.

Maximize button ☐
The button in the middle of the three buttons located at the right end of the title bar on a restored window. This button enlarges a window to its greatest possible size. When you maximize a window, the Maximize button is replaced by the *Restore button.*

menu bar
The bar located under the title bar that lists the available menu items for the open document or folder.

Minimize button ▬
The button located on the right side of the menu bar and/or title bar that you can click to reduce a window to a taskbar button.

Restore button
The button in the middle of the three buttons located at the right end of the menu bar and/or title bar on a maximized window. This button returns a maximized window to its previous size. When you restore a maximized window, the Restore button is replaced by the *Maximize button.*

sizing handle
An area in the bottom-right corner of windows that can be sized.

Standard toolbar
A row of buttons that provides quick access to frequently used commands.

status bar
The bar at the bottom of a program or folder window. It displays information about the program or folder, and it can be turned on and off from the View menu.

title bar
The horizontal bar at the top of a window that provides the name of the open *document* and/or *program.*

Web Page view
A feature that displays a picture and the name of the selected item in the top-left corner of the workspace. It also displays information about the selected item in the bottom-left corner of the workspace.

window
A rectangle that holds a dialog box, folder, program, or document.

window border
The boundary that marks the edges of a window and can be used to size that window.

window title
The name of a window, located just to the right of the *Control menu button.* The document name, if any, is listed along with the program name.

workspace
The inner part of a window where the work in a *document* or *program* is carried out.

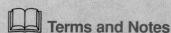 **Terms and Notes**

accessories
Supplemental, built-in programs that come with Windows 98.

NOTE: Depending on your hardware (i.e., modem or network capabilities), some accessories may not be displayed in Windows or, if displayed, you may not be able to use them. Certain other programs are not installed if you chose the Typical option during installation.

Windows Accessories

In addition to being an operating system, Windows 98 offers many kinds of built-in programs called **accessories**. There are programs for:

- games
- general use
- multimedia
- Internet
- communications
- system tools

Each Windows program has an icon to help you identify it quickly. Many accessory icons are shown below.

Game Programs

 FreeCell

 Hearts

 Minesweeper

 Solitaire

General-Use Programs

 Paint to create pictures.

 WordPad to write and format documents.

 Notepad to write and view documents.

 Calculator to make calculations.

 Imaging to perform basic tasks with faxes and scanned pictures.

Multimedia Programs

 ActiveMovie Control to play video and audio multimedia files.

 CD Player to play compact disks.

 Media Player to play multimedia files.

 Sound Recorder to record, edit, and play sound files.

 Volume Control to adjust the sound level.

Internet Programs

 Internet Explorer to browse the World Wide Web.

 Microsoft NetMeeting to hold digital conversations with people around the world.

 Outlook Express to communicate online with e-mail and newsgroups.

 Address Book to store contact information.

 FrontPage Express to edit Web pages.

Communications Programs

 Dial-Up Networking to connect to a computer (and its network) using a modem.

 Direct Cable Connection to connect to a computer using a cable.

 Briefcase to synchronize files used on more than one computer.

 Phone Dialer to place calls from your computer.

System Tools

 Disk Cleanup to free up space on your hard drive.

 Disk Defragmenter to speed up your hard disk.

 FAT 32 Converter to change your hard disk from FAT 16 to the FAT 32 system.

 Maintenance Wizard to help you get the best performance from your system.

 Scan Disk to detect and repair disk errors.

 Scheduled Tasks to run tasks (such as Disk Defragmenter) when it's most convenient for you.

 System Information to gather system configuration information.

 System File Checker to review your system files to make sure they are all correct.

 Welcome to Windows to introduce you to your computer's new programs and features.

TOPIC 8 • Controlling Windows

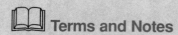

Terms and Notes

commands
Instructions that you issue, causing an action to be carried out.

control keys
Certain keys (Shift, Ctrl, and Alt) that are used in combination with other keys to issue commands. Also called *modifier keys*.

keyboard
The device used to enter data and issue commands to the computer.

keyboard shortcuts
Key combinations that are used to activate certain commands as an alternative to using the *mouse*.

mouse
A small, hand-held device used to control the *pointer* on the screen and issue commands to the computer.

pointer
The arrow-shaped cursor on the screen that moves with the *mouse* as you slide it over a flat surface. The pointer's shape changes depending on the job it is doing (or can do) at the current time. Also called *arrow pointer* or *mouse pointer*.

Common Pointer Shapes

SHAPE	NAME
	arrow *the standard shape*
	background *system is working in the background*
	help *describes selected item*
	busy *signals for you to wait*
	unavailable *cannot perform action*
	hand *selects hyperlinks*
	I-beam *selects text*
	move *moves windows*
	sizing *sizes windows*

Controlling Windows

You can control Windows using **commands**, which are instructions that cause an action to be carried out.

The Windows graphics environment is designed to take advantage of the mouse as a method of issuing commands, though commands can often be issued from the keyboard also. (There are usually several different ways to issue commands.) While the large variety of command choices can lead to confusion for beginners, it offers enough flexibility to meet the requirements of many different Windows users.

The Mouse

The **mouse** is a small, hand-held device that is used to control the pointer on the screen. The **pointer** is the arrow on the screen that moves with the mouse as you slide it over a flat surface. The pointer shape changes depending on the job it is doing (or can do) at the current time.

A mouse usually has at least two buttons: the **primary mouse button** (usually the left button) and the **secondary mouse button** (usually the right button).

There are six main mouse actions:

Point — Move the mouse until the tip of the mouse pointer is over the item you want.

Click — Press and quickly release the left mouse button.

Right-click — Press and quickly release the *right* mouse button.

Double-click — Press and quickly release the left mouse button twice.

IMPORTANT: When instructed to click or double-click, always use the left mouse button unless otherwise instructed.

Drag — Point to an item while you hold down the left mouse button, slide the pointer to a new location, and release the mouse button.

Right-drag — Point to an item while you hold down the *right* mouse button, slide the pointer to a new location, and release the mouse button.

Bullshit Bingo

Do you keep falling asleep in meetings and seminars? What about those long and boring conference calls? Here is a way to change all of that!

How to play: Check off each block when you hear these words during a meeting, seminar, or phone call. When you get five blocks horizontally, vertically, or diagonally, stand up and shout **BULLSHIT**!!

Paradigm	Strategic Fit	Gap Analysis	Best Practice	Bottom Line
Revisit	Bandwidth	Path Forward	Out of the Loop	Benchmark
Value-Added	Proactive	Win-Win	Think Outside the Box	Fast Track
Result-Driven	Empower [or] Empowerment	Knowledge Base	Total Quality [or] Quality Driven	Touch Base
Mindset	Customer Focus[ed]	Key Learning	Game Plan	Leverage

Testimonials from satisfied players:

"I had only been in the meeting for five minutes when I won." -Jack W. - Boston

"My attention span at meetings has improved dramatically." -David D. - Florida

"What a gas. Meetings will never be the same for me after my first win." -Bill R - New York City

"The atmosphere was tense in the last process meeting as 14 of us waited for the 5th box." -Ben G. - Denver

"The speaker was stunned as eight of us screamed 'Bullshit' for the third time in 2 hours." - Kathleen Atlanta

Bullshit Bingo

Do you keep falling asleep in meetings and seminars? What about those long and boring conference calls? Here is a way to change all of that!

How to play: Check off each block when you hear these words during a meeting, seminar, or phone call. When you get five blocks horizontally, vertically, or diagonally, stand up and shout **BULLSHIT**!!

Paradigm	Strategic Fit	Gap Analysis	Best Practice	Bottom Line
Revisit	Bandwidth	Path Forward	Out of the Loop	Benchmark
Value-Added	Proactive	Win-Win	Think Outside the Box	Fast Track
Result-Driven	Empower [or] Empowerment	Knowledge Base	Total Quality [or] Quality Driven	Touch Base
Mindset	Customer Focus[ed]	Key Learning	Game Plan	Leverage

Testimonials from satisfied players:

"I had only been in the meeting for five minutes when I won." -Jack W. - Boston

"My attention span at meetings has improved dramatically." -David D. - Florida

"What a gas. Meetings will never be the same for me after my first win." -Bill R - New York City

"The atmosphere was tense in the last process meeting as 14 of us waited for the 5th box." -Ben G. - Denver

"The speaker was stunned as eight of us screamed 'Bullshit' for the third time in 2 hours." - Kathleen Atlanta

The Keyboard

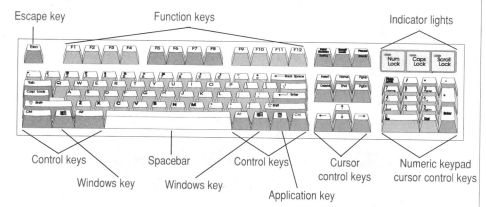

Escape key · Function keys · Indicator lights

Control keys · Spacebar · Control keys · Cursor control keys · Numeric keypad cursor control keys

Windows key · Windows key · Application key

The **keyboard** is used to enter data and to issue commands to the computer.

The twelve keys located across the top of the keyboard that are labeled F1 through F12 are called **function keys**.

Control keys (Shift, Ctrl, and Alt) are used in combination with other keys to issue commands.

Keyboard shortcuts are key combinations that can be used to activate certain commands as an alternative to using the mouse. A menu command that has a keyboard shortcut available will display its key combination to the right of its command name.

Using Keys Together

When two keys are used together to issue a command, a plus sign (+) is shown between the keys. For example: Alt + Tab.

To issue this command, you should press and hold down Alt, tap Tab, and then release Alt.

Using Keys in Succession

Keys are used in succession when two or more keys are pressed one after the other to issue a command. Keys used in succession are illustrated with a comma separating them. For example: F4, M, E. Press each key in succession.

Four Special Keys

Esc (the Escape key) is used to back out of situations. Occasionally you find yourself in a place you don't want to be; the Escape key will often get you out of these situations without doing any damage to your work or the computer.

F1 is used to get Help.

(the Windows key) Some keyboards have this key, which is used to open the Start menu quickly.

(the Application key) Some keyboards have this key, which is used to open shortcut menus for the active object quickly.

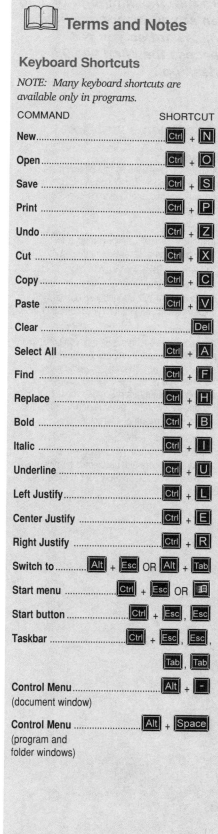

Terms and Notes

Keyboard Shortcuts

NOTE: Many keyboard shortcuts are available only in programs.

COMMAND	SHORTCUT
New	Ctrl + N
Open	Ctrl + O
Save	Ctrl + S
Print	Ctrl + P
Undo	Ctrl + Z
Cut	Ctrl + X
Copy	Ctrl + C
Paste	Ctrl + V
Clear	Del
Select All	Ctrl + A
Find	Ctrl + F
Replace	Ctrl + H
Bold	Ctrl + B
Italic	Ctrl + I
Underline	Ctrl + U
Left Justify	Ctrl + L
Center Justify	Ctrl + E
Right Justify	Ctrl + R
Switch to	Alt + Esc OR Alt + Tab
Start menu	Ctrl + Esc OR ⊞
Start button	Ctrl + Esc, Esc
Taskbar	Ctrl + Esc, Esc, Tab, Tab
Control Menu (document window)	Alt + -
Control Menu (program and folder windows)	Alt + Space

EXERCISE 1 • Start Windows 98

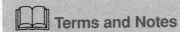

Terms and Notes

dialog box
A special kind of window that offers different controls for you to manipulate in order to change the performance or appearance of a document or program.

log on
To identify yourself to your computer (with a *user name* and a *password*) and open the Windows 98 desktop.

Logon screen
The opening Windows 98 dialog box that appears when you first turn your computer on.

password
A combination of characters that you type, when prompted, in order to access Windows (or another feature). Characters appear as small *x*'s when you type. The Password feature is a security measure that prevents access to a Windows network (or other feature) without the correct combination of characters.

user name
The name given to a Windows user. Using different identifiers and passwords for different people allows each operator's work to be kept secure.

IMPORTANT: When instructed to click *or* double-click, *always use the left mouse button unless otherwise instructed.*

Begin with the computer turned off.

1 **Turn on the power to your computer system:**

- **Turn on** the monitor and computer.

  NOTE: On some computer systems, the monitor is plugged into the computer so you only need to turn on the computer.

  After a few minutes of booting, the Logon screen appears—a dialog box that asks for your user name and password.

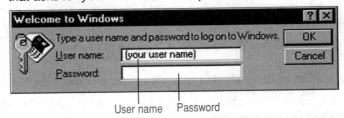

User name   Password

NOTE: You may have a different Logon screen.

- IF your system is networked, the Logon screen may be different; it may ask for a password to log on to the network.

- IF someone previously disabled the Password feature, it is possible that no Welcome to Windows dialog box appears asking for a password.

- IF the Windows desktop appears *(see Topic 5, The Desktop)*, skip the steps below and **go on** to Exercise 2.

2 **Enter your password:**

NOTES: If Windows is being started for the first time since it was installed, you will be asked to enter a User *name and to create a* Password *of your choice. Be sure to remember the password (you may want to write it down and put it in a safe place) for use in future exercises.*

To add other Windows users, you can enter a new User *name and then create a new* Password *at the Welcome to Windows dialog box.*

- **Type** the correct name in the User name text box if it is not already there.

- **Type** the correct password in the Password text box.

  The letters you type appear as small x's.

- **Click** OK .

  The Windows desktop appears. If the Welcome to Windows 98 dialog box appears, see the notes at the bottom of this page.

  NOTE: If you typed an incorrect password, the dialog box will reappear so you can try again.

OR

Cancel the Logon screen:

NOTE: If you cancel the Welcome to Windows dialog box to access the Windows desktop on a computer that you have previously used a password to log on to, you may not be able to open files that you saved during earlier, password-protected sessions.

- **Click** Cancel , or **press** Esc .

  The Windows desktop appears.

  NOTES: If the Welcome to Windows 98 dialog box appears, click the Close button in the dialog box title bar to close it, and then click the No button so the dialog box doesn't automatically reopen.

  If you want to go through the Welcome to Windows 98 tutorial at some other time, you can always access it by clicking Start, Programs, Accessories, System Tools, and finally, Welcome To Windows.

1 **Open the Start menu:**

- **Click** **Start** (the Start button).
  The Start menu opens.

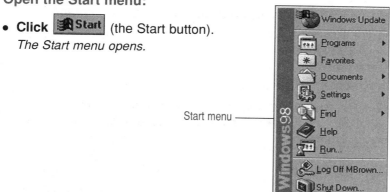

Start menu ——

2 **Open submenus:**

NOTE: A submenu opens whenever you point to a menu item that is followed by a right-pointing arrowhead (▶).

- **Point** to **Find** ▶ until the Find menu opens.

—— Find menu

- **Point** to **Settings** ▶ until the Settings menu opens.

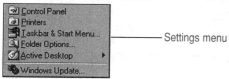

—— Settings menu

- **Point** to **Documents** ▶ until the Documents menu opens.
  A menu appears displaying the names of the last 15 documents used in alphabetical order.
- **Point** to **Favorites** ▶ until the Favorites menu opens.
- **Point** to **Programs** ▶ until the Programs menu opens.
- **With** the Programs menu still open, **point** to **Accessories** ▶ until the Accessories menu opens.
- IF *Accessories* does *not* appear at the top of the Programs menu and a directional arrowhead (▲) does, **point** to ▲ until the Accessories menu appears.

  Top of Programs Menu

  | Internet Explorer ▶ | —— Up arrowhead

  NOTE: When a menu contains more items than will fit in the panel allowed for that menu, an up arrowhead will appear at the top of the menu and/or a down arrowhead will appear at the bottom of the menu.
- **Move** the mouse pointer off of the menus.
  The menus remain open.

3 **Close menus:**

- **Click** an empty space on the desktop. (Do not click a menu item or another object on the desktop.)
  The menus close.

To open a menu and display the items within it.

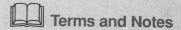 **Terms and Notes**

directional arrowhead ▶
A small arrowhead that appears at the beginning and/or end of menus and toolbars to indicate that there are more items than you can presently see on the menu or toolbar. Point to the arrowhead to scroll through the menu or toolbar items.

menu
A drop-down or pop-up list of items from which you may choose only one at a time.

menu item
One of the choices on a *menu*.

submenu
A menu that cascades out from another menu. A right-pointing arrowhead on a menu item indicates that a submenu will appear when you point to it.

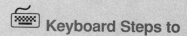 **Keyboard Steps to**

Open the Start Menu

Press Ctrl + Esc.

OR

Press Alt + S (Start).

OR

Press ⊞ (the Windows key).

Choose a Menu Item

Type the *underlined letter* of the desired menu item.

OR

Type the *first letter* of the desired menu item.
NOTE: If more than one item starts with the same letter, press the letter again until the desired menu item is highlighted, then press the Enter key.

OR

Press ↑↓ (arrow keys) to select an item.

Close an Open Menu

Press Esc.

EXERCISE 3 • Start a Program

To use Windows 98 to run a program.

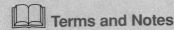

Terms and Notes

bar
The term *bar* is used to define window stripes (e.g., the title bar, menu bar, and status bar).

launch
To start a program. The terms *run* and *open* are also used frequently.

program
A set of instructions that your computer follows to perform one specific task such as word processing or creating a graphic. While the term *application* is used a lot in Windows, this book uses the term *program* more often.

taskbar
The *bar* that appears by default on the bottom of the desktop and lets you quickly start programs, switch between tasks, and access the tools (and toolbars) of your choice.

taskbar button
A button located on the taskbar that represents an open program. Each taskbar button displays the program icon and name of each open program.

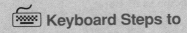

Keyboard Steps to

Start a Program

—USING THE START MENU—

1. Press [Ctrl] + [Esc].

   OR

   Press [Alt] + [S] (Start).

   OR

   Press [▦] (the Windows key).

2. **Type** the *underlined letter* of the desired menu item.

   OR

   Type the *first letter* of the desired menu item.

   NOTE: If more than one item starts with the same letter, press the letter again until the desired menu item is highlighted, then press the Enter key.

3. **Repeat** step 2 until you reach and open the desired program.

Start a Program

There are other phrases that are used to mean *start a program* (or application):

- launch a program
- open a program
- run a program

In this exercise, you will work your way through the Start menu, the Programs menu, and finally the Accessories menu to find and then start two Windows 98 accessory programs.

1 **Start Calculator:**

- **Click** [Start], **point** to Programs, then **point** to Accessories.

- **Click** [Calculator].

   The Calculator program opens. Notice that its program icon and name appear on the taskbar as a button.

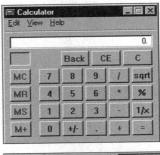

Calculator taskbar button

2 **Start WordPad:**

- **Click** [Start], **point** to Programs, then **point** to Accessories.

- **Click** [WordPad].

   The WordPad program opens. Notice that its program icon and name appear on the taskbar as a button.

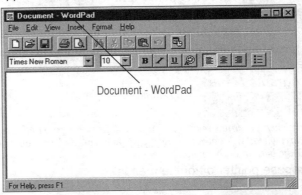

Document - WordPad

NOTE: When you name a WordPad document, that name will replace the word Document in the title bar.

WordPad taskbar button

3 - **Go on** to Exercise 4 without stopping.

Exit a Program

You can exit programs several different ways. You can use the:

- Close button
- Control menu button
- File menu

Control menu button   Close button

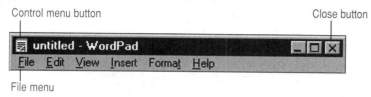

File menu

WARNING: If you make any kind of change in a program (for example, draw a line in Paint or type a word in WordPad), when you exit, a dialog box appears asking if you want to save the current changes. If this happens in this lesson, click the No button to exit without saving the changes.

Continue from Exercise 3 without stopping.

1 **Exit a program using the Close button:**

With WordPad still open:

- **Click** ▼ (the WordPad Close button), located on the right side of the title bar.

  WordPad closes; Calculator remains open.

2 **Exit a program using the Control menu button:**

- **Click** ▦ (the Calculator Control menu button), located on the left side of the title bar.

  The Calculator Control menu drops down.

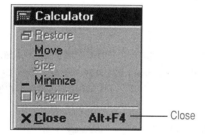

- **Click** Close.

  Calculator closes.

3 **Exit a program by double-clicking the Control menu button:**

- **Start** Calculator (review, Exercise 3).
- **Double-click** ▦ (the Calculator Control menu button), located on the left side of the title bar.

  Calculator closes.

4 **Exit a program using the File menu:**

- **Start** WordPad (review, Exercise 3).
- **Click** File, then **click** Exit.

  WordPad closes.

5 **Exit a program using any method:**

- **Start** Paint (review, Exercise 3), and then **exit** Paint.
- **Start** Notepad, and then **exit** Notepad.

To use Windows 98 to close a program, removing it from the computer's working memory (RAM).

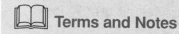 **Terms and Notes**

Close
A command that lets you quit a window. *Close* means essentially the same as *exit*; however, traditionally the term *exit* refers to quitting a program, while the term *close* refers to quitting everything except a program, for example, a dialog box, a document, or a folder window. The Close command is found in the Control menu and in a folder window's File menu.

Close button ▼
A button located at the right end of a document and/or program title bar that you click to close a window.

Control menu
A menu with items that you use to manipulate a document and/or program window (Restore, Move, Size, Minimize, Maximize, and Close). It is opened by clicking the *Control menu button* or by right-clicking the desired document's or program's taskbar button.

Control menu button
An icon on the left side of the title bar that opens the *Control menu*. The icon for the Control menu button matches the file type icon.

Exit
A command that lets you quit a Windows program. The Exit command is found in a program's File menu.

RAM (random-access memory)
The workspace area of the computer that temporarily holds the instructions (software or programs) and information (data or commands) you give it. When you turn the computer off, everything in RAM disappears. Also called *memory* or *working memory*.

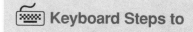 **Keyboard Steps to**

Exit a Program

Press ⬚Alt⬚ + ⬚F4⬚.

OR

1. Press ⬚Alt⬚ + ⬚Space⬚.
2. Press ⬚C⬚ (Close).

OR

1. Press ⬚Alt⬚ + ⬚F⬚ (File).
2. Press ⬚X⬚ (Exit).

EXERCISE 5 • Maximize a Window

To enlarge a window to its greatest possible size.

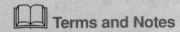 **Terms and Notes**

bar
The term *bar* is used to define window stripes (e.g., the title bar, menu bar, and status bar).

desktop
The opening screen in Windows 98 that contains a few objects, the Start button, and the *taskbar*. The button shown above is the Show Desktop button on the Quick Launch toolbar.

Maximize button
The button in the middle of the three buttons located at the right end of the title bar on a restored window. This button enlarges a window to its greatest possible size. When you maximize a window, the Maximize button is replaced by the *Restore button*.

Restore button
The button in the middle of the three buttons located at the right end of the menu bar and/or title bar on a maximized window. This button returns a maximized window to its previous size. When you restore a maximized window, the Restore button is replaced by the *Maximize button*.

taskbar
The *bar* that appears by default on the bottom of the *desktop* and lets you quickly start programs, switch between tasks, and access the tools (and toolbars) of your choice.

Keyboard Steps to

Maximize a Window

1. Press **Alt** + **Space**.
2. Press **X** (Ma*x*imize).

1 Start a program (WordPad):
- **Start** WordPad (review, Exercise 3, step 2).
- IF the Restore button is displayed in the middle of the series of buttons in the top-right corner of WordPad, **click** (the Restore button) so WordPad will *not* be maximized.
  WordPad is a restored (unmaximized) window.

Restored (Unmaximized) Window

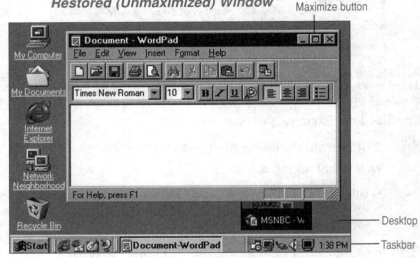

2 Maximize a window (WordPad):
- **Click** (the Maximize button).
  OR
  Double-click the title bar.
  OR
  Click the WordPad Control menu button, then **click** Ma*x*imize.
  WordPad enlarges to its greatest size, leaving only the taskbar displayed at the bottom of the desktop. The Maximize button changes to the Restore button.

Maximized Window

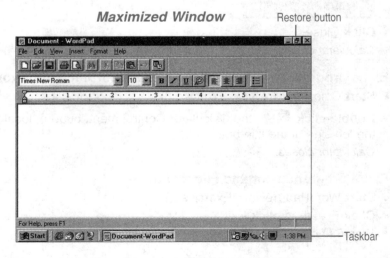

3 • **Go on** to Exercise 6 without stopping.

Continue from Exercise 5 without stopping.

1 **Restore a window (WordPad):**

- **Click** (the Restore button).
  OR
  Double-click the title bar.
  OR
  Click the Control menu button, then **click** Restore.
  WordPad returns to its previous size. The Restore button is replaced by the Maximize button.

Restored Window

Maximize button

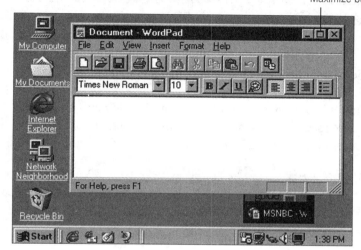

2
- **Maximize** the WordPad window again (review, Exercise 5, step 2).
- **Restore** the WordPad window again (review, step 1).
- **Exit** WordPad (review, Exercise 4).

3
- **Start** Paint (review, Exercise 3).
- **Maximize** Paint.
- **Restore** Paint.
- **Exit** Paint.

4 **Open a window that has a dimmed Maximize button:**
- **Start** Calculator.
- **Notice** that the Maximize button in Calculator is dimmed. This is because Calculator is a program that cannot be maximized. A dimmed command cannot be used.

Dimmed Maximize button

- **Exit** Calculator.

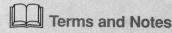

To return a maximized window to its previous size.

📖 **Terms and Notes**

dimmed command
A command or button that cannot be used in the current situation. It is displayed in gray instead of in black or in color.

Restore button 🗗
The button in the middle of the three buttons located at the right end of the menu bar and/or title bar on a maximized window. This button returns a maximized window to its previous size. When you restore a maximized window, the Restore button is replaced by the Maximize button.

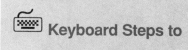 **Keyboard Steps to**

Restore a Window

1. Press Alt + Space .

2. Press Enter .

   OR

   Press R (Restore).

EXERCISE 7 • Minimize a Window

To shrink a window to a taskbar button.

📖 Terms and Notes

Minimize button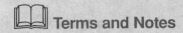
The button located on the right side of a menu bar and/or title bar that you can click to reduce a window to a taskbar button.

pressed
A 3-D effect in which a button (or other item) appears "sunken," indicating it is selected (or active). See *unpressed*, below.

task
An open, but not necessarily active, program.

taskbar
The bar that appears by default at the bottom of the desktop and lets you quickly start programs, switch between tasks, and access the tools (and toolbars) of your choice.

taskbar button
A button located on the *taskbar* that represents an open program. Each taskbar button displays the program icon and name of each open program.

NOTE: Don't confuse taskbar buttons with Quick Launch toolbar buttons or system tray icons—both of which are also on the taskbar. (See Topic 11, The Taskbar.)

unpressed
A 3-D effect in which a button (or other item) appears "raised," indicating it is deselected (or inactive). See *pressed*, above.

Begin with the desktop displayed and no taskbar buttons on the taskbar.

NOTE: You will be instructed to start most exercises with the introductory sentence above.

1 **Start a program:**
- **Start** WordPad (review, Exercise 3).

  WordPad opens; a WordPad taskbar button appears, and it is pressed.

  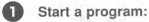

- **Notice** the Minimize button on the right end of the title bar.

  Minimize button

2 **Minimize a window:**
- **Click** ▬ (the Minimize button).
  OR
  Click the Control menu button, then **click** Mi<u>n</u>imize.
  The WordPad window shrinks to a taskbar button.
- **Notice** that the WordPad taskbar button appears unpressed.

3 **Activate a minimized window:**
- **Click** 📄 Document-WordPad (the WordPad taskbar button).
  The WordPad program opens into a window.
- **Notice** that the WordPad taskbar button appears to be pressed again.

4 **Minimize and restore a window using the taskbar:**
- **Click** 📄 Document-WordPad (the WordPad taskbar button).
  WordPad shrinks to an unpressed taskbar button.
- **Click** 📄 Document-WordPad (the WordPad taskbar button).
  WordPad opens into a window.

5
- **Exit** WordPad (review, Exercise 4).
  WordPad closes; the WordPad taskbar button disappears.

6
- **Start** Calculator.
- **Minimize** Calculator (review step 2).
- **Activate** the minimized Calculator (review step 3).
- **Exit** Calculator.

⌨ Keyboard Steps to

Minimize a Window

1. Press `Alt` + `Space`.

2. Press `N` (Mi<u>n</u>imize).

Begin with the desktop displayed and with no taskbar buttons on the taskbar.

NOTE: If any taskbar buttons are visible, click each button and exit each program.

1 **Open three programs:**
- **Start** WordPad, **start** Notepad, and then **start** Calculator.
  As each program opens, its taskbar button appears. The Calculator taskbar button is active (pressed).

2 **Switch between tasks using the click-on-window method:**
- **Click** the WordPad or Notepad window.
  The clicked window moves to the front, hiding part or all of the Calculator.

3 **Switch between tasks using the taskbar button method:**

NOTE: You may not be able to see the entire program name on the taskbar button. If you point to the button, however, its full name will appear.

Taskbar button's full name

- **Click** the Calculator taskbar button.
  Calculator moves to the front.
- **Click** the WordPad taskbar button.
  WordPad moves to the front.
- **Click** the Notepad taskbar button.
  Notepad moves to the front.

4 **Maximize Notepad and WordPad:**
- **Maximize** Notepad (review, Exercise 5).
  Notepad now hides both the Calculator and WordPad.
- **Click** the WordPad taskbar button.
  WordPad moves to the front.
- **Maximize** WordPad.
  WordPad now hides both the Calculator and Notepad.

5 **Switch between tasks using the cycle-through-icons method:**
- **Press and hold** Alt while tapping Tab. Watch the screen as icons of the open tasks are displayed. Each press of the Tab key moves the icon outline while the name of the selected task appears below the set of icons.
- **Release** both keys when Calculator is selected.

- **Switch** to Notepad using the cycle-through-icons method.
- **Switch** to WordPad using the cycle-through-icons method.

6 • **Exit** WordPad, **exit** Notepad, then **exit** Calculator.

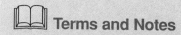

To move between open programs.

📖 **Terms and Notes**

active window
The window whose title bar is highlighted (i.e., in color–not gray), indicating that it is currently in use.

Four Ways to Switch Tasks

- **Click** the desired window itself (if it is visible).
- **Click** the desired taskbar button.
- **Press** Alt + Esc to cycle through open windows.
- **Press** Alt + Tab to cycle through icons of open windows.

 Keyboard Steps to

Switch Tasks

Cycle through open windows:

Press Alt + Esc until the program window you want moves to the front.

Cycle through window icons:

Press Alt + Tab until the icon of the program you want is outlined and its name is displayed below the icons.

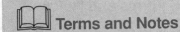

To change the location of a window using both the mouse and the keyboard.

📖 **Terms and Notes**

drag
A mouse action in which you complete the following steps:
- Point to the item to move.
- Hold down the left mouse button.
- Slide the arrow pointer to the desired location.
- Release the mouse button.

move pointer ✥
The four-headed arrow that appears when you click (or point to) some areas, for example, the small area to the immediate right of a sizing handle on the taskbar. Once the move pointer appears, the Move procedure is available.

title bar
The horizontal bar at the top of a window that provides the name of the open document and/or program.

⌨ **Keyboard Steps to**

Move a Window

1. **Select** the desired window.

2. **Press** `Alt` + `Space`.

3. **Press** `M` (Move).

4. **Press** `↑↓←→` (arrow keys) to move window as desired.

5. **Press** `Enter`.

Begin with the desktop displayed and no taskbar buttons on the taskbar.

1
- **Start** Calculator (review, Exercise 3).

2 **Move a window using drag:**
- **Point** to the Calculator's title bar.
- **Press and hold** the left mouse button.
- **Drag** the window to the bottom-right corner of the desktop.
- **Release** the mouse button.

3
- **Move** the Calculator window to the top-right corner of the desktop.
- **Move** the Calculator window to the center of the desktop.

4 **Move a window using the keyboard:**
With the Calculator window active (its title bar highlighted):
- **Press** `Alt` + `Space` to open the Calculator's Control menu.
- **Press** `M` (Move).
  The move pointer appears in the center of the title bar.
- **Press** `→` (right arrow) until the window reaches the right side of the desktop.
  The arrow pointer replaces the move pointer.
- **Press** `↓` (down arrow) until the window reaches the bottom of the desktop.
- **Press** `Enter`.

5
- **Follow** the directions in step 4 to move the Calculator window back to the center of the desktop.
- **Exit** Calculator (review, Exercise 4).

6
- **Start** WordPad.
- IF WordPad is maximized, **click** the Restore button to return WordPad to its previous size.
- **Move** WordPad to the bottom-left corner of the desktop.
- **Move** WordPad to the top-right corner the desktop.
- **Exit** WordPad.
- **Start** WordPad. (Did WordPad remember its last position?)
  WordPad opens in the location in which it was last positioned.
- **Move** WordPad to the bottom-left corner of the desktop with part of it not visible—off the desktop.
- **Exit** WordPad.
- **Start** WordPad. (Did WordPad remember its last position?)
  WordPad does not remember its last position if part of it was off the desktop.
- **Exit** WordPad.

Begin with the desktop displayed and with no taskbar buttons on the taskbar.

Notepad Window (Sized Small)

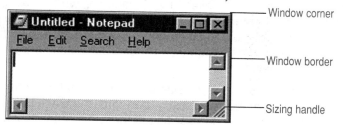

Window corner
Window border
Sizing handle

1 **Size a window using the window border:**
- **Start** Notepad.
- **Point** to the right border of the Notepad window until the sizing pointer (↔) appears.
- **Drag** the window's right border to the right about an inch.

2 **Size a window using the sizing handle:**
- **Point** to the sizing handle in the bottom-right corner of the Notepad window until the diagonal sizing pointer (↖) appears.
- **Drag** the sizing pointer up and left about an inch.

3 **Size a window as small as it will go:**
- **Size** the Notepad window as small as you can.
  Notepad can be sized so small that only its Control menu button, partial name, and Minimize, Maximize, and Close buttons appear.

- **Exit** Notepad and then **start** it again.
  Notice that Notepad does not keep its small size, but instead returns to its default size.
- **Exit** Notepad.

4 **Try to size a window that cannot be sized:**
- **Start** Calculator and **point** to the window border.
- **Notice** that the sizing pointer does not appear because Calculator cannot be sized. **Notice** also that Calculator's borders are narrower than the borders of windows that can be sized.
- **Exit** Calculator.

5 **Size a window (Paint):**
- **Start** Paint. (IF it is maximized, restore it [review, Exercise 6].)
- **Enlarge** the Paint window using the sizing handle.
- **Size** the Paint window as small as possible using the sizing handle.
  Paint keeps a size that is large enough to display its tools and color palette.
- **Exit** Paint. (IF asked to save, click No)
- **Start** Paint again.
  Paint keeps its previous size.
- **Size** Paint so it is about twice as wide as it is high.
- **Exit** Paint. (IF asked to save, click No)

To increase or decrease the area of a window.

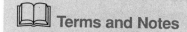 **Terms and Notes**

sizing handle
An area in the bottom-right corner of windows that can be sized. It is used to size windows. You can size a window using any of its corners. However, because the bottom-right corner has a sizing handle that covers a large sizing area, the arrow pointer changes to a sizing pointer more easily than it does in other window corners.

sizing pointer
The arrow pointer becomes a double-headed arrow when you point to a sizing handle or certain borders. The sizing pointer is used to size a window or the taskbar. Sizing pointers can appear in any of the following forms:

↕ vertical
Appears on the top or bottom window border.

↔ horizontal
Appears on the right or left window border.

↖ diagonal
Appears on the top-left or bottom-right corner of a window.

↗ diagonal
Appears on the bottom-left or top-right corner of a window.

⌨ **Keyboard Steps to**

Size a Window
1. **Select** the desired window.
2. **Press** Alt + Space .
3. **Press** S (Size).
4. **Press** ↑↓ (arrow keys) once in the direction of the border to size.
5. **Press** ↑↓ (arrow keys) until the desired size is obtained.
6. **Press** Enter .

EXERCISE 11 • Scroll Through a Window

To use scroll bars to view data in a window that is beyond the window's borders.

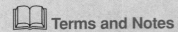 **Terms and Notes**

scroll
To move through a document or list box using a *scroll bar*.

scroll arrows
The arrows at each end of a *scroll bar*. Used to *scroll* through the contents of a document or list box.

scroll bar
The bar that appears at the right and/or bottom edge of a window or list box when the contents are not completely visible. Each scroll bar contains two *scroll arrows* and a proportional *scroll box*.

scroll box
The box in a *scroll bar*. It shows two things:
- The *position* of the information displayed in relation to the entire document or list. For example, if the scroll box is in the center of the *scroll bar*, you are looking at the center of the document or list.
- The *size* of the entire document in relation to the screen size. For example, if the scroll box takes up a large part of the *scroll bar*, you can see most of the entire document or list; but, if the scroll box takes up just a little part of the scroll bar, you can see only a small portion of the entire document or list.

Keyboard Shortcuts

ACTION	PRESS
Character left	←
Character right	→
Line up	↑
Line down	↓
Screen up	Page Up
Screen down	Page Down
Beginning of document	Ctrl + Home
End of document	Ctrl + End

Look at Scroll Bars

Below are illustrations showing **scroll bars**, **scroll arrows**, and **scroll boxes**. In Windows 98, scroll boxes are *proportional*, which means that their size is related to the amount of information in the document. The larger the scroll box, the smaller the document; the smaller the scroll box, the larger the document. No scroll bars are displayed if all the information in a document is visible in the window.

In the illustration below, the size of the horizontal (bottom) scroll box is over half the length of the scroll bar. Therefore, the scroll box is telling you that the window is displaying over half of the width of the text in the document.

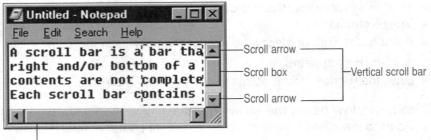

Large scroll box (small document)

In the illustration below, the horizontal scroll box has been moved as far right as possible. Notice that the text inside the dashed box is some of the same text that appears in the illustration above. You can see that the small Notepad window displays a little over half the text in the document.

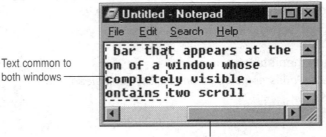

Scroll box (moved as far right as it can go)

Begin with the desktop displayed and with no taskbar buttons on the taskbar.

1
- **Start** Help. (Click **Start**, then click ⊘ Help .)
- **Click** the Index tab.
  The Index tab of Windows Help moves to the front.
- **Notice** the size of the scroll box in the left pane scroll bar.
  NOTE: The very small scroll box tells you there are many more screens of information.

Small scroll box (large document)

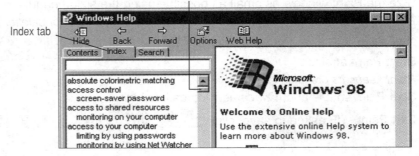

2 **Scroll up and down one line at a time (vertical scroll bar):**
Using the left pane:
- **Click** the bottom scroll arrow once.
  The list scrolls down (i.e., text moves up) one line.
- **Click** the bottom scroll arrow about ten times and watch as new items come into view one line at a time at the bottom of the screen.
- **Click** the top scroll arrow several times and watch as new items come into view one line at a time at the top of the screen.

3 **Scroll up and down one screen at a time (vertical scroll bar):**
Using the left pane:
- **Notice** the name of the item at the bottom of the workspace.
- **Click** the scroll bar between the scroll box and the bottom scroll arrow.
  The list scrolls down a full screen with the line that was previously at the bottom of the workspace now at the top of the workspace.
  NOTE: This feature helps you be certain that you did not miss any data as you move through windows one screen at a time.
- **Click** the scroll bar above the bottom scroll arrow five more times, and watch as the succeeding items in the list come into view one screen at a time (i.e., the list scrolls down).
- **Click** the scroll bar between the scroll box and the top scroll arrow, and watch as the preceding items on the list come into view one screen at a time (i.e., the list scrolls up).

4 **Scroll to a general location (vertical scroll bar):**
Using the left pane:
- **Drag** the scroll box to the middle of the scroll bar.
  The Index displays the middle of the list.
- **Drag** the scroll box to the bottom of the scroll bar.
  The Index displays the end of the list.
- **Drag** the scroll box to the top of the scroll bar.
  The Index displays the beginning of the list.
- **Exit** Help (review, Exercise 4).

5
- **Open** Control Panel. (Click 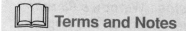 **Start**, point to **Settings** ▶, then click **Control Panel**.)
- **Size** the Control Panel window to about 6" tall by 3" wide (review, Exercise 10).
- **Click** the right scroll arrow (in the horizontal scroll bar) until the scroll box moves to the right side of the horizontal scroll bar.
- **Click** the vertical scroll bar in the space above the bottom scroll arrow but below the scroll box.
- **Drag** the horizontal scroll box slowly to the left side and watch the contents of the window scroll left.
- **Drag** the vertical scroll box slowly to the top and watch the contents of the window scroll up.
- **Drag** the horizontal scroll box slowly left and right and the vertical scroll box slowly up and down a few times and watch what happens.
- **Exit** Control Panel.

EXERCISE 12 • Exit Windows 98

To close Windows 98 and either return to the Logon screen or shut down your computer.

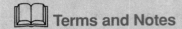 **Terms and Notes**

IMPORTANT: Always shut down Windows 98 before you turn off your computer.

log off
To use the Log Off feaure to do the following:
- Close all programs.
- Disconnect your computer from the network (if you are on one).
- Return Windows 98 to the *Logon screen* so you or someone else can log on again.

log on
To identify yourself to your computer (with a user name and a password) and open the Windows 98 desktop.

Logon screen
The opening Windows 98 dialog box that appears when you first turn your computer on.

shut down
To use the Shut Down feature to quit Windows 98 properly so the computer can safely be turned off.

Three Ways to Exit Windows 98

- **Log Off**
  This procedure closes all programs and prepares your computer to be used by someone else. A new user enters his/her name and password to access Windows 98.

- **Restart Windows 98**
  This procedure restarts Windows 98 and returns you to the *Logon screen*. This option is sometimes used to clear the computer's working memory (*RAM*).

- **Shut Down Windows 98**
  This procedure prepares your computer to be turned off. Don't turn your computer off until you get a message that tells you that it is safe to do so. Some computers, however, turn themselves off automatically without displaying this message.

⌨ **Keyboard Steps to**

Shut Down the Computer

1. Press `Ctrl` + `Esc` OR `⊞` (the Windows key).

2. Press `U` (Sh<u>u</u>t Down).

3. Press `S` (<u>S</u>hut Down).

4. Press `Enter`.

5. **Turn off** the computer.

Begin with the desktop displayed and with no taskbar buttons on the taskbar.

① **Log off and return to the Logon screen:**

- **Click** `Start`, then **click** `Log Off [your user name]`.
  The Log Off Windows dialog box appears, asking if you are sure you want to log off.
- IF you don't have the <u>L</u>og Off option, **skip** to step 2.
- **Click** `Yes`, or **press** `Enter`.
  Windows 98 closes, and the Logon screen appears:

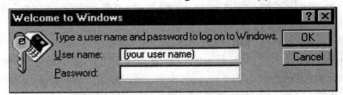

- **Log on** to Windows 98 (review, Exercise 1).

② **Restart your computer:**

- **Click** `Start`, then **click** `Shut Down...`.
  The Shut Down Windows dialog box appears:

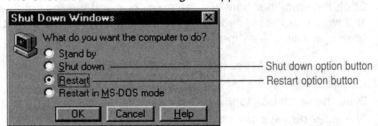

Shut down option button
Restart option button

- **Click** the <u>R</u>estart option button, then **click** `OK`.
  The computer closes everything, then it restarts and displays the Logon screen.
- **Log on** to Windows 98 (review, Exercise 1).

③ **Shut down your computer:**

- **Click** `Start`, then **click** `Shut Down...`.
  The Shut Down Windows dialog box appears.
- **Click** the <u>S</u>hut down option button (to select it).
- **Click** `OK`.
  The Shut Down Windows screen appears:

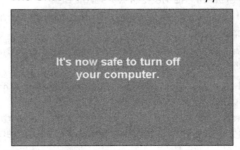

It's now safe to turn off your computer.

NOTE: Many newer computers automatically turn the computer off without displaying the Shut Down Windows screen.

④ **Turn off** the computer (IF your computer does not automatically turn off).

Begin with the computer off.

1 **Start** Windows.

2 **Click** the Start button.

3 **Point** to Settings.

4 **Click** Control Panel.

5 **Maximize** the Control Panel window.

6 **Restore** the Control Panel window.

7 **Minimize** the Control Panel window.

8 **Click** the Control Panel taskbar button to activate the Control Panel window again.

9 **Click** the Control Panel taskbar button to minimize the Control Panel window again.

10 **Click** the Control Panel taskbar button to reactivate the Control Panel window.

11 **Exit** the Control Panel window.

12 **Start** WordPad. (IF it is maximized, restore it.)

13 **Start** Paint. (IF it is maximized, restore it.)

14 **Start** Calculator.

15 **Switch** to Paint.

16 **Maximize** Paint.

17 **Switch** to WordPad.

18 **Maximize** WordPad.

19 **Switch** to Paint using the cycle-through-icons method (press ⎇Alt + ⇥Tab).

20 **Switch** to Calculator using the taskbar button method.

21 **Switch** to WordPad using whichever method you prefer.

22 **Minimize** WordPad.

23 **Switch** to Paint.

24 **Minimize** Paint.

25 **Activate** WordPad.

26 **Restore** WordPad.

27 **Exit** WordPad.

Continued on the next page

Windows Basics

Tasks Reviewed:
- Start Windows 98
- Open and Close Menus
- Start a Program
- Exit a Program
- Maximize a Window
- Restore a Window
- Minimize a Window
- Switch Tasks
- Move a Window
- Size a Window
- Scroll Through a Window
- Exit Windows 98

REMINDER: When you exit a program, if you made any kind of change in that program (for example, drew something in Paint or typed a word in WordPad), a dialog box will appear asking: Do you want to save the current changes? *If this happens in this lesson, click the No button to exit without saving the changes.*

Continued from the previous page

(28) **Activate** Paint.

(29) **Switch** to Calculator.

(30) **Exit** Calculator.

(31) **Exit** Paint.

(32) **Log off** of Windows 98 and then **log on** again (IF your computer has the Log Off option).

(33) **Restart** Windows 98.

(34) **Log on** to Windows 98.

(35) **Shut down** Windows 98.

(36) **Turn off** the computer (IF your computer does not automatically turn off).

Lesson One Worksheets (1 and 2) are on pages 301 and 302.

Lesson Two

Programs and Dialog Boxes

Table of Contents

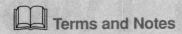

Terms and Notes

common dialog boxes
Dialog boxes, such as Open, Save As, and Print, which are basically the same in many different programs. Common dialog boxes make it easier for you to learn new programs.

controls
The elements in a *dialog box* that ask for information from the user in order for the dialog box to complete its task. Such elements include:

- check boxes
- command buttons
- drop-down list box
- list box
- option buttons
- slider
- spin box
- tabs
- text box

dialog box
A special kind of *window* that offers different *controls* for you to manipulate in order to change the performance or appearance of a document or program.

tabs
In connection with dialog boxes, *tabs* refer to the "flaps" at the top of a series of separate groups of settings (sometimes called *pages*) that appear in some dialog boxes, particularly in Properties dialog boxes.

window
A rectangle that holds a dialog box, folder, program, or document.

WARNINGS: If you accidentally open a dialog box that you do not want to be in, the safest thing for you to do is click the Cancel button or press the Escape key—both of which allow you to back out of dialog boxes without making changes.

Pressing the Enter key while in a dialog box will usually activate the settings and close the dialog box since the OK command button is usually preselected.

What are Dialog Boxes?

Dialog boxes are windows that contain one or more different kinds of **controls** that you can use to:

- Change the performance of a program (such as how often a file is saved).
- Change the appearance of a document (such as changing the font).

There are a lot of different kinds of **windows** in Windows 98, and that can be confusing to new users. For example, there are program windows, folder windows, and dialog box windows. You can quickly tell if a window is a dialog box, however, because, while it has a Help button and a Close button in the top-right corner, it does *not* have a Maximize or Minimize button.

Some dialog boxes are very similar from one program to another. These **common dialog boxes**, such as Open, Save As, and Print, make it easier to learn new programs.

You can make as many changes as you wish in a dialog box, then you usually click the OK button to close the dialog box and activate the new settings. In the dialog box below, however, you would click the Open button to activate the new settings.

The Open Dialog Box

Drop-down list box

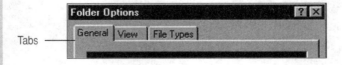

NOTE: This dialog box uses an Open button rather than an OK button to activate its command.

Text box

File name:
Files of type:

Command buttons

Drop-down list box

Tabbed Dialog Boxes

Some dialog boxes use **tabs** to organize the many settings that are available to you. Each tab is always visible, making it easy for you to keep track of where you are. To switch between them, simply click the tab you want.

Folder Options

Tabs — General | View | File Types

Dialog Box Controls

Command buttons   Carry out an action, such as:

OK **OR** Cancel

Text box   A box that provides space for typing any information needed to carry out a command.

File name:

Check boxes

Square boxes next to the items in a list from which you may select as many as desired. Selected check boxes contain check marks.

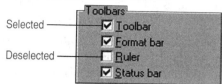

Selected ——

Deselected ——

Option buttons

The circles next to the items in a list from which you may select only one. A selected option button contains a dot in its circle.

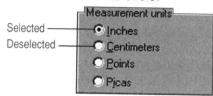

Selected ——

Deselected ——

List box

A box that displays a list of options from which you can choose only one. Scroll to view additional options.

——Scroll bar

Drop-down list box

Similar to a list box, except that a drop-down list box must be opened by clicking it or its arrow. Drop-down list boxes are usually found in small or crowded dialog boxes.

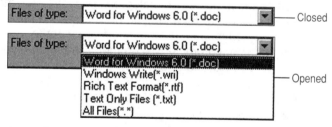

——Closed

——Opened

Spin box

A text box containing a preset value which can be adjusted incrementally by clicking its up or down arrow as desired. (A new value can also be typed in.)

NOTE: A spin box is also called an increment box.

Slider

Lets you set a value within a continuous range.

Terms and Notes

file
Data or program instructions that are saved on a disk as a named unit.

filename
The name you give to data that is stored on a disk.

filename extension
The period and, usually but not always, three characters at the end of a filename (for example, .doc, .txt, .gif). Also called *file extension*.

file type
The kind of file that is created by a particular program. Files are defined by the programs they are created in. Every file type has an icon associated with it; occasionally, a file type has more than one icon associated with it.

program
A set of instructions that your computer follows to perform one specific task, such as word processing. Also called *application*.

NOTE: Files, filenames, and file associations are covered in greater depth in Topic 14, Files and Filenames.

What are File Types?

In Lesson Two, you will be creating, saving, printing, and opening documents. Saving a document creates a **file** on a disk. The kind of **program** you use to create the file determines what is known as the document's **file type**.

When you save a document, you give it a **filename**; the program you are using automatically assigns the document a **filename extension** and an icon. The filename extension and the icon identify the document's file type and thus associate the document with the program in which it was created (in most cases). Some file types, however, can be opened in more than one program. Further, some programs can open more than one file type. Windows 98 recognizes file types by their filename extensions (which are usually hidden to you), but you can identify file types by their icons.

When you save a file in Notepad, it adds the filename extention *.txt.* When you save a file in WordPad, it adds the filename extension *.doc.* Because both WordPad *and* Microsoft Word use .doc as their default file type, there can be some confusion with the .doc file type icon. If you have Microsoft Word on your computer, WordPad will use the Microsoft Word icon rather than the WordPad icon when you save a document in WordPad. Notepad and WordPad file type icons are illustrated below.

 Notepad icon for .txt file types

 WordPad icon for .doc file types if you *do not* have Microsoft Word

 WordPad icon for .doc file types if you *do* have Microsoft Word

In Exercise 19, you will first start a program (Notepad or WordPad) and then use the Open dialog box to open a document. In later exercises, you will open files without starting the program first; when you do, Windows 98 will automatically start the correct program based on the document's file type.

The workspace in the Open dialog box displays only those files that match the file type shown in the Files of type drop-down list box—even though there may be files of other types in that folder. If you want to open a document with a different file type, you must first change the Files of type drop-down list box to the file type you want to open. Therefore, if you want to open a text file in WordPad, you must first change the Files of type drop-down list box setting to *Text Documents (*.txt)* since WordPad's default is to use the *Word for Windows (*.doc)* file type.

Notepad's Open Dialog Box

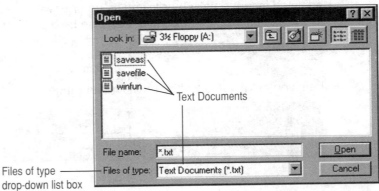

Begin with the desktop displayed and with no taskbar buttons on the taskbar.

1 **Open Notepad and type a sentence:**
- **Start** Notepad (review, Exercise 3).
  Notepad opens.
- **Type:** Now is the time for all good computer users to learn Windows 98.
- **Press** Home to move the cursor to the beginning of the sentence.

2 **Use a dialog box:**
- **Click** Search, then **click** Find.
  The Find dialog box opens with the cursor blinking in the Find what text box.

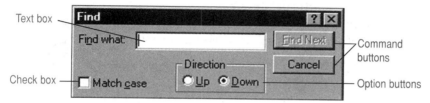

- **Type:** good in the Find what text box.
- **Click** the Match case check box (to select it).
  A check mark appears in the check box.
- **Click** the Match case check box again (to deselect it).
  The check mark disappears.
- **Click** the Up option button (to select it).
  A dot appears in the circle next to Up; the dot disappears in the circle next to Down.
- **Click** the Down option button (to select it).
  The dot disappears from the Up option button and appears in the Down option button.
- **Click** Find Next .
  The word good is highlighted where it occurs in the sentence.
- **Click** Find Next again.
  A small dialog box appears saying: Cannot find "good."
- **Click** OK .
  The small dialog box disappears.
- **Click** X (the Close button) in the Find dialog box.
  The Find dialog box closes.

3 **Exit Notepad:**
- **Exit** Notepad (review, Exercise 4).
  A dialog box appears with a warning:

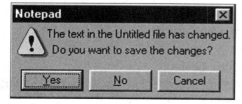

- **Click** No (you do *not* want to save the changes).
  Notepad closes.

To open a dialog box, make changes to the settings, and activate those changes.

⌨ Keyboard Steps to

Open a Dialog Box
1. Press Alt .
2. **Type** the *underlined letter* of the desired menu item which is followed by an ellipsis (...).

Cancel a Dialog Box (and Any Changes You Made in It)
Press Esc .

Move Within a Dialog Box
Press Tab to move forward.
OR
Press Shift + Tab to move backward.

Type Information in a Text Box
1. Press Tab to move to the desired text box.
2. **Type** the desired information.

Select a List Box Item
1. Press Tab to move to the desired list box.
2. Press Alt + ↓ to open a drop-down list.
   AND/OR
   Press ↑↓ to select the desired item.

Select/Deselect a Check Box
1. Press Tab to move to the desired check box.
2. Press Space to select or deselect the item as desired.

Select an Option Button
1. Press Tab to move to the desired option button area.
2. Press ↑↓ to select the desired option.

Choose a Command Button
1. Press Tab to move to the desired command button.
2. Press Enter to accept it.

Complete Original Command
1. Press Tab to move to the OK command button.
2. Press Enter to accept it.

EXERCISE 15 • Use a Properties Dialog Box

To open an object's Properties dialog box, make changes to the settings, and activate those changes.

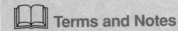 **Terms and Notes**

object
One of the many things that you use when working with the computer system—items such as:

- files
- programs
- folders
- shortcuts
- disk drives

- Control Panel tools
- My Computer
- Network Neighborhood
- The Recycle Bin
- My Briefcase

NOTE: As used here, object is really just another catch-all term for an item, element, thing, or what-cha-ma-call-it. The terms object and object-oriented also have a more formal computer-related meaning that is not used in this book.

properties
Characteristics of an *object;* for example, the color scheme on the desktop is one of the desktop's properties. Changing the properties for an object lets you customize that object.

Properties dialog box
A special kind of dialog box that groups the settings for a specific object's properties.

right-click
Press and quickly release the right mouse button.

tabs
In connection with dialog boxes, *tabs* refer to the "flaps" at the top of a series of separate groups of settings (sometimes called *pages*) that appear in some dialog boxes, particularly Properties dialog boxes.

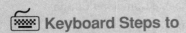 **Keyboard Steps to**

Move Through Dialog Box Tabs

Move forward through tabs:

Press `Ctrl` + `Tab`.

Move backward through tabs:

Press `Ctrl` + `Shift` + `Tab`.

What is a Properties Dialog Box?

A **Properties dialog box** is a special kind of dialog box that lets you change the settings that are associated with an **object**, for example, the desktop or a printer.

Most Properties dialog boxes have **tabs** that organize the different groups of settings related to the object.

You can usually open the Properties dialog box for an object by right-clicking the object and then selecting Properties from the shortcut menu that appears.

Begin with the desktop displayed and with no taskbar buttons on the taskbar.

1 Open a shortcut menu:

- **Right-click** a blank space anywhere on the desktop.
  A shortcut menu appears that has an option for desktop properties.

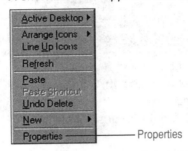
— Properties

2 Open a Properties dialog box (Display Properties):

- **Click** Properties.
  The Display Properties dialog box opens with the Background tab selected.

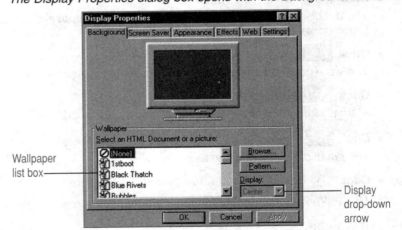

Wallpaper list box

Display drop-down arrow

3 Move through tabs in a Properties dialog box:

WARNING: Do not make changes on any of the tabs.

- **Click** the Screen Saver tab.
  The Screen Saver tab moves forward.
- **Click** the Appearance tab.
  The Appearance tab moves forward.
- **Click** each of the remaining tabs: the Effects, Web, and Settings tabs.
  Each tab moves to the front when you click it.
- **Click** the Background tab.
  The Background tab moves forward.

4 **Change the desktop wallpaper:**

IMPORTANT: Notice the current wallpaper so you can return to it later! Look in the Wallpaper list box and write down the selected option. If your screen is a solid color, the Wallpaper option is (None).

- **Scroll** through the Wallpaper list box and look at the names of the wallpapers that are available.
- **Click** *Red Blocks* to select (highlight) it.

  The screen display preview on the Background tab shows small red blocks.

  NOTE: If you cannot find Red Blocks, use a different wallpaper.

- **Click** the Display drop-down arrow (or list box), then **click** Tile.
- **Click** Apply.

  The desktop changes to red blocks.

- **Click** the Background wallpaper name that you wrote down at the beginning of step 4. (If you don't know what it was, select *[None]* at the top of the list.)
- **Click** Apply.

  The desktop changes back to its original wallpaper (or [None]).

5 **Change the screen saver:**

IMPORTANT: Notice the current screen saver setting so you can return to it later! Look in the Screen Saver drop-down list box and write down the selected option.

- **Click** the Screen Saver tab.
- **Click** the Screen Saver drop-down arrow (or list box).

  The list box drops down.

- **Press** Ctrl + Home to go to the top of the list, *(None).*
- **Press** ↓ (down arrow) once so *3D Flower Box* is selected.

  The screen display preview on the Screen Saver tab shows the selected screen saver.

- **Press** ↓ (down arrow) slowly, looking at the sample of each screen saver in the display, until you reach the bottom of the list box.
- **Click** *Curves and Colors*, then **click** Preview.

  The entire screen displays the Curves and Colors screen saver.

- IF the preview doesn't stop, **click** anywhere to stop the display and return to the dialog box.
- **Click** the Screen Saver drop-down arrow (or list box).
- **Click** the screen saver name that you wrote down at the beginning of step 5. (If you don't know what it was, select *[None]* at the top of the list.)

6 **Cancel a Properties dialog box:**

- **Click** Cancel.

  The Display Properties dialog box disappears.

  NOTES: Clicking the Cancel button will reverse any changes you made in the dialog box—except for instances in which you already clicked the Apply button.

  Clicking the OK button will activate any and all of the changes you made, even if you did not click the Apply button at the time you made the change.

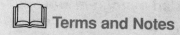
Terms and Notes

NOTES: Because this book is used most often in training settings, many instructors like to keep a stable operating environment. Therefore, you will usually be directed to leave settings the way they were when you started—or to undo changes that you are asked to make during the course of an exercise. If you wish to make changes to your personal computer, however, you may use these instructions to help you do so.

Display Properties is a good example of a dialog box that uses a preview to display the changes you make in the dialog box.

EXERCISE 16 • Use a Program

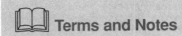
Begin with the desktop displayed and with no taskbar buttons on the taskbar.

1 **Use a program's workspace:**
- **Start** Notepad.
- **Maximize** Notepad.
- **Type** the following text, pressing the Enter key where indicated:

Notepad is a program (also called an application) that is used `Enter` to create and edit unformatted text files. An unformatted text `Enter` file is a file that contains only ASCII text characters (letters, `Enter` numbers, and symbols) and a few codes, such as a carriage return. `Enter` `Enter` WordPad is a simple word processor. WordPad has automatic `Enter` word wrap, so you do not have to press Enter at the end of each `Enter` line (as you do in Notepad). You press Enter only at the end `Enter` of short lines and paragraphs in WordPad. `Enter` `Enter`

- **Press** `Ctrl` + `Home` to move to the beginning of the document.
- **Press** `End` to move to the end of the line.
- **Press** `Home` to move to the beginning of the line.
- **Press** `Ctrl` + `End` to move to the end of the document.
- **Press** `Ctrl` + `Home` to move back to the beginning of the document.

2 **Open menus:**
- **Click** File.
  The File menu drops down:

- **Point** to Edit.
  The Edit menu drops down:

- **Point** to Search.
  The Search menu drops down:

- **Point** to Help.
  The Help menu drops down:

- **Click** outside the menu to close it.

3 **Go on** to Exercise 17 without stopping.

Common Dialog Boxes

This exercise uses a dialog box that is common to other programs in Windows 98: the Save As dialog box. After you learn to use the Save As dialog box here, you will know how to save in other Windows 98 programs as well.

Saving on Drive A:

This book instructs you to save your files on drive A: because there are many instances (especially in a training setting) in which it is better not to save files on the hard disk. While you are instructed to save on drive A:, if you *have* a drive B:, you may substitute drive B: for drive A: throughout this book if you prefer.

IMPORTANT: You need a blank, formatted floppy disk for your data in this exercise.

Continue from Exercise 16 without stopping.

1 **Open the Save As dialog box:**
- **Click** File, then **click** Save (or Save As).
The Save As dialog box opens.

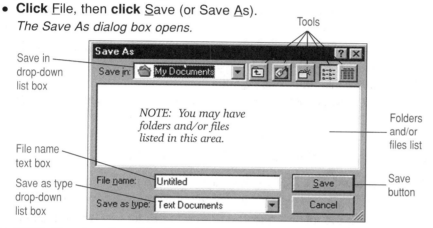

NOTE: There is no Save dialog box—just a Save command. The Save command will save changes to the document that you are working on if it has already been saved (i.e., has a name). However, when you save a new, untitled document, Windows automatically opens the Save As dialog box so you can name your file.

2 **Save a document on drive A:**
- **Insert** your blank, formatted disk into drive A:.
- **Click** the Save in drop-down list box.
The list opens to reveal the available options. (Your list may be different.)

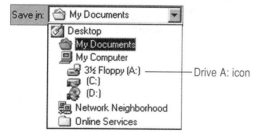

- **Click** 3½ Floppy (A:).
The drive A: icon appears in the Save in drop-down list box.
- **Click** the File name text box.
The cursor appears in the text box.
- **Delete** any characters in the File name text box.

To use the Save As dialog box to: name and save a new file, resave an already named file, or rename and save an existing file on a disk.

Terms and Notes

Three Ways to Save a Document
- **Click** File, then **click** Save.
- **Press** Ctrl + S (not in Notepad).
- **Click** 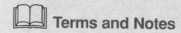 (the Save button) on the toolbar (not available in Notepad).

NOTE: The Save command opens the Save As dialog box the first time you save a document. If the document is already named, the Save command simply updates the saved file—incorporating any changes you've made to the document without asking for confirmation. To save a document with a different name, you must use the Save As command.

document
A file that consists of data created in a program, such as a letter typed in WordPad or a picture drawn in Paint. Also called *data file*.

floppy disk
A removable, magnetically coated diskette on/from which information can be stored and retrieved.

NOTES: 3½" disks are referred to as floppy—even though you can't bend them—as a hold over from the days of 5¼" disks which really were floppy. The term, floppy, helps distinguish external disks (that you insert into a floppy disk drive) from the internal hard disk that comes built into your computer.

Although it used to be common to sell programs on floppy disk, today most programs come on CD-ROMs. When 3½" disks are used to store data files, they are sometimes called data disks.

program file
A file containing a set of instructions that your computer follows to perform a task, such as word processing. Also called *application file*.

Save
The command that saves changes to a previously named document or opens the Save As dialog box so you can save a new document.

Save As
A command that opens the Save As dialog box, which lets you save a new document or rename a previously saved one.

Continued on the next page

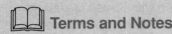
associated file
A file that has been identified as belonging to a certain program, such as .txt with Notepad, .bmp with Paint, or .doc with Microsoft Word. When you open an associated file, the program related to that file also opens automatically.

default
An automatic setting in a program.

IMPORTANT: When you use Save As to save a file with a name that matches an existing filename, you get this message:

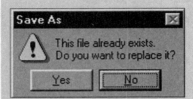

You DO NOT get this message when you resave a previously named document using the Save command; Windows automatically updates the existing file with the changes.

Keyboard Steps to

Save a Previously Named File

SHORTCUT: Ctrl + S

NOTE: The keyboard shortcut above is not available in Notepad.

1. **Press** Alt + F (File).

2. **Press** S (Save).

Save a New File or Rename a File

1. **Press** Alt + F (File).

2. **Press** A (Save As).

3. **Type** the filename.

    —IF you want to change the file location:

    • **Press** Alt + I (Save in).

    • **Press** ↓ (down arrow).

    • **Press** ↑↓ (up or down arrow) to highlight the desired location.

    • **Press** Enter.

4. **Press** Enter.

Continued from the previous page

• **Type**: savefile (Do not put a period at the end; Notepad automatically adds the extension *.txt* to the filename, associating it with the program.)
   NOTE: Folders, files, and filenames are covered in Lessons Four and Five.

• **Click** Save .
   The dialog box closes, the file is saved on the floppy disk in drive A:, and the filename appears on the title bar.

   Filename

   ```
   🗿 savefile - Notepad
   File  Edit  Search  Help
   ```

3 **Resave (update) a previously named file:**

• **Press** Ctrl + End to move the cursor to the end of the document.
   NOTE: Be sure to leave one blank line between the previous text and the new text.

• **Type** the following text, pressing the Enter key where indicated:
   The Save command either resaves a previously named document or Enter opens the Save As dialog box so you can name and save a new Enter document. Enter Enter

• **Click** File, then **click** Save.
   The drive A: light goes on as the revised document is resaved, updating the file.
   NOTE: The program automatically remembers the filename and location that you set previously.

4 **Rename and save a previously named file:**

• **Press** Ctrl + End to move the cursor to the end of the document.
   NOTE: Be sure to leave one blank line between the previous text and the new text.

• **Type** the following text, pressing the Enter key where indicated:
   The Save As... command opens a dialog box to let you either name Enter and save a new document or rename and save a previously named Enter document. Enter Enter

• **Click** File, then **click** Save As.
   The Save As dialog box opens with the previous filename highlighted in the File name text box, with the cursor blinking at the end of the filename, and 3½" Floppy (A:) in the Save in drop-down list box.

   Previous filename

• **Type**: saveas
   The new filename replaces the existing one.
   NOTES: When text is highlighted in a text box, it is automatically deleted when you start typing over it. If you press the Home key, the End key, or an arrow key, the highlighting disappears and the text remains so that you can edit it if you wish.

• **Click** Save .
   A copy of the document is saved on the floppy disk in drive A: with a new filename. The document with the original filename remains on the floppy disk as well.

5 **Go on** to Exercise 18 without stopping.

The New Command

The New command is common to most Windows 98 Accessory programs. If unsaved data exists in a program, the New command displays a dialog box asking if you want to save the changes. If you click Yes, the Save As dialog box opens and you can save the file in the desired location with the desired filename. If you click No, the workspace will be cleared without saving the changes.

Continue from Exercise 17 without stopping.

1 Clear the workspace:
- **Click** File, then **click** New.
  The workspace clears.
- IF a dialog box appears asking if you want to save the changes,
  click No (you do *not* want to save them).

2 Clear a workspace with unsaved data and save the data:
- **Type**: Windows is a user-friendly program.
- **Click** File, then **click** New.
  The following dialog box appears:

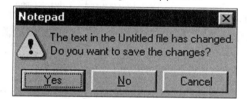

- **Click** Yes (you do want to save the changes).
  The Save As dialog box appears with the cursor in the highlighted File name text box.
- **Type**: winfun
- **Notice** that *Floppy (A:)* remains in the Save in drop-down list box. It will stay there until you either open a file or exit Notepad.
- **Click** Save .
  The file is saved on the floppy disk in drive A: and the workspace clears.

3 Clear a workspace with unsaved data and do *not* save the data:
- **Type**: Windows has many features that are common to all Windows programs.
- **Click** File, then **click** New.
  Again, a dialog box appears telling you that changes were made and asking if you want to save the changes.
- **Click** No (you do *not* want to save the changes).
  The workspace clears, and your document was not saved.

4 Remove and label your floppy disk:
- **Remove** your data disk from drive A:.
- **Label** your disk: DATA DISK 1. Also, put your name on your floppy disk and store it in a safe place.
  NOTE: You will need your data disk throughout this book. A separate disk will be used for the Practice Exercises at the end of each lesson.

5
- **Exit** Notepad.

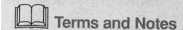

To clear the workspace so that you can start a new document.

📖 **Terms and Notes**

Three Ways to Create a New Document
- **Click** File, then **click** New.
- **Press** [Ctrl] + [N] (not in Notepad).
- **Click** [ ] (the New button) on the toolbar (not available in Notepad).

common commands
Commands such as New, Save, and Print that work the same way in most Windows programs.

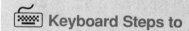

⌨ **Keyboard Steps to**

Clear the Workspace and Save

1. **Press** [Alt] + [F] (File).
2. **Press** [N] (New).
   A dialog box appears asking if you want to save the changes.
   —IF you are using WordPad, the New dialog box asks you to choose the type of document you want to create. Press the Enter key to accept *Word 6 Document*.
3. **Press** [Enter] to activate the Yes command button.
   The Save As dialog box appears.
4. **Type** a filename in the File name text box.
   —IF you want to change the file location:
   - **Press** [Alt] + [I] (Save in).
   - **Press** [↓] (down arrow).
   - **Press** [↑↓] (up or down arrow) to select the desired location.
   - **Press** [Enter] .
5. **Press** [Enter] to activate the Save command button.

Clear the Workspace Without Saving

1. **Press** [Alt] + [F] (File).
2. **Press** [N] (New).
3. **Press** [N] (No).

EXERCISE 19 • Open a Document

To use the Open dialog box to copy a file from a disk to a program's workspace.

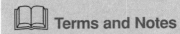 **Terms and Notes**

Three Ways to Open a Document

- **Click** File, then **click** Open.
- **Press** Ctrl + O (not in Notepad).
- **Click** 📂 (the Open button) on the toolbar (not available in Notepad).

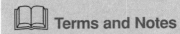 **Keyboard Steps to**

Open a Document

SHORTCUT: Ctrl + O
NOTE: The keyboard shortcut above is not available in Notepad.

1. **Press** Alt + F (File).
2. **Press** O (Open).
   The Open dialog box appears.
   —IF you want to change the location to Look in:
   - **Press** Alt + I (Look in).
   - **Press** ↓ (down arrow).
   - **Press** ↑↓ (up or down arrow) to highlight the desired location.
   - **Press** Enter.
   —IF you want to change the type of file the program will display:
   - **Press** Alt + T (Files of type).
   - **Press** ↓ (down arrow).
   - **Press** ↑↓ (up or down arrow) to highlight the desired file type.
   - **Press** Enter.
3. **Press** Alt + N (File name).
4. **Type** the filename of the file you want to open.
5. **Press** Enter to activate the Open command button.

Begin with the desktop displayed and with no taskbar buttons on the taskbar.

1 **Access the Open dialog box:**
- **Start** and **maximize** Notepad.
- **Click** File, then **click** Open.
  The Open dialog box appears.
- **Notice** its similarity to the Save As dialog box (review, Exercise 17).

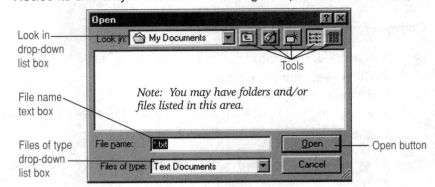

2 **Locate a file to open:**
- **Insert** DATA DISK 1 in drive A:.
- **Click** the Look in drop-down list box.
  The list opens to display the available options.

- **Click** 💾 3½ Floppy (A:).
  The files on drive A: appear in the workspace.

3 **Open a document:**
Click 📄 winfun, then **click** ⬜ Open.
OR
Double-click 📄 winfun.
The winfun.txt file opens in the Notepad workspace.

4 **Open the saveas file:**
- **Clear** the workspace (review, Exercise 18).
- **Click** File, **click** Open, **click** saveas, then **click** ⬜ Open.

5 **Open a new file when a program contains an unchanged file:**

If the existing file in Notepad has not been changed, when you start a new file, the existing file disappears and the new file opens into the program.

- **Open** *savefile* (review, step 4).

  The saveas file closes and savefile appears in the Notepad window.

6 **Open a new file when a program contains a changed file:**

- **Move** the cursor to the end of the document.
- **Type**: I am changing this file by typing this text.
- **Access** the Open dialog box (review, step 1).

  A dialog box appears asking if you want to save the changes.

- **Click** [No] (you do *not* want to save the changes. Note, however, that you could save the changes at this point if you wanted to.)

  The Open dialog box appears.

- **Open** *winfun*, then **exit** Notepad.

7 **Open a Notepad document in WordPad:**

- **Start** WordPad.
- IF the WordPad toolbar is not displayed, **click** <u>V</u>iew, then **click** <u>T</u>oolbar.

  WordPad opens with the toolbar displayed.

WordPad Standard Toolbar

- **Maximize** WordPad, if it is not already maximized.
- **Click** 🖙 (the Open button) on the Standard toolbar.

  Notice that the Open dialog box for WordPad looks like the Open dialog box for Notepad.

- **Change** the Look <u>i</u>n drop-down box to Floppy (A:) (review, step 2).

  None of your files are displayed since WordPad is currently looking for only .doc files. (See Topic 10, Program File Types.)

8 **Change the file type in the Open dialog box:**

Notice that the Files of <u>t</u>ype drop-down list box defaults to *Word for Windows (*.doc)* for WordPad. You, on the other hand, want to open a document created in Notepad. Remember that the file type associated with Notepad is *Text Documents (*.txt)*.

- **Click** the Files of type drop-down list box.

  Text Documents (*.txt) —

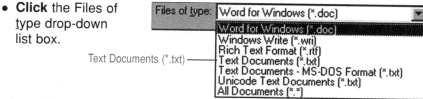

- **Click** the Text Documents (*.txt) option.

  Your files now appear in the list box.

- **Open** *saveas*.
- **Restore** and then **exit** WordPad.
- **Remove** DATA DISK 1 from drive A:.

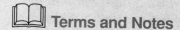

Terms and Notes

associated file
A file that has been identified as belonging to a certain program, such as .txt with Notepad, .bmp with Paint, or .doc with Microsoft Word. When you open an associated file, the program related to that file also opens automatically.

changed file
A file that has had some kind of modification—either the file is new or the file has been edited in some way since it was last saved. See *unchanged file*, below.

toolbar
A row of buttons, usually along the top or bottom of the screen by default, that provides quick access to frequently used commands, tasks, or other objects such as Internet addresses and hyperlinks.

unchanged file
A file that has not been modified (edited) since it was last saved. See *changed file*, above.

WordPad
An accessory program shipped with Microsoft Windows 98. WordPad is a simple word processor that provides only basic formatting features.

EXERCISE 20 • Print a Document

To make a hard copy of the data with or without the help of the Print dialog box.

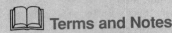 **Terms and Notes**

ASSUMPTION: It is assumed that your printer has been properly installed.

Three Ways to Print a Document

- **Click** File, then **click** Print.
- **Press** Ctrl + P (not in Notepad).
- **Click** 🖨 (the Print button) on the toolbar (not available in Notepad).

Print dialog box

Considered a *common dialog box* along with Open and Save As. Contains three sections: Printer, Print range, and Copies. The Print range and Copies sections are used mainly for multiple page documents. The commands in each section are summarized below:

Printer section

- **Name**   Lists the printers that are set up on your computer.
- **Status**   Shows if printer is ready.
- **Type**   Shows selected printer name.
- **Where**   May show printer location.
- **Comment**   May show data about printer.
- **Print to file**   Prints to a file instead of a printer.
- **Properties button**   Opens a Properties dialog box in which you may set options for the selected printer. Options vary with different printers.

Print range section

- **All**   Prints the entire document.
- **Pages**   Prints the indicated range of pages.
- **Selection**   Prints the highlighted data.

Copies section

- **Number of copies**   Prints the number of copies you set.
- **Collate**   Specifies if you want the copies grouped. This option is available only if more than one copy is set.

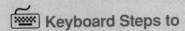 **Keyboard Steps to**

Print a Document

SHORTCUT: Ctrl + P

1. **Press** Alt + F (File).
2. **Press** P (Print).
3. **Press** Enter to accept OK.

NOTE: Notepad does not use a Print dialog box to print because it is a text editor (i.e., not a word processor) and, therefore, does not use special printing codes. All other programs in Windows make a Print dialog box available when you print, however. Since the purpose of this exercise is to use a Print dialog box, you are instructed to print using WordPad instead of Notepad.

Begin with the desktop displayed and with no taskbar buttons on the taskbar.

①
- **Start** and **maximize** WordPad.
- **Insert** DATA DISK 1 in drive A:.
- **Access** the Open dialog box (review, Exercise 19, step 1).
- **Change** Files of type to *Text Documents (*.txt)* (review, Exercise 19, step 8).
- **Change** to drive A: (review, Exercise 19, step 2), then **open** *saveas*.

② **Print a document using the Print dialog box:**
- **Make sure** that your printer is turned on and ready to receive data.
- **Click** File, then **click** Print.
  The Print dialog box opens.

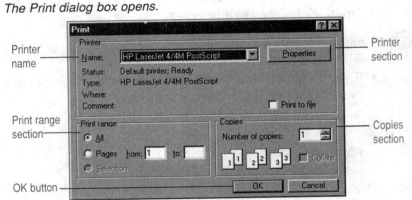

- **Notice** that the default setting for the Print range section is All and the default setting for the Copies section is a single copy. These are the settings used most often.

- **Click** OK .
  The saveas file is printed.

> Notepad is a program (also called an application) that is used
> to create and edit unformatted text files. An unformatted text
> file is a file that contains only ASCII text characters (letters,
> numbers, and symbols) and a few codes, such as a carriage return.
>
> WordPad is a simple word processor. WordPad has automatic
> word wrap, so you do not have to press Enter at the end of each
> line (as you do in Notepad). You press Enter only at the end
> of short lines and paragraphs in WordPad.
>
> The Save command either resaves a previously named document or
> opens the Save As dialog box so you can name and save a new
> document.
>
> The Save As... command opens a dialog box to let you either name
> and save a new document or rename and save a previously named
> document.

③ **Print a document using the toolbar:**
NOTE: If the toolbar is not displayed, click View, then click Toolbar.
- **Click** 🖨 (the Print button) on the Standard toolbar.
  The saveas file is printed again, this time without opening the Print dialog box.
- **Exit** WordPad without saving (if asked), and **remove** DATA DISK 1.

Begin with the desktop displayed and with no taskbar buttons on the taskbar.

1 **Open the Page Setup dialog box:**
- **Start** and **maximize** WordPad.
- **Click** **File**, then **click** Page Setup.
  The Page Setup dialog box opens.

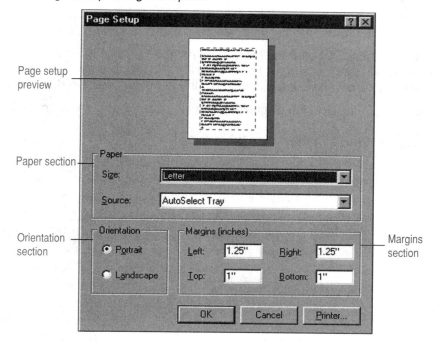

2 **Highlight options in the Size drop-down list box:**
- **Click** the Size drop-down list box.
  The Size drop-down list box opens.
- **Notice** the current setting in the Size drop-down list box (probably *Letter*).
- **Press** ⬇ until you reach the bottom of the list, then **press** ⬆ until you reach the top of the list.
  The page setup preview changes with each page size.
- **Click** the original definition (probably *Letter*).

3 **Change the page orientation:**
- **Click** the Landscape option button.
  The page setup preview changes to a landscape orientation.
- **Click** the Portrait option button.
  The page setup preview returns to a portrait orientation.

4 **Change the page margins:**
- **Click** the Left margin text box, then **change** the setting to 2".
- **Click** the Right margin text box, then **change** the setting to .5".
- **Click** the Bottom margin text box, then **change** the setting to 3".
  The page setup preview changes to reflect each margin change.

5 **Cancel the Page Setup dialog box:**
- **Click** [Cancel] to close the dialog box without activating changes.
- **Exit** WordPad.

To make changes in the Page Setup dialog box and notice how the page setup preview displays those changes.

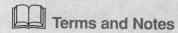 **Terms and Notes**

NOTE: Page Setup is a good example of a dialog box that uses a preview to display the changes you make in the dialog box.

landscape
A page orientation in which the paper is wider than it is tall, as are typical landscapes.

portrait
A page orientation in which the paper is taller than it is wide, as are typical portraits.

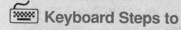 **Keyboard Steps to**

Change Page Setup (WordPad)
1. Press [Alt] + [F] (File).
2. Press [U] (Page Setup).
3. Choose options below as desired:

Paper size
- Press [Alt] + [Z] (Size).
- Press [Alt] + [↓] (down arrow).
- Press [↑↓] (up or down arrow) to highlight the desired paper definition.
- Press [Enter].

Paper source
- Press [Alt] + [S] (Source).
- Press [Alt] + [↓] (down arrow).
- Press [↑↓] (up or down arrow) to highlight the desired paper source.
- Press [Enter].

Page orientation
- Press [Alt] + [O] (Portrait) OR
  Press [Alt] + [A] (Landscape).

Paper margins
- Press [Alt] + [L] (Left) OR
  Press [Alt] + [R] (Right) OR
  Press [Alt] + [T] (Top) OR
  Press [Alt] + [B] (Bottom).
- Type the desired setting.
4. Press [Enter] to accept OK.

EXERCISE 22 • Use WordPad

To create and edit a document in WordPad using simple formatting features.

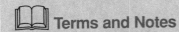 **Terms and Notes**

alignment
The horizontal placement of paragraphs or lines of text. One can align text to the left, center, or right. Also called *justification*.

font design
A complete set of characters designed in a specific style, such as Arial or Times New Roman. Also called *font face*.

font styles
Font characteristics, such as bold, italic, and underline, that are used for text emphasis.

pressed
A 3-D effect in which a button (or other item) appears "sunken," indicating it is selected (or active).

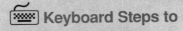 **Keyboard Steps to**

Highlight (Select) a Word

1. **Place** the cursor before the word to highlight. *(See Keyboard Steps, Exercise 16.)*
2. **Press** Ctrl + Shift + → to highlight the word. (Press the right arrow key again to highlight two words.)

Change the Font Style

1. **Highlight** the desired word *(see above)*.
2. **Choose** one of the following font styles:
   - **Press** Ctrl + B (Bold).
   - **Press** Ctrl + I (Italic).
   - **Press** Ctrl + U (Underline).

   NOTE: Use the same procedure to change from a font style to regular text.

Change the Text Alignment

1. **Place** the cursor in the paragraph (or line) to align. *(See Keyboard Steps, Exercise 16.)*
2. **Choose** one of the following text alignments:
   - **Press** Ctrl + L (Align Left).
   - **Press** Ctrl + E (Center).
   - **Press** Ctrl + R (Align Right).

Undo a Change

Press Ctrl + Z (Undo).

As mentioned before, WordPad is a simple word processor and Notepad is a text editor. With WordPad you can use the formatting features listed below:

- **font designs** such as Times New Roman and Arial
- **font sizes** (The default size is 10 point, but you can make fonts larger or smaller as desired.)
- **font styles** such as bold, italics, and underline
- **font colors**
- **text alignments** such as left align, center, and right align

Notepad does not offer the features listed above. Although the two programs create different kinds of file types, WordPad is able to open the simple Notepad files. Notepad, however, cannot open the more complex WordPad files.

Begin with the desktop displayed and with no taskbar buttons on the taskbar.

1
- **Start** and **maximize** WordPad.
- **Type** the following text, pressing the Enter key where indicated:

  When WordPad is started, the cursor (a blinking vertical line) is displayed in the top left corner of the workspace. The cursor is called an insertion point because it shows where the next character you type will be inserted. You create a document by typing. Press the ENTER key only at the end of short lines and paragraphs or to insert blank lines. WordPad will automatically move a word to the next line when the word is too long to fit on the present line. Enter Enter You can move the insertion point by using the arrow keys or the mouse. The mouse pointer shape appears as an I-Beam in the WordPad workspace. To move the cursor with the mouse, you can move the I-Beam to the desired location AND CLICK THE MOUSE BUTTON. Enter Enter

2 **Save a document on drive A:**
- **Insert** DATA DISK 1, then **click** 💾 (the Save button) on the toolbar.
  The Save As dialog box opens.
- **Change** to Floppy (A:) (review, Exercise 17, step 2).
- **Save** the document; name it create (review, Exercise 17, step 2).
  The document is saved and you are returned to the WordPad workspace.

3 **Change text alignments:**
- **Click** in the first paragraph.
- **Notice** the alignment buttons on the Formatting toolbar.
  The Align Left button is pressed; the text is even on the left margin and ragged on the right margin.

  Align Left button

- **Click** in the second paragraph, then **click** ≡ (the Align Right button).
  All the lines of text in the paragraph are even on the right margin and ragged on the left margin.
- **Click** in the third paragraph, then **click** ≡ (the Center button).
  All the lines of text in the paragraph are centered.

4 **Change font styles:**
- **Double-click** WordPad (in the first line), then **click** (the Bold button).
  The word is first highlighted and then bolded. (You can see the bold effect better when the word is no longer highlighted.)

- **Double-click** cursor (in the first line), then **click** [I] (the Italic button).
  The word becomes italicized.
- **Double-click** insertion (in the second line), then **press** [Shift] while you **click** point (to highlight both words), then click [I] (the Italic button).
  The two words, insertion point, *become italicized.*
- **Double-click** vertical (in the first line), then **click** [U] (the Underline button).
  The word becomes underlined.

5 Change font and font size:
  - **Double-click** character (in the second line).
  - **Click** the Font drop-down arrow on the Formatting toolbar.

  Font drop-down list box ——[Times New Roman ▼]—— Drop-down arrow

  The Font drop-down list box opens, displaying all available fonts.
  - **Scroll** toward the top of the list and **click** Arial.
    The font changes to Arial, a plain font that has no serifs.
  - **Click** the Font Size drop-down arrow.

  Font Size drop-down list box ——[10 ▼]—— Drop-down arrow

  The Font Size drop-down list box opens, displaying a variety of font sizes.
  - **Click** 16.
    The font size changes to 16 point; the default size is 10 point.

6 Resave and print:
  - **Click** [💾] (the Save button) on the Standard toolbar.
    The document changes are resaved without opening the Save As dialog box.
  - **Click** [🖨] (the Print button) on the Standard toolbar.
    The document is printed without opening the Print dialog box.

When **WordPad** is started, the *cursor* (a blinking <u>vertical</u> line) is displayed in the top left corner of the workspace. The cursor is called an *insertion point* because it shows where the next character you type will be inserted.

You create a document by typing. Press the ENTER key only at the end of short lines and paragraphs or to insert blank lines. WordPad will automatically move a word to the next line when the word is too long to fit on the present line.

You can move the insertion point by using the arrow keys or the mouse. The mouse pointer shape appears as an I-Beam in the WordPad workspace. To move the cursor with the mouse, you can move the I-Beam to the desired location AND CLICK THE MOUSE BUTTON.

---

7 Change font color:
  - **Double-click** character (in the second line).
  - **Click** [🖊] (the Color button) on the Formatting toolbar, then **click** [■ Fuchsia].
  - **Click** anywhere in the workspace to deselect the word.
    The word, character, *becomes fuchsia.*

8 Undo a change:
  - **Click** [↶] (the Undo button) on the Standard toolbar.
  - **Click** anywhere in the workspace to deselect the word.
    The word, character, *changes back to black.*

9
  - **Remove** DATA DISK 1 and **exit** WordPad without saving changes.

Programs and Dialog Boxes

Tasks Reviewed:
- Use a Dialog Box
- Use a Properties Dialog Box
- Use a Program
- Save a Document
- Start a New Document
- Open a Document
- Print a Document
- Page Setup
- Use WordPad

IMPORTANT: You need a new blank, formatted floppy disk just for the Practice Exercises. Your printer must be turned on and ready to receive data to complete step 3, below.

Begin with the desktop displayed and with no taskbar buttons on the taskbar.

1
- **Start** and **maximize** WordPad.
- **Type:** The Find dialog box is opened differently in WordPad than it is in Notepad.
- **Move** the cursor to the beginning of the document.
- **Open** the Find dialog box. (Click Edit, then click Find.)
- **Find** all instances of the word, in, using the dialog box controls.
- **Cancel** the Find dialog box.
- **Exit** WordPad without saving.

2
- **Right-click** the desktop, then **click** Properties to open the Display Properties dialog box.
- **Access** the different tabs, ending with the Background tab in front.
- **Change** the wallpaper to *Circles*, **change** the Display setting to *Tile*, then **click** Apply .
- **Change** the wallpaper to any other design of your choice, then **click** Apply .
- **Change** the wallpaper to *(None)* at the top of the list, then **click** Apply .
- **Cancel** the Display Properties dialog box.

3
- **Start** and **maximize** Notepad.
- **Open** each of the menus on the menu bar.
- **Type** the following, pressing the Enter key where indicated:

Notepad is a text editor. A text editor is a program that operates in ASCII file format and that you use to create unformatted text files. ASCII stands for American Standard Code for Information Interchange. [Enter][Enter]

- **Label** your blank disk: DATA DISK 2 (Practice), and put your name on it.
- **Insert** DATA DISK 2 into drive A:.
- **Save** the document on DATA DISK 2 in drive A:. **Name** it text1.
- **Type** the following, pressing the Enter key where indicated:

Text files contain only ASCII text characters (letters, numbers, and symbols) and a few codes such as carriage returns. Unformatted [Enter] text files do not contain formatting codes such as underline and [Enter] bold. [Enter][Enter]

- **Save** the document as a new file on drive A:. **Name** it text2.
- **Click** File, then **click** Print.

```
Notepad is a text editor.  A text editor is a program that operates
in ASCII file format and that you use to create unformatted text
files.  ASCII stands for American Standard Code for Information
Interchange.

Text files contain only ASCII text characters (letters, numbers,
and symbols) and a few codes such as carriage returns.  Unformatted
text files do not contain formatting codes such as underline and
bold.
```

4
- **Clear** the workspace (i.e., start a new document).
- **Open** *text1,* then **clear** the workspace again.
- **Type**: Whether you think you can, or whether you think you can't, you are right.
- **Clear** the workspace and save the document. **Name** it cando.
- **Type**: Previous practice prevents poor performance.
- **Clear** the workspace without saving the document this time, then **exit** Notepad.

5
- **Start** and **maximize** WordPad.
- **Open** the Notepad file, *text1.*
  REMEMBER: You must first change Files of type to Text Documents (*.txt).
- **Print** the document using the Print button on the Standard toolbar.

> Notepad is a text editor. A text editor is a program that operates in ASCII file format and that you use to create unformatted text files. ASCII stands for American Standard Code for Information Interchange.

- **Clear** the workspace. **Click** [OK] in the New dialog box.

6
- **Type** the following text using the formatting features shown below:

> In WordPad, you can use **bold** and *italic* and <u>underline</u>.
> You can also use left, center, or right alignment in paragraphs.
> And you can use a wide variety of font **designs** and sizes.
>
> Align center   Align right   Use 16-point Arial Rounded font.

- **Save** the document on drive A:. **Name** it format.
- **Change** the font color of the word, *designs*, to red.
- **Undo** the change.
- **Print** the document, then **clear** the workspace without saving the changes.

7
- **Open** the Page Setup dialog box.
- **Change** the page orientation to landscape.
- **Change** all the margins to 2".
- **Notice** the page setup preview in the dialog box.
- **Change** the left and right margins to 1.25".
- **Change** the top and bottom margins to 1".
- **Change** the page orientation back to portrait.
- **Cancel** the Page Setup dialog box, then **exit** WordPad.

8
- **Remove** DATA DISK 2 from drive A:.

Lesson Two Worksheet (3) is on page 303.

NEXT
LESSON

Lesson Three
The Taskbar

Table of Contents

TOPIC 11 • The Taskbar

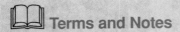 Terms and Notes

bar
The term *bar* is used to define window stripes (e.g., the title bar, menu bar, and status bar). In addition, *bar* is also used to define certain special Windows 98 features (e.g., the Explorer bar, Channel bar, and Address bar).

system tray
The area at the right end of the *taskbar* that displays system icons and offers easy access to (and information about) those system features.

taskbar
The bar that appears by default on the bottom of the desktop and lets you quickly start programs, switch between tasks, and access the tools (and toolbars) of your choice.

taskbar button
A button located on the *taskbar* that represents an open program. Each taskbar button displays the program icon and name of each open program.

NOTE: Don't confuse taskbar buttons with Quick Launch toolbar buttons or system tray icons—both of which are also on the taskbar.

What is the Taskbar?

The **taskbar** is the bar at the bottom of the desktop with the following items:
- Start button on the left end
- Quick Launch toolbar (which can be removed)
- Taskbar button area
- System tray at the right end

The taskbar is easily customized, so yours may look different from the illustration of the default taskbar below.

Taskbar without Taskbar Buttons

Start button   Quick Launch toolbar   Taskbar button area   System tray

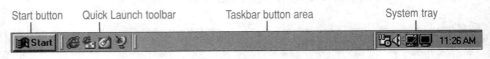

Taskbar with Taskbar Buttons

Taskbar buttons

What Does the Taskbar Do?

Use the taskbar to:
- Switch between open programs
- Arrange windows
- Control programs
- Access the Web
- Access the desktop
- Change the system date and time
- Change the speaker volume
- Schedule tasks

You can customize the taskbar by:
- Putting toolbars (and **bars**) on the taskbar, including: Quick Launch, Address, Links, and Desktop
- Creating your own new toolbar
- Hiding toolbar button names (text labels)
- Hiding the taskbar
- Moving the taskbar
- Sizing the taskbar

The Start Button

The taskbar's Start button lets you carry out many basic Windows 98 tasks:
- View a list of *Programs*
- Start *Programs*
- Open your *Favorites* folder
- Open *Documents*
- Change computer *Settings*
- *Find* Files or Folders
- Get *Help*
- Use the *Run* command
- *Log Off* of Windows
- *Shut Down* the computer

Begin with the desktop displayed and with no taskbar buttons on the taskbar.

1 Move the taskbar to the right edge of the desktop:
- **Point** to a blank space on the taskbar.
- **Drag** the pointer up and right until the taskbar jumps to the right edge of the desktop.

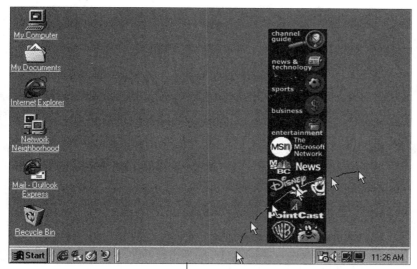

Taskbar (default position)

- **Release** the mouse button.
  The taskbar jumps to the right edge of the desktop.

Taskbar

2
- **Follow** the procedure in step 1 to **move** the taskbar back to the bottom of the desktop.
- **Move** the taskbar to the top of the desktop.
- **Move** the taskbar to the left edge of the desktop.
- **Move** the taskbar back to the bottom of the desktop.

To drag the taskbar to one of the four edges of the desktop.

📖 **Terms and Notes**

move pointer ✛
The four-headed arrow that appears when you point to (or click) some areas, for example, the small area to the immediate right of a sizing handle on the taskbar. Once the move pointer appears, the Move procedure is available.

⌨ **Keyboard Steps to**

Move the Taskbar

1. Press `Ctrl` + `Esc` , `Esc` .

2. Press `Alt` + `Space` .
   A Control menu appears.

3. Press `M` (Move).
   The move pointer appears in the middle of the taskbar.

4. Use `↔` (arrow keys) to move the arrow pointer until the taskbar appears in the desired position on the desktop.

5. Press `Enter` .

EXERCISE 25 • Size the Taskbar

To change the dimensions of the taskbar.

📖 Terms and Notes

NOTES: This feature is useful when you have so many taskbar buttons on the taskbar that they become difficult to identify.

You can size the taskbar to take up as much as half of the desktop.

WARNING: New users sometimes accidentally size the taskbar until it disappears. See step 5 for directions to recover the taskbar.

arrow pointer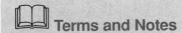
The arrow-shaped cursor on the screen that moves with the mouse as you slide it over a flat surface. The pointer's shape changes depending on the job it is doing (or can do) at the current time. Also called *mouse pointer*.

sizing pointer ↔
The arrow pointer becomes a double-headed arrow when you point to a sizing handle or certain borders. The sizing pointer is used to size a window or the taskbar.

⌨ Keyboard Steps to

Size the Taskbar

1. Press `Ctrl` + `Esc`, `Esc`.

2. Press `Alt` + `Space`.
   A Control menu appears.

3. Press `S` (Size).

4. Press `↑` (up arrow).
   The sizing pointer appears.

5. Press `↑` (up arrow) to increase the taskbar to the desired size.
   OR
   Press `↓` (down arrow) to decrease the taskbar to the desired size.

6. Press `Enter`.

Begin with the desktop displayed and with no taskbar buttons on the taskbar.

1 **Change the taskbar size:**
  - **Point** to the upper edge of the taskbar until the arrow pointer changes to a sizing pointer.

Sizing pointer

  - **Drag** the sizing pointer up until the taskbar doubles in size.
  - **Release** the mouse button.
    The taskbar is sized to twice its original size.

2 **Return the taskbar to its original size (one layer):**
  - **Point** to the upper edge of the taskbar until the arrow pointer changes to a sizing pointer.
  - **Drag** the sizing pointer down until the taskbar returns to its original size.
  - **Release** the mouse button.
    NOTE: If you accidentally move the taskbar until it disappears, see step 5 to recover it.

3 **Change the size of the taskbar on the side of the desktop:**
  - **Move** the taskbar to the right edge of the desktop (review, Exercise 24, step 1).
  - **Point** to the left edge of the taskbar until the arrow pointer changes to a sizing pointer.
  - **Drag** the sizing pointer left until the taskbar doubles in size.
  - **Release** the mouse button.
  - **Size** the taskbar back to its original size.
  - **Move** the taskbar back to the bottom of the desktop.

4 **Size the taskbar until you cannot see it:**
  Since this procedure can happen accidentally, it is useful to do it purposely now and use step 5 to recover the taskbar.
  The taskbar should be in its default position and size—at the bottom of the desktop and one layer thick.
  - **Point** to the upper edge of the taskbar until the arrow pointer changes to a sizing pointer.
  - **Drag** the sizing pointer down to the bottom of the desktop.
  - **Release** the mouse button.
    The taskbar seems to disappear, but it actually becomes a thin line at the bottom of the desktop.

5 **Recover the taskbar:**
  - **Point** to the bottom of the desktop until the pointer changes to a double-headed arrow.
  - **Drag** the double-headed arrow up until the taskbar appears, then **release** the mouse button.

Begin with the desktop displayed and with no taskbar buttons on the taskbar.

1 **Open the Taskbar Properties dialog box using the taskbar:**
- **Right-click** an empty space on the taskbar.
  The taskbar shortcut menu opens.
- **Click** Properties.
  The Taskbar Properties dialog box opens with the Taskbar Options tab in front.

Auto hide
check box

Apply button
(dimmed)

2 **Hide the taskbar:**
- **Click** the Auto hide check box (to select it).
  The Auto hide, Always on top, and Show clock check boxes should be selected (checked) and the Apply button should no longer be dimmed.
- **Click** 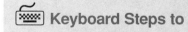, then **close** the Taskbar Properties dialog box.
  The taskbar disappears.
- IF the taskbar doesn't disappear, **click** the desktop.

3 **Display the taskbar temporarily:**
- **Move** the pointer to the bottom of the screen until the taskbar appears.
  When the arrow pointer reaches the bottom of the screen, it turns into a sizing pointer and then the taskbar appears.
- **Move** the pointer up the screen until the taskbar disappears.
- IF the taskbar doesn't disappear, **click** the desktop.

4 **Open the Taskbar Properties dialog box using the Start menu:**
- **Click** **Start**, **point** to Settings, then **click** Taskbar & Start Menu.
  The Taskbar Properties dialog box opens.

5 **Change the Auto hide option so the taskbar is always visible:**
- **Click** the Auto hide check box (to deselect it).
  The check mark disappears from the Auto hide check box.
- **Click** OK .
  The taskbar reappears and the Taskbar Properties dialog box closes.

To reduce the taskbar to a thin line at the bottom of the desktop so that it is displayed only when the pointer gets near it and it hides again when the pointer moves away.

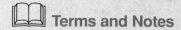 **Terms and Notes**

NOTE: If you want the taskbar to be accessible when you run a maximized program, be sure that both the Always on top and the Auto hide check boxes are selected.

dimmed command
A command or button that cannot be used in the current situation. It is displayed in gray instead of in black or in color.

sizing pointer ←→
The arrow pointer becomes a double-headed arrow when you point to a sizing handle or certain borders. The sizing pointer is used to size a window or the taskbar.

⌨ **Keyboard Steps to**

Show/Hide the Taskbar

1. **Press** Ctrl + Esc .
   OR
   Press ⊞ (the Windows key).
   The Start menu opens.
2. **Press** S (Settings).
   The Settings menu opens.
3. **Press** T (Taskbar & Start Menu).
   The Taskbar Properties dialog box opens.
4. **Press** Alt + U (Auto hide) to select or deselect the check box as desired.
5. **Press** Enter .

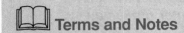

EXERCISE 27 • Arrange Windows

To use the taskbar menu commands to position the windows in the desktop so that they can all be seen.

📖 **Terms and Notes**

cascade
To resize and layer windows on the desktop so that the title bar of each window is visible.

tile horizontally
To resize and arrange the windows on the desktop one on top of the other so that each window displays part of its workspace.

tile vertically
To resize and arrange the windows on the desktop side by side so that each window displays part of its workspace.

NOTE: If you are using Windows 95 with Internet Explorer 4 installed, your Paint icon (shown on the taskbar in step 2) may look like this: 🖋 rather than this: 🎨.

Begin with the desktop displayed and with no taskbar buttons on the taskbar.

1 • **Start** the following programs: WordPad, Calculator, Notepad, Paint.

2 **Open the taskbar's shortcut menu:**

Empty space

• **Right-click** an empty space on the taskbar.
   NOTE: Empty spaces on the taskbar can be very small. However, if you are precise, you can click at the end of the taskbar buttons or even between them. If you don't get the correct menu at first, try again.
   The taskbar shortcut menu opens. The commands in the menu may vary slightly, depending upon conditions at any given time.

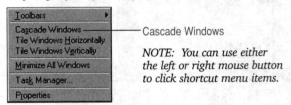

— Cascade Windows

NOTE: You can use either the left or right mouse button to click shortcut menu items.

3 **Cascade windows:**
• **Click** Cascade Windows.
   The windows on the desktop cascade.

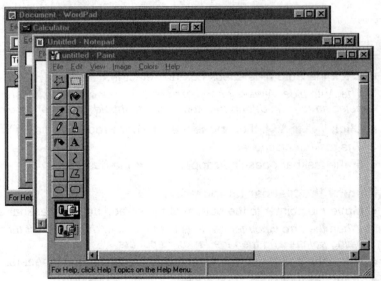

4 **Undo the Cascade command:**
• **Right-click** an empty space on the taskbar.
   The taskbar shortcut menu opens.

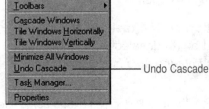

— Undo Cascade

• **Click** Undo Cascade.
   The windows return to their previous sizes and positions.

5 **Tile windows horizontally:**
- **Right-click** an empty space on the taskbar.
- **Click** Tile Windows Horizontally.
  The windows tile unevenly.
- **Exit** Calculator, then **exit** Paint.
- **Right-click** an empty space on the taskbar.
- **Click** Tile Windows Horizontally again.
  The two windows are positioned one above the other and are equal in size.

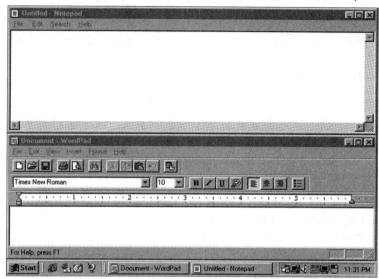

- **Right-click** an empty space on the taskbar, then **click** Undo Tile.
  The windows return to their previous sizes and positions.

6 **Tile windows vertically:**
- **Right-click** an empty space on the taskbar.
- **Click** Tile Windows Vertically.
  The two windows are positioned side by side and are equal in size.

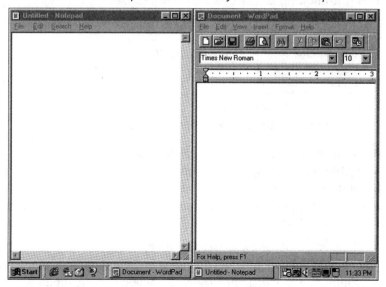

7 • **Exit** WordPad and Notepad.

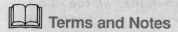

Keyboard Steps to

Arrange Windows

—WITH MORE THAN ONE WINDOW OPEN—

1. **Press** `Ctrl` + `Esc`, `Esc`.
   The Start button is selected.

2. **Press** `Tab`.
   The Start button is no longer selected and, although there is no indication of it, the taskbar is selected.

3. **Press** `Shift` + `F10`.
   The taskbar shortcut menu opens.

4. **Choose** a way to arrange windows:
   - **Press** `S` (Cascade Windows).
   - **Press** `H` (Tile Windows Horizontally).
   - **Press** `E` (Tile Windows Vertically).
   - **Press** `U` (Undo Cascade [or Tile]).

EXERCISE 28 • Show the Desktop

To minimize all the open programs and display the desktop using the Show Desktop button and the taskbar shortcut menu.

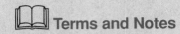 **Terms and Notes**

Quick Launch toolbar
A toolbar that appears next to the Start button on the taskbar (by default) and contains buttons for the following frequently used features: Internet Explorer, Outlook Express, desktop, and channels.

taskbar button
A button located on the taskbar that represents an open program. Each taskbar button displays the program icon and name of each open program.

ToolTip
A pop-up box that displays the name of, and/or information about, a button or an icon.

Begin with the desktop displayed and with no taskbar buttons on the taskbar.

1
- **Start** Calculator, then **start** and **maximize** Notepad.
- **Start** WordPad, then **start** WordPad again.
- **Start** and **maximize** Paint.

2 Display a ToolTip:

- **Point** to 📝 (the Show Desktop button) on the Quick Launch toolbar.
  The Show Desktop button is selected and a ToolTip appears.

3 Quickly access the desktop:

- **Click** 📝 (the Show Desktop button).
  The open windows are all minimized and the desktop is displayed.

- **Click** 📝 (the Show Desktop button) again.
  The open windows are all restored to their previous sizes and locations, hiding the desktop.

4 Access the desktop using the taskbar shortcut menu:
- **Right-click** an empty space on the taskbar.
  The taskbar shortcut menu opens.

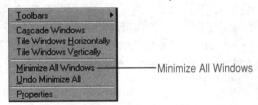

- **Click** Minimize All Windows.
  The open windows are all minimized and the desktop is displayed.
- **Right-click** an empty space on the taskbar.
  The taskbar shortcut menu opens.

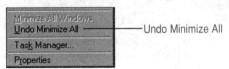

- **Click** Undo Minimize All.
  The windows return to their previous sizes and positions.

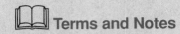 **Keyboard Steps to**

Access the Desktop

—WITH ONE OR MORE WINDOW(S) OPEN—

1. **Press** [Ctrl] + [Esc], [Esc].
   The Start button is selected.

2. **Press** [Tab].
   The taskbar is selected.

3. **Press** [Shift] + [F10].

   OR

   Press [▤] (the Application key).
   The taskbar shortcut menu opens.

4. **Press** [M] (Minimize All Windows).

5 Access the desktop when a dialog box is open:
- **Right-click** an empty space on the taskbar.
- **Click** Properties.
- **Notice** that the Taskbar Properties dialog box does not have a taskbar button.
- **Click** 📝 (the Show Desktop button).
  The open windows are all minimized and the desktop is displayed.
- **Notice** that the Taskbar Properties dialog box disappears.

6 • **Go on** to Exercise 29 without stopping.

Continue from Exercise 28 without stopping.

① **Restore and minimize Paint from the taskbar:**

- **Click** the Paint taskbar button, identified by its icon 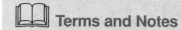 or .
  Paint is displayed on the desktop and it is active.
- **Click** the Paint taskbar button again.
  Paint is reduced to a taskbar button (i.e., minimized) again.
- **Notice** that the Taskbar Properties dialog box appears on the desktop.
  NOTE: An open dialog box does not have a taskbar button. When you use the Show Desktop button to access the desktop, an open dialog box disappears when the open tasks are minimized. That dialog box will reappear on the desktop when you click the Show Desktop button again or when you restore a task. If the restored task covers the dialog box, you can see the dialog box by minimizing the task.
- **Close** the Taskbar Properties dialog box.

② **Close minimized windows using the Control menu:**
- **Right-click** the Paint taskbar button.
  The Control menu for Paint opens.
- **Click** Close.
  The Paint taskbar button disappears and Paint is closed.

③ **Close open programs using the taskbar:**
- **Click** the Calculator taskbar button.
  Calculator is displayed on the desktop and it is active.
- **Click** the Notepad taskbar button.
  Notepad is displayed on the desktop and it is active.
- **Right-click** the Calculator taskbar button, then **click** Close.
  Calculator is closed.
- **Right-click** the Notepad taskbar button, then **click** Close.
  Notepad is closed.
- **Click** one of the WordPad taskbar buttons.
- **Type**: I am going to close this program from the taskbar.
- **Right-click** the pressed WordPad taskbar button.
- **Click** Close.
  A dialog box asks if you want to save changes to the document.
- **Click** No (to close WordPad without saving).
- **Close** the remaining WordPad program window from the taskbar.

④ **Hide and display a dialog box from the taskbar:**
- **Right-click** the desktop, then **click** Properties.
  The Display Properties dialog box opens.
- **Click** (the Show Desktop button).
  The Display Properties dialog box disappears.
- **Click** (the Show Desktop button) again.
  The Display Properties dialog box reappears.
- **Close** the Display Properties dialog box.

To use taskbar buttons to access the program Control menu and select commands.

📖 **Terms and Notes**

active window
The window whose title bar is highlighted (i.e., in color—not gray), indicating that it is currently in use.

Control menu
A menu with items that you use to manipulate a program or folder window (e.g., Restore, Move, Size, Minimize, Maximize, and Close). The Control menu can be opened by clicking the Control menu button on the left side of the title bar or by right-clicking a window's taskbar button.

pressed
A 3-D effect in which a button (or other item) appears "sunken," indicating it is selected (or active).

⌨ **Keyboard Steps to**

Control Programs from the Taskbar
—WITH ONE OR MORE WINDOW(S) OPEN—

1. **Press** Ctrl + Esc, Esc, Esc.
   The Start button is selected.
2. **Press** Tab, Tab.
   The Start button is no longer selected and, although there is no indication of it, the taskbar button section of the taskbar is selected.
3. **Press** until the taskbar button for the program you want to control is selected.
4. **Press** Shift + F10.
   OR
   Press (the Application key).
   The Control menu for the program opens.
5. **Choose** a way to control the program:
   - **Press** R (Restore).
   - **Press** M (Move).
   - **Press** S (Size).
   - **Press** N (Minimize).
   - **Press** X (Maximize).
   - **Press** C (Close).

NOTE: Some options may be dimmed, depending on whether the task is currently restored, maximized, or minimized.

Terms and Notes

directional arrowhead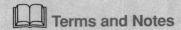
A small arrowhead that appears at the beginning and/or end of menus and *toolbars* to indicate that there are more menu items than you can presently see on the menu or toolbar. Point to the arrowhead to scroll through the menu or toolbar items.

taskbar toolbars
Another tool that offers several ways to customize Windows 98 and make it easier for you to use. While you can create a toolbar of the items in any folder, four useful toolbars appear on the Toolbars submenu by default for easy access:

- The **Address bar** allows you to type a Web-page address (URL) or a folder location and then press Enter to go to it.
- The **Links toolbar** provides shortcuts to useful Web sites.
- The **Desktop toolbar** contains all the shortcuts on your desktop.
- The **Quick Launch toolbar** has shortcuts to frequently used features, such as Internet Explorer, Outlook Express (for e-mail and newsgroups), Channels, and the Desktop (minimizes all open tasks and displays the desktop).

toolbar
A row of buttons, usually along the top or bottom of the screen by default, that provides quick access to frequently used commands, tasks, or other objects such as Internet addresses and hyperlinks.

⌨ Keyboard Steps to

Add a Toolbar to the Taskbar

1. Press `Ctrl` + `Esc`, `Esc`, `Tab`.
   The taskbar is selected.
2. Press `Shift` + `F10`.
   The taskbar shortcut menu opens.
3. Press `T` (*Toolbars*).
   The Toolbars menu appears.
4. **Type** the *underlined letter* for the desired toolbar.

Begin with the desktop displayed and with no taskbar buttons on the taskbar.

1 Add a toolbar to the taskbar:
- **Right-click** an empty space on the taskbar.
  The taskbar shortcut menu appears.
- **Point** to Toolbars.
  The Toolbars submenu appears.

- **Click** Desktop.
  The Desktop toolbar appears on the taskbar.

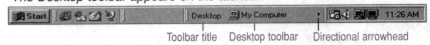

2 Scroll through hidden toolbar buttons:
- **Click** the directional arrowhead at the right end of the Desktop toolbar.
  The first button disappears and the next button appears.
- **Click** the right arrowhead until you have seen all the Desktop toolbar buttons.
  A directional arrowhead now appears at the left side of the buttons.
- **Click and hold down** the left directional arrowhead until the first button appears.
- **Notice** that the toolbar title (Desktop) always stays at the left end of the taskbar toolbar.

3 Hide toolbar text labels and title:
- **Right-click** [Desktop] (the Desktop toolbar title).
  The toolbar shortcut menu appears.

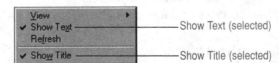

- **Click** Show Text (to deselect it).
  The toolbar labels disappear and several icons now appear on the Desktop toolbar.
- **Right-click** [Desktop] (the Desktop toolbar title) again.
- **Click** Show Title (to deselect it).
  The toolbar title disappears and even more icons appear on the Desktop taskbar toolbar.

4 Display a ToolTip and open a desktop folder:
- **Point** to 🖳 (the My Computer button) until its ToolTip appears.

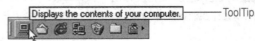

- **Click** 🖳 (the My Computer button).
  The My Computer folder window opens.
- **Close** the My Computer folder window.

⑤ Show toolbar labels and title:

- **Right-click** the sizing handle.
  NOTE: *When you right-click, the button should not be selected (i.e., raised).*

Sizing handle ──── 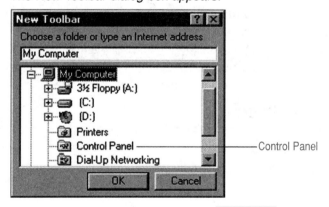 ──── Icon is flat.

  The toolbar shortcut menu opens.

- **Click** Sho<u>w</u> Title (to select it).
  The toolbar title, Desktop, appears.

- **Right-click** [Desktop], then **click** Show Te<u>x</u>t (to select it).
  The toolbar button labels appear.

- IF only [Desktop] appears, **double-click** it to display the buttons and their labels.

⑥ Deselect a taskbar toolbar:

- **Right-click** [Desktop].
- **Point** to <u>T</u>oolbars, then **click** <u>D</u>esktop (to deselect it).
- IF the Confirm Toolbar Close dialog box appears, **click** [OK].
  The Desktop toolbar disappears from the taskbar.

⑦ Add a new toolbar to the taskbar:

NOTE: *Use the New Toolbar dialog box to add a toolbar to the taskbar. This toolbar can contain either a folder or the Internet address of your choice.*

- **Right-click** an empty space on the taskbar.
- **Point** to <u>T</u>oolbars, then **click** <u>N</u>ew Toolbar.
  The New Toolbar dialog box appears.

New Toolbar dialog box:

Choose a folder or type an Internet address

My Computer

- 🖳 My Computer
  - ⊞ 🖫 3½ Floppy (A:)
  - ⊞ 💾 (C:)
  - ⊞ 🖴 (D:)
  - 🖻 Printers
  - 🖻 Control Panel ──── Control Panel
  - 🖻 Dial-Up Networking

[OK] [Cancel]

- **Click** 🖻 Control Panel , then **click** [OK].
- **Hide** the toolbar text labels (review, step 3).
- **Scroll** through the hidden toolbar buttons (review, step 2).
- **Show** the toolbar text labels (review, step 5).

⑧ Close a toolbar:

- **Right-click** [Control Panel], then **click** <u>C</u>lose.
- IF the Confirm Toolbar Close dialog box appears, **click** [OK].
  The Control Panel toolbar disappears from the taskbar.

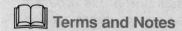

Terms and Notes

flat
The smooth, level appearance of icons on many toolbars in Windows 98. When you point to a flat toolbar icon, it becomes *raised* and looks like a button. See *raised*, below.

new taskbar toolbars
Toolbars that you can create on the taskbar to show the contents of any folder desired.

raised
A 3-D effect in which a toolbar icon that is normally *flat* is defined as a button when you point to it. If you rest the arrow pointer on a button, a ToolTip appears. See *flat*, above.

EXERCISE 31 • Manipulate a Taskbar Toolbar

To size and move different areas and toolbars on the taskbar.

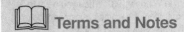 Terms and Notes

move pointer ⊕
A four-headed arrow that appears when you point to (or click) some areas, for example, the small area to the immediate right of a sizing handle on the taskbar. Once the move pointer appears, the Move procedure is available.

sizing handle
An area in the bottom-right corner of windows that can be sized. It is used to size windows. You can size a window using any of its corners. However, because the bottom-right corner has a sizing handle that covers a large sizing area, the arrow pointer changes to a sizing pointer more easily than it does in other window corners. Sizing handles are also available for taskbar toolbars (and taskbar "areas") on the left-hand side of toolbar titles.

sizing pointer
The arrow pointer becomes a double-headed arrow when you point to a sizing handle or certain borders. The sizing pointer is used to size a window or the taskbar. Sizing pointers can appear in any of the following forms:

↕ vertical
Appears on the top or bottom window border.

↔ horizontal
Appears on the right or left window border.

↘ diagonal
Appears on the top-left or bottom-right corner of a window.

↗ diagonal
Appears on the bottom-left or top-right corner of a window.

Begin with the desktop displayed and with no taskbar buttons on the taskbar.

1 Size a toolbar using the sizing handle:
- **Add** the Desktop toolbar to the taskbar (review, Exercise 30, step 1).
- **Point** to the sizing handle until the arrow pointer changes to a sizing pointer.

- **Press and hold down** the left mouse button.
  The sizing pointer now displays a set of parallel lines between the arrowheads.

- **Drag** the sizing handle to the right as far as it will go, then **release** the mouse button.
  Only the toolbar title, Desktop, remains.

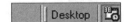

- **Drag** the Desktop toolbar sizing handle to the left and **release** the button when the toolbar stops.
- **Notice** that the Desktop toolbar stops before it reaches the taskbar button sizing handle, thereby leaving room for taskbar buttons.

2 Size a toolbar using the move pointer:
- **Click** `Desktop` **and hold down** the left mouse button.
  The arrow pointer turns into a move pointer.

- **Drag** the Desktop toolbar right until it stops.
- **Double-click** `Desktop`.
  The Desktop toolbar slides as far left as it can go.
- **Double-click** `Desktop` again.
  The Desktop toolbar slides as far right as it can go.

3 Move a toolbar:
- **Click** `Desktop` **and hold down** the mouse button.
- **Drag** the Desktop toolbar left and **notice** that it quits following at some point. (Don't release the button.)

- **Keep dragging** the move pointer until it is just left of the taskbar button sizing handle and then **release** it.
  The Desktop toolbar switches places with the taskbar button area.

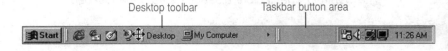

- **Click and hold** on the space immediately to the right of the *taskbar button area* sizing handle. There is a very small area that will produce the move pointer.

Move pointer

- **Drag** the move pointer to the left of the Desktop toolbar until it is just left of the taskbar button sizing handle and then **release** it.

- **Double-click** Desktop .

  Your taskbar should now match the illustration below:

4 **Scroll through taskbar buttons:**
- **Start** the following programs: Calculator, Notepad, Paint, and WordPad.

  Taskbar buttons do not appear for every program; however, scroll arrows appear to indicate that more taskbar buttons are available.

  Click to scroll to the left.   Click to scroll to the right.

- **Click** the bottom scroll arrow to scroll to the *right.*
- **Click** the top scroll arrow to scroll to the *left.*

5 **Size the taskbar to double its original size:**
- **Point** to the upper edge of the taskbar until the arrow pointer becomes a sizing pointer. **Drag** the sizing pointer up until the taskbar doubles in size.

  The taskbar buttons spread into the top row, and the Desktop toolbar fills the bottom row.

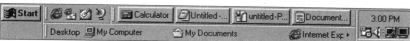

- **Point** to Desktop and **hold down** the left mouse button.
  The arrow pointer becomes a move pointer.

Move pointer

- **Drag** the move pointer to the top row as illustrated above.

  When you release the mouse button, the taskbar areas are divided into sections that include both rows.

- **Scroll** to the *right* end of the Desktop toolbar. (Click the right directional arrowhead until you get to the end.)

- **Scroll** back to the *left* end of the Desktop toolbar.
- **Return** the taskbar to its original size (review, Exercise 25, step 2).

![Start taskbar illustration]

6 - **Close** the Desktop toolbar (review, Exercise 30, step 6).
- **Close** each program using its taskbar button (review, Exercise 29, step 2).

  There are no taskbar buttons left on the taskbar.

EXERCISE 32 • Create a Floating Toolbar

To move toolbars from the taskbar to the desktop.

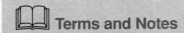

Terms and Notes

floating toolbar
A toolbar that you have dragged from the taskbar to an unanchored position on your desktop.

Begin with the desktop displayed and with no taskbar buttons on the taskbar.

1 **Float a toolbar on the desktop:**
- **Add** the Desktop toolbar to the taskbar (review, Exercise 30, step 1).
- **Drag** up, placing it about two inches from the top of the desktop.

   As you drag the toolbar onto the desktop, the move pointer changes to an arrow pointer with a small rectangle attached.

   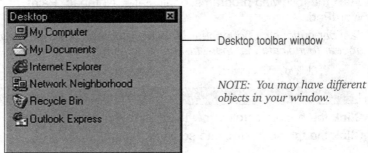
   ———Arrow pointer with small rectangle attached

- **Release** the mouse button.

   The Desktop toolbar is now a window on the desktop.

Desktop	☒
🖥️ My Computer	
📁 My Documents	
🌐 Internet Explorer	
🖧 Network Neighborhood	
🗑️ Recycle Bin	
📧 Outlook Express	

   ———Desktop toolbar window

   NOTE: You may have different objects in your window.

2 **Change the size of toolbar icons:**
- **Right-click** an empty space on the right side of the Desktop toolbar window.

   The toolbar shortcut menu appears.
- **Point** to <u>V</u>iew, then **click** Large (to select it).

   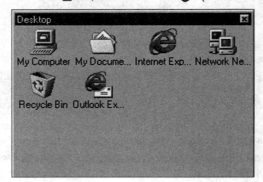

3 **Move a toolbar to the top of the desktop:**
- **Drag** the Desktop toolbar window's title bar to the top of the desktop.

   The Desktop toolbar is docked on the top of the desktop window.

- **Drag** the Desktop toolbar back onto the desktop using its title.

   The Desktop toolbar is once again a window on the desktop.
- **Right-click** an empty space in the Desktop toolbar window. (You may have to right-click close to the right or bottom window border.)

   The shortcut menu appears.
- **Point** to <u>V</u>iew, then **click** S<u>m</u>all (to select it).

4 Size a floating toolbar:

- **Right-click** an empty space in the Desktop toolbar window.
- **Click** Show Te<u>x</u>t (to deselect it).
  The text labels disappear.
- **Point** to the bottom of the Desktop toolbar window until the arrow pointer becomes a sizing pointer.
- **Drag** the bottom border up until all the blank space is gone.
  The floating Desktop toolbar becomes a row:

- **Drag** the bottom border back down to its original size.

5 Add more toolbars to the floating toolbar:

- **Right-click** an empty space in the Desktop toolbar window.
- **Point** to <u>T</u>oolbars, then **click** <u>A</u>ddress.
  The Address bar is added to the Desktop toolbar, and the window's title changes to Toolbar.
- **Right-click** an empty space in the Toolbar window.
- **Point** to <u>T</u>oolbars, then **click** <u>L</u>inks.
  The Links toolbar is added to the other floating toolbars.

Toolbar ———
Toolbar sizing handles

——— Desktop toolbar
——— Address bar
——— Links toolbar

- **Drag** the Address bar sizing handle (i.e., the handle *above* the Address bar) down until the Desktop toolbar icons are visible.
- **Drag** the Links toolbar sizing handle down until the Address bar appears.
  The Toolbar window looks something like this:

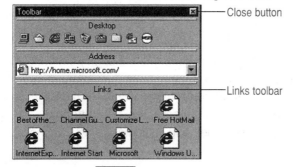
——— Close button
——— Links toolbar

- **Double-click** Links .
  The Desktop toolbar and the Address bar no longer display their data.

6 Close the Toolbar window:

- **Click** the Close button (on the title bar).
- IF the Confirm Toolbar Close dialog box appears, **click** 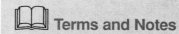 .
  All the toolbars close.

Terms and Notes

Address bar
In Windows 98 folders and programs, a drop-down text box that lets you access a Web page or a location on your computer by typing or selecting an address or path.

bar
The term *bar* is used several ways:
- to define window stripes (e.g., the title bar, menu bar, and status bar)
- to define certain features (e.g., the Explorer bar, Channel bar, and Address bar). While the Address bar is included in the Toolbars menus as a toolbar that you can hide or display, it is not, strictly speaking, considered a toolbar.

Links toolbar
The toolbar that provides quick access to commonly used Web sites.

The Taskbar

Tasks Reviewed:
- Move the Taskbar
- Size the Taskbar
- Hide the Taskbar
- Arrange Windows
- Access the Desktop
- Control Programs from the Taskbar
- Add a Toolbar to the Taskbar
- Manipulate a Taskbar Toolbar
- Create a Floating Toolbar

Begin with the desktop displayed and with no taskbar buttons on the taskbar.

1
- **Move** the taskbar to the left side of the desktop.
- **Move** the taskbar to the top of the desktop.
- **Move** the taskbar back to the bottom of the desktop.

2
- **Size** the taskbar to double its original size (two layers).
- **Size** the taskbar back to one layer.
- **Move** the taskbar to the left side of the desktop.
- **Size** the taskbar to two layers.
- **Size** the taskbar to its original size.
- **Move** the taskbar back to the bottom of the desktop.
- **Size** the taskbar until it becomes a narrow line at the bottom of the desktop.
- **Size** the taskbar to its original size (one layer).

3
- **Open** the Taskbar Properties dialog box using the taskbar.
- **Click** the Auto hide check box (to select it), then **click** ☐ OK ☐.
- **Click** an empty space in the middle of the desktop.
- **Move** the pointer down until the taskbar appears.
- **Move** the pointer up and down a few times.
- **Open** the Taskbar Properties dialog box again using the Start button.
- **Change** the Auto hide option to its original setting (i.e., the taskbar is always visible).
- **Click** ☐ OK ☐.

4
- **Start** WordPad, Calculator, Notepad, and Paint.
- **Arrange** the windows using the Cascade command.
- **Undo** the Cascade command.
- **Exit** Calculator and Paint.
- **Arrange** the windows in a vertical tile order.
- **Undo** the tile arrangement.
- **Arrange** the windows in a horizontal tile order.
- **Undo** the tile arrangement.
- **Exit** WordPad and Notepad.
  There shouldn't be any taskbar buttons on the taskbar.

5
- **Start** WordPad and Calculator.
- **Start** and **maximize** Notepad and Paint.
- **Access** the desktop using the Show Desktop button.
- **Return** all the programs to their original states using the Show Desktop button.

6 **Use the taskbar buttons to:**
- **Close** WordPad.
- **Restore** Notepad, then **minimize** Notepad.
- **Restore** Paint, then **close** Paint.
- **Minimize** Calculator.

- **Maximize** Notepad.
- **Close** Calculator and Notepad.

  There shouldn't be any taskbar buttons on the taskbar.

7
- **Add** the Desktop toolbar to the taskbar.
- **Scroll** through the Desktop toolbar's hidden toolbar buttons.
- **Display** and **read** the ToolTip for the Recycle Bin.
- **Hide** the Desktop toolbar's text labels.
- **Hide** the Desktop toolbar title.
- **Show** the Desktop toolbar title.
- **Show** the Desktop toolbar's text labels, then **close** the Desktop toolbar.
- **Add** a new toolbar, My Computer, to the taskbar.
- **Scroll** to the end of the My Computer toolbar.
- **Close** the My Computer toolbar.

8
- **Add** the Desktop toolbar to the taskbar.
- **Size** the Desktop toolbar as small as it will go using the sizing handle.
- **Size** the Desktop toolbar as large as it will go using the double-click method.
- **Move** the Desktop toolbar in front of the taskbar button area.
- **Move** the taskbar button area in front of the Desktop toolbar.
- **Size** the Desktop toolbar as large as it will go.
- **Start** the following programs: Calculator, Notepad, Paint, and WordPad.
- **Scroll** through the taskbar buttons.
- **Size** the taskbar to two layers (double it).
- **Drag** the Desktop toolbar to the top layer.
- **Size** the taskbar to one layer.
- **Close** all of the programs, but leave the Desktop toolbar open.

9
- **Drag** the Desktop toolbar onto the desktop to create a floating toolbar.
- **Change** the size of the Desktop toolbar icons to Large, then back to Small.
- **Add** the Address bar to the the floating Desktop toolbar.
- **Close** the Toolbar window.

  Lesson Three Worksheet (4) is on page 304.

NEXT
LESSON

Lesson Four
Folder Windows

Table of Contents

Terms and Notes

Classic style
The Windows 95 approach to working with folders, icons, and the desktop. It includes:
- browsing windows using separate windows
- click-to-select/double-click-to-open browsing
- icon titles that are *not* underlined

See also *Web style*, below.

folder 📁
A structure that holds files and/or subfolders that are stored on a disk. A folder can also contain other objects, such as printers and disk drives. (Folders have traditionally been called *directories*.)

Folder Options
The command that switches between Web-style and Classic-style browsing environments.

folder window
A window that displays the contents of a folder (or certain other objects, such as disk drives). Folder windows offer many of the same folder-managing features as Windows Explorer. Click a folder (if Web-style browsing is enabled) to open its window and see what is in it.

Internet icon
The button at the right end of the menu bar, illustrated with a Windows flag, that accesses the Internet when clicked.

Web style
The Web-page approach to working with folders, icons, and the desktop. It includes:
- browsing windows using the same window
- point-to-select/click-to-open browsing
- underlined icon titles
- enabling Web-related content in folders and on the desktop

See also *Classic style*, above.

Windows 98 Folder Windows

Folder windows display the contents of **folders.** Folder windows have several standard Windows elements: Minimize, Maximize, and Close buttons; a menu bar, toolbar, and status bar; and a Control menu button.

Windows 98 added the following new elements to folder windows to make it easier for you to access the Internet and get information from within a folder window:

- Internet icon
- Address bar
- Links toolbar
- Favorites menu
- Go menu
- Explorer bars
- Web Page view
- Back, Forward, and Up buttons

Folder Styles

In addition to adding new elements, Windows 98 lets you choose from two different browsing environments that affect how you view and work with all folders and icons as well as Windows Explorer and the desktop: **Classic style** (Windows 95) and **Web style**. The **Folder Options** command, located in folder windows (<u>V</u>iew, Folder <u>O</u>ptions) and in the Start menu (Start, <u>S</u>ettings, <u>F</u>older Options), opens the Folder Options dialog box. In this dialog box, you can switch between the two folder styles; or, if you wish, you can customize the Windows 98 environment to create a mixture of the Web style and Classic style.

Below is a table that shows how each folder option works depending on your choice of browsing environment.

FOLDER OPTION	WEB STYLE	CLASSIC STYLE
Active Desktop	Uses the Active Desktop.	Uses the standard, Windows 95 desktop.
Browse folders	Opens each folder in the *same* window.	Opens each folder in its *own* window.
View Web content in folders	Turns on Web Page view in all folders automatically.	Does *not* turn on Web Page view in folders.
Click items as follows	Point to select an item; click to open it.	Click to select an item; double-click to open it.
Underline items	Icon titles are underlined, as they are in Internet Explorer.	Icon titles are *not* underlined.

Web-Style Browsing

In this book, you will usually be instructed to use the Web-style environment. The most noticeable feature of the Web-style environment is the underlining of icon titles which makes it possible for you to select an object by pointing to it and to open an object by clicking it once. *(See the illustration on the next page.)*

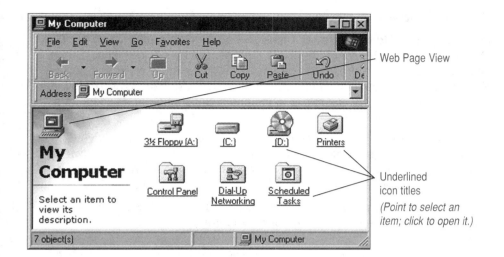

Web Page View

Underlined
icon titles
*(Point to select an
item; click to open it.)*

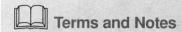 **Terms and Notes**

Active Desktop
The Windows 98 desktop that consists of two
layers: one layer on which you can display
standard desktop objects, and a second layer
on which you can display HTML objects.

Web Page view
A feature in folder windows (and Windows
Explorer) that displays:
- a picture of the selected item in the
  top-left corner of the workspace
- the selected item's name
- information about the selected item
  along the left side of the workspace
While this feature is turned on automatically in
Web-style mode, it can be used in Classic-style
mode as well.

View as Web Page

Another new folder feature in Windows 98 is Web Page view. However, don't
confuse this feature with the Active Desktop feature that is turned on by
selecting the similarly named command, *View As Web Page*, from the desktop
shortcut menu. Both features are automatically turned on when you choose
the Web-style browsing environment, and both can be turned off individually at
any time. Below is a description of the two different Web Page view
commands—one for folder windows and one for the desktop—including a
description of how each feature affects the browsing environment and how
you can turn either one on or off.

- **the View, as Web Page command in folder windows.**

  Displays a section on the left side
  of the workspace that names the
  folder you are in and shows
  information about the selected item
  in that folder. *(See the folder window
  illustration above.)*

  You can turn any folder window's
  View, as Web Page feature on and
  off independently of the Web-style
  command by clicking View, and
  then clicking as Web Page.

View, as Web
Page command
(folder window)

- **the Active Desktop, View As Web Page command on the desktop
  shortcut menu.**

  Changes the desktop so it can
  display Web pages.

  From the desktop, you can turn
  the Active Desktop on and off
  independently of the Web-style
  command by right-clicking the
  desktop, pointing to Active Desktop,
  and then clicking View As Web Page.

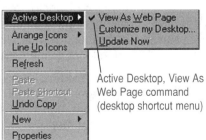

Active Desktop, View As
Web Page command
(desktop shortcut menu)

Terms and Notes

special folder
A folder designed to hold specific items, for example, My Computer, drive C:, and My Documents.

Special Folders

Folders are used to organize your files and other folders *(see Topic 15, Disk Drives and Folders)*. Most folders are represented by a folder icon. Some **special folders** are represented by a folder with a picture on it; and some objects that act as special folders do not have a folder icon at all. Below are illustrations of some special folder icons and a description of each folder's function.

Desktop—the *logical* top-level folder, in contrast to drive C:, which is the *actual* top-level folder *(see Topic 16, Windows 98 Structure)*. It holds My Computer, My Documents, and other folders and shortcuts.

My Computer—the quick route to the disk drives, folders, files, and other objects on your computer system.

(C:)—the top-level (or root) folder on your computer. Drive C: usually holds all the other folders in the computer, including the Desktop folder.

Floppy A:—the floppy disk drive folder. Floppy drive A: holds the data files stored on the removable floppy disk currently inserted.

Printers—adds a new printer setup or changes settings for an existing printer.

Control Panel—personalizes your computer by letting you change various settings, such as your screen display, system date/time, mouse settings, passwords, etc.

Dial-Up Networking—shares information with another computer, even if your computer is not on a network.

Scheduled Tasks—contains tasks that you tell the computer to run when it's easiest for you; for example, you may schedule a job like defragmenting the hard drive to take place in the middle of the night.

My Documents—provides you with a handy place to store documents. Windows 98 accessory programs such as WordPad and Paint automatically store documents in the My Documents folder unless you change the default storage location.

Favorites—holds frequently used Web-page addresses and paths so you can easily access Web sites and items on your computer. You can further organize your favorites into subfolders of the Favorites folder.

Group folders—folders that are found primarily within the Programs folder that hold groups of program shortcuts. They represent menu items that appear in the Programs submenu of the Start menu.

History—lists Web sites that you have visited.

Today

Today (or weekday name)—organizes your history (list) of visited Web sites by placing those sites into folders that are labeled with the days of the week on which the sites were visited.

Downloaded Program Files

Downloaded Program Files—the default location where Windows 98 stores downloaded Active X and Internet-related programs.

Channels

Channels—contains a list of Web sites that have the ability to automatically deliver information from the Internet to your computer.

Subscriptions

Subscriptions—contains a list of your subscriptions to Web sites and channels.

Network Neighborhood

Network Neighborhood—the entry point to other computers on your network. If you are not on a network, this folder icon may not appear on your desktop.

Recycle Bin

Recycle Bin—holds "deleted" documents in case you change your mind and want to restore them. Once you empty the Recycle Bin, however, you can no longer restore these documents.

My Briefcase

My Briefcase—keeps your documents up-to-date between PCs.

EXERCISE 34 • Change the Folder Style

To switch between the Web-style and Classic-style browsing environments when working with folders and icons.

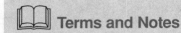 Terms and Notes

Classic style
The Windows 95 approach to working with folders, icons, and the desktop. It includes:
- browsing windows using separate windows
- click-to-select/double-click-to-open browsing
- icon titles that are *not* underlined
See also *Web style*, below.

Folder Options dialog box
The dialog box in which you can switch between Web-style and Classic-style browsing environments for folders and icons. You can open the Folder Options dialog box in two ways:
- **Click** the Start button, **point** to Settings, then **click** Folder Options.
- From any folder window, **click** View, then **click** Folder Options.

My Computer 🖥
A special folder (with an icon that appears on the desktop by default) that gives you a quick route to the disk drives, folders, files, and other objects on your computer system.

ToolTip
A pop-up box that displays the name of, and/or information about, a button or an icon.

Web style
The Web-page approach to working with folders, icons, and the desktop. It includes:
- browsing windows using the same window
- point-to-select/click-to-open browsing
- underlined icon titles
- enabling Web-related content in folders and on the desktop
See also *Classic style*, above.

Begin with the desktop displayed and with no taskbar buttons on the taskbar.

1 **Change to Web-style folders and icons using the Start menu:**

- **Click** 🏁 **Start**, **point** to 🖳 Settings, then **click** 🔍 Folder Options... .
  The Folder Options dialog box opens.

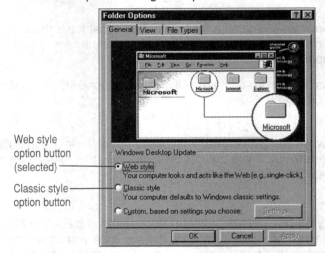

Web style
option button
(selected)

Classic style
option button

- **Click** the Web style option button (to select it), then **click** [OK].
- IF the Single-click dialog box appears, **click** Yes, then **click** [OK].
  The icon titles on the desktop are underlined. The desktop is active.

2 **Select a Web-style icon:**
- **Point** to the My Computer desktop icon until a ToolTip appears.
  My Computer is selected and the arrow pointer changes to a hand.

My Computer icon   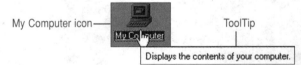   ToolTip

- **Move** the pointer to a blank area on the desktop.
  My Computer remains selected.
- **Select** the My Documents icon and **read** the ToolTip.
- **Select** the Internet Explorer icon and **read** the ToolTip.
- **Select** the Recycle Bin icon and **read** the ToolTip.

3 **Open a folder:**

- **Click** My Computer (the My Computer icon).
  The My Computer folder window opens.
- **Notice** the illustration of the My Computer folder window on the next page.
- IF your folder window has no:
  - Standard toolbar—**click** View, **point** to Toolbars, then **click** Standard Buttons.
  - Address bar—**click** View, **point** to Toolbars, then **click** Address Bar.
  - Links toolbar—**click** View, **point** to Toolbars, then **click** Links.

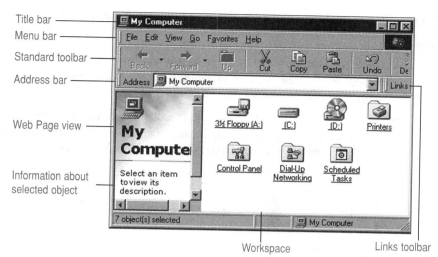

Title bar
Menu bar
Standard toolbar
Address bar

Web Page view

Information about
selected object

Workspace

Links toolbar

Keyboard Steps to

Open the Folder Options Dialog Box

—WITHOUT A FOLDER WINDOW OPEN—

1. Press `Ctrl` + `Esc`.

   OR

   Press `⊞` (the Windows key).
   The Start menu opens.

2. Press `S` (Settings).
   The Settings menu opens.

3. Press `F` (Folder Options).
   The Folder Options dialog box opens.

—WITH A FOLDER WINDOW OPEN—

1. Press `Alt` + `V` (View).

2. Press `O` (Folder Options).
   The Folder Options dialog box opens.

Change Folder Options Style

—FROM FOLDER OPTIONS DIALOG BOX—

1. Press `Alt` + `W` (Web style).

   OR

   Press `Alt` + `C` (Classic style).

2. Press `Enter`.

**Open the My Computer Folder
Window**

—WITH THE DESKTOP DISPLAYED—

1. Press `Ctrl` + `Esc`, `Esc`.

2. Press `Tab`, `Tab`, `Tab` until an item on
   the desktop is selected.
   *NOTE: Press the Tab key as many
   times as necessary until an item on
   the desktop is selected.*

3. Press `M` until the My Computer icon
   is selected.

4. Press `Enter`.

4 **Change to Classic-style folders and icons using the Start menu:**
- **Close** the My Computer folder window.

- **Click** 🏁**Start**, **point** to ⚙ **Settings**, then **click** 🔍 **Folder Options...**.
  The Folder Options dialog box opens (see previous page).

- **Click** the Classic style option button (to select it), then **click** OK .
  *The icon titles on the desktop are no longer underlined and the desktop
  is no longer active.*

- **Click** the My Computer icon to select it.

- **Double-click** the My Computer icon to open it.
  *The icon titles are no longer underlined and Web Page view is no
  longer enabled.*

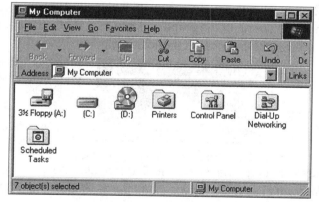

5 **Change back to Web-style folders and icons using the View menu:**

In this step, you will access the Folder Options dialog box from a folder
window rather than from the Start menu.

- **Click** View, then **click** Folder Options.
  The Folder Options dialog box opens (see previous page).

- **Click** the Web style option button (to select it), then **click** OK .
  The icon titles are underlined, but Web-view elements may not appear.

- IF Web-view elements do not appear, **close and reopen** the My
  Computer folder window.

- **Close** the My Computer folder window.

To notice what happens when you select and open objects in a folder window.

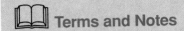 **Terms and Notes**

path
The route to an object; it consists of the disk drive, folder, subfolders (if any), and the filename (if the path is to a file).

subfolder
A folder contained within another folder.

WARNING: The point-to-select procedure works only if the workspace (in a folder window) or the desktop is selected. If you point to an object when the workspace or desktop is not selected, the arrow pointer will change into a hand and the object's hyperlink will turn blue, but the object will not become selected (highlighted). Simply click the desktop or a folder workspace to select it.

Begin with the desktop displayed and with no taskbar buttons on the taskbar.

1 **Select objects in a folder window:**

• **Click** My Computer to open its folder window.

  Notice that the title of the folder window is My Computer and that My Computer also appears in the Address bar.

• **Point** to 💾 (the drive C: icon) to select it and **read** the information.

  The (C:) icon is highlighted. Information about drive C: appears under the Web-view icon, and there may be a scroll bar.

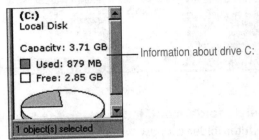
Information about drive C:

• **Select** the Printers icon and **read** the information about it.
• **Select** the Control Panel icon and **read** the information about it.
• **Click** the Address bar, then **point** to (C:).

  The arrow pointer turns into a hand and the icon title turns blue, but the icon is not selected.

• **Click** the My Computer workspace, then **point** to the (C:) icon in the workspace.

  Now the drive C: icon is selected.

2 **Open objects in a folder window:**

• **Click** 💾 (the drive C: icon) to open its folder window.
• **Notice** that (C:) opens in the same window that My Computer was in.
• **Notice** the following features in the folder window:

The **title bar** changes to (C:).

The **Back button** is no longer dimmed.

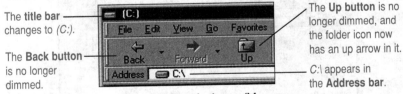

The **Up button** is no longer dimmed, and the folder icon now has an up arrow in it.

C:\ appears in the **Address bar**.

• **Open** the Program Files folder window. (You may need to scroll through the window to find the folder.)
  – *The Program Files folder opens in the same window that (C:) was in.*
  – Program Files *appears in the title bar.*
  – *The Address bar shows the path to the Program Files folder.*

• **Open** the Accessories folder window.
  – *The Accessories folder opens in the same window that (C:) was in previously.*
  – Accessories *appears in the title bar.*
  – *The Address bar shows the path to the Accessories folder.*

3 • **Go on** to Exercise 36 without stopping.

 **Keyboard Steps to**

Select Objects in a Folder Window

1. **Press** Tab until an icon in the folder workspace is selected.

2. **Press** (arrow keys) to select the desired object.

Open Objects in a Folder Window

1. **Select** the desired object *(see above)*.

2. **Press** Enter.

Continue from Exercise 35 without stopping.

1 **Go back to the previous folder:**

- **Point** to 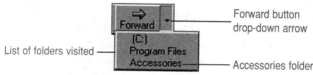 (the Back button).
  The Back button becomes active (it is raised and its arrow turns blue) and its ToolTip appears.

Back button

ToolTip
Tells where the Back button will take you.

- **Click** the Back button.
  The Program Files folder appears in the window.
- **Click** the Back button again.
  Drive C: appears in the window.
- **Click** the Back button again.
  The My Computer folder appears in the window.

2 **Go forward to the last folder on the list:**
- **Click** the Forward button drop-down arrow.
  A list of locations drops down, displaying the folders that have been opened during the session.

Forward button drop-down arrow

List of folders visited

Accessories folder

- **Click** Accessories.
  The Accessories folder appears in the window.

3 **Go back to an intermediate location:**
- **Click** the Back button drop-down arrow.
  A list of the locations you've visited drops down.

Back button drop-down arrow

List of folders visited

- **Click** (C:).
  The window displays the contents of drive C:.
- **Click** the Forward button *twice* to go forward to the Accessories folder.

4 **Go up one folder level at a time:**

- **Click** 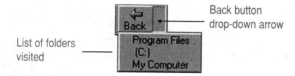 (the Up button).
  The window displays the folder that is one level up from the Accessories folder, in this case, Program Files.
- **Notice** that the Address bar kept everything except the previous folder, Accessories.
- **Click** the Up button again.
  The window displays the contents of drive C:.
- **Click** the Up button once again.
  The window displays the contents of the My Computer folder.
- **Close** the My Computer folder window.

To move through folders that have been opened during a single session.

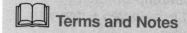 **Terms and Notes**

Back button
Moves back to a previous view when navigating through folder windows.

Forward button
Moves ahead to a previous view when navigating through folder windows.

Up button
When navigating through folder windows, moves to the folder that is up one level from the open folder on the system hierarchy.

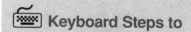 **Keyboard Steps to**

Go Back
SHORTCUT: Alt + [left arrow]
1. Press Alt + G (Go).
2. Press B (Back).

Go Forward
SHORTCUT: Alt + [right arrow]
1. Press Alt + G (Go).
2. Press F (Forward).

Go Up One Level
SHORTCUT: Backspace
1. Press Alt + G (Go).
2. Press U (Up One Level).

To open menus on the menu bar and examine the menu items in them. To see how the File menu changes depending on the object that is selected when you open it.

Begin with the desktop displayed and with no taskbar buttons on the taskbar.

1 **Look at the folder menus:**
- **Click** My Computer to open it.
- **Click** the File menu to open it, then **point** to the remaining menus, examining each one as it opens.
  Each menu drops down.

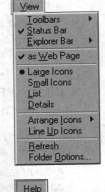

- **Click** outside the menu bar to deselect the menus.

2 **Look at the File menu for drive C:**
- **Select** the drive C: icon.
- **Click** the File menu to open it.
  Because the File menu changes depending on which item is selected, the menu items in the File menu have changed to include additional commands that are relevant to drive C:. There may be different items in your menu.
- **Click** the File menu again to close it.

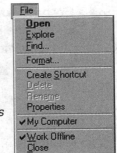

3 **Look at the File menu for a folder:**
- **Open** the drive C: folder window (review, Exercise 35, step 2).
- **Select** the Program Files folder.
- **Click** the File menu to open it.
  The menu items in the File menu have changed to include commands that are relevant to folders. There may be different items in your menu.
- **Click** the File menu again to close it.

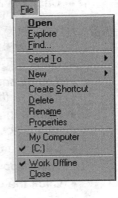

4 • **Close** the (C:) folder window.

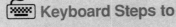 **Keyboard Steps to**

Toggle Access to the Menu Bar

—WITH A FOLDER WINDOW OPEN—

Press Alt.
The File menu becomes a button or changes from a button to a flat area.

Open a Menu

Press Alt + *the underlined letter* in the name of the menu you want to open; for example, to open the File menu, press the Alt key + F.
NOTE: These steps can be performed either together.

Close an Open Menu

Press Esc.

Begin with the desktop displayed and with no taskbar buttons on the taskbar.

To examine some of the different shortcut menus available in folder windows.

1 **Look at the shortcut menu for drive C:**

- **Open** My Computer.

- **Right-click** ▭ (the drive C: icon).
  The shortcut menu for drive C: appears. It has menu items that are similar to those in step 2 in the previous exercise.

- **Click** outside the shortcut menu to close it.

Open
Explore
Find...
Format...
Create Shortcut
Properties

2 **Look at the shortcut menu for the Printers folder:**

- **Right-click** Printers (the Printers folder icon).
  The shortcut menu for the Printers folder appears.

- **Click** outside the shortcut menu to close it.

Open
Explore
Capture Printer Port...
End Capture...
Create Shortcut

3 **Look at the shortcut menu for the Control Panel folder:**

- **Right-click** Control Panel (the Control Panel folder icon).
  The shortcut menu for the Control Panel folder appears.

- **Click** outside the shortcut menu to close it.

Open
Explore
Create Shortcut

4 **Look at the shortcut menu for a regular folder:**

- **Open** the drive C: folder. (Click its icon.)

- **Right-click** Program Files (the Program Files folder icon).
  The shortcut menu for regular folders appears.

- **Click** outside the shortcut menu to close it.

Open
Explore
Find...
Send To ▶
Cut
Copy
Create Shortcut
Delete
Rename
Properties

5 **Look at the shortcut menu for the workspace:**

- **Right-click** the workspace.
  The shortcut menu for the drive C: workspace appears.

- **Click** outside the shortcut menu to close it.

View ▶
Customize this Folder...
Arrange Icons ▶
Line Up Icons
Refresh
Paste
Paste Shortcut
New ▶
Properties

6 - **Close** the (C:) folder window.

To hide and display toolbars and toolbar text labels. To customize toolbars by moving them around.

Begin with the desktop displayed and with no taskbar buttons on the taskbar.

1
- **Open** My Computer.
- IF your folder window has no:
  - Standard toolbar—**click** View, **point** to Toolbars, then **click** Standard Buttons.
  - Address bar—**click** View, **point** to Toolbars, then **click** Address Bar.
  - Links toolbar—**click** View, **point** to Toolbars, then **click** Links.
- IF the My Computer window is maximized, **restore** it.
- **Size** the window until the entire Standard toolbar is visible.

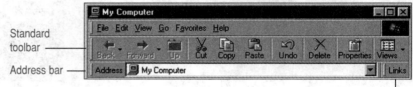

Standard toolbar

Address bar

Links toolbar

2 **Hide toolbars:**
- **Click** View, then **point** to Toolbars.
  The Toolbars menu opens.

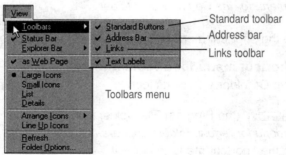

Standard toolbar
Address bar
Links toolbar

Toolbars menu

- **Click** Address Bar (to deselect it).
  The Address bar is hidden.
- **Hide** the Standard toolbar.
- **Hide** the Links toolbar.

3 **Display toolbars:**
- **Click** View, **point** to Toolbars, then **click** Standard Buttons (to select it).
  The Standard toolbar is redisplayed.
- **Display** the Address bar.
- **Display** the Links toolbar.

4 **Hide toolbar text labels:**
- **Click** View, **point** to Toolbars, then **click** Text Labels.
  The toolbar text labels are hidden.

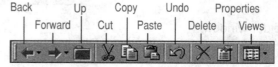

Back   Up   Copy   Undo   Properties
   Forward   Cut   Paste   Delete   Views

- **Size** the window to the width of the shorter Standard toolbar, as shown above.

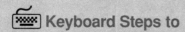 **Keyboard Steps to**

Toggle Toolbars and/or Text Labels On and Off

—WITH A FOLDER WINDOW OPEN—

1. **Press** Alt + V (View).

2. **Press** T (Toolbars).
   The Toolbars menu opens.

3. **Turn on/off** desired toolbar option (a check mark by an option means it is selected):
   - **Press** S (Standard Buttons).
   - **Press** A (Address Bar).
   - **Press** L (Links).
   - **Press** T (Text Labels).

⑤ **Size and move toolbars:**

- **Double-click** the word *Links* on the Links toolbar, if necessary, to slide it open (display its contents).

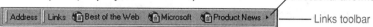

Directional arrowhead

Links toolbar

- **Scroll** to the end of the Links toolbar.
- **Double-click** the word *Links* on the Links toolbar again to close it.
  The Links toolbar slides as far right as it can go.

- **Hold down** the mouse button while pointing to the word *Links* so that the arrow pointer changes to a move pointer.
- **Drag** the move pointer to the right end of the Standard toolbar.

Use move pointer to drag the Links toolbar.

The Links toolbar moves to the right end of the Standard toolbar.

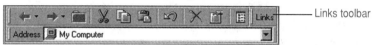

Links toolbar

- **Drag** the Links toolbar under the Address bar.
  The Links toolbar opens under the Address bar.

Links toolbar

- **Drag** the Links toolbar up and over to the right end of the menu bar.
  The Links toolbar appears on the right end of the menu bar.

Links toolbar

- **Drag** the Address bar to the left side of the Links toolbar on the menu bar.
  The Address bar appears next to the Links toolbar on the menu bar.

Address bar   Links toolbar

- **Double-click** the Address bar.
  The Address bar slides open.

Address bar   Links toolbar

⑥ **See how folder windows keep their settings:**

- **Close** the My Computer folder window, then **open** it again.
- **Notice** that the toolbars are the way you left them.

⑦
- **Return** the toolbars to their default settings. *(See the illustration in step 1.)*
- **Display** the toolbar text labels.
- **Close** the My Computer folder window.

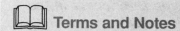

EXERCISE 40 • Use the Address Bar to Find Folders

To type an address in the Address bar drop-down text box.

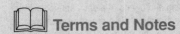

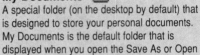 **Terms and Notes**

Address bar
A drop-down text box that lets you access a Web page or a location on your computer by typing or selecting an address or path.

AutoComplete
A feature in the Address bar that automatically completes an address when you begin to enter a previously typed address.

My Documents
A special folder (on the desktop by default) that is designed to store your personal documents. My Documents is the default folder that is displayed when you open the Save As or Open dialog box in Windows accessory programs.

NOTE: You will be instructed to use the My Documents folder in Exercise 52.

Begin with the desktop displayed and with no taskbar buttons on the taskbar.

1 **Use the Address bar drop-down list:**
- **Open** My Computer.
- **Click** the Address bar drop-down arrow.
  The Address bar drop-down list appears.
- **Notice** that the list is similar to the Look in list in the Open dialog box.

- **Click** (C:).
  The window changes to drive C:.
- **Click** the Address bar drop-down arrow, then **click** My Documents.
  The window changes to the My Documents folder.
- **Click** the Address bar drop-down arrow, then **click** Desktop.
  The window changes to the Desktop folder.
- **Click** the Address bar drop-down arrow, then **click** My Computer.
  The window changes to the My Computer folder.

2 **Type a folder path in the Address bar using AutoComplete:**
With the Address bar selected:
- **Type:** c:
  The entire address for drive C: appears in the Address bar. The text that Windows automatically entered to finish the address is highlighted.
- **Press** End to move to the end of the line, then **type:** prog
  The entire address for the Program Files folder appears in the Address bar. The text that Windows automatically entered is highlighted.

- **Press** End to move to the end of the line, then **type:** \a
  The entire address for the Accessories folder appears in the Address bar. The text that Windows automatically entered is highlighted.

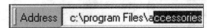

- **Press** Enter to open the folder.
  The Accessories folder opens.
- **Close** the Accessories folder window.

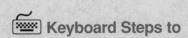 **Keyboard Steps to**

Open the Address Bar List

—WITH A FOLDER WINDOW OPEN—

1. **Press** Tab until the Address bar is selected.

2. **Press** Alt + ↓ (down arrow).
   The Address bar drop-down list opens.

3. **Press** ↑/↓ (up or down arrow) to select the desired location.

4. **Press** Enter .

Begin with the desktop displayed and with no taskbar buttons on the taskbar.

1
- **Open** My Computer.
- IF the folder window is maximized, **restore** it.
- **Click** View.
- IF as Web Page does not have a check mark by it, **click** as Web page to select it; otherwise, **click** View to close the menu.

2 **Size the folder window to display entire Web Page view:**
- **Select** the (C:) icon by pointing to it.
- **Size and move** the window as necessary to see the My Computer icon and the information about (C:) on the left side of the window.

Window is sized big enough to show the icon...

...and display information about drive C:.

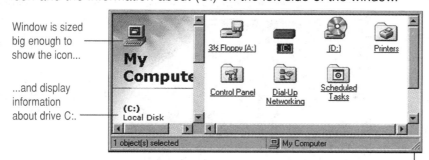

Sizing handle

3 **Show Web Page view at the top of the window:**
- **Drag** the sizing handle left until the My Computer icon disappears. *Just the label,* My Computer, *remains at the top.*

Window is sized so small that the icon disappears...

...and there is no information about drive C:.

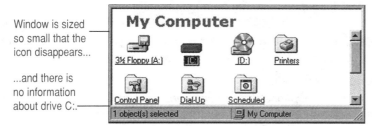

- **Drag** the sizing handle right until the My Computer icon and the information about (C:) is visible once again *(see step 2).*

4 **Turn Web Page view off and on:**
- **Click** View, then **click** as Web Page to deselect it. *Web Page view disappears.*

Web Page view is turned off.

- **Click** View, then **click** as Web Page to select it. *Web Page view reappears.*

5
- **Close** the My Computer folder window.

To demonstrate the two Web Page view displays and to turn Web Page view off and on.

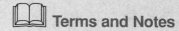 **Terms and Notes**

Web Page view
A feature in folder windows (and Windows Explorer) that displays:
- a picture of the selected item in the top-left corner of the workspace
- the selected item's name
- information about the selected item along the left side of the workspace

When a folder window is sized too small to display all the items listed above, Web Page view displays only the title of the folder window across the top of the workspace.

While Web Page view is turned on automatically in Web-style mode, it can be used in Classic-style mode as well.

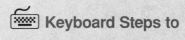 **Keyboard Steps to**

Toggle Web Page View Off and On

—WITH A FOLDER WINDOW OPEN—

1. **Press** `Alt` + `V` (View).
2. **Press** `W` (as Web Page).

To turn on a feature that displays underlined icon titles only when you point at them.

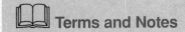 **Terms and Notes**

NOTE: *This feature offers the best of two worlds: Web-style browsing (point-to-select/click-to-open browsing) without the clutter of underlined icon titles (Classic style).*

Begin with the desktop displayed and with no taskbar buttons on the taskbar.

1 **Change to underline icon titles only when you point at them:**
- **Open** My Computer.
- **Click** View, then **click** Folder Options.
  The Folder Options dialog box opens.
- **Click** the *Custom, based on settings you choose* option button, then **click** Settings.
  The Custom Settings dialog box opens.
  NOTE: *The Custom Settings dialog box defaults to the style that was last used, in this case, Web style. Notice that in each section of the Custom Settings dialog box, the top option is selected; these are the Web-style default settings. The bottom options are the Classic-style default settings. In this section, you can blend the Web and Classic styles.*

NOTE: *The last section of the Custom Settings dialog box offers two underlining options when the Single-click to open an item (point to select) option button is selected.*

Underline icon titles only when I point at them option button

- **Click** the *Underline icon titles only when I point at them* option button to select it.
- **Click** OK.
  The Folder Options dialog box appears with the Custom, based on settings you choose option button still selected.
- **Close** the Folder Options dialog box.
  Icon titles in My Computer (and on your desktop) are no longer underlined.

2 **Select an icon:**
- **Point** to the Printers icon and **notice** that the title turns blue and becomes underlined.
- **Move** the pointer away from the icon (but not to another icon) and **notice** that the Printers icon remains selected.
- **Point** to the Control Panel icon to select it.
- **Click** the drive C: icon.
  The Drive C: folder window still opens with one click.

3 **Return to the default, Web-style browsing option:**
- **Click** View, then **click** Folder Options.
- **Click** the Web style option button (to select it), then **click** OK.
  All icon titles are now underlined again.
- **Close** the (C:) folder window.

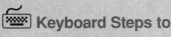 **Keyboard Steps to**

Underline Icon Titles as You Point

—WITH A FOLDER WINDOW OPEN—

1. Press Alt + V (View).

2. Press O (Folder Options).
   The Folder Options dialog box opens.

3. Press U (Custom, based on settings you choose).

4. Press S (Settings).

5. Press P (Underline icon titles only when I point at them).

6. Press Enter, Enter.

Begin with the desktop displayed and with no taskbar buttons on the taskbar.

1 **Add a background picture to a folder:**
- **Open** My Computer, then **open** (C:).
- **Right-click** an empty area in the (C:) workspace.
- **Click** Customize this Folder.
  The Customize this Folder wizard appears.

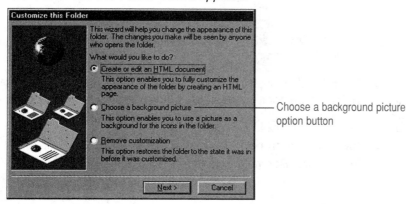

Choose a background picture option button

- **Click** the *Choose a background picture* option button (to select it), then **click** [Next >].
- **Click** Clouds.bmp (*not* CLOUD.GIF), then **click** [Next >].
  The next screen appears, congratulating you and showing your choice.
- **Click** [Finish].
  The Clouds background appears in the drive C: workspace.

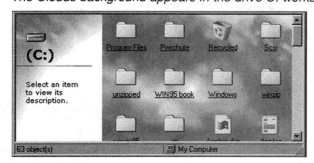

2 **View another folder background:**
- **Click** the Program Files icon.
  The Program Files folder window opens. It does not have a background.
- **Click** the Up button to return to the (C:) folder window.
  The Clouds background reappears.

3 **Remove a background picture from a folder:**
- **Right-click** the workspace, then **click** Customize this Folder.
- **Click** the Remove customization option button (to select it), then **click** [Next >].
  The next screen warns that you are about to remove the folder customization.
- **Click** [Next >], then **click** [Finish].
  The (C:) folder window background is removed.
- **Close** the (C:) folder window.

To customize a folder by putting a background in its workspace.

📖 **Terms and Notes**

wizard
A tool that walks you through a complex task step by step.

NOTES: The Customize feature changes only the folder you are working in; other folders remain unchanged.

My Computer does not offer the Customize feature.

⌨ **Keyboard Steps to**

Add a Background Picture

—WITH A FOLDER WINDOW OPEN—

1. **Press** [Alt] + [V] (View).
2. **Press** [C] (Customize this Folder).
   The Customize this Folder wizard opens.
3. **Press** [C] (Choose a background picture).
4. **Press** [N] (Next).
5. **Press** [↓] (down arrow) to select the desired picture.
6. **Press** [Alt] + [N] (Next).
7. **Press** [Enter].

Remove a Background Picture

—WITH A FOLDER WINDOW OPEN—

1. **Press** [Alt] + [V] (View).
2. **Press** [C] (Customize this Folder).
   The Customize this Folder wizard opens.
3. **Press** [R] (Remove customization).
4. **Press** [N] (Next).
5. **Press** [N] (Next).
6. **Press** [Enter].

EXERCISE 44 • View Explorer Bars

To work offline (stay off the Internet) while opening Explorer bars in a folder window.

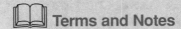

Terms and Notes

NOTE: This exercise is an introduction to working offline; it gives you a strategy for staying offline when you encounter a situation in which Windows 98 tries to put you online automatically. Using the Internet will be covered in Lessons 12 and 13.

Explorer bars
A way to browse through a list of Web links—such as those in Search, Favorites, History, and Channels.

NOTES: Explorer bars are used in folder windows as another way to access the Web quickly. Only the Favorites Explorer bar can access a computer location.

You may not be able to view the Search Explorer bar in offline mode.

hyperlink
Text or graphics that, when clicked, connect(s) to one of the following:
- another place on the same Web page.
- another Web page on the same Web site.
- another Web page on a different Web site.

In Windows 98, hyperlinks are also used to connect one location to another within your computer system. When you point to a hyperlink, the arrow pointer becomes a hand. Also called a *link*.

offline
Not connected to the Internet.

work offline mode
A condition in which you can view Web pages (and Web-page objects) that are stored on the computer without being connected to the Internet.

Begin with the desktop displayed and with no taskbar buttons on the taskbar.

1 **Select the Work Offline feature:**
- **Open** My Computer, then **click** File.
  The File menu drops down. Work Offline may or may not be selected:

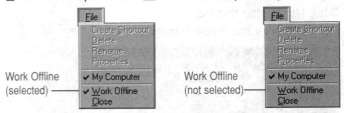

- IF Work Offline does *not* have a check mark beside it, **click** Work Offline (to select it); otherwise, **click** File again to close the menu.

2 **Open the Channels Explorer bar:**
- **Click** View, then **point** to Explorer Bar.
  The Explorer Bar menu opens:

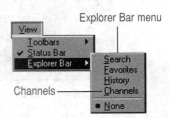

- **Click** Channels.
  The Channels Explorer bar opens:

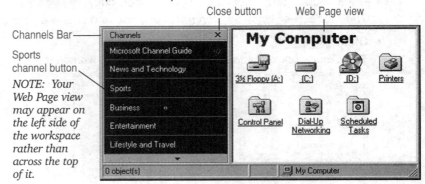

- **Click** the Sports channel button.
  The Sports channel category appears in the workspace because there is a Sports Web page already stored on your computer; notice the Address bar. Your screen may be different from the one shown below.

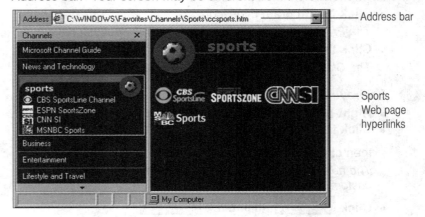

3 **Stay offline when Windows 98 automatically opens the Web:**

- **Click** the Microsoft Channel Guide channel button at the top of the Channels Explorer bar.

  The following dialog box appears:

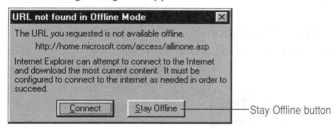

Stay Offline button

- IF the message below appears instead, **click** the blue underlined text, *here*.

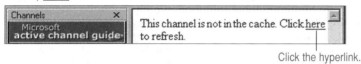

Click the hyperlink.

- **Click** Stay Offline .

4 **Close an Explorer bar using the Close button:**

- **Click** ✕ (the Close button) at the top of the Channels Explorer bar.
  The Channels Explorer bar closes.

5 **Open the Favorites Explorer bar:**

- **Click** the Back button twice to go back to the My Computer folder window.
- **Click** View, **point** to Explorer Bar, then **click** Favorites.
  The Favorites Explorer bar opens.
  NOTE: Your menu items may differ, and your Web Page view may appear on the left side of the workspace rather than across the top of it.

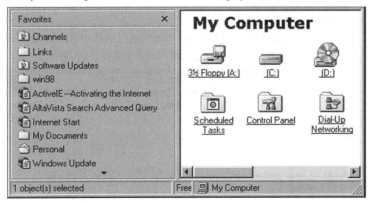

6 **Close an Explorer bar using the menu:**

- **Click** View, **point** to Explorer Bar, then **click** None (to select it).
  The Favorites Explorer bar closes.
- **Close** the My Computer folder window.

⌨ **Keyboard Steps to**

Select the Work Offline Feature

—WITH A FOLDER WINDOW OPEN—

1. **Press** Alt + F (File).

2. IF Work Offline is already selected,

   press Alt to close the menu; otherwise,

   press W (Work Offline) to select it.

View Explorer Bar

—WITH A FOLDER WINDOW OPEN—

1. **Press** Alt + V (View).

2. **Press** E (Explorer Bar).
   The Explorer Bar menu opens.

3. **Choose** desired Explorer bar:

   - **Press** S (Search).

   - **Press** F (Favorites).

   - **Press** H (History).

   - **Press** C (Channels).

NOTE: IF the URL not found in the Offline Mode *dialog box appears, press the S key (Stay Offline).*

Turn Off Explorer Bar

—WITH A FOLDER WINDOW OPEN—

1. **Press** Alt + V (View).

2. **Press** E (Explorer Bar).
   The Explorer Bar menu opens.

3. **Press** N (None).

To change the way objects are displayed in the workspace.

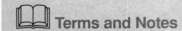 **Terms and Notes**

Folder Window Objects Can Be Displayed Four Ways

- **Large Icons**
  Displays objects as large icons.
- **Small Icons**
  Displays objects as small icons in a left-to-right order.
- **List**
  Displays objects as small icons in a top-to-bottom order.
- **Details**
  Displays objects as small icons in a top-to-bottom order with information about each object in the window.

Begin with the desktop displayed and with no taskbar buttons on the taskbar.

1
- **Open** My Computer.
- **Size** and **move** the window until the entire Standard toolbar is displayed.

2 **View objects as large icons:**
- **Click** the Views button drop-down arrow.

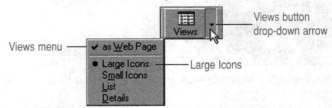

- **Click** Large Icons.
  NOTE: As you may have gathered from working with the View, Explorer Bar submenu in the previous exercise, you cannot deselect a menu item with a dot next to it by clicking that item. A group of menu items that uses a dot to indicate the selected status is similar to a group of option buttons in a dialog box—only one item can be selected. In other words, you must select the desired option to deselect the option you no longer wish to use.
  The objects are displayed as large icons.

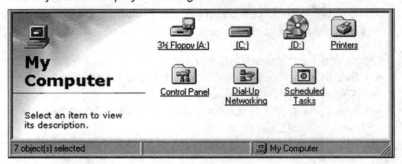

3 **View objects as small icons:**
- **Click** the Views button drop-down arrow, then **click** Small Icons.
  The objects are displayed as small icons in a left-to-right order.

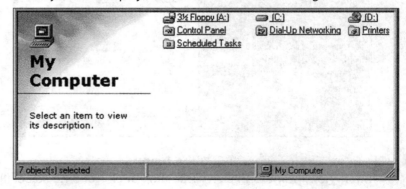

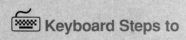 **Keyboard Steps to**

Change Icon View

—WITH A FOLDER WINDOW OPEN—

1. Press **Alt** + **V** (View).
2. **Choose** desired icon view:
   - **Press** **G** (Large Icons).
   - **Press** **M** (Small Icons).
   - **Press** **L** (List).
   - **Press** **D** (Details).

4 **View objects in a list:**
- **Click** the Views button drop-down arrow, then **click** List.
  The objects are displayed as small icons in a top-to-bottom order. (See illustration at the top of the next page.)

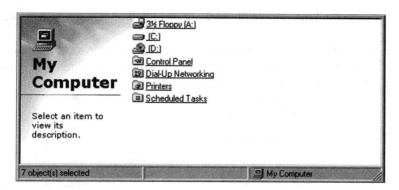

5 View objects showing details:
- **Click** the Views button drop-down arrow, then **click** Details.

  The objects are displayed in a list with the following information: Name, Type, Total Size, and Free Space.

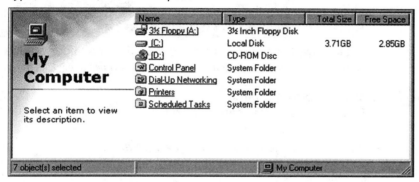

6 Cycle through icon views using the Views button:

- **Click**  (the Views button) on the Standard toolbar.

  The icon view changes to Large Icons.
- **Click** the Views button again.

  The icon view changes to Small Icons.
- **Click** the Views button again.

  The icon view changes to List.
- **Click** the Views button once again.

  The icon view changes to Details.

7 Change icon view using the shortcut menu:
- **Right-click** the workspace, then **point** to View.

View ▶	✔ as Web Page	— View menu
Arrange Icons ▶	Large Icons	
Line Up Icons	Small Icons	
	List	— List
Refresh	● Details	

- **Click** List.

  The icon view changes to List.
- **Right-click** the workspace, **point** to View, then **click** Large Icons.

  The icon view changes to Large Icons.
- **Close** the My Computer folder window.

EXERCISE 46 • Arrange Icons

To sort objects in a folder window (or in Windows Explorer) by name, size, type, or date modified.

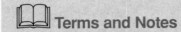

Terms and Notes

NOTES: *While most folder windows can arrange objects by name, type, size, or date, the My Computer folder window can arrange icons by drive letter, type, size, or free space.*

If you are using Windows 95 and have Internet Explorer 4 installed, the warning message shown in step 1 may not appear.

Keyboard Steps to

Arrange Icons

—WITH A FOLDER WINDOW OPEN—

1. **Press** Alt + V (View).

2. **Press** I (Arrange Icons).

3. **Choose** a way to arrange icons:
   - **Press** N (by Name).
   - **Press** T (by Type).
   - **Press** Z (by Size).
   - **Press** D (by Date).

NOTE: *In My Computer, you can arrange objects by Drive Letter, Type, Size, or Free Space rather than the choices shown above.*

Toggle Auto Arrange

—WITH A FOLDER WINDOW OPEN—

1. **Press** Alt + V (View).

2. **Press** I (Arrange Icons).

3. **Press** A (Auto Arrange).

NOTE: *When Auto Arrange is selected, a check mark appears in front of the option.*

Begin with the desktop displayed and with no taskbar buttons on the taskbar.

1 • **Open** My Computer, **open** (C:), then **open** the Windows folder.
The Windows folder appears, but its contents are hidden and there is a warning message.

Warning

Click the
Show Files
hyperlink.

• **Click** Show Files, then **maximize** the Windows folder window.
NOTE: *You may need to scroll to find the blue, underlined Show Files hyperlink.*

2 **Arrange icons by name:**
• **Right-click** the Windows workspace.
The shortcut menu appears.
• **Point** to Arrange Icons, then **click** by Name.
All the folders, and then all the files, are arranged alphabetically from left to right.
• **Scroll** through the objects by clicking *below* the scroll box many times.
• **Scroll** back to the top of the folder window by clicking *above* the scroll box several times.

3 **Change the way objects are viewed:**
• **Click** the View menu, then **click** Small Icons.
The objects are displayed as small icons and are listed alphabetically from left to right across the top.
• **Click** the View menu, then **click** List.
The objects are displayed as small icons and are listed alphabetically from top to bottom.
• **Scroll** through the window by clicking to the *right* of the scroll box many times.
• **Scroll** back to the left of the folder window by clicking to the *left* of the scroll box.

4 **Arrange icons by type:**
• **Right-click** the workspace, **point** to Arrange Icons, then **click** by Type.
The icons are listed alphabetically by type and then alphabetically within their types.
• **Scroll** through the window until you find groups of identical icons.
• **Notice** the group of Paint icons (bitmap images): or ⬛.
All the bitmap icons are listed alphabetically.
• **Notice** the small group of HTML document icons 🗐.
All the Microsoft HTML Document 4.0 icons are listed alphabetically.

5 View file information:
- **Click** the <u>V</u>iew menu, then **click** <u>D</u>etails.

  Headings are displayed across the top of the workspace.

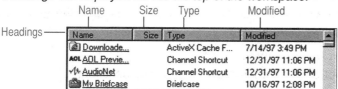

- **Scroll** through the window and notice the different file types and the icons that represent them.

6 Arrange objects using column headings:
- **Click** `Name` (the Name heading).

  The objects are sorted alphabetically (A to Z) by name; all the folders are listed first, then all the files.
- **Scroll** through the window to see the alphabetized folders and files.
- **Click** `Name` again.

  The objects are sorted in descending order (Z to A) by name.
- **Click** `Size` (the Size heading) twice.

  The objects are sorted in descending order (9 to 0) by size.
- **Click** `Modified` (the Modified heading).

  The objects are sorted in ascending order (newest to oldest) by the date last modified; all the folders are listed first, then all the files.
- **Scroll** through the window and **notice** how objects are sorted.
- **Click** `Views` (the Views button).

  The objects change to large icons.
- **Click** `Up` (the Up button) twice.

  The My Computer folder window appears.

7 Auto Arrange icons:
- **Right-click** the workspace, then **point** to Arrange <u>I</u>cons.
- IF <u>A</u>uto Arrange has a check mark next to it, **click** <u>A</u>uto Arrange to deselect that option; otherwise, **click** outside the menu to close it without selecting <u>A</u>uto Arrange.
- **Move** the Control Panel icon about one-half inch (but not onto another icon).
- **Move** the Control Panel icon back to its original position.
- **Right-click** the workspace, **point** to Arrange <u>I</u>cons, then **click** <u>A</u>uto Arrange (to select it).

  The next time you look at the Arrange <u>I</u>cons menu, the <u>A</u>uto Arrange option will have a check mark by it.
- **Move** the Control Panel icon about one-half inch.

  The icon jumps back to its original position (or possibly switches places with another icon).
- **Right-click** the workspace, **point** to Arrange <u>I</u>cons, then **click** <u>A</u>uto Arrange (to deselect it).
- **Restore** and then **close** the My Computer folder window.

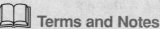 **Terms and Notes**

Auto Arrange
A command that prevents desktop and folder icons from being moved out of their aligned positions.

NOTE: If you want to move icons around but can't, deselect the <u>A</u>uto Arrange command.

sort
When you arrange icons using the View menu or the shortcut menu, you can sort files only from A-Z or 0-9 (ascending). When you arrange icons using column headings, however, you can sort files from Z-A or 9-0 (descending) as well as in ascending order.

File Type Icons

ICON	FILE TYPE
	Bitmap image
	document Find file
	execution file
	font file
	generic icon
	GIF image
	Help file
	Microsoft HTML document 4.0
	Microsoft Word document
	MIDI Sequence
	text file
	TrueType Font file
	WAV file

NOTE: You probably won't find all of these file type icons in the Windows folder.

Folder Windows

Tasks Reviewed:
- Change the Folder Style
- Select and Open Objects in Folders
- Use Back, Forward, and Up Buttons
- Look at Folder Menus
- Look at Shortcut Menus
- Manage Toolbars
- Use the Address Bar to Find Folders
- Turn Web Page View Off and On
- Underline Icon Titles as You Point
- Change a Folder Background
- View Explorer Bars
- Change Icon View
- Arrange Icons

Begin with the desktop displayed and with no taskbar buttons on the taskbar.

1
- **Change** to Classic-style folders and icons using the Start menu.
- **Select** My Computer, then **open** My Computer.
- **Change** back to Web-style folders and icons using the View menu.
- **Close** My Computer.

2
- **Open** My Computer.
- **Select** drive C:, then **read** the information about it.
- **Open** drive C:.
- **Open** the Windows folder. (You may need to scroll to find it.)
- **Go back** to My Computer.
- **Go forward** to the Windows folder.
- **Go up** one level at a time to My Computer.

3
- **Look** at each of the menus on the menu bar.
- **Select** drive C:, then **look** at the File menu.
- **Open** drive C:.
- **Select** the Program Files folder, then **look** at the File menu.
- **Go back** to My Computer.

4
- **Look** at the shortcut menu for drive C:.
- **Look** at the shortcut menu for the Printers icon.
- **Open** drive C:.
- **Look** at the shortcut menu for the Program Files icon.
- **Look** at the shortcut menu for the workspace.
- **Close** drive C:.

5
- **Open** My Computer.
- **Turn off** the Links and Standard toolbars as well as the Address bar.
- **Turn on** the Links and Standard toolbars as well as the Address bar.
- **Turn off** the toolbar text labels.
- **Move** the Links toolbar below the Address bar.
- **Move** the Address bar to the right end of the menu bar.
- **Move** the Links toolbar to the right end of the Standard toolbar.
- **Move** the Address bar under the Standard toolbar.
- **Move** the Links toolbar to the right end of the Address bar.
- **Open** the Links toolbar using the double-click method, then **scroll** to the end of it.
- **Close** the Links toolbar using the double-click method.
- **Close** the Address bar and then **open** it.
- **Turn on** the toolbar text labels.

6
- **Go to** My Documents **using** the Address bar.
- **Go to** My Computer **using** the Address bar.

7
- **Turn off** Web Page view.
- **Turn on** Web Page view.
- **Size** the My Computer folder window small enough so that the My Computer icon and the description section aren't visible.
- **Size** the My Computer folder window large enough to make the My Computer icon and the description section visible.

⑧ • **Change** to underline icon titles only when you point at them.
   • **Select** a few icons so you can see how they become underlined.
   • **Change** back to Web-style folders and icons using either method desired.

⑨ • **Open** drive C:.
   • **Change** the folder background to BACKGRND.GIF (or the picture of your choice).
   • **Remove** the background picture.
   • **Go back** to My Computer.

⑩ • **Select** the Work Offline feature. (Make sure it has a check mark by it.)
   • **View** the Channels Explorer bar.
   • **Select** (click) the Business channel button.
   • **Select** (click) the Microsoft Channel Guide channel button.
   • IF a message appears in the workspace that says, *Click here to refresh*, **click** here.
   • **Stay offline** when Windows says it can't find the URL.
   • **Close** the Channels Explorer bar.
   • **Go back** to My Computer.

⑪ • **Size** the My Computer folder window until you can see the entire Standard toolbar.
   • **View** the objects as small icons using the shortcut menu.
   • **View** the objects in a list using the shortcut menu.
   • **View** the objects showing details using the shortcut menu.
   • **View** the objects as large icons using the shortcut menu.
   • **Cycle through** icon views using the Views button.

⑫ • **Open** drive C:, **open** Windows, then **click** Show Files.
   • **Maximize** the Windows folder window, and **arrange** the objects by name.
   • **View** objects in a list.
   • **Arrange** icons alphabetically by type, then **scroll** through the objects.
   • **View** file information.
   • **Arrange** icons by name from Z to A using the headings.
   • **Arrange** icons by size using the headings.
   • **Arrange** icons alphabetically by name from A to Z using the headings.
   • **Go back** to My Computer, then **view** the objects as large icons.
   • **Move** the Printers folder about one-half inch, then **move** it back.
   • **Turn on** Auto Arrange, and **move** the Printers folder about one-half inch.
   • **Turn off** Auto Arrange, and **arrange** icons by drive letter.
   • **Restore** and then **close** the My Computer folder window.

Lesson Four Worksheet (5) is on page 305.

NEXT
LESSON

Lesson Five
More Folder Windows

Table of Contents

TOPIC 14 • Files and Filenames

Terms and Notes

associated file
A file that has been identified as belonging to a certain program, such as .txt with Notepad, .bmp with Paint, or .doc with Microsoft Word. When you open an associated file, the program related to that file also opens automatically.

document
A file that consists of data created in a program, such as a letter typed in WordPad or a picture drawn in Paint. Also called *data file*.

file
Data or program instructions that are saved on a disk as a named unit.

filename
The name you give to data that is stored on a disk.

filename extension
The period and, usually but not always, three characters at the end of a filename.

file types
Files are defined by the programs that they are created in. Every file type has an icon associated with it. Below are examples of file types and their icons:

 Bitmap image

 document Find file

 execution file

 font file

 generic icon

 help file

 Microsoft HTML Document 4.0

 Microsoft Word document

 MIDI Sequence

 text file

 TrueType Font file

long filename
A filename that is up to 255 characters long and *can* contain spaces and most symbols.

program file
A file containing a set of instructions that your computer follows to perform a specific task, such as word processing.

short filename
A filename that is no longer than eight characters, can contain a filename extension, but *cannot* contain spaces or certain symbols.

Files

A **file** is a collection of data that is given a **filename** and stored on a disk. Some of the file-managing jobs that Windows 98 helps you perform are:

- name
- rename
- save
- resave
- open
- print
- copy
- move
- paste
- delete
- view
- browse
- organize
- create shortcuts

Files are identified and categorized in various ways. Most files you work with are either:

- **program files** (instructions that perform a task), or
- **data files** (information created in a program, such as a letter).

Conventional File-Naming Rules

Files have traditionally been named using the following rules:

- A filename can be no longer than eight characters.
- You cannot use these characters: . " / \ [ ] : * | < > + = ; , ?
- You cannot use a space.
- You can use an optional filename extension of a period (.) and up to three characters.

Long Filenames

You are not confined to the conventional file-naming rules when naming files created with Windows 98 programs. Below are rules for long filenames:

- A filename can be up to 255 characters.
- You cannot use these characters: . " / \ < > ? *
- You can use a space.
- You can use an optional filename extension of a period (.) and up to three characters.

When you save a file with a long filename, Windows 98 saves not only the long filename you specify, but a shorter version of that name which meets the conventional file-naming rules listed above. Any programs you may have that cannot read long filenames will access these files using their shorter filenames.

Filename Extensions

Filename extensions are usually used to identify groups of related file types. There are certain standard extensions that have special meanings:

.exe (execution)	program files
.sys (system)	files that work with your hardware
.txt (text)	text files
.bmp (bitmap)	associated with Paint
.doc (document)	associated with Microsoft Word or WordPad

Windows 98 hides filename extensions by default, but you can still identify file types by their icons (see the side panel).

Where are Files Stored?

All files are stored on disk in **folders**. *(See the next page for more information about folders.)*

Files
Folder

Disk Drives

Disk drives are used to store files. Your computer system comes with at least two disk drives: one **floppy disk drive**, named drive A:, and one **hard disk drive**, typically named drive C:. You may also have a second floppy disk drive, usually named drive B:. Today, computers also have a **CD-ROM drive**, frequently named drive D:. CD-ROMs can hold much more information than a floppy disk. However, most CD-ROMs cannot store your files; they are only used to read very large amounts of data stored on them.

Many of today's computer systems come with a Zip or Jazz disk drive. These drives use disks that can hold much more data than a floppy disk. This extra capacity is needed for the very large files created by many of today's high-tech programs. These drives are especially useful for making backups and transporting files.

Folders

Folders are created on disks (especially the hard disk) to efficiently organize the many files that are stored on disks. Folders may also hold other folders (sometimes referred to as **subfolders**) which, in turn, may hold still more files and folders. The resulting multilevel structure forms a **hierarchy**, that is, a system of folders ranked one above the other. In Windows 98, folders are always marked with a folder icon 📁. Windows 98 uses the term *folder* to describe what used to be called *directories*. *(See also Topic 23, A Look at Structure.)*

The illustration below shows a simplified structure of folders on drive C:. Notice that all the folders below the Start Menu folder are group folders. **Group folders** represent submenus that branch off of primarily the Programs menu.

Structure of Folders on the Hard Disk

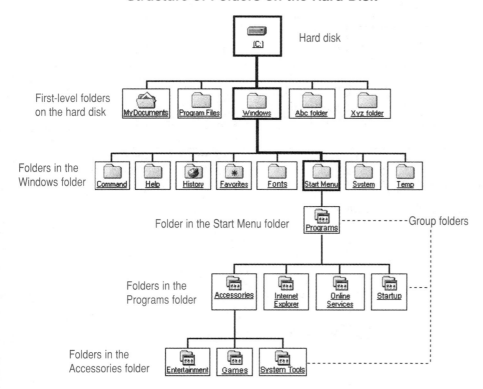

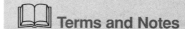 **Terms and Notes**

CD-ROM drive
A drive that retrieves information from removable, read-only optical disks that can store relatively large amounts of data when compared to regular floppy disks.

disk
Media on which information is stored and retrieved in named units called *files.*

disk drive
A mechanical device used to transfer information back and forth between the computer's memory and a disk.

floppy disk
A removable, magnetically coated diskette on/from which information can be stored and retrieved.

floppy disk drive
A hardware component of your computer system. A drive used to transfer information back and forth between the RAM and a floppy disk.

folder
A structure that holds files and/or other folders *(subfolders)* that are stored on a disk. A folder can also contain other objects, such as printers and disk drives. (Folders have traditionally been called *directories.*)

group folder
A folder within the Start Menu folder that holds groups of program shortcuts and other folders; they each represent menus within the Start menu.

hard disk drive
A built-in storage device that has a nonremovable disk (a fixed disk) with a large capacity.

hierarchy
A system of things (or people) ranked one above the other. With regard to computers, the term *hierarchy* describes the multilevel structure of folders and subfolders on a disk. In the case of Windows 98, it further describes the multilevel structure of objects on the entire computer system. This structure is also referred to as a *tree.*

subfolder
A folder contained within another *folder.*

TOPIC 16 • Windows 98 Structure

Terms and Notes

browse
To look at files, folders, disks, printers, programs, documents, and other objects on your computer system.

desktop
The opening screen in Windows 98 that contains a few objects, the Start button, and the taskbar. The button shown above is the Show Desktop button on the Quick Launch toolbar. It's also the desktop icon in Windows Explorer.

My Computer
A special folder (with an icon that appears on the desktop by default) that gives you a quick route to the disk drives, folders, files, and other objects on your computer system.

Network Neighborhood
An object that may appear on the desktop; it lets you browse through other computers on your network.

Display Hidden Files and Folders

1. **Open** Windows Explorer.
2. **Click** the View menu.
3. **Click** Folder Options.
4. **Click** the View tab.
5. **Click** Show all files option button.
6. **Click** the OK button.
(For more information, see Exercise 105, Display Hidden Files and Folders.)

Windows 98 Structure Consists of More than Disks and Folders

Microsoft has designed Windows 98 with networking capabilities (using Network Neighborhood). If you are connected to a network, you will be able to access folders and files on computers other than your own.

The **desktop** is the heart of Windows 98. The illustration below shows the desktop at the top of the Windows structure. From the desktop, you can choose to look at folders and files in **My Computer** or **Network Neighborhood**.

The desktop is the logical—but not physical—top of the Windows 98 structure; it acts like the top of the structure, but the Desktop folder is actually a hidden folder located on drive C:. While this fact is of little concern to most users, it may reduce confusion for others.

In the illustration below, dashed lines around the hard disk (C:) structure distinguish it from the Windows logical structure above the hard disk. The heavy lines show the route from the desktop to the Start Menu folder. The Start Menu folder represents the Start menu on your desktop. The group folders below the Start Menu folder represent cascading menus that branch off of the Start menu. Keep this structure in mind when you are **browsing** folders.

Windows 98 Structure

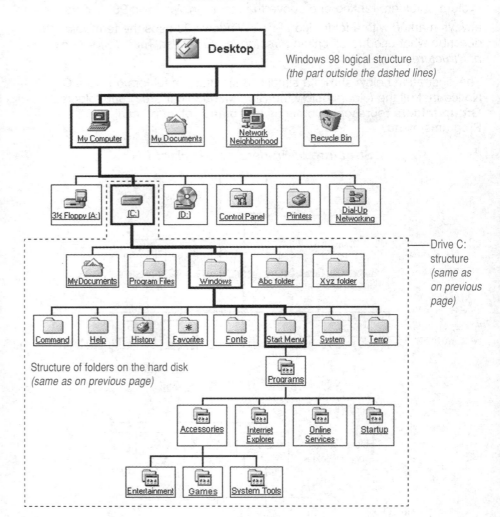

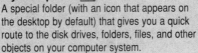

The My Computer Folder Window

From **My Computer**, you can work your way to any resource on your computer. My Computer is a special folder *(see Topic 13, Special Folders)* whose icon is located at the top-left corner of your desktop. My Computer is at the top of your local computer structure. Every object in My Computer opens a **folder window** that displays the object's contents.

My Computer icon

NOTE: Your desktop may display different icons.

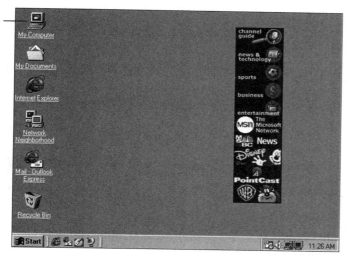

My Computer and other folder windows are a smaller version of Windows Explorer (the file-managing program covered in Lesson Eight). Folder windows and Windows Explorer offer many of the same features, some of which were already covered in Lesson Four:

- Select and open objects
- Back, Forward, and Up buttons
- Menu bars and shortcut menus
- Toolbars
- Explorer bars
- Icon views and arrangements

Folder window features covered in this lesson include:

- Change disk drives
- Start Windows Explorer
- Start a program
- Open a document
- My Documents
- Create and delete folders
- Move files into a folder
- Favorites

My Computer Folder Window

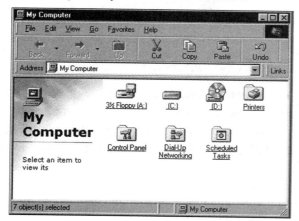

NOTE: The contents of your My Computer folder may differ from this one.

Terms and Notes

folder window
A window that displays the contents of a folder (or certain other objects, such as disk drives). Folder windows offer many of the same folder-managing features as Windows Explorer. Click a folder (if Web-style browsing is enabled) to open its window and see what is in it.

My Computer
A special folder (with an icon that appears on the desktop by default) that gives you a quick route to the disk drives, folders, files, and other objects on your computer system.

To switch between drive C: and drive A: in My Computer.

Begin with the desktop displayed and with no taskbar buttons on the taskbar.

① **Change to drive C:**
- **Open** My Computer.
- **Click** ▭ (the drive C: icon).
  The drive (C:) folder window opens:

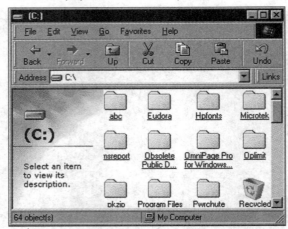

② **Change to drive A:**
- **Click** the Up button.
- **Insert** DATA DISK 1 into drive A:.

- **Click** 3½ Floppy (A:) (the drive A: icon).
  The Floppy (A:) folder window opens:

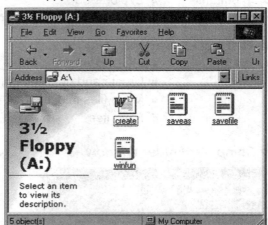

NOTE: Your WordPad icons may be different.

③ **Change drives using the Address bar:**
- **Click** the Address bar drop-down arrow, then **click** (C:).
- **Click** the Address bar drop-down arrow, then **click** Floppy (A:).
- **Click** the Address bar drop-down arrow, then **click** My Computer.

④
- **Close** the My Computer folder window.
- **Remove** DATA DISK 1 when you're through working. (You will need it again in Exercise 51.)

⌨ **Keyboard Steps to**

Change Disk Drives from My Computer

—WITH MY COMPUTER OPEN—

1. **Press** Tab until an icon in the folder workspace is selected.

2. **Press** ⬆⬇ (arrow keys) to select the desired disk drive icon.

3. **Press** Enter.
   The disk drive opens.

Begin with the desktop displayed and with no taskbar buttons on the taskbar.

1 **Open Windows Explorer from My Computer:**
- **Open** My Computer.
- **Right-click** drive C:, then **click** <u>E</u>xplore.
- **Maximize** the Explorer window if it is not already maximized.
  Windows Explorer opens with the title, Exploring - (C:), *in the title bar.*
  NOTE: *Your drive C: may have a name before the drive designation, (C:).*

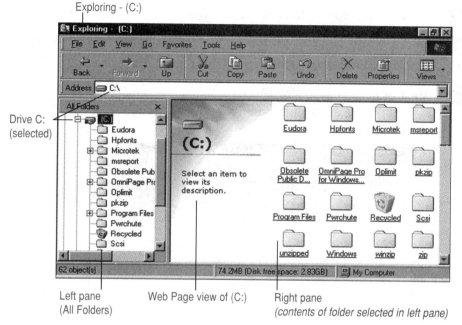

Exploring - (C:)

Drive C: (selected)

Left pane (All Folders)　　Web Page view of (C:)　　Right pane *(contents of folder selected in left pane)*

Windows Explorer is divided into two panes. The **left pane** displays the Windows hierarchy (All Folders); the **right pane** displays the contents of the selected folder in the left pane (it resembles a folder window). The Explorer title bar names the folder that is selected in the left pane. Explorer and folder windows have the same menus on the menu bar—the one notable exception being the <u>T</u>ools menu which is only found in Windows Explorer. You will learn more about Explorer in Lessons Eight and Nine.

2 **Select a different object in the left pane:**
- **Scroll** to the top of the left pane.
- **Click** My Computer at the top of the left pane to select it.
  The Explorer title bar name changes from Exploring - (C:) *to* Exploring - My Computer, *and the right pane displays the contents of My Computer.*
- **Close** Windows Explorer, then **close** My Computer.

3 **Open Windows Explorer from the desktop:**
  You can open Windows Explorer by right-clicking any folder. When Windows Explorer opens, the contents of the right-clicked folder will appear in the right pane.
- **Right-click** My Computer, then **click** <u>E</u>xplore.
  Windows Explorer opens with the title, Exploring - My Computer, *in the title bar.*
- **Close** Windows Explorer.

To right-click the My Computer icon to open Windows Explorer.

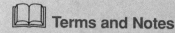 **Terms and Notes**

Windows Explorer
The Windows 98 program that you can use to look at and manage objects in your computer system, including remote computers if your system is networked. The *left pane* displays All Folders (a hierarchy of folders); the *right pane* displays the contents of the folder that is selected in the left pane.

NOTE: *Don't confuse Windows Explorer (the file-managing program) with Internet Explorer (the Web-browsing program). Windows Explorer is sometimes simply called* Explorer.

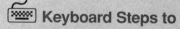 **Keyboard Steps to**

Open Windows Explorer from My Computer

—WITH MY COMPUTER OPEN—

1. Press `Tab` until an icon in the folder workspace is selected.
2. Press `←↓↑→` (arrow keys) to select the drive C: icon.
3. Press `Alt` + `F` (<u>F</u>ile).
4. Press `E` (<u>E</u>xplore).
   The Explorer opens.

Open Windows Explorer Using the My Computer Icon

—WITH THE DESKTOP DISPLAYED—

1. Press `Ctrl` + `Esc`, `Esc`.
2. Press `Tab`, `Tab`, `Tab`.
3. Press `←↓↑→` (arrow keys) to select My Computer.
4. Press `Shift` + `F10`.
   OR
   Press `📄` (the Application key).
5. Press `E` (<u>E</u>xplore).

EXERCISE 50 • Start a Program from a Folder

To start a program from a folder you opened while browsing with My Computer.

Why Start a Program from a Folder?

This method is useful for starting programs that are not on the <u>P</u>rograms menu, or for starting a program you see in a folder and decide you want to start immediately.

Begin with the desktop displayed and with no taskbar buttons on the taskbar.

1 • **Open** My Computer.

2 **Change to a folder that holds a program:**
  • **Open** (C:), **open** the Program Files folder, then **open** the Accessories folder.
  Mspaint and WordPad are in the Accessories folder.

3 **Start and then exit WordPad:**
  • **Click** WordPad to start (open) it.
  WordPad opens:

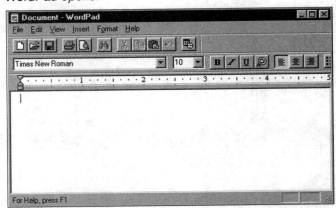

  • **Exit** WordPad.

4 **Start and then exit Calculator:**
  • **Go back** to drive C: (review, Exercise 36).
  • **Open** the Windows folder, then **click** <u>Show Files</u>.

  • **Scroll** until you find <u>Calc</u> (the Calculator icon).
  • **Click** the Calc icon to start it.
  Calculator opens:

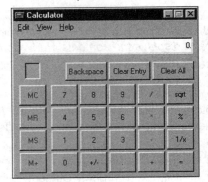

  • **Exit** Calculator.
  • **Close** the Windows folder window.

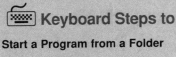 **Keyboard Steps to**

Start a Program from a Folder

—WITH DESIRED PROGRAM ICON DISPLAYED—

1. **Press** `Tab` until an icon in the folder workspace is selected.

2. **Press** (arrow keys) to select the desired program icon.

3. **Press** `Enter` to start the program.

Why Open a Document from a Folder?

Opening a document from a folder is convenient because Windows starts the associated program when it opens the document. If you are browsing, it is nice to be able to open the document you want without delay.

Begin with the desktop displayed and with no taskbar buttons on the taskbar.

1
- **Open** My Computer.

2 **Open a document on drive A:**
- **With** DATA DISK 1 inserted, **open** Floppy (A:).
- **Click** saveas.
  Notepad starts with saveas open.
- **Exit** Notepad.

3 **Open a drawing on drive C:**
- **Go back** to My Computer, then **open** drive C:.
- **Open** the Windows folder, then **click** Show Files.

- **Scroll** until you find Forest (the Forest icon).
- **Click** Forest to open it.
  NOTE: If you cannot find Forest, open another file with a bitmap (.bmp) icon: 🖼️ *or* 🖼️.
  Paint starts with Forest.bmp open:

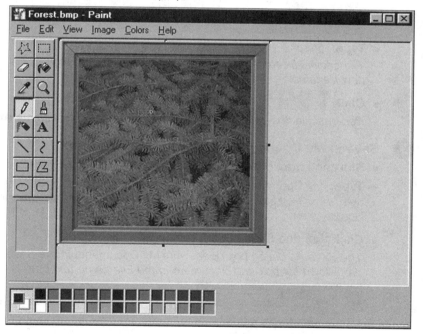

4
- **Exit** Paint.
- **Close** the Windows folder window.
- **Remove** DATA DISK 1 when you're through working. (You will need it again in Exercise 53.)

To open a data file and its associated program from a folder window.

 Keyboard Steps to

Open a Document from a Folder

—WITH DESIRED DOCUMENT ICON DISPLAYED—

1. **Press** `Tab` until an icon in the folder workspace is selected.

2. **Press** `↕` (arrow keys) to select the desired document icon.

3. **Press** `Enter` to open the document.

To save and open files in the default folder, My Documents.

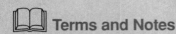 **Terms and Notes**

filename extension
The period and, usually but not always, three characters at the end of a filename (for example, .doc, .txt, .gif).

long filename
A filename that is up to 255 characters long and can contain spaces and most symbols.

My Documents
A special folder (on the desktop by default) that is designed to store your personal documents. My Documents is the default folder that is displayed when you open the Save As or Open dialog box in Windows accessory programs.

NOTE: The My Documents folder is displayed on the desktop, but it is physically a subfolder of drive C:—you will see it in both places.

Why Save Files in My Documents?

The My Documents folder was designed as a convenient location for users to save their personal files on their computers' hard drives. Furthermore, most Windows 98 programs use My Documents as the default folder in which to save files. However, in order to keep you from making permanent changes on your hard drive, you will be directed to save files in the My Documents folder in this exercise, and then you will be directed to move those files to your data disk in Exercise 53.

Begin with the desktop displayed and with no taskbar buttons on the taskbar.

1
- **Start** and **maximize** Notepad.
- **Type** the following text, pressing the Enter key where indicated:

  My Documents is the default folder to save files in. You will `Enter` save and open files in My Documents. Then you will move them `Enter` to your floppy data disk. `Enter`

2 **Save a document in My Documents using a long filename:**
- **Click** File, then **click** Save.

The Save As dialog box opens with My Documents *in the Save in drop-down list box and* Untitled *in the File name text box.*

NOTE: There may be additional files in the workspace.

- **Type:** personal file 1
  The original filename disappears and personal file 1 *becomes the new filename.*
- **Click** [Save], then **exit** Notepad.
  Personal file 1 is saved as a text document with a .txt filename extension.

3 **Save in My Documents from a different program:**
- **Start** and **maximize** WordPad.
- **Type:** My Documents is the default folder to save files in for WordPad as well as for Notepad. Other Microsoft software automatically saves files in My Documents also.
- **Click** 💾 (the Save button) on the Standard toolbar.
  The Save As dialog box opens with My Documents *in the Save in drop-down list box and* Document *in the File name text box.*

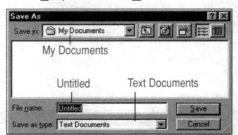
Document

Word for Windows 6.0

NOTE: The default settings in the File name and Save as type text boxes in WordPad's Save As dialog box are the only elements that are different from those in the Notepad Save As dialog box.

- **Type:** personal file 2 in the File name text box, then **click** [Save].
  Personal file 2 is saved as a Word document with a .doc filename extension.

4 **Open a file in My Documents:**

- **Click** 🗋 (the New button) on the Standard toolbar.
  The New dialog box opens.

- **Click** [OK] to accept *Word Document*.

- **Click** 📂 (the Open button) on the Standard toolbar.
  The Open dialog box appears with My Documents *in the Look in drop-down list box and* personal file 2 *in the workspace.*

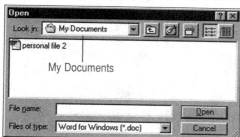

My Documents

NOTE: *Your workspace may have other files and/or folders, and you may need to scroll to find personal file 2.*

- **Click** personal file 2, then **click** [Open].
  The personal file 2 document opens in WordPad.

5 **Open a text file from My Documents:**

- **Click** 🗋 (the New button) on the Standard toolbar.
  The New dialog box appears.

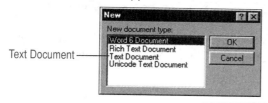

Text Document

- **Click** Text Document, then **click** [OK].

- **Click** 📂 (the Open button) on the Standard toolbar.

- IF Word for Windows (*.doc) appears in the Files of type list box, **click** the Files of type drop-down arrow, then **click** *Text Documents (.txt).*
  The Open dialog box appears and personal file 1 *appears in its workspace.*

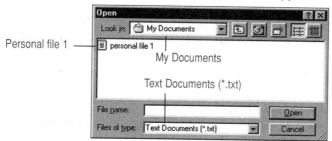

Personal file 1

My Documents

Text Documents (*.txt)

- **Click** personal file 1, then **click** [Open].
  The personal file 1 document opens in WordPad.

6
- **Exit** WordPad.
- **Go on** to Exercise 53 without stopping.

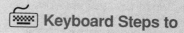 **Keyboard Steps to**

Save a File in My Documents

—WITH NEW TEXT IN AN OPEN PROGRAM—

1. **Press** [Alt] + [F] (File).

2. **Press** [A] (Save As).
   The Save As dialog box opens.

3. **Type** the desired filename.

4. **Press** [Enter] to activate the Save command button.

Open a File from My Documents

—WITH AN EMPTY WORKSPACE IN AN OPEN PROGRAM—

1. **Press** [Alt] + [F] (File).

2. **Press** [O] (Open).
   The Open dialog box appears with My Documents *in the Look in drop-down list box.*

3. **Type** the desired filename.

4. **Press** [Enter] to activate the Open command button.

Change File Type in Open Dialog Box

—FROM THE OPEN DIALOG BOX—

1. **Press** [Alt] + [T] (Files of type).

2. **Press** [↓] (down arrow).
   The Files of type list box drops down.

3. **Press** [↑↓] (up or down arrow) to highlight the desired file type.

4. **Press** [Enter].

To use the cut-and-paste method to transfer a file from one folder window to another.

 Terms and Notes

NOTES: *In this exercise, you will transfer the files you saved in My Documents to the Floppy (A:) folder so you don't leave files on the hard drive.*

While there are Cut and Paste buttons on the Standard toolbar, in this exercise you will use the shortcut menu to cut and paste.

clipboard
A temporary storage area in the computer's memory used to hold information that is being cut/copied and pasted.

cut
To transfer information (a file or section of highlighted text) from its current location to the *clipboard* where it remains until it is pasted or replaced when another item is cut or copied.

paste
To copy information from the *clipboard* into a folder or document. Paste leaves the information in the clipboard so it can be pasted again (until you replace it with newly cut/copied data).

 Keyboard Steps to

Cut a File from a Folder

—WITH A FOLDER WINDOW OPEN FROM WHICH TO CUT THE FILE—

1. **Select** the file you want to cut *(see page 72).*

2. **Press** `Ctrl` + `X` (Cut).
   The cut file becomes dimmed.

Paste a File in Floppy (A:)

—WITH A FLOPPY DISK IN DRIVE A:—

1. **Press** `Tab` until the Address bar is selected.

2. **Press** `↓` (down arrow) to open the Address bar drop-down list.

3. **Press** `↓` (down arrow) until Floppy (A:) is selected.

4. **Press** `Enter`.

5. **Press** `Ctrl` + `V` (Paste).
   The cut file appears in the Floppy (A:) folder.

Go Back to the Previous Folder

1. **Press** `Alt` + `G` (Go).

2. **Press** `B` (Back).

Continue from Exercise 52 without stopping.

① **Open and size two folder windows:**
- **Open** My Computer.
- **Click** the Address bar drop-down arrow, then **click** My Documents.
- **Size and move** the My Documents folder window as shown below.
- **Open** My Computer again.
- **With** DATA DISK 1 inserted, **open** Floppy (A:).
- **Size and move** the Floppy (A:) folder window as shown below.

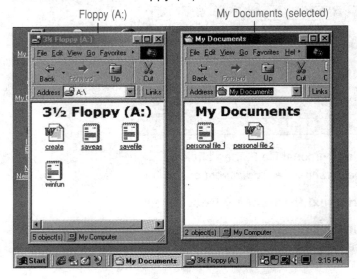

② **Cut a file from My Documents and paste it into Floppy (A:):**
- **Right-click** personal file 1 (in the My Documents folder window), then **click** Cut.
  The personal file 1 icon becomes dimmed.

Icon *before* you right-click   Icon *when* you right-click   Icon *after* you cut

- **Right-click** the Floppy (A:) workspace, then **click** Paste.
  The Moving dialog box appears briefly and personal file 1 *appears in the Floppy (A:) folder window and disappears from the My Documents folder window.*

③ **Cut and paste a file with just one folder window displayed:**
- **Close** the Floppy (A:) folder window.
- **Right-click** personal file 2 (in the My Documents folder window), then **click** Cut.
  The personal file 2 icon becomes dimmed.
- **Click** the Address bar drop-down arrow, then **click** Floppy (A:).
  The Floppy (A:) folder window appears.
- **Right-click** the Floppy (A:) workspace, then **click** Paste.
  Personal file 2 *appears in the Floppy (A:) folder window and disappears from the My Documents folder window (although you can't see it disappear since the My Documents folder is closed).*

④
- **Close** the Floppy (A:) folder window.
- **Remove** DATA DISK 1 or **go on** to Exercise 54.

Begin with the desktop displayed and with no taskbar buttons on the taskbar.

1 • **With** DATA DISK 1 inserted, **open** My Computer, then **open** Floppy (A:).

2 Create a folder:
- **Click** a blank area of the workspace to be sure no object is selected.
- **Click** <u>F</u>ile, **point** to <u>N</u>ew, then **click** <u>F</u>older.

    OR

    Right-click the workspace, **point** to <u>N</u>ew, then **click** <u>F</u>older.

    A new folder appears in the workspace and is named New Folder; *a cursor is blinking at the end of the folder name.*

- **Type**: My Folder

    The original name, New Folder, *disappears and* My Folder *becomes the new folder's name.*

- **Press** Enter.

    The folder is still selected.

3 Open a new folder:

- **Press** Enter again.

    My Folder opens and it is empty:

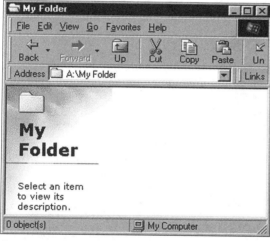

- **Click** the Up button.

    My Folder now appears as an icon in the Floppy (A:) folder window.

4 Delete a new folder:

- **Right-click** My Folder, then **click** <u>D</u>elete.

    The Confirm Folder Delete dialog box opens, asking: Are you sure you want to remove the folder 'My Folder' and all its contents?

- **Click** Yes.

    The Deleting... dialog box appears briefly, then My Folder disappears from the workspace.

5 • **Create** My Folder again *(see step 2)*, but do *not* delete it this time.

6 • **Go on** to Exercise 55 without stopping.

Keyboard Steps to

Create a Folder

—WITH A FOLDER WINDOW OPEN—

1. **Press** Alt + F (<u>F</u>ile).
2. **Press** N (<u>N</u>ew).
3. **Press** F (<u>F</u>older).
4. **Type** the desired folder name.
5. **Press** Enter.

Delete a Folder

—WITH A FOLDER WINDOW OPEN—

1. **Press** Tab until an icon in the folder workspace is selected.
2. **Press** (arrow keys) to select the folder you want to delete.
3. **Press** Alt + F (<u>F</u>ile).
4. **Press** D (<u>D</u>elete).
    The Confirm Folder Delete dialog box appears.
5. **Press** Y (<u>Y</u>es).

EXERCISE 55 • Drag and Drop Files

To move files from one folder to another by dragging them.

Terms and Notes

drag
A mouse action in which you complete the following steps:
- Point to the item to move.
- Hold down the left mouse button.
- Slide the arrow pointer to the desired location.
- Release the mouse button.

drag and drop
A procedure in which you drag an object and drop it onto another object to perform a task, for example, to move, copy, delete, or print a document.

Keyboard Steps to

Move a Document into a Folder

—WITH THE FLOPPY (A:) FOLDER WINDOW OPEN—

1. Press **Tab** until an icon in the folder workspace is selected.

2. Press **↑↓←→** (arrow keys) to select the file you want to move.

3. Press **Ctrl** + **X** (Cut).
   The icon becomes dimmed.

4. Press **↑↓←→** (arrow keys) to select the folder into which you want to move the cut file.

5. Press **Enter** to open the desired folder.

6. Press **Ctrl** + **V** (Paste).

Continue from Exercise 54 without stopping.

1
- **Arrange** icons by name (review, Exercise 46, step 2).
- **Size** the Floppy (A:) folder window so you can see all its objects.

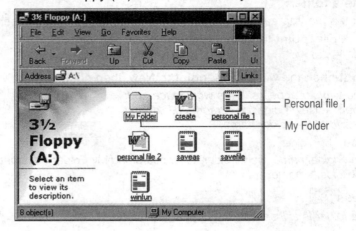

2 **Move a file into the My Folder window:**
- **Drag** personal file 1 onto the My Folder icon until My Folder is selected.
- **Drop** personal file 1 onto My Folder.
  Personal file 1 moves into My Folder and disappears from the Floppy (A:) folder window.

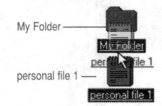

- **Drag and drop** personal file 2 onto My Folder.
  Personal file 2 moves into My Folder and disappears from the Floppy (A:) folder window.

3 **Look at the files in the My Folder window:**
- **Open** My Folder.
  The two files you just moved are displayed in the My Folder window:

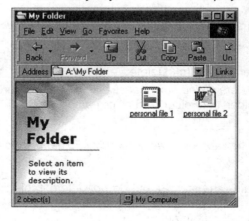

4
- **Close** the My Folder window.
- **Remove** DATA DISK 1 or **go on** to Exercise 56.

Printing from a Folder

When you print a document from a folder window, Windows 98 automatically:

- starts the associated program,
- opens the data file,
- prints the data file,
- closes the data file, and
- exits the program.

Begin with the desktop displayed and with no taskbar buttons on the taskbar.

1
- **Open** My Computer.
- **With** DATA DISK 1 inserted, **open** Floppy (A:).
- **Open** My Folder.

2 **Print a Text Document (.txt) from a folder window:**
- **Make sure** the printer is turned on and ready to receive data.
- **Right-click** personal file 1.

  The shortcut menu opens; Print is the second command in the menu.
- **Click** Print.

  Notepad starts, personal file 1 opens and is printed, and Notepad closes.

```
                    personal file 1

My Documents is the default folder to save files in.  You will
save and open files in My Documents.  Then you will move them
to your floppy data disk.




                       Page 1
```

3 **Print a Word for Windows document (.doc) from a folder window:**
- **Make sure** the printer is turned on and ready to receive data.
- **Right-click** personal file 2, then **click** Print.

  WordPad starts, personal file 2 opens and is printed, and WordPad closes.

  NOTE: If you have Microsoft Word on your computer, Word will start instead of WordPad.

> My Documents is the default folder to save files in for WordPad as well as for Notepad. Other Microsoft software automatically saves files in My Documents also.

4
- **Close** the My Folder window.
- **Remove** DATA DISK 1 or **go on** to Exercise 57.

To make a hard copy of a document that is in a folder.

⌨ **Keyboard Steps to**

Print a Document from a Folder

—WITH THE DESIRED FOLDER WINDOW OPEN—

1. **Press** `Tab` until an icon in the folder workspace is selected.
2. **Press** `↑↓` (arrow keys) to select the document you want to print.
3. **Press** `Alt` + `F` (File).
4. **Press** `P` (Print).

EXERCISE 57 • Use Favorites

To add, delete, and organize frequently used folders in the Favorites menu.

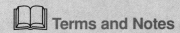 **Terms and Notes**

dimmed command
A command or button that cannot be used in the current situation. It is displayed in gray instead of in black or in color.

directional arrowhead
A small arrowhead that appears at the beginning and/or end of menus and toolbars to indicate that there are more menu items than you can presently see on the menu or toolbar. Click the arrowhead to scroll through the menu or toolbar items.

Favorites menu
A list of frequently used Web sites and/or folders that you can easily access from the Start menu, all folder windows, Windows Explorer, or Internet Explorer.

NOTE: If there are a lot of items on your Favorites menu, you may have to scroll the menu (use the directional arrowhead at the top and/or bottom of the menu) to find the desired item.

shortcut
An icon containing a direct route to a specific object and displaying a small jump arrow on its lower-left corner.

What is Favorites?

Favorites is a feature that offers users a quick way to access their favorite Web pages on the Internet and perform other Internet-related tasks (covered in Lessons Twelve and Thirteen). In this exercise, however, you will learn how Favorites also offers a way to reach favorite locations on your computer quickly.

Begin with the desktop displayed and with no taskbar buttons on the taskbar.

1
- **Open** My Computer.
- **With** DATA DISK 1 inserted, **open** drive A:, then **open** My Folder.

2 **Examine Favorites:**
- **Click** the F*a*vorites menu (to open it).
- **Point** to Channels and **look** at the menu that opens.
- **Point** to Links and **look** at the menu that opens.

3 **Add an item to the Favorites list:**
- **With** the F*a*vorites menu still open, **click** *A*dd to Favorites.
  The Add Favorite dialog box opens. (Since you are adding a folder, the Internet options are dimmed.)

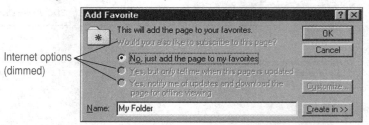

- **Click** | OK |.
  *A shortcut to My Folder is added to the F*a*vorites menu.*
- **Click** the F*a*vorites menu.
  *The new item, My Folder, appears at the bottom of the F*a*vorites menu.*
- **Close** the My Folder window.

4 **Open a favorite from the Start menu:**
- **Click** | Start |, **point** to F*a*vorites, then **click** My Folder.
  The My Folder window opens.
- **Close** the My Folder window.

5 **Open a favorite from a folder:**
- **Open** My Computer, **open** drive C:, then **open** Windows.
- **Click** F*a*vorites, then **click** My Folder.
  The My Folder window opens.

6 **Add another folder to Favorites:**
- **Click** the Up button to go to the Floppy (A:) folder window.
- **Click** F*a*vorites, **click** *A*dd to Favorites, then **click** | OK |.
  *Floppy (A:) is added to the F*a*vorites menu.*
- **Click** the F*a*vorites menu.
  *Now you have added shortcuts to two folders in the F*a*vorites menu; Floppy (A:) appears at the bottom of the F*a*vorites menu and My Folder is placed in alphabetical order.*

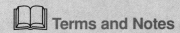 **Keyboard Steps to**

Add a Folder to Favorites

—WITH THE DESIRED FOLDER WINDOW OPEN—

1. **Press** [Alt] + [A] (F*a*vorites).
2. **Press** [A] (*A*dd to Favorites).
   The Add Favorite dialog box opens.
3. **Press** [Enter].
   *The folder is added to the F*a*vorites menu.*

7 **Create a new folder in the Favorites menu:**
- **With** the Favorites menu still open, **click** Organize Favorites.

  The Organize Favorites dialog box opens:

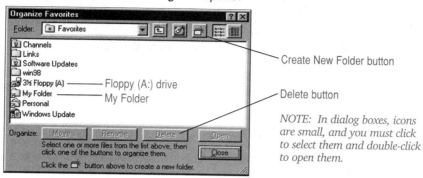

Create New Folder button

Floppy (A:) drive
My Folder

Delete button

NOTE: In dialog boxes, icons are small, and you must click to select them and double-click to open them.

- **Click** 🗂 (the Create New Folder button).
- **Type:** My Stuff, and **press** Enter.

8 **Organize Favorites:**
- **Drag** My Folder and **drop** it onto My Stuff.

  My Folder is moved into the My Stuff folder and disappears from the workspace.
- **Drag** Floppy (A:) and **drop** it onto My Stuff.

  Floppy (A:) is moved into the My Stuff folder and disappears from the workspace.
- **Double-click** My Stuff to open it.

  My Folder and Floppy (A:) are displayed in the My Stuff window.
- **Close** the Organize Favorites dialog box, then **close** Floppy (A:).

9 **Open a favorite from the Start menu:**
- **Click** 🏁 Start,
  point to Favorites,
  point to My Stuff, then
  click My Folder.

  My Folder opens.

My Folder

10 **Delete a folder on the Favorites menu:**
- **Click** Favorites, then **click** Organize Favorites.

  The Organize Favorites dialog box opens.
- **Click** the My Stuff folder to select it.
- **Hold down** Shift and click the Delete button.

  NOTE: Holding down the Shift key when you delete an object keeps Windows from sending it to the Recycle Bin.
  The Confirm Folder Delete dialog box opens.
- **Click** Yes.

  My Stuff and its contents (the shortcuts to My Folder and Floppy [A:]) are deleted. The actual My Folder and Floppy (A:) folders are not deleted, just the shortcuts to them.
- **Close** the Organize Favorites dialog box, then **close** My Folder.
- **Remove** DATA DISK 1 or **go on** to Exercise 58.

📖 **Terms and Notes**

NOTE: If you have a lot of favorites, it is helpful to organize them by creating one or more folders to put them in. Doing this keeps your Favorites menu orderly and your items easy to find.

EXERCISE 58 • Use Quick View

To take a quick look at a document's contents and use some basic Quick View features.

 Terms and Notes

Quick View

A simple program that lets you look at the contents of a file quickly, without opening the program in which that file was created. Quick View appears on the menu only if there is a *viewer* available for the type of file you select and if it has been installed. (The Typical install does not install Quick View.)

Install Quick View

If Quick View is not on your system, you may want to install it since it is a very useful program. Quick View requires 1.3 Mb of hard disk space.

WARNING: Do not do this procedure if the computer you are using is not your own.

1. **Click** the Start button.
2. **Point** to Settings.
3. **Click** Control Panel.
4. **Click** the Add/Remove Programs icon.
5. **Click** the Windows Setup tab.
6. **Click** Accessories.
7. **Click** the Details button.
8. **Scroll** until you see Quick View.
9. **Click** the Quick View check box.
   A check mark appears in the box.
10. **Click** the OK button.
11. **Click** the OK button again.
    The Insert Disk dialog box asks for a certain Windows 98 disk.
12. **Insert** the CD-ROM.
13. **Click** the OK button.
    The Copying Files dialog box and then the Start Menu Shortcuts dialog box each appear for a short time as the files are added to Windows 98 on your computer.
14. **Close** the Control Panel folder window.

 Keyboard Steps to

Use Quick View

—WITH A FOLDER WINDOW OPEN—

1. **Press** `Tab` until an icon in the folder workspace is selected.
2. **Press** `↕↔` (arrow keys) to select the file you want to view.
3. **Press** `Alt` + `F` (File).
4. **Press** `Q` (Quick View).

WARNING: The Quick View program may not have been installed when Windows 98 was installed. If it was not, SKIP this exercise. If the computer you are working on is your own, however, you can follow the instructions in the left column to install Quick View if desired.

Begin with the desktop displayed and with no taskbar buttons on the taskbar.

1
- **Open** My Computer.
- **With** DATA DISK 1 inserted, **open** Floppy (A:).

2 **Look at a document using Quick View:**
- **Right-click** the winfun icon.

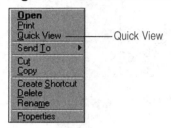

- **Click** Quick View.
  The Quick View program opens with the winfun text displayed.

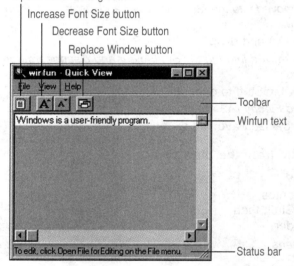

- IF the Quick View program above does not appear, skip to Exercise 59.

3 **Look at the Quick View menus:**
- **Click** the File menu.
- **Move** the arrow pointer over the View and Help menus also, examining each menu as it opens.

4 Change the font size in the Quick View workspace:

- **Click** **A˙** (the Increase Font Size button—the large A) twice.
  The text size increases noticeably.
- **Click** **A˅** (the Decrease Font Size button—the small A) twice.
  The text returns to its original size.
- **Click** **A˅** (the Decrease Font Size button—the small A) twice again.
  The text size decreases noticeably.
- **Click** **A˙** (the Increase Font Size button—the large A) twice.
  The text returns to its original size.
  NOTE: The default font for Quick View is Arial 10 point. The font you select affects Quick View only, not the text in the file.

5 Open a file in Quick View:

- **Click** 📄 (the Open File for Editing button) on the toolbar.
  Notepad opens with the winfun document in it and Quick View closes.
- **Exit** Notepad.
- **Click** the Up button to return to the My Computer folder window.

6 Look at a graphic file using Quick View:

- **Open** (C:), **open** the Windows folder, then **click** <u>Show Files</u>.
- **Scroll** until you find the Gold Weave icon, then **right-click** it.
  NOTE: If you can't find Gold Weave, open any other file with a bitmap (.bmp) icon 🏠 or 🖼️.
- **Click** <u>Quick View</u>.
  The Quick View program opens with Gold Weave displayed.

7
- **Exit** Quick View, then **close** the Windows folder window.
- **Remove** DATA DISK 1 or **go on** to Exercise 59.

More Folder Windows

Tasks Reviewed:
- Change Disk Drives with My Computer
- Start Windows Explorer from My Computer
- Start a Program from a Folder
- Open a Document from a Folder
- Use the My Documents Folder
- Cut and Paste Files
- Create and Delete Folders
- Drag and Drop Files
- Print from a Folder
- Use Favorites
- Use Quick View

Begin with the desktop displayed and with no taskbar buttons on the taskbar.

You will need DATA DISK 2 for this practice exercise.

1
- **Open** My Computer.
- **Open** (C:).
- **Go back** (or up) to My Computer.
- **Insert** DATA DISK 2 (for Practice Exercises), and **open** Floppy (A:).
- **Go back** (or up) to My Computer.

2
- **Select** (C:) (point to it).
- **Open** Windows Explorer from My Computer (using the [C:] icon).
- **Scroll** to the top of the left pane.
- **Select** the Desktop icon. (In the left pane, you must click to select.)
- **Close** Windows Explorer and **close** My Computer.
- **Open** Windows Explorer using the My Computer icon.
- **Close** Windows Explorer.

3
- **Open** My Computer, **open** (C:), **open** Program Files, then **open** Accessories.
- **Start** WordPad from the Accessories folder.
- **Exit** WordPad.
- **Go back** to (C:).
- **Open** the Windows folder. (Remember to click Show Files.)
- **Start** Calculator from the Windows folder.
- **Exit** Calculator.

4
- **Open** Floppy (A:) using the Address bar.
- **Open** cando.
- **Exit** Notepad.
- **Go back** to Windows.
- **Open** Metal Links.
- **Exit** Paint.
- **Close** the Windows folder.

5
- **Start** and **maximize** Notepad.
- **Type**: I am going to save a file in My Documents.
- **Save** the document in My Documents; **name it** personal file 3.
- **Exit** Notepad.
- **Start** and **maximize** WordPad.
- **Type**: Now I am going to save a WordPad document in My Documents.
- **Save** the document in My Documents; **name it** personal file 4.
- **Start** a new WordPad document. (Click the New button on the Standard toolbar.)
- **Open** personal file 4.
- **Start** a new text document.
- **Open** personal file 3. (Remember to change Files of type to *Text Documents [*.txt]*.)
- **Exit** WordPad.

6
- **Open** My Computer.
- **Open** My Documents using the Address bar.
- **Size and move** the My Documents folder window so it fits in the right half of the desktop.
- **Open** My Computer again.
- **With** DATA DISK 2 inserted, **open** Floppy (A:).
- **Size and move** the Floppy (A:) folder window so it fits in the left half of the desktop.
- **Cut** <u>personal file 3</u> from My Documents and **paste** it into Floppy (A:).
- **Close** the Floppy (A:) folder window.
- **Cut** <u>personal file 4</u> from the My Documents folder window.
- **Open** Floppy (A:) using the Address bar.
- **Paste** <u>personal file 4</u> into the Floppy (A:) folder window.

7
- **Size** the Floppy (A:) folder window a little wider.
- **Create** a new folder; name it My Holder.
- **Open** <u>My Holder</u>.
- **Go back** (or up) to Floppy (A:).
- **Delete** the My Holder folder.
- **Create** the My Holder folder, but do *not* delete it this time.

8
- **Arrange** icons in the Floppy (A:) folder window by name.
- **Size** the Floppy (A:) window so you can see all the objects in it.
- **Drag** <u>personal file 3</u> **and drop** it onto My Holder.
- **Drag** <u>personal file 4</u> **and drop** it onto My Holder.
- **Open** <u>My Holder</u> and **look** at the files in it.

9
- **Print** personal file 3 from the My Holder window.

```
                        personal file 3
   I am going to save a file in My Documents.




                          Page 1
```

- **Print** personal file 4 from the My Holder window.

```
   Now I am going to save a WordPad document in My Documents.

```

10
- **Add** <u>My Holder</u> to the F<u>a</u>vorites menu.
- **Close** the My Holder window.
- **Open** My Holder using F<u>a</u>vorites on the Start menu.
- **Go up** to Floppy (A:).
- **Add** Floppy (A:) to the F<u>a</u>vorites menu.
- **Create** a new folder in the F<u>a</u>vorites menu; name it Mine. (Click F<u>a</u>vorites, click <u>O</u>rganize Favorites, then click the Create New Folders button.)

Continued on the next page

Continued from the previous page

- **Move** the shortcut icons for My Holder and Floppy (A:) into Mine using either the drag-and-drop or cut-and-paste method.
- **Close** the Organize Favorites dialog box.
- **Close** the Floppy (A:) folder window.
- **Open** My Holder using F<u>a</u>vorites on the Start menu.
- **Open** the Organize Favorites dialog box.
- **Delete** the Mine folder and its contents from the F<u>a</u>vorites menu.
- **Close** the Organize Favorites dialog box.

- **Go up** to Floppy (A:).
- **Look** at cando using Quick View.
- IF you don't have the Quick View program, **close** Floppy (A:), **remove** DATA DISK 2 from drive A:, and **skip** the rest of this step.
- **Increase** the workspace font size twice.
- **Decrease** the workspace font size twice to return to the original font size.
- **Close** Quick View.
- **Go up** to My Computer.
- **Open** (C:), then **open** the Windows folder.
- **Look** at CLOUD*S* (*not* CLOUD) using Quick View.
- **Exit** Quick View.
- **Close** the Windows folder.
- **Remove** DATA DISK 2.

Lesson Five Worksheet (6) is on page 306.

Lesson Six
The Desktop

Table of Contents

TOPIC 18 • The Heart of Windows 98

The Desktop is the Heart of Windows 98

The Windows 98 desktop is more than:

- the large workspace you see when you start Windows,
- the hierarchical structure managed by the shell, or
- the background upon which a few graphic objects and the taskbar appear.

The desktop is the heart of Windows 98. The idea behind the Windows 98 desktop is that you can use it pretty much the way you use your personal desktop at home—to keep important items at your fingertips. Just as you put your computer, printer, clock, phone, folders, and documents on your real desktop, you can do the same with your Windows 98 desktop. Furthermore, you can decorate it to fit your mood; you can even scan your favorite picture and put it on the desktop.

While the computer system is structured with many levels (a hierarchy), by using shortcuts on the desktop, that structure seems to disappear. You can design a logical structure (grouping of files and folders) to meet your individual needs.

A Traditional Desktop

The Windows 98 Desktop

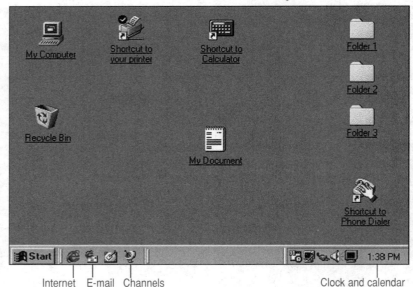

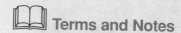

Shortcuts Are Powerful and Efficient

A **shortcut** is an icon you create that contains a path (a direct route) to a specific object (the target). The **target** object might be a document, program, folder, disk drive, or printer. A shortcut is easily identified by the **jump arrow** that appears on the lower-left corner of its icon.

Shortcuts are powerful because they offer quick access to frequently used objects while Windows does all the work of keeping track of what you are doing. Shortcuts are efficient because when you use a shortcut to jump from one place to another you do *not* have to:

- remember folder and subfolder names,
- work through a lot of menus,
- open a lot of folders, or
- type out a long path name.

Creating a shortcut can be as easy as using the Find feature to locate the object you want and then dragging the object onto the desktop. While you can place shortcuts just about anywhere, often the most practical place to put them is on the desktop, where they are handy.

While shortcuts let you jump to different locations without appearing to follow the actual **path**, behind the scenes Windows keeps track of your movements—as you can see in the Shortcut to Calc Properties dialog box below. To view a shortcut object's path, open the shortcut's **Properties dialog box**, click the Shortcut tab, and look at the Target text box.

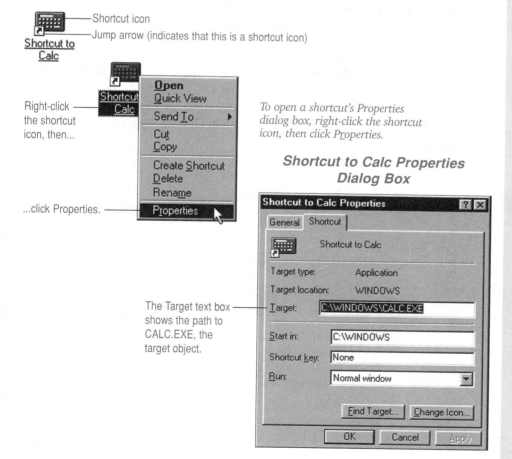

Shortcut icon
Jump arrow (indicates that this is a shortcut icon)

Shortcut to Calc

Right-click the shortcut icon, then...

...click Properties.

To open a shortcut's Properties dialog box, right-click the shortcut icon, then click Properties.

Shortcut to Calc Properties Dialog Box

The Target text box shows the path to CALC.EXE, the target object.

Terms and Notes

NOTES: Do not confuse shortcuts as described in this topic with (right-click) shortcut menus, or keyboard shortcuts.

You can create more than one shortcut to an object.

jump arrow
A small arrow that appears on the lower-left corner of *shortcut icons*, thereby distinguishing them from other icons.

path
The route to an object; it consists of the disk drive, folder, subfolders (if any), and the filename (if the path is to a file).

Properties dialog box
A special kind of dialog box that groups the settings for a specific object's properties.

shortcut
An icon containing a direct route to a specific object and displaying a small *jump arrow* on its lower-left corner. Click the shortcut icon to quickly open the file or program it represents. You can customize your desktop by creating shortcuts to the documents and programs you use most often.

target
The path (including the name) to the object to which a shortcut is pointing.

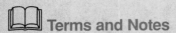
document
A file that consists of data created in a program, such as a letter typed in WordPad or a picture drawn in Paint. Also called *data file*.

document-centric
A system that focuses on documents and their contents rather than on the programs used to create those documents.

Documents Are Central

As we have seen in Topics 18 and 19, the desktop is the heart of Windows 98, and shortcuts can be powerful and efficient tools in this environment. Throughout this book, however, you will notice that the center of activity is usually the **document**. Much of what you do on your computer system revolves around producing documents of one kind or another. Realizing this, Microsoft designed Windows 98 to be **document-centric**, that is, centered around documents rather than the programs used to create them.

Different Ways to Open a Document

Using the Documents menu:
- click the Start button,
- point to the Documents menu, and
- click the document (if it is one of the last 15 documents used).

Using the File menu:
- open a program,
- click the File menu, and
- click the document (if it is one of the last four documents used).

Using the Open dialog box:
- open a program,
- click File, then click Open,
- find the folder the document is in, and finally,
- click the filename, then click OK.

Clicking a document file icon:
- click a document file icon on the desktop or in folder windows (when in Web-style mode).
  OR
  double-click a document file icon (when in Classic-style mode or in dialog boxes).

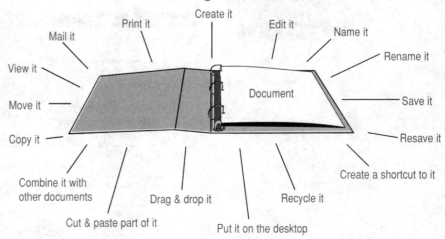

File-Management Tasks

Mail it · Print it · Create it · Edit it · Name it · View it · Rename it · Move it · Document · Save it · Copy it · Resave it · Combine it with other documents · Drag & drop it · Recycle it · Create a shortcut to it · Cut & paste part of it · Put it on the desktop

The Documents Menu

When you open the Documents menu, you can see up to 15 of your most recently used (i.e., saved and/or opened) documents. The My Documents folder is displayed where it is easy to access, at the top of the Documents menu. The My Documents folder was designed as a handy place to put your personal documents.

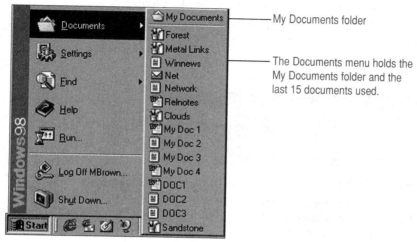

— My Documents folder

— The Documents menu holds the My Documents folder and the last 15 documents used.

Documents on the File Menu

The last four documents you opened and/or saved are listed near the bottom of the File menu in most programs. Simply click a document listed on the File menu to open it.

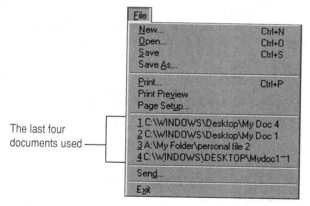

The last four documents used —

Click a Document File Icon

The illustration below shows documents in the Floppy (A:) folder window.

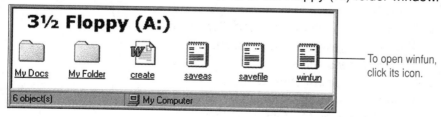

— To open winfun, click its icon.

To create an icon containing a direct route to a specific object.

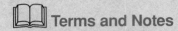 **Terms and Notes**

YOU MAY WANT TO COMPLETE LESSON SIX IN ONE SESSION.

Exercises 60-71 make changes to the desktop that are reversed in Exercise 72. If you are in a training environment and if you do not have a separate user profile, you may want to complete Lesson Six in one session so the desktop will remain unchanged for the next user.

Four Ways to Create a Shortcut

The procedure to create a shortcut may be slightly different depending upon where the target object is located. So, although there are several ways to create a shortcut, not every method works for every object.

- **Right-click** an object.
- **Drag** an object.
- **Right-drag** an object.
- **Right-click** the desktop (or a folder's workspace).

command line

The text box where you enter the *path* to the desired file or folder.

path

The route to an object; it consists of the disk drive, folder, subfolders (if any), and the filename (if the path is to a file). For example, C:\WINDOWS\CALC is the path to the Calculator program. If long folder names or filenames are used in a path, the path must be enclosed in quotes ("). For example, "A:\My Folder\personal file 3.doc" is the path to the document file, *personal file 2*, on drive A:. *(See Topic 14, Files and Filenames, for more information.)*

right-drag

- Point to the item to move.
- Hold down the *right* mouse button.
- Slide the arrow pointer to desired location.
- Release the mouse button.

shortcut

An icon containing a direct route to a specific object and displaying a small jump arrow on its lower-left corner. Click the shortcut icon to quickly open the file or program it represents. You can customize your desktop by creating shortcuts to the documents and programs you use most often.

target

The path (including the name) to the object to which a shortcut is pointing.

Begin with the desktop displayed and with no taskbar buttons on the taskbar.

1 **Create a shortcut by right-clicking an object:**
- **Right-click** the desktop, then **point** to Arrange Icons.
- IF Auto Arrange has a check mark next to it, **click** Auto Arrange to deselect it; otherwise, **click** outside the shortcut menu to close it.
- **Open** My Computer, then **open** the Printers folder.
- **Right-click** the printer (the default printer, if there is more than one).

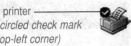
Default printer
(has a circled check mark in the top-left corner)

- **Click** Create Shortcut.

The Shortcut dialog box appears:

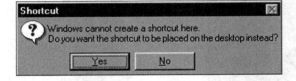

- **Click** [Yes], then **close** the Printers folder window.

The Shortcut to [your printer] *icon is displayed on the desktop at the end of the main group of icons.*

Shortcut to [your printer] icon
Shortcut to HP LaserJet 4-4...

2 **Create a shortcut for a program by dragging it to the desktop:**

NOTE: Dragging a program to the desktop creates a program shortcut; dragging a document to the desktop moves (or copies) the document to the desktop. To create a document shortcut, you must right-drag it to the desktop (see step 3, below).

- **Open** My Computer, **open** (C:), then **open** the Windows folder. (Remember to **click** Show Files.)
- **Move** and **size** the Windows folder window until the top-right corner of the desktop is visible.

- **Scroll** until you find Calc (the Calculator icon).
- **Drag** the Calc icon to the top-right corner of the desktop.

A shortcut icon appears on the desktop:

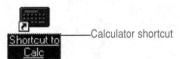
Calculator shortcut

- **Close** the Windows folder window.
- **Click** a blank space on the desktop to deselect Shortcut to Calc.

3 **Create a shortcut for a document by right-dragging it:**
- **Insert** DATA DISK 1 in drive A:.
- **Open** My Computer, then **open** Floppy (A:).
- **Right-drag** savefile to the desktop.

A shortcut menu appears.

- **Click** Create Shortcut(s) Here.

A shortcut to savefile is created.

- **Close** the Floppy (A:) folder window.

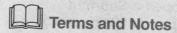

4 **Create a shortcut by right-clicking the desktop:**

NOTE: The shortcut icon will appear where you right-click the desktop.

- **Right-click** an empty space on the desktop, **point** to New, then **click** Shortcut.

  The Create Shortcut dialog box opens with the cursor blinking in the Command line text box.

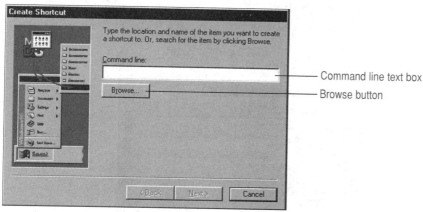

— Command line text box
— Browse button

- **Click** Browse... .

  The Browse dialog box opens; it looks like the Open dialog box.

- **Open** Floppy (A:). (Click Look in list box, then click Floppy [A:]).
- **Change** Files of type to *All Files*.
- **Double-click** My Folder to open it.

  The files in My Folder appear in the workspace.

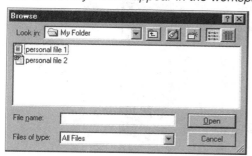

NOTE: While you can open folders with a single click when you are in a folder window, you must double-click a folder (or click it, then click the Open button) to open it when you are in a dialog box such as Open, Close, Save As, or Browse.

- **Click** personal file 2, then **click** Open .

  The name of the object that the shortcut points to (the target) appears in the Command line text box of the Create Shortcut dialog box.

— Target

- **Click** Next > .

  The Select a Title for the Program dialog box appears with personal file 2 *in the text box.*

- **Click** Finish to accept the default name.

  The shortcut to personal file 2 appears on the desktop; the icon probably looks like one of the two icons shown on the right:

 OR

personal file 2   personal file 2

5 - **Remove** DATA DISK 1 or **go on** to Exercise 61.

📖 **Terms and Notes**

NOTES: The Create Shortcut dialog box may not appear if you are on a network and using separate user profiles. In that case, you can open My Computer, Floppy (A:), and My Folder and create a shortcut by right-dragging personal file 2 to the desktop.

Notice that the filename in the Command line text box includes a three-letter filename extension (see Topic 14, Files and Filenames). Most files are assigned a filename extension even though those extensions are usually not visible to you.

⌨ **Keyboard Steps to**

Create a Printer Shortcut

1. **Open** My Computer *(see page 71)*.
2. **Open** the Printers folder *(see page 72)*.
3. **Select** the desired printer *(see page 72)*.
4. **Press** `Alt` + `F` (File).
5. **Press** `S` (Create Shortcut).
6. **Press** `Y` (Yes).
7. **Close** all the open folders.

Create a Calculator Shortcut

1. **Open** My Computer *(see page 71)*.
2. **Press** `Tab` until the Address bar is selected.
3. **Press** `↓` (down arrow) to open the drop-down list.
4. **Press** `Home` to select Desktop.
   The Desktop folder opens.
5. **Press** `Enter`.
6. **Press** `Alt` + `F` (File).
7. **Press** `N` (New).
8. **Press** `S` (Shortcut).
   The Create Shortcut dialog box opens.
9. **Press** `Alt` + `R` (Browse).
   The Browse dialog box opens.
10. **Press** `Shift` + `Tab` to select the workspace.
11. **Press** `↔` (arrow keys) to find and select the Windows folder.
12. **Press** `Enter` to open the Windows folder.
13. **Press** `C` until Calc is highlighted.
14. **Press** `Enter`, `Enter`, `Enter`.
15. **Press** `Alt` + `Space`, `C` (Close) to close the My Computer folder.

EXERCISE 61 • Look at Shortcut Properties

To open a Shortcut Properties dialog box and examine the information.

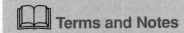

Terms and Notes

Properties dialog box
A special kind of dialog box that groups the settings for a specific object's properties.

target
The path (including the name) to the object to which a shortcut is pointing.

Some Shortcut Properties

- type of file
- location of file
- size of file
- MS-DOS name
- date file was created
- date file was modified
- date file was last accessed
- attributes for the file
- target file type
- target file location
- target file name
- folder to start in (contains the original item)
- shortcut keys for shortcut
- kind of window the file will run in: normal, maximized, or minimized

Keyboard Steps to

Look at a Shortcut Properties Dialog Box

1. **Press** Tab until an item on the desktop is selected.

2. **Press** ↑↓ (arrow keys) to select the desired shortcut.

3. **Press** Alt + Enter.

4. **Press** Ctrl + Tab until the Shortcut tab moves forward.

5. **Press** Esc to cancel the Properties dialog box.

Begin with the desktop displayed and with no taskbar buttons on the taskbar.

1 Look at the Calculator shortcut properties:
- **Right-click** the Shortcut to Calc icon, then **click** Properties.
  The Shortcut to Calc Properties dialog box opens:

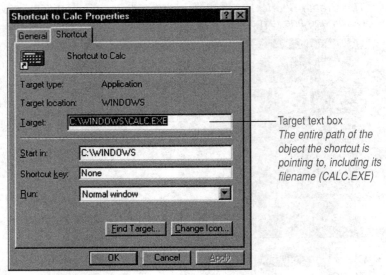

Target text box
The entire path of the object the shortcut is pointing to, including its filename (CALC.EXE)

- **Click** the General tab.
  The General tab moves to the front.
- **Notice** that the location of the shortcut is in the Desktop folder.

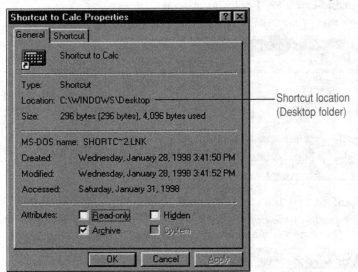

Shortcut location
(Desktop folder)

2 Use context-sensitive help to get information about properties:
- **Click** the Shortcut tab.
- **Click** [?] (the Help button) on the title bar, then **click** Target.
  A pop-up window opens with information about the Target text box.

> Displays the name of the item that the shortcut points to. There are many types of items that a shortcut can point to, such as a file, folder, printer, part of a document, or a computer on your network.

- **Read** the information, then **click** anywhere to close the pop-up window.

- **Right-click** Target location, then **click** 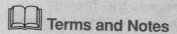 What's This? .

  A pop-up window opens with information about the Target location text box.

  > Displays the location of the original item that the shortcut points to.

- **Get** context-sensitive help for the remaining items using the method you prefer.
- **Close** the Shortcut to Calc Properties dialog box.

3 Look at document shortcut properties:

- **With** DATA DISK 1 inserted, **right-click** the Shortcut to savefile icon, then **click** P_roperties.

  The Shortcut to savefile Properties dialog box opens:

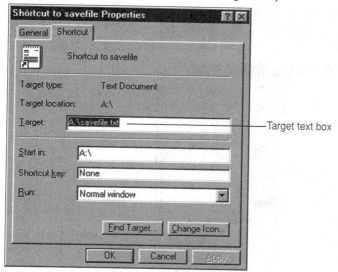

— Target text box

- **Read** the information.
- **Close** the Shortcut to savefile Properties dialog box.

4 Look at printer shortcut properties:

- **Right-click** the *Shortcut to [your printer]* icon.
- **Click** P_roperties.

  The Shortcut to [your printer] Properties *dialog box is opened.*

- **Read** the information.
- **Click** the General tab.
- **Read** the information.
- **Close** the *Shortcut to [your printer] Properties* dialog box.

5
- **Remove** DATA DISK 1 when you're through working. (You will need it again in Exercise 68.)

📖 Terms and Notes

NOTES: Examining shortcut properties helps you understand how shortcuts work.

Notice that the filename in the T_arget text box of the Properties dialog box includes a three-letter filename extension (see Topic 14, Files and Filenames). Most files are assigned a filename extension even though those extensions are usually not visible to you. Windows 98 uses filename extensions to associate a file with a program.

EXERCISE 62 • Clear the Documents Menu

To access the Taskbar Properties dialog box and empty the Documents menu of all previously used documents.

Begin with the desktop displayed and with no taskbar buttons on the taskbar.

① **Look at documents in the Documents menu:**

- **Click** [Start], **point** to Documents, and **look** at the documents on the menu.

  The Documents menu displays the last 15 documents used and offers you a quick way to open the My Documents folder (see Topic 20, Documents).

- **Click** an empty space on the desktop to close the menus.

② **Open the Taskbar Properties dialog box:**

- **Click** [Start], **point** to Settings, then **click** Taskbar & Start Menu.
  OR
  Right-click the taskbar, then **click** Properties.

③ **Clear the Documents menu:**

- **Click** the Start Menu Programs tab.

  The Start Menu Programs tab moves to the front:

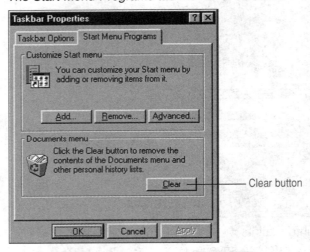

Clear button

- **Click** [Clear], then **click** [OK].

④ **Look at documents in the Documents menu again:**

- **Open** the Documents menu.

  The Documents menu is cleared of all documents; only the My Documents folder is displayed.

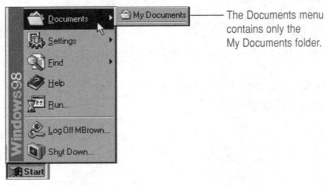

The Documents menu contains only the My Documents folder.

- **Close** the Start menu.

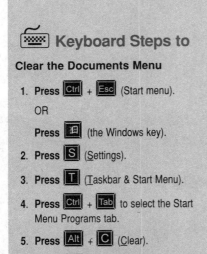

⌨ Keyboard Steps to

Clear the Documents Menu

1. Press `Ctrl` + `Esc` (Start menu).
   OR
   Press `⊞` (the Windows key).

2. Press `S` (Settings).

3. Press `T` (Taskbar & Start Menu).

4. Press `Ctrl` + `Tab` to select the Start Menu Programs tab.

5. Press `Alt` + `C` (Clear).

6. Press `Esc`.

Begin with the desktop displayed and with no taskbar buttons on the taskbar.

1 **Create a document:**

- **Start** WordPad.

  Type: Much of what you do on your computer system is centered around producing documents of one kind or another. Microsoft designed Windows 98 to be document-centric, that is, centered around documents rather than the programs used to create the documents.

- **Press** [Ctrl] + [S] (Save).

  The Save As dialog box opens.

2 **Save a document on the desktop using a long filename:**

- **Click** [↑] (the Up One Level button) until *Desktop* is displayed in the Save in drop-down list box.

- **Delete** the information in the File name text box.

- **Type:** My Doc 1

  The Save As dialog box looks similar to this:

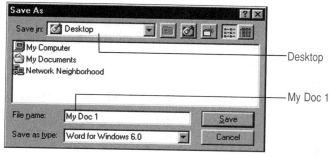

- **Click** [Save].

3 - **Print** My Doc 1.

> Much of what you do on your computer system is centered around producing documents of one kind or another. Microsoft designed Windows 98 to be document-centric, that is, centered around documents rather than the programs used to create the documents.

4 **Locate a document's icon on the desktop:**

- **Exit** WordPad.

  The document appears on the desktop, probably using one of the two icons below and appearing at the end of the main group of icons.

   OR
  My Doc 1   My Doc 1

- *WARNING: IF the filename displays the extension, .doc, the next exercise will not perform as expected. To hide the filename extension, you need to:*

  —**Open** My Computer, **click** *View,* **click** *Folder Options,* then **click** the View tab.

  —**Click** the Hide file extensions for known file types *check box* (to select it).

  —**Click** [OK], then **close** My Computer.

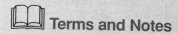

*To choose **Desktop** in the Save in drop-down list box of the Save As dialog box so a document can be saved on the desktop.*

📖 Terms and Notes

long filename
A filename that is up to 255 characters long and can contain spaces and most symbols. *(See Topic 14, Files and Filenames.)*

⌨ Keyboard Steps to

Save a Document on the Desktop

1. **Start** WordPad (or another program).
2. **Create** a document.
3. **Press** [Alt] + [F] (File).
4. **Press** [A] (Save As).
5. **Press** [Alt] + [I] (Save in).
6. **Press** [↓] (down arrow) to open the drop-down list.
7. **Press** [Page Up] to select Desktop.
8. **Press** [Enter].
9. **Press** [Alt] + [N] (File name).
10. **Type** a filename.
11. **Press** [Enter].
12. **Exit** WordPad (or the program started in step 1).

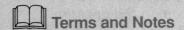

EXERCISE 64 • Create a Document from the Desktop

To create a new document from the desktop.

📖 **Terms and Notes**

WARNING: If file extensions are displayed, this exercise will not perform as expected; when you try to change the filename, you will get a warning dialog box. If you get a warning dialog box about changing the filename extension, click the No button, press the Escape key, press the Delete key, then click the Yes button. Perform the procedure in the warning in step 4 of Exercise 63 and start this exercise again.

Begin with the desktop displayed and with no taskbar buttons on the taskbar.

1 **Create a new document from the desktop:**
- **Right-click** an empty space on the desktop, **point** to New, then **click** Text Document.

  The New Text Document icon is selected on the desktop (where you right-clicked, above) with the cursor blinking at the end of the highlighted filename.

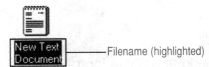
——Filename (highlighted)

2 **Rename a newly created document:**

With the original filename still highlighted from the step above:
- **Type:** My Doc 2 then **press** ⏎.

  The new name replaces the original one, and the icon remains highlighted.

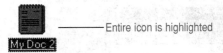
——Entire icon is highlighted

- **Click** an empty space on the desktop.

  The highlighting on the icon disappears, but the icon title still has a dotted line around it—a sign that this was the last icon selected.

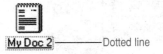
——Dotted line

- **Point** to My Doc 1 to select it.

  My Doc 1 is selected, and the dotted line disappears from My Doc 2.

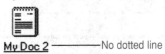
——No dotted line

3 **Open a newly created, empty document:**
- **Click** My Doc 2.

  Notepad opens with an empty screen and the title, My Doc 2 - Notepad, in the title bar.

4 **Edit a document and save the changes:**
- **Type** the following text, pressing the Enter key only where indicated:

  The idea behind the Windows 98 desktop is that you can use it ⏎ pretty much the way you use your personal desktop. You can put ⏎ your computer, clock, phone, folders, and documents on the ⏎ Windows 98 desktop. You can decorate it to fit your mood, and ⏎ even scan your favorite picture and put it on the desktop.

- **Click** File, then **click** Save.

  The document on the desktop is updated.

- **Exit** Notepad.

Begin with the desktop displayed and with no taskbar buttons on the taskbar.

Drag and drop a document from the desktop onto the printer:

- **Make sure** the printer is turned on and ready to receive data.

- **Drag and drop** 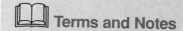 onto your printer's shortcut icon.
  My Doc 2 is printed. (If you watch, you will see Notepad open, My Doc 2 open, the document get sent to the printer, and the document and Notepad close.)

My Doc 2

The idea behind the Windows 98 desktop is that you can use it
pretty much the way you use your personal desktop. You can put
your computer, clock, phone, folders, and documents on the
Windows 98 desktop. You can decorate it to fit your mood, and
even scan your favorite picture and put it on the desktop.

Page 1

To drag and drop a document icon onto your printer shortcut so the document can be printed quickly.

Terms and Notes

drag and drop
A procedure in which you drag an object and drop it onto another object to perform a task, for example, to move, copy, delete, or print a document.

EXERCISE 66 • Create a Folder on the Desktop

To use the two methods available for creating new folders on the desktop.

Begin with the desktop displayed and with no taskbar buttons on the taskbar.

1 **Create a folder on the desktop:**
- **Right-click** an empty space on the desktop.
  The shortcut menu appears.
- **Point** to New, then **click** Folder.
  The New Folder icon is selected on the desktop (where you right-clicked, above) with the cursor blinking at the end of the highlighted folder name.

- **Type:** My Tools then **press** Enter.
  The My Tools folder icon is selected on the desktop.

2 **Create a folder from the Save As dialog box:**
- **Open** Notepad.
- **Type:** You can create a new folder when you save a document. When you are in the Save As dialog box, simply click the Create New Folder button, type the folder's name, and then press Enter.
- **Click** File, then **click** Save As.
- **Click** 🔼 (the Up One Level button) until *Desktop* appears in the Save in drop-down list box.
- **Click** 📁 (the Create New Folder button).
  The New Folder appears at the end of the list of files in the workspace with its name highlighted.
- **Type:** My Docs then press Enter.
  The My Docs folder is selected in the workspace.
- **Press** Enter again to open the My Docs folder.
- **Type:** My Doc 3 in the File name text box, then **click** .
- **Exit** Notepad.
  The My Docs folder appears on the desktop at the end of the main group of icons.

3 **Open a newly created folder:**
- **Click** My Docs.
  My Docs opens and displays the newly created document, My Doc 3.

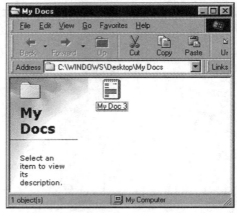

- **Close** the My Docs folder window.

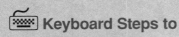 **Keyboard Steps to**

Create a Folder on the Desktop

1. **Open** My Computer *(see page 71).*
2. **Press** Tab until the Address bar is selected.
3. **Press** ⬇ (down arrow) to open the drop-down list.
4. **Press** Home to select Desktop.
5. **Press** Enter.
   The Desktop folder opens.
6. **Press** Alt + F (File).
7. **Press** N (New).
8. **Press** F (Folder).
9. **Type** a new folder name, if desired.
10. **Press** Enter.
11. **Press** Alt + F4.

Begin with the desktop displayed and with no taskbar buttons on the taskbar.

To organize desktop objects, and to line up icons.

1
- **Right-click** an empty space on the desktop, then **point** to Arrange Icons.
- IF Auto Arrange has a check mark by it, **click** Auto Arrange to deselect it; otherwise, **click** outside the menu to close it.

2 **Move objects around on the desktop:**
- **Drag** the desktop objects you have created in this lesson (documents, folders, and shortcuts) to the top-right half of the desktop, next to the Channel bar, so the icons are in the approximate order shown below:

Top-Right Corner of the Desktop

NOTE: The Channel bar may not be displayed on your desktop.

3 **Line up the icons on the desktop:**
- **Right-click** an empty space on the desktop, then **click** Line Up Icons.
  The icons are evenly aligned.
  NOTE: You may need to adjust the icons a second or third time and use the Line Up Icons command again to get icons to look like the illustration below.

Top-Right Corner of the Desktop

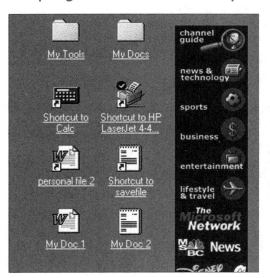

EXERCISE 68 • Open a Document by Clicking its Filename

To open a document (and the program to which it belongs) by clicking the document's icon.

Begin with the desktop displayed and with no taskbar buttons on the taskbar.

1 **Open a document on the desktop:**

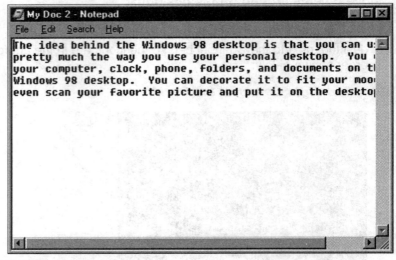

• **Click** My Doc 2 on the desktop.
  My Doc 2 opens in Notepad.

• **Exit** Notepad.
• **Insert** DATA DISK 1 into drive A:, if it's not already there.

2 **Open a document using a shortcut:**
• **Click** the personal file 2 shortcut icon.
  Personal file 2 opens in WordPad, Microsoft Word, or possibly some other program.
• **Exit** the program that personal file 2 opened into.

3 **Open a document in a desktop folder:**
• **Open** the My Docs folder.
• **Click** <u>My Doc 3</u>.
  My Doc 3 opens in Notepad.
• **Exit** Notepad.
• **Close** the My Docs folder window.

4 **Open a document on a floppy disk:**
• **Open** My Computer.
• **Open** Floppy (A:).
• **Click** <u>winfun</u>.
  Winfun opens in Notepad.
• **Exit** Notepad.
• **Close** the Floppy (A:) folder window.

5 • **Remove** DATA DISK 1 when you're through working. (You will need it again in Exercise 72.)

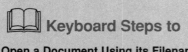 **Keyboard Steps to**

Open a Document Using its Filename

1. **Press** `Ctrl` + `Esc` , `Esc` .

2. **Press** `Tab` , `Tab` , `Tab` until an item on the desktop is selected.

3. **Press** `↑↓` (arrow keys) until the document icon to open is selected.

4. **Press** `Enter` .

—FROM A FOLDER WINDOW—

1. **Press** `Tab` until an icon in the folder workspace is selected.

2. **Press** `↑↓` (arrow keys) to select the document icon to open.

3. **Press** `Enter` .

Begin with the desktop displayed and with no taskbar buttons on the taskbar.

1 **Quickly access a recently used document:**

- **Click** 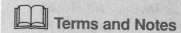, then **point** to Documents.

  The Documents menu displays the documents you have used since you cleared the Documents menu in Exercise 62.

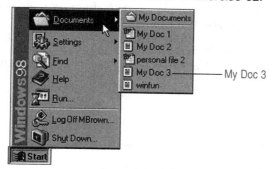

— My Doc 3

- **Click** My Doc 3.

  The document opens in Notepad, the program in which it was created.

2 **Print a document:**

- **Make sure** the printer is turned on and ready to receive data.
- **Print** My Doc 3.

> My Doc 3
>
> You can create a new folder when you save a document. When you are in the Save As dialog box, simply click the Create New Folder button, type the folder's name, and then press Enter.
>
> Page 1

- **Exit** Notepad (without saving, if asked).

3 **Quickly access another recently used document:**

- **Click** 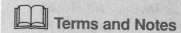, then **point** to Documents.
- **Click** My Doc 1.

  The document opens in WordPad or Microsoft Word.

- **Exit** WordPad or Microsoft Word (without saving, if asked).

To open a document (and the program to which it belongs) by clicking the document listed in the Documents menu.

📖 Terms and Notes

Documents menu
A menu on the Start menu that holds the My Documents folder and up to 15 of the documents you have used most recently.

NOTE: When you open a document from the Documents menu, it opens into the program it is associated with by file type— not necessarily the program it was created in. For example, a document created in WordPad will open into Microsoft Word if Word is installed on your computer.

⌨ Keyboard Steps to

Open a Document from the Documents Menu

1. **Press** Ctrl + Esc .

   OR

   Press 🔲 (the Windows key).

2. **Press** D (Documents).

3. **Press** ↑↓ (up or down arrow) to highlight the desired document.

4. **Press** Enter .

To start a program and use its File menu to open one of the last four documents used.

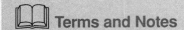

Terms and Notes

NOTE: When you start WordPad (and many other programs), you can easily open one of the last four documents you used by clicking the desired document in the File menu. Notepad, however, is one program whose File menu does not display its recently used documents. Remember though that you can always open any of the last 15 documents used by opening the Documents menu in the Start menu.

Begin with the desktop displayed and with no taskbar buttons on the taskbar.

1 **Create a shortcut to WordPad on the desktop:**
- **Right-click** an empty space on the desktop, **point** to <u>N</u>ew, then **click** <u>S</u>hortcut.
  The Create Shortcut dialog box appears.
- **Type:** "c:\program files\accessories\wordpad.exe" (with the quotes and the space) in the <u>C</u>ommand line text box.
- **Click** Next >, then **click** Finish.
  A WordPad shortcut appears where you right-clicked the desktop.

Wordpad

2 **Create a WordPad document and save it on the desktop:**
- **Click** the WordPad shortcut to start WordPad.
- **Type:** WordPad remembers the last four documents you used with it. You can easily open one of those documents by using the File menu.
- **Click** <u>F</u>ile, then **click** <u>S</u>ave.
- **Click** (the Up One Level button) until *Desktop* is displayed in the Save <u>i</u>n drop-down list box.
- **Type:** My Doc 4 in the File <u>n</u>ame text box, then **click** <u>S</u>ave.
- **Exit** WordPad.
  The new document, My Doc 4, appears as an icon on the desktop.

3 **Open recently used documents using WordPad's File menu:**
- **Start** WordPad by clicking its shortcut on the desktop.
- **Click** <u>F</u>ile.
  The <u>F</u>ile menu opens:

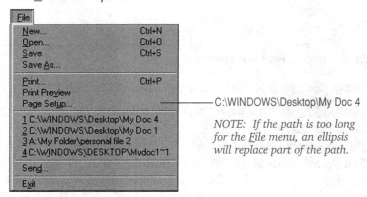

— C:\WINDOWS\Desktop\My Doc 4

NOTE: If the path is too long for the <u>F</u>ile menu, an ellipsis will replace part of the path.

- **Click** C:\WINDOWS\Desktop\My Doc 4.
  My Doc 4 opens into WordPad.
- **Exit** WordPad.

4 **Open a document by dragging it onto a program:**
- **Locate** the WordPad shortcut icon and <u>My Doc 4</u> on the desktop.
- **Drag and drop** <u>My Doc 4</u> onto the WordPad shortcut.
  My Doc 4 opens into WordPad.
- **Exit** WordPad.

Keyboard Steps to

Open a Document from the File Menu

1. Press [Alt] + [F] (File).

2. Press [↓] (down arrow) until the desired document is highlighted.

3. Press [Enter].

Organizing Your Desktop

Organizing your desktop can put the objects you use most frequently within easy reach. Simply create one or more folders and then move shortcuts and documents into folders as desired; for example, you may want to put all the documents relating to a certain project in one folder. You may even want to create subfolders to further organize your documents.

Begin with the desktop displayed and with no taskbar buttons on the taskbar.

1 **Move an object into a folder:**

- **Drag and drop** My Doc 4 onto the My Docs folder.

My Doc 4 ——— ——— My Docs folder

- **Drag and drop** the WordPad shortcut onto the My Tools folder.

2 **Move a group of objects into a folder:**

NOTES: In this step, you will select a group of icons so you can move them all at one time. When you select a group of objects, start with the pointer away from all of the objects. (If you start too close to an object, you will move the object instead of selecting it.)

When you drag the group, drag with the pointer on one of the objects rather than in the space between the selected objects. If you accidentally deselect the group when you try to drag it, try the procedure again.

When you are ready to drop the group of icons, be sure the folder name is highlighted before you release the mouse button.

- **Select** Shortcut to Calc, Shortcut to [your printer], personal file 2, and Shortcut to savefile, and **release** the mouse button when the area is selected.

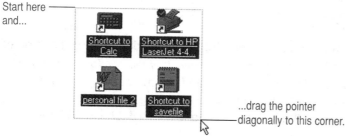

Start here and...

...drag the pointer diagonally to this corner.

- **Drag and drop** the group of icons onto the My Tools folder.

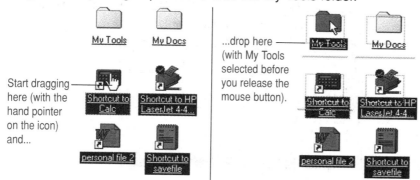

Start dragging here (with the hand pointer on the icon) and...

...drop here (with My Tools selected before you release the mouse button).

- **Select** My Doc 1 and My Doc 2.
- **Drag and drop** them onto the My Docs folder.

  All the objects you created are removed from the desktop except the My Tools and My Docs folders.

To arrange shortcuts and files on the desktop in a useful order by putting them into folders.

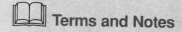 **Terms and Notes**

subfolder
A folder contained within another folder.

EXERCISE 72 • Use Cut and Paste to Move Objects

To move objects from the desktop into the Floppy (A:) folder so that the desktop is restored to its condition before Lesson Six.

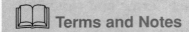 **Terms and Notes**

NOTE: Exercises in this book are designed to leave no permanent changes to Windows 98. Lesson Six is the longest section in which changes remain in place.

Two Ways to Move Objects

- Drag and drop
- Cut and paste

When you use the drag-and-drop method, objects are:
- *moved* if you drag and drop objects onto the same disk drive, but
- *copied* if you drag objects from one disk drive and drop them onto another disk drive.

When you use the cut-and-paste method, objects are:
- *moved* when you cut and paste on different disk drives as well as when you cut and paste on the same disk drive.

Why Use Cut and Paste Instead of Drag and Drop in this Exercise?

Since you want to *move* the folders from the desktop (on drive C:) to drive A: (a different disk drive), you should use cut and paste rather than drag and drop.

⌨ Keyboard Steps to

Select an Object on the Desktop

1. Press `Ctrl` + `Esc`, `Esc`.
2. Press `Tab`, `Tab`, `Tab`.
3. Press `↕↔` (arrow keys) to select a shortcut, file, or folder.

Move Folders Using Cut and Paste

1. **Select** the folder to move. *(See Select an Object on the Desktop, above, or Select Objects in a Folder, page 72.)*
2. Press `Ctrl` + `X` (Cut). *The icon is dimmed.*
3. **Open** a destination folder.
4. Press `Ctrl` + `V` (Paste). *The icon appears in the folder.*

Begin with the desktop displayed and with no taskbar buttons on the taskbar.

1 **Open Floppy (A:):**
- **Open** My Computer.
- **With** DATA DISK 1 inserted, **open** Floppy (A:).
- **Move** the Floppy (A:) folder window so you can see the My Tools and My Docs folder icons on the top of the desktop.

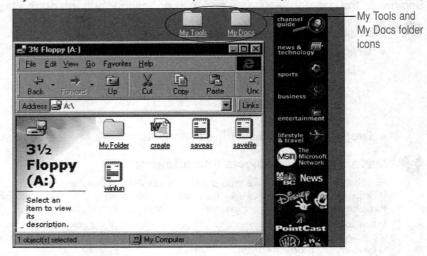

My Tools and My Docs folder icons

2 **Cut folders from the desktop and paste them into Floppy (A:):**
- **Right-click** the My Tools folder icon, then **click** Cut. *The folder is dimmed and its icon title is highlighted.*

Cut (dimmed) My Tools folder icon

- **Right-click** the Floppy (A:) folder window workspace, then **click** Paste. *The Moving... dialog box shows that the My Tools folder is moving.*
- **Cut** the My Docs folder icon from the desktop and **paste** it into the Floppy (A:) folder window as well.
- **Arrange** the icons by name (review, Exercise 46, step 2).

3 **Look at the contents of a copied folder:**
- **Click** the My Docs folder in the Floppy (A:) folder window. *My Docs opens with four documents in it:*

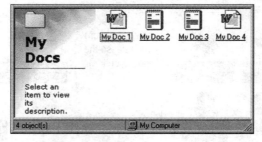

- **Click** 🔼 (the Up One Level button) to go back to Floppy (A:).
- **Click** the My Tools folder in the Floppy (A:) folder window. *My Tools opens with five shortcuts in it.*
- **Close** the My Tools folder, and **remove** DATA DISK 1. *The desktop looks like it did at the beginning of Lesson Six.*

Begin with the desktop displayed and with no taskbar buttons on the taskbar.

You will need DATA DISK 2 for this practice exercise.

1
- **Create** a shortcut to your printer on the desktop.
- **Insert** DATA DISK 2 in drive A:.
- **Create** a shortcut to text2 (saved on drive A:) on the desktop.
- **Close** the Floppy (A:) folder window.

2
- **Look** at the properties for *Shortcut to text2*.
- **Read** the information in both the Shortcut and General tabs.
- **Close** the *Shortcut to text2 Properties* dialog box.

3
- **Look** at the <u>D</u>ocuments menu.
- **Clear** the <u>D</u>ocuments menu, then **look** at it again.
- **Close** the Taskbar Properties dialog box.

4
- **Start** and **maximize** WordPad.
- **Type:** On the Start menu, Documents is listed before Programs (as you move up). When you open the Documents menu, you will find the My Documents folder and a list of up to 15 of the most recently used documents.
- **Save** the file on the desktop; **name** it DOC1.
- **Exit** WordPad.

5
- **Right-click** an empty space on the desktop and create a new text document; **name** it DOC2.
- **Open** DOC2, then **maximize** Notepad.
- **Type** the following text, pressing the Enter key where indicated:

  Shortcuts are powerful because they let you have quick access to [Enter]
  all the objects you need. Meanwhile, Windows does all the work [Enter]
  by keeping track of what you are doing. [Enter]
- **Save** the document, then **exit** Notepad.

6
- **Print** DOC2 using the drag-and-drop method.

  ```
              Doc2

  Shortcuts are powerful because they let you have quick access to
  all the objects you need.  Meanwhile, Windows does all the work
  by keeping track of what you are doing.
  ```

7
- **Create** a folder on the desktop; **name** it My Things.
- **Start** Notepad and **type** the following text, pressing the Enter key where indicated:

  When you save a document, you can create a folder and save the [Enter]
  document in it. To place that folder on the desktop, you must [Enter]
  first click the "Up One Level" button until "Desktop" appears in [Enter]
  the "Save in" list box. [Enter]
- **Click** <u>F</u>ile, then **click** Save <u>A</u>s.

Continued on the next page

The Desktop

Tasks Reviewed:
- Create a Shortcut
- Look at Shortcut Properties
- Clear the Documents Menu
- Save a Document on the Desktop
- Create a Document from the Desktop
- Use Drag and Drop to Print
- Create a Folder on the Desktop
- Arrange the Desktop
- Open a Document by Clicking Its Filename
- Open a Document from the Documents Menu
- Open a Document from the File Menu
- Organize the Desktop
- Use Cut and Paste to Move Folders

Continued from the previous page

- **Select** Desktop in the Save i̲n drop-down list box.
- **Create** a folder; **name** it Docs.
- **Open** the new Docs folder.
- **Save** the new document in the Docs folder; **name** it DOC3.
- **Exit** Notepad.

8
- **Arrange** the new icons as shown below, then **line up** the icons.

9
- **Open** DOC2 by clicking its filename, then **exit** Notepad.
- **Open** text2 by clicking its shortcut, then **exit** Notepad.
- **Open** the Docs folder, **open** DOC3, then **exit** Notepad and **close** the Docs folder window.

10
- **Open** DOC3 using the D̲ocuments menu.
- **Print** DOC3, then **exit** Notepad.

11
- **Start** WordPad.
- **Open** DOC1 using the F̲ile menu (shown as C:\Windows\Desktop\Doc1).
- **Print** DOC1, then **exit** WordPad.

> On the Start menu, Documents is listed before Programs (as you move up). When you open the Documents menu, you will find the My Documents folder and a list of up to 15 of the most recently used documents.

12
- **Select** the two shortcuts (to your printer and to text2).
- **Drag and drop** the group of selected icons onto the My Things folder.
- **Select** DOC1 and DOC2, then **drag and drop** them onto the Docs folder.
- **Open** the My Things folder and look at the two shortcuts in it, then **close** the folder window.
- **Open** the Docs folder and look at the three documents in it, then **close** the folder window.

13
- **Open** the Floppy (A:) folder, then **move** the Floppy (A:) folder window so you can see the My Things and Docs folders.
- **Cut** the My Things folder and **paste** it in the Floppy (A:) folder window.
- **Cut** the Docs folder and **paste** it in the Floppy (A:) folder window.
- **Arrange** the icons in the Floppy (A:) folder window by name.
- **Close** the Floppy (A:) folder window.
- **Remove** DATA DISK 2.

Lesson Six Worksheet (7) is on page 307.

Lesson Seven
More Desktop

Table of Contents

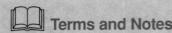 Terms and Notes

Active Desktop
The Windows 98 desktop that consists of two layers: one layer on which you can display standard desktop objects, and a second layer on which you can display *HTML* objects.

HTML (Hypertext Markup Language)
The programming language used to create Web pages so that they can be viewed, read, and accessed by any computer running on any type of operating system.

Internet Explorer
The Windows 98, Web-browsing program with a built-in interface to the *Active Desktop* and with many easy-to-use features that open the door to the world of information on the Internet.

standard desktop
A place to put objects (such as icons for shortcuts, folders, and files) for quick and easy access. The standard desktop cannot, however, display *HTML* objects.

Web browser
A program that lets you access the Web and view Web pages. Also called *browser*.

Web-page object
An object that appears in Web pages, such as text, a hyperlink, a graphic image, or an animated graphic image.

work offline mode
A condition in which you can view Web pages (and Web-page objects) that are stored on the computer without being connected to the Internet.

The Standard Desktop

The **standard desktop** is a place to put objects for fast, easy access. Such objects include:

- the Start button
- the taskbar
- the My Computer, My Documents, Internet Explorer, Network Neighborhood, and Recycle Bin icons
- shortcuts to your most frequently used programs
- folders that hold groups of related objects
- documents that you want to keep handy

The Active Desktop

The **Active Desktop** adds another layer to the standard desktop. The Active Desktop is an HTML background layer that can display HTML objects—either from the Web or on your own hard drive. **HTML (Hypertext Markup Language)** is a common computer-programming language used to format Web pages. **Web browsers**, such as **Internet Explorer**, understand HTML. The Active Desktop can also understand HTML. It is the HTML background layer that defines the Active Desktop.

When your desktop is active, you can put **Web-page objects** on it, such as:

- the Channel bar
- headlines for breaking news stories
- tickers for stock quotes
- weather reports
- an HTML document created in Notepad
- graphics

The Active Desktop with Web-Page Objects

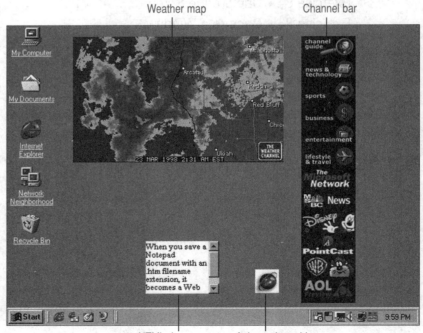

Weather map   Channel bar

HTML document created in Notepad   Animated graphic

In this lesson, you will be working with some Web elements and using Internet Explorer in work offline mode (not connected to the Web). In Lessons 9 and 10, you will connect to the Internet if you have an Internet connection.

Begin with the Active Desktop displayed and no taskbar buttons on the taskbar.

1 **Turn the Active Desktop off:**

- **Right-click** an empty space on the desktop, then **point** to <u>A</u>ctive Desktop.

  The Active Desktop submenu opens:

View As Web Page (selected)

- IF there is *no* check mark beside View As <u>W</u>eb Page, **click** outside the shortcut menu to close it; otherwise, **click** View As <u>W</u>eb Page to deselect it.

  The Active Desktop is turned off; the standard desktop appears.

2 **Turn the Active Desktop on:**

- **Right-click** an empty space on the desktop.
- **Point** to <u>A</u>ctive Desktop, then **click** View As <u>W</u>eb Page (to select it).

  The Active Desktop is turned on. The Internet Explorer Channel bar appears on the desktop.

Channel bar (a Web-page object)

- IF the Channel bar does not appear, see the note on the right.

To add the Active Desktop layer to (and to remove the Active Desktop layer from) the standard desktop.

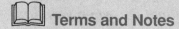 **Terms and Notes**

NOTE: *For the rest of the exercises in this book, you should remain in Active Desktop mode unless otherwise instructed.*

WARNING: *Occasionally the Active Desktop does not function correctly and a white background titled* Active Desktop Recovery *may appear. To return to the Active Desktop:*

- **Click** <u>Restore My Active Desktop</u>. *The Microsoft Internet Explorer dialog box appears.*
- **Click** the <u>Y</u>es button to restore your Active Desktop settings.

If the Active Desktop still does not function correctly, or if you are missing icons from your system tray, you should restart your computer to clear the computer's working memory (RAM) and restart your computer with fresh settings.

NOTE: *IF the Channel bar does not appear, complete the following steps:*

- **Right-click** an empty space on the desktop.
- **Point** to <u>A</u>ctive Desktop.
- **Click** <u>C</u>ustomize my Desktop.
- **Click** the Internet Explorer Channel Bar check box (to select it).
- **Click** [OK].

Keyboard Steps to

Switch Between Standard Desktop and Active Desktop

1. **Press** `Ctrl` + `Esc` (Start menu).
   OR
   Press `⊞` (the Windows key).
2. **Press** `S` (<u>S</u>ettings).
3. **Press** `A` (<u>A</u>ctive Desktop).
4. IF a check mark is already showing by View As <u>W</u>eb Page, **press** `W` (View As <u>W</u>eb Page) to turn the Active Desktop off.
   OR
   IF there is no check mark by View As <u>W</u>eb Page, **press** `W` (View As <u>W</u>eb Page) to turn the Active Desktop on.

EXERCISE 75 • Work Offline

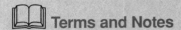

To select the Work Offline feature so your computer will not connect to the Internet when you open Internet Explorer. To use Full Screen view and the Channel bar when working offline.

 Terms and Notes

Full Screen view
A View menu option in Internet Explorer in which only one bar is displayed (at the top), leaving the entire screen available for Internet content.

Internet icon
The button at the right end of the menu bar illustrated with a Windows flag that accesses the Internet when clicked.

View Channels button
A button on the taskbar's Quick Launch toolbar that opens Internet Explorer in Full Screen view and displays the Channel bar.

NOTE: The Channel bar that appears in Internet Explorer and in folder windows displays the same channels as the Channel bar on the Active Desktop.

work offline mode
A condition in which you can view Web pages (and Web-page objects) that are stored on the computer without being connected to the Internet.

NOTE: When you're working offline, Internet Explorer will stay offline until you deselect the Work Offline menu option. However, sometimes a dialog box appears and offers you the opportunity to Connect or to Stay Offline.

Why Work Offline?

Some Windows 98 users may have no access, or restricted access, to the Internet. **Working offline** lets you use Internet Explorer to examine aspects of Web pages and Web-page objects without actually connecting to the Internet.

Begin with the Active Desktop displayed and no taskbar buttons on the taskbar.

1 **Change to working offline:**
  • **Open** My Computer
  • **Click** File.
    The File menu drops down and displays whether you are working offline or not.

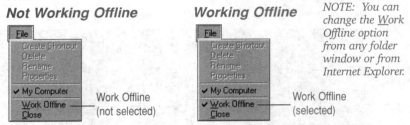

NOTE: You can change the Work Offline option from any folder window or from Internet Explorer.

  • IF there is *no* check mark next to Work Offline, **click** Work Offline to select it; otherwise, **click** outside the File menu to close it.
  • **Close** the My Computer folder window.
    You may not see any change, but you are now working offline.

2 **Open Internet Explorer in offline mode:**
    NOTE: The View Channels button is used in this exercise not to explore channels, but as an easy method to open Internet Explorer in Offline mode and Full Screen view.

  • **Click**  (the View Channels button) on the taskbar Quick Launch toolbar.
  • IF the *URL not found in Offline Mode* dialog box appears,

    click [Stay Offline] .
    Internet Explorer opens in Full Screen view. Except for the workspace, only the Standard toolbar (without text labels), the Internet icon, and the Close and Minimize buttons appear. Even the taskbar is hidden.

NOTE: The contents of the window will vary depending upon the conditions:
  — *Your workspace may contain a message that says:* Unable to retrieve Webpage in Offline mode.
  — *Your workspace may contain a message that says:* This channel is not in the cache. Click here to refresh.
  — *Your workspace may contain a previously retrieved and stored "Microsoft Active Channel Guide" Web page.*

③ Secure the Channel bar:
- **Point** to the left side of the workspace.
  The Channel bar slides into view, if it's not already there.
- IF the push pin on the Channel bar is flat, **click** the push pin to press it in; otherwise, do nothing.
- **Point** to the right side of the workspace.
  The Channel bar stays "pinned" in place.
- **Click** the push pin to "unpin" the Channel bar.
  The push pin changes from pressed to flat.

Flat push pin

| Channels | 📌 × |

| Channels | 🔘 × |

Pressed push pin

④ Display and hide the Channel bar:
- **Point** to the middle of the workspace.
  The Channel bar slides out of view on the left side of the workspace.
- **Point** to the left side of the workspace.
  The Channel bar slides back into view.

⑤ Display and hide the taskbar:
- **Point** to the bottom of the workspace until the taskbar is displayed.
- **Point** to the middle of the workspace.
  The taskbar hides again.

⑥ Turn Full Screen view off:
- **Click** 🔲 (the Fullscreen button) on the Standard toolbar.
  The Internet Explorer window gets smaller. The title bar, menu bar, Address bar, and Links bar appear. Text labels appear on the Standard toolbar. The Channel bar is displayed on the left side of the workspace.

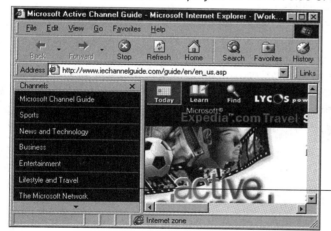

NOTE: The contents on the right side of your workspace may differ from the workspace shown here.

Channel bar

- **Maximize** the Internet Explorer window.
  The window still has all the same bars and toolbars.

⑦ Turn Full Screen view on:
- **Click** 🔲 Fullscreen (the Fullscreen button) on the Standard toolbar.
  The window is in Full Screen view. All the bars and toolbars except the Standard toolbar disappear.
- **Close** the Internet Explorer window by clicking its Close button.

EXERCISE 76 • Create a Web-Page Object

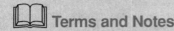
Begin with the Active Desktop displayed and no taskbar buttons on the taskbar.

1 **Save a Notepad .txt document on the desktop:**
- **Start** Notepad, then **type:** When you save a Notepad document with an .htm filename extension, it becomes a Web page object.
- **Click** File, then **click** Save As.
- **Click** the Save in drop-down list box, then **click** 📁 Desktop .
- **Click** the File name text box, **delete** the text, then **type:** mypage
- **Click** [Save] .
  The document is saved on the desktop with a .txt icon; it is not yet a Web-page object.

2 **Save a Notepad .htm document on the desktop:**
- **Click** File, then **click** Save As.
- **Type:** myweb.htm in the File name text box, then **click** [Save] .
  The document is saved on the desktop with an .htm icon; it is now a Web-page object.
- **Exit** Notepad, and **notice** the new desktop icons.
  The two new documents you created appear at the end of the main group of icons.

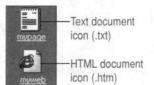
—Text document icon (.txt)

—HTML document icon (.htm)

NOTE: The unformatted text document that Notepad creates can easily be read as an HTML document. If, however, you create a document in WordPad and open it as an HTML document, you will see a lot of symbols that represent formatting codes which the Web browser can't understand.

3 **Open new documents:**
- **Click** mypage.
  Mypage opens into Notepad.
- **Exit** Notepad.
- **Click** myweb.
  Myweb opens into Internet Explorer because it is an HTML document.

Title bar

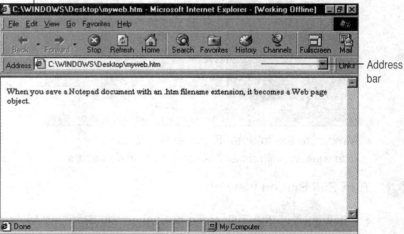

- **Notice** that the title bar and the Address bar both display the name of the document, including its path.
- **Exit** Internet Explorer.

Add a Web-Page Object to the Desktop • EXERCISE 77

Begin with the Active Desktop displayed and no taskbar buttons on the taskbar.

1 **Add a new Web-page object to the desktop:**

- **Right-click** an empty space on the desktop, **point** to <u>A</u>ctive Desktop, then **click** <u>C</u>ustomize my Desktop.

  The Display Properties dialog box opens with the Web tab selected.

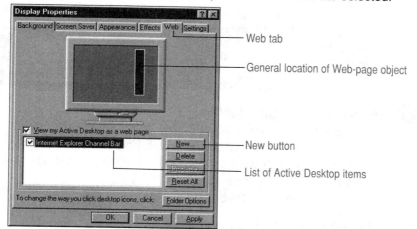

— Web tab

— General location of Web-page object

— New button

— List of Active Desktop items

- **Click** New... .
- **IF** a dialog box asks: ...*connect to the gallery now?*, **click** No .

  The New Active Desktop Item dialog box opens.
- **Click** Browse... .

  The Browse dialog box appears.
- **Click** the Look <u>i</u>n drop-down list box to open it, then **click** Desktop.
- **Click** myweb, then **click** <u>O</u>pen .
- **Click** OK in the New Active Desktop Item dialog box.

  The new Web-page object appears in the Web-page list box and on the desktop preview in the Display Properties dialog box.

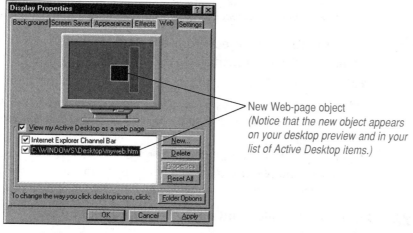

— New Web-page object
(Notice that the new object appears on your desktop preview and in your list of Active Desktop items.)

- **Click** OK .

  The new Web-page object appears on the desktop in the same location shown in the desktop preview.

Continued on the next page

To put a new Web-page object on the desktop, manipulate it, and then delete it.

⌨ Keyboard Steps to

Add a Web-Page Object to the Desktop

1. **Press** `Ctrl` + `Esc`, `Esc` (Start button).

   OR

   Press `⊞` (the Windows key).

2. **Press** `Tab` three times (or until the desktop is selected).

3. **Press** `Shift` + `F10` (desktop shortcut menu).

   OR

   Press `▤` (the Application key).

4. **Press** `R` (<u>P</u>roperties).

5. **Press** `Ctrl` + `Tab` until the Web tab is selected (in front).

6. **Press** `Alt` + `N` (<u>N</u>ew).

   —IF a dialog box asks ...*connect to the gallery now?*, **press** `Alt` + `N` (<u>N</u>o).

7. **Press** `Alt` + `B` (<u>B</u>rowse).

8. **Press** `Alt` + `I` (Look <u>i</u>n).

9. **Press** `↓` (down arrow) to open the list box.

10. **Press** `↑↓` (up or down arrow) to select *(C:)*, then **press** `Enter`.

11. **Press** `Tab` to get to the workspace.

12. **Press** `↑↓↔` (arrow keys) to select the Windows folder, then **press** `Enter`.

13. **Press** `↑↓↔` (arrow keys) to select the Web folder, then **press** `Enter`.

14. **Press** `↑↓↔` (arrow keys) to select the desired Web-page document, then **press** `Enter`.

15. **Press** `Tab`, `Tab` to select the OK button.

16. **Press** `Enter` to accept the Web file, leave the Browse dialog box, and return to the Display Properties dialog box.

17. **Press** `Enter` again to put the Web-page object on the desktop.

Continued from the previous page

2 **Move the Web-page object to the right side of the desktop:**
- **Find** the new Web-page object. (It may be hidden behind other icons.)
- **Point** to the new Web-page object until a gray border appears around it.
- **Drag and drop** the title bar of the Web-page object next to the Channel bar.
  In a few seconds, the gray border disappears from the Web-page object.

Gray border and title bar for the Web-page object  Gray border disappears from the Web-page object

3 **Resize a Web-page object:**
- **IF** there is a scroll bar, **scroll** to the bottom of the document.
- **Point** to the left edge of the new Web-page object until the gray border appears and the arrow pointer turns into a sizing arrow.
- **Drag** the edge left about one inch.
  The entire text of the Web-page object is displayed.

4 **Close the new Web-page object:**
- **Point** to the new Web-page object until its gray title bar appears.
- **Click** ☒ (the Close button).
  The Web-page object disappears.

5 **Put a Web-page object back on the desktop:**
- **Open** the Display Properties dialog box (see step 1, first bullet).
  The Display Properties dialog box opens; the new Web-page object is not selected.

New Web-page object (not selected) ☑ Internet Explorer Channel Bar ☐ C:\WINDOWS\Desktop\myweb.htm

- **Click** the check box next to *C:\WINDOWS\Desktop\myweb.htm* to select it, then **click** OK .
  The new Web-page object is displayed on the screen where it last appeared.

6 **Delete a Web-page object from the desktop list:**
- **Open** the Display Properties dialog box again.
- **Click** *C:\WINDOWS\Desktop\myweb.htm* to highlight it, then **click** Delete .
  A dialog box asks if you are sure you want to delete this item from your Active Desktop.
- **Click** Yes , then **click** OK .
  The Web-page object is deleted from the desktop and from the list of Active Desktop items.

7 **Cut a group of files and paste them into Floppy (A:):**
- **Insert** DATA DISK 1 into drive A:.
- **Select** mypage and myweb on the desktop (review, Exercise 71, step 2).
- **Right-click** one of the selected icons, then **click** Cut.
- **Open** My Computer, then **open** Floppy (A:).
- **Right-click** the Floppy (A:) workspace, then **click** Paste.
- **Close** the Floppy (A:) window, then **remove** DATA DISK 1.

Begin with the Active Desktop displayed and no taskbar buttons on the taskbar.

To use a background wallpaper that was created using HTML.

1 **Open the Display Properties dialog box:**
- **Right-click** an empty space on the desktop, then **click** P̲roperties.
  The Display Properties dialog box opens with the Background tab selected.
- **Notice** which wallpaper is currently being used.
- **Scroll** to the bottom of the Wallpaper list box.
  An HTML wallpaper (Windows98) appears at the bottom of the list.

Enlargement of HTML icon

Windows98 wallpaper

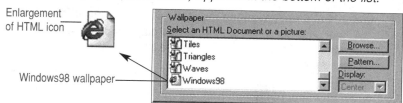

2 **Select an HTML desktop background:**
- **Click** Windows98.
  In the dialog box, the Windows98 wallpaper appears in the desktop preview.

Preview of selected wallpaper (Windows98)

- **Click** OK.
  The new desktop background appears:

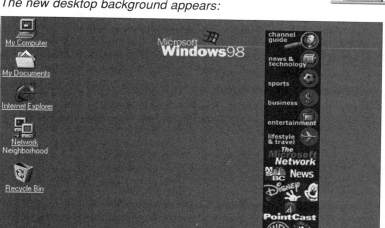

3 **Return the desktop background to its previous wallpaper:**
- **Right-click** an empty space on the desktop, then **click** P̲roperties.
- **Click** the wallpaper that was being used before you changed it.
  OR
  Click ⊘ (None) (the first item in the Wallpaper list box).
- **Click** OK.
  The original desktop background reappears.

⌨ **Keyboard Steps to**

Change to an HTML Wallpaper

1. **Press** Ctrl + Esc, Esc (Start button).
2. **Press** Tab three times (or until the desktop is selected).
3. **Press** Shift + F10 (desktop shortcut menu).
   OR
   Press ▤ (the Application key).
4. **Press** R (P̲roperties).
5. **Press** ↓ (down arrow) to until you reach the desired wallpaper with an HTML icon.
6. **Press** Enter.

To open the Programs folder and create a subfolder within it. The subfolder will then be displayed as a submenu in the Programs menu.

 Terms and Notes

directional arrowhead
A small arrowhead that appears at the beginning and/or end of menus and toolbars to indicate that there are more items than you can presently see on the menu or toolbar. Point to the arrowhead to scroll through the menu or toolbar items. See also *submenu*.

menu
A drop-down or pop-up list of items from which you may choose only one at a time.

Programs menu
A submenu of the Start menu that holds programs and submenus which contain groups of related programs.

submenu
A menu that cascades out from another menu. A right-pointing arrowhead on a menu item indicates that a submenu will appear when you point to it. See also *directional arrowhead*.

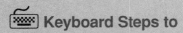 **Keyboard Steps to**

Add a Submenu to the Programs Menu

1. Press `Ctrl` + `Esc`, `Esc` (Start button).

2. Press `Shift` + `F10` (Start button shortcut menu).

3. Press `O` (Open).

4. IF the workspace is not selected, **press** `Tab` until it is selected.

5. Press `↑↓` (arrow keys) until the Programs folder is selected.

6. Press `Enter`.
   The Programs folder window opens.

7. Press `Alt` + `F` (File).

8. Press `N` (New).

9. Press `F` (Folder).

10. **Type** the desired folder name.

11. Press `Enter`.

Begin with the Active Desktop displayed and no taskbar buttons on the taskbar.

① **Open the Programs folder:**

- **Right-click** [Start], then **click** <u>O</u>pen.
  The Start Menu folder window opens.
- **Open** the Programs folder.
  The Programs folder window opens.

② **Create a submenu:**

- **Right-click** the workspace, **point** to <u>N</u>ew, then **click** <u>F</u>older.
  A new program folder named New Folder *appears with a cursor blinking at the end of the name. The new folder will appear where you right-clicked the desktop.*

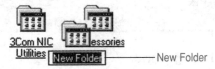
—— New Folder

NOTE: The menus and submenus that open from the Start button are in fact folders and subfolders on your hard drive. The Programs folder is a special folder, as indicated by the picture of a group of six program files on the front of the folder icon.

- **Type:** My Submenu then **press** `Enter`.
  The folder name changes to My Submenu.
- **Close** the Programs folder window.

③ **Open the new submenu on the Start menu:**

- **Click** [Start], then **point** to <u>P</u>rograms.
  The <u>P</u>rograms *menu opens.*
- **Locate** My Submenu.
- IF you don't see My Submenu in the <u>P</u>rograms menu, **point** to and/or **click** the directional arrowhead at the bottom of the <u>P</u>rograms menu until you find My Submenu.

—— Directional arrowhead

My Submenu may be displayed at the bottom of the <u>P</u>rograms *menu or it may be displayed alphabetically among group windows toward the bottom of the* <u>P</u>rograms *menu.*

—— My Submenu

- **Point** to My Submenu.
  My Submenu displays [Empty] *because you haven't put anything in your submenu yet.*

——[Empty] menu

- **Click** outside of the menu to close it.

④ - **Go on** to Exercise 80 without stopping.

Continue from Exercise 79 without stopping.

1 **Open the Taskbar Properties dialog box:**

- **Right-click** an empty space on the taskbar, then **click** P<u>r</u>operties.
- **Click** the Start Menu Programs tab.

  The Start Menu Programs tab is selected, and the top half displays the Customize Start menu section.

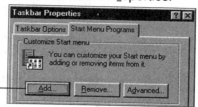

Add button

2 **Add a program to My Submenu:**

- **Click** <u>A</u>dd... , **click** B<u>r</u>owse... , then **double-click** Windows.
- **Scroll** to find 🖉 Notepad, **double-click** it, then **click** <u>N</u>ext > .

  The Select Program Folder dialog box opens.

- **Scroll** to find 🖼 My Submenu , **click** it, then **click** <u>N</u>ext > .

  The Select a Title for the Program dialog box opens with Notepad *in the text box.*

- **Click** Finish .

  The Taskbar Properties dialog box remains open.

3 **Look at the new program in the menu:**

- **Open** My Submenu (review, Exercise 79, step 3).

  Notepad appears in My Submenu.

- **Close** the menus by clicking the desktop.

4 **Add more programs to My Submenu:**

- In the Taskbar Properties dialog box, **click** <u>A</u>dd... , **click** B<u>r</u>owse... , then **double-click** the Windows folder.
- **Scroll** to find Calc, **double-click** it, then **click** <u>N</u>ext > .
- **Scroll** to find My Submenu, **click** it, then **click** <u>N</u>ext > .
- **Type:** Calculator then **click** Finish .
- In the Taskbar Properties dialog box, **click** <u>A</u>dd... , then **click** B<u>r</u>owse... .
- **Open** the Program Files folder, then **open** the Accessories folder.
- **Double-click** WordPad, then **click** <u>N</u>ext > .
- **Click** My Submenu, then **click** <u>N</u>ext > .
- **Type:** WordPad (with a capital P), then **click** Finish .
- **Close** the Taskbar Properties dialog box.
- **Open** My Submenu, **look** at the three programs, then **close** the menus.

  The Calculator and WordPad programs are added to My Submenu:

5 • **Go on** to Exercise 81 without stopping.

To locate programs and select them so they are displayed in a menu.

⌨ **Keyboard Steps to**

Add Notepad to a Menu

1. **Press** Ctrl + Esc (Start menu).

   OR

   Press 🏁 (the Windows key).

2. **Press** S (Settings).

3. **Press** T (Taskbar & Start Menu).

4. **Press** Ctrl + Tab to select the Start Menu Programs tab.

5. **Press** Alt + A (Add).

6. **Press** Alt + R (Browse).

7. **Press** Shift + Tab to move into the workspace.

8. **Press** ↑↓ (arrow keys) to highlight the Windows folder.

9. **Press** Enter .

10. **Press** N until Notepad is selected.

11. **Press** Enter .

12. **Press** Alt + N (Next).

13. **Press** ↑↓ (up or down arrow) to highlight the desired submenu.

14. **Press** Alt + N (Next).

15. **Type** a new name for Notepad, if desired.

16. **Press** Enter to finish.

17. **Press** Esc to close the Taskbar Properties dialog box.

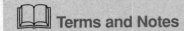

EXERCISE 81 • Move Items Within a Menu

To change the order of menu items by dragging them into the desired position.

📖 **Terms and Notes**

WARNING: With Windows 98, it is easy to drag Start menu items within menus and off of menus. While this is a handy feature, you need to be aware of how easy it is to rearrange items on your menu accidentally by dragging them.

Continue from Exercise 80 without stopping.

1 Open a menu:
- **Open** My Submenu using the Start button.

  The items in My Submenu are displayed.

  NOTE: If your My Submenu items are in a different order than those illustrated here, use these steps as a guide and move the icons until they appear as illustrated in step 4.

Notepad ——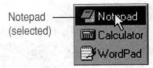

2 Move a menu item within the menu:
- **Point** to Notepad.

  Notepad is selected.

Notepad
(selected)

- **Drag** Notepad down until a line appears under Calculator.

  A heavy outline appears around Notepad, another heavy line appears under Calculator, and a small rectangle is attached to the bottom of the arrow pointer.

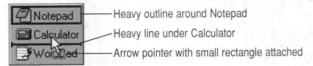
—— Heavy outline around Notepad
—— Heavy line under Calculator
—— Arrow pointer with small rectangle attached

- **Release** the mouse button.

  Notepad switches places with Calculator.

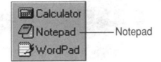
—— Notepad

3 Move WordPad to the top of the menu:
- **Drag** WordPad to the top of the menu.

  A heavy line appears at the top of the menu.

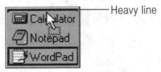
—— Heavy line

- **Release** the mouse button.

  WordPad moves to the top of the menu and the other items move down.

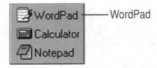
—— WordPad

4 Move a submenu within the Programs menu:
- **Drag** My Submenu up until it is in alphabetical order in the list of submenus.

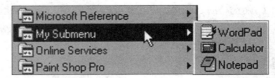

NOTE: The submenus on your machine, other than My Submenu, are probably different from those shown here.

- **Close** the menus by clicking an empty space on the desktop.

Begin with the Active Desktop displayed and no taskbar buttons on the taskbar.

1 **Remove a menu item:**
- **Open** the Taskbar Properties dialog box and **select** the Start Menu Programs tab (review, Exercise 80, step 1).
- **Click** [Remove...].
  The Remove Shortcuts/Folders dialog box opens.
- **Click** [+] (the plus sign) to the left of My Submenu.
  The plus sign turns into a minus sign, and My Submenu expands to reveal the program shortcuts within it.

Minus sign ——— 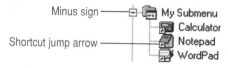 ——— My Submenu / Calculator / Notepad / WordPad
Shortcut jump arrow ———

NOTE: The program icons have jump arrows indicating that they are really just shortcuts to the programs, not the programs themselves.

- **Click** Calculator, then **click** [Remove...].
- **Close** the Remove Shortcuts/Folders dialog box.
- **Close** the Taskbar Properties dialog box.

2 **Delete a menu item:**
- **Open** My Submenu using the Start button.
- **Right-click** Notepad, then **click** Delete.
  The Confirm File Delete dialog box appears.
- **Click** [Yes].
  Notepad is deleted from the menu.

3 **Move a menu item to the desktop:**
- **Open** My Submenu using the Start button.
- **Point** to WordPad.

- **Drag** WordPad to the desktop.
  A heavy line appears around WordPad, and a small rectangle is attached to the bottom of the arrow pointer.

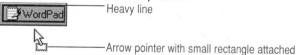
Heavy line
Arrow pointer with small rectangle attached

- **Release** the mouse button.
  The WordPad shortcut is moved to the desktop and the menus close.

4 **Move a submenu to the desktop:**
- **Open** the Programs menu using the Start button.
- **Drag** My Submenu to the desktop.
  The My Submenu menu (now a folder) is moved to the desktop and the menus close.

To use different procedures to delete items from a menu. To move items from the Start menu to the desktop.

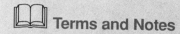 **Terms and Notes**

collapse
To hide the folders contained in an object. Objects that can be collapsed have a minus sign (-) beside them.

expand
To display the unseen folders contained in an object. Objects that can be expanded have a plus sign (+) beside them.

⌨ **Keyboard Steps to**

Remove a Program from a Menu

1. **Press** Ctrl + Esc (Start menu).
   OR
   Press ⊞ (the Windows key).
2. **Press** S (Settings).
3. **Press** T (Taskbar & Start Menu).
4. **Press** Ctrl + Tab to select the Start Menu Programs tab.
5. **Press** Alt + R (Remove).
6. **Press** ↓ (down arrow) until the desired submenu is selected.
7. **Press** → (right arrow) to expand the submenu, displaying the items within it.
8. **Press** ↓ (down arrow) until the desired program is selected.
9. **Press** Alt + R (Remove).
10. **Press** Enter to activate the Close command button.
11. **Press** Esc to close the Taskbar Properties dialog box.

To add programs and folders to the Quick Launch toolbar. To remove programs and folders from the Quick Launch toolbar.

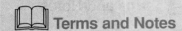 Terms and Notes

directional arrowhead
A small arrowhead that appears at the beginning and/or end of menus and toolbars to indicate that there are more items than you can presently see on the menu or toolbar. Point to the arrowhead to scroll through the menu or toolbar items.

Quick Launch toolbar
A toolbar that appears next to the Start button on the taskbar (by default) and contains buttons for frequently used features.

FEATURE	BUTTON NAME
Internet Explorer	Launch Internet Explorer Browser
Outlook Express	Launch Outlook Express
desktop	Show Desktop
channels	View Channels

WARNING: If the Quick Launch toolbar does not appear on the taskbar, right-click an empty space on the taskbar, point to Toolbars, then click Quick Launch.

NOTE: The program name and the file/icon name differ for the Paint program.

Begin with the Active Desktop displayed and no taskbar buttons on the taskbar.

1 **Put a desktop shortcut on the Quick Launch toolbar:**
- **Drag** the WordPad shortcut (that you dragged onto the desktop in Exercise 82) onto the Quick Launch toolbar until a vertical line appears on the Quick Launch toolbar.

The WordPad icon is dimmed and a vertical line shows where the icon will appear.
- **Release** the mouse button.

The WordPad shortcut is copied to the Quick Launch toolbar, and since there is an extra icon on the menu, a directional arrowhead appears so you can scroll to reveal the other icons.

— WordPad icon
— Right arrowhead

- **Drag** the sizing handle to display all the Quick Launch icons.
  OR
  Double-click very precisely (not on the icon) right here.
  — Sizing handle

2 **Put a desktop folder on the Quick Launch toolbar:**
- **Drag** the My Submenu folder onto the Quick Launch toolbar immediately *left* of the WordPad icon.

The My Submenu folder icon appears on the Quick Launch toolbar.

3 **Put a program on the Quick Launch toolbar:**
- **Open** My Computer, **open** (C:), **open** Program Files, then **open** Accessories.
- **Drag** Mspaint onto the Quick Launch toolbar immediately *left* of the My Submenu icon. *(See note in side column.)*

The Paint icon appears on the Quick Launch toolbar; Mspaint remains in the folder window.
- **Size** the Quick Launch toolbar to show all the icons.
- **Close** the Accessories folder window.

4 **Start a program from the Quick Launch toolbar:**
- **Click** WordPad on the Quick Launch toolbar to start it, then **exit** WordPad.
- **Click** Paint to start it, then **exit** Paint.

5 **Delete an icon on the Quick Launch toolbar:**
- **Drag** the Paint icon from the Quick Launch toolbar onto the desktop.
  The Shortcut to Mspaint icon moves from the toolbar to the desktop.
- **Right-click** the WordPad icon on the Quick Launch toolbar, **click** Delete, then **click** [Yes] (you do want to send it to the Recycle Bin).
- **Right-click** the My Submenu folder icon on the Quick Launch toolbar, **click** Delete, then **click** [Yes].
  The new icons are removed from the Quick Launch toolbar.
- **Size** the Quick Launch toolbar to show just the icons.
  The Quick Launch toolbar appears as it did when you started this exercise.

Begin with the Active Desktop displayed and no taskbar buttons on the taskbar.

1 **Arrange desktop icons:**

- **Drag** those icons that were left on the desktop from Exercises 82 and 83 next to the Channel bar so they look something like the illustration on the right:

  NOTE: If you can't move the icons, deselect Auto Arrange and try again (see Exercise 46, step 7).

- **Right-click** an empty space on the desktop, then **click** Line Up Icons.
  The icons snap into alignment.

2 **Capture the desktop:**

- **Press** [Print Scrn] (the Print Screen key, on the top row of keys).
  Nothing seems to happen, but if all went well, an image of the screen was copied to the clipboard.

3 **Paste the screen capture into WordPad:**

- **Click** the WordPad shortcut icon, then **maximize** the WordPad window.
- **Click** [icon] (the Paste button) on the Standard toolbar.
  The captured screen image appears in the WordPad workspace.
- **Press** [End] to deselect the image.
- **Scroll** to the top of the image.

4 **Print the screen capture:**

- **Make** sure the printer is turned on and ready to receive data.
- **Click** [icon] (the Print button) on the Standard toolbar.
  The screen capture is printed. Your image may have different icons.

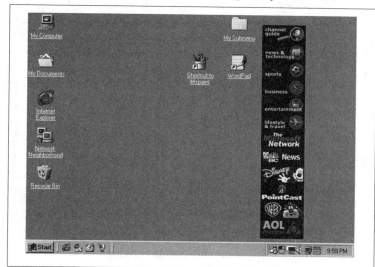

- **Exit** WordPad without saving the document.

To copy an image of the entire screen, paste it into WordPad, and print the image.

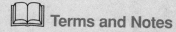 **Terms and Notes**

clipboard
A temporary storage area in the computer's memory used to hold information that is being cut/copied and pasted.

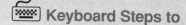 **Keyboard Steps to**

Capture the Screen

Press [Print Scrn].

Print a Capture

1. **Start WordPad:**
   - Press [Ctrl] + [Esc].
     OR
     Press [⊞] (the Windows key).
   - Press [P] (Programs).
   - Press [A] until the Accessories menu is selected (probably the first time).
   - Press [Enter].
   - Press [W] to open WordPad.

2. **Paste the capture into WordPad:**
   - Press [Ctrl] + [V] (Paste).
     OR
     Press [Alt] + [E], [P] (Edit, Paste).

3. **Print the document:**
   - Press [Ctrl] + [P] (Print).
   - Press [Enter].

4. **Exit WordPad:**
   - Press [Alt] + [Space], [C] (Close).
     OR
     Press [Alt] + [F4] (Close).
     OR
     Press [Alt] + [F], [X] (File, Exit).

EXERCISE 85 • Capture a Window

To copy an image of the active window, paste it into WordPad, and print the image.

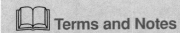 **Terms and Notes**

active window
The window whose title bar is highlighted (i.e., in color—not gray), indicating that it is currently in use.

clipboard
A temporary storage area in the computer's memory used to hold information that is being cut/copied and pasted.

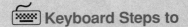 **Keyboard Steps to**

Capture a Window

1. **Open** or **select** the desired window.

2. Press **Alt** + **Print Scrn**.

Print a Capture

1. Start WordPad:
   - Press **Ctrl** + **Esc**.
     OR
     Press **⊞** (the Windows key).
   - Press **P** (Programs).
   - Press **A** until the Accessories menu is selected (probably the first time).
   - Press **Enter**.
   - Press **W** to open WordPad.

2. Paste the capture into WordPad:
   - Press **Ctrl** + **V** (Paste).
     OR
     Press **Alt** + **E**, **P** (Edit, Paste).

3. Print the document:
   - Press **Ctrl** + **P** (Print).
   - Press **Enter**.

4. Exit WordPad:
   - Press **Alt** + **Space**, **C** (Close).
     OR
     Press **Alt** + **F4** (Close).
     OR
     Press **Alt** + **F**, **X** (File, Exit).

Begin with the Active Desktop displayed and no taskbar buttons on the taskbar.

1 **Open a window:**
- **Open** My Computer.
- **With** DATA DISK 1 inserted, **open** Floppy (A:).
- **Arrange** the icons by name (review, Exercise 46, step 2).

2 **Capture a window:**
NOTE: While capturing the screen copies the image of the entire screen, capturing a window captures the image of just the active window.

- Press **Alt** + **Print Scrn**. (Hold down the Alt key, tap the Print Screen key, and then release the Alt key.)
  Nothing seems to happen, but if all went well, an image of the Floppy (A:) folder window was copied to the clipboard.
- **Close** the Floppy (A:) folder window, and **remove** DATA DISK 1 from drive A:.

3 **Paste the window capture into WordPad:**
- **Start** and **maximize** WordPad.
- **Right-click** an empty space on the workspace, then **click** Paste.
  The captured window image appears in the WordPad workspace.

4 **Print the window capture:**
- **Make** sure the printer is turned on and ready to receive data.
- **Click** 🖨 (the Print button) on the Standard toolbar.
  The window capture is printed.

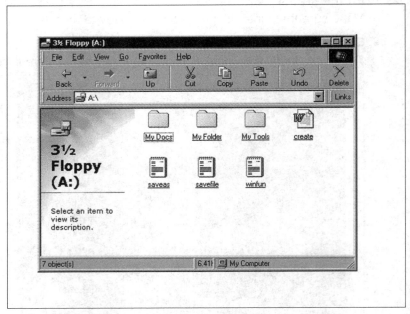

- **Exit** WordPad without saving the document.

Begin with the Active Desktop displayed and no taskbar buttons on the taskbar.

1 **Rename a shortcut, then undo the change:**
- **Right-click** the Shortcut to Mspaint icon on the desktop, then **click** Rename.

  A box appears around the icon title which is also highlighted.
- **Type:** Paint and **press** Enter.
- **Right-click** an empty space on the desktop.

  A shortcut menu appears.

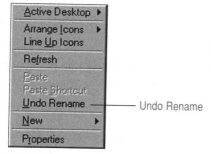
— Undo Rename

- **Click** Undo Rename.

  The icon title changes back to Shortcut to Mspaint.

2 **Perform three file operations:**

CHANGE ICON TITLE
- **Right-click** the Shortcut to Mspaint icon, then **click** Rename.
- **Type:** Paintbrush and press Enter.

MOVE SHORTCUT INTO FOLDER
- **Drag and drop** the Paintbrush shortcut icon onto the My Submenu folder icon.

DELETE ICON
- **Right-click** the WordPad shortcut icon, then **click** Delete.

  The Confirm File Delete dialog box appears.
- **Click** [Yes] (you do want to send it to the Recycle Bin).

3 **Undo a series of file operations:**

UNDO LAST ACTION (DELETE)
- **Right-click** an empty space on the desktop, then **click** Undo Delete.

  The WordPad shortcut icon appears at the end of the list of icons on the desktop.

UNDO MIDDLE ACTION (MOVE)
- **Right-click** an empty space on the desktop, then **click** Undo Move.

  The Paintbrush shortcut icon appears at the end of the list of icons on the desktop.

UNDO FIRST ACTION (RENAME)
- **Right-click** an empty space on the desktop, then **click** Undo Rename.

  The Paintbrush shortcut's icon title returns to Shortcut to Mspaint.

4
- **Drag** the WordPad shortcut icon and the Shortcut to Mspaint icon back to their previous positions, to the left of the Channel bar.

To reverse a file operation or a series of file operations.

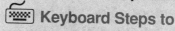 **Keyboard Steps to**

Select an Object on the Desktop
1. **Press** Ctrl + Esc , Esc .
2. **Press** Tab , Tab , Tab .
3. **Press** ↕ to select a shortcut, file, or folder.

Change an Object on the Desktop
Rename an icon:
1. **Select** an object on the desktop.
2. **Press** Shift + F10 .
3. **Press** M (Rename).
4. **Type** the new icon name.
5. **Press** Enter .

Delete an icon:
1. **Select** an object on the desktop.
2. **Press** Shift + F10 .
3. **Press** D (Delete).
4. **Press** Y (Yes).

Copy and paste a shortcut or document:
1. **Select** an object on the desktop.
2. **Press** Ctrl + C (Copy).
3. **Change** to a new location, if desired.
4. **Press** Ctrl + V (Paste).

Move a shortcut or document:
1. **Select** an object on the desktop.
2. **Press** Ctrl + X (Cut).
   The icon is dimmed.
3. **Open** a different folder.
4. **Press** Ctrl + V (Paste).
   The icon appears in the folder.
5. **Return** to the first folder.
   The original icon has disappeared.

Undo an action:
1. **Press** Ctrl + Esc , Esc .
2. **Press** Tab , Tab , Tab .
3. **Press** Shift + F10 (desktop shortcut menu).
4. **Press** U , U (Undo [action]) where *action* represents Delete, Rename, Move, or Copy. IF undoing a copy:

   press Y (Yes) and skip step 5.
5. **Press** Enter .

Close the open folders:
1. **Press** Alt + Tab to select an open folder.
2. **Press** Alt + F4 .

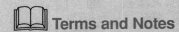

EXERCISE 87 • Use the Recycle Bin

To send objects to be deleted to the Recycle Bin, to restore objects in the Recycle Bin, and to empty the Recycle Bin.

To send objects to be deleted to the Recycle Bin, to restore objects in the Recycle Bin, and to empty the Recycle Bin.

📖 **Terms and Notes**

Recycle Bin
A special folder on the desktop whose icon looks like a wastebasket. The Recycle Bin temporarily holds "deleted" files so you can restore them if you change your mind. But, once you empty the Recycle Bin, you cannot restore (or Undo Delete for) any items that were in it.

NOTE: Objects in the Recycle Bin take up space on your hard drive. If you need more disk space, empty your Recycle Bin. Even if you do not yet need more space, it is a good idea to check and empty the Recycle Bin periodically.

Begin with the Active Desktop displayed and no taskbar buttons on the taskbar.

1 **Empty the Recycle Bin using the shortcut menu:**
- **Right-click** the Recycle Bin icon, **click** Empty Recycle <u>B</u>in, then
  click 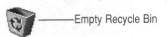 .
- IF the Empty Recycle <u>B</u>in command is dimmed, **click** outside the shortcut menu to close it.
  The Recycle Bin is now empty; there is no trash showing.

  ♻ ——————Empty Recycle Bin

2 **Move a shortcut into the Recycle Bin:**
- **Drag and drop** the WordPad shortcut icon onto the Recycle Bin icon.
  The Confirm File Delete dialog box asks if you want to send 'WordPad' to the Recycle Bin.
- **Click** 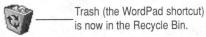 .
  The shortcut disappears and the Recycle Bin now displays trash.

  ♻ ——————Trash (the WordPad shortcut)
  is now in the Recycle Bin.

- **Move** the My Submenu folder to the Recycle Bin.

3 **Delete an item (put it in the Recycle Bin):**
- **Right-click** the Shortcut to Mspaint icon, then **click** <u>D</u>elete.
  The Confirm File Delete dialog box appears:

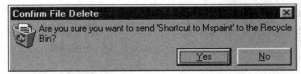

- **Click** <u>Yes</u> .
  Shortcut to Mspaint is moved to the Recycle Bin.

4 **Open the Recycle Bin folder window:**
- **Click** the Recycle Bin icon.
  The Recycle Bin folder window opens and reveals the items you "deleted."
- **Scroll** through and **read** the brief description of the Recycle Bin in the left side of the window.

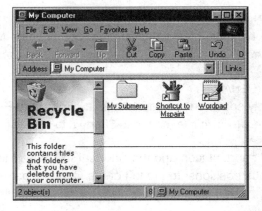

Brief description of the Recycle Bin

152 Lesson Seven • More Desktop

5 **Restore objects in the Recycle Bin:**

- **Drag** the WordPad shortcut icon onto the desktop.

  The shortcut icon is moved from the Recycle Bin folder window to the desktop. When you drag the icon to the desktop, the Recycle Bin folder window is deselected, as indicated by its gray title bar.

- **Click** the Recycle Bin folder window to activate it.

  NOTE: When the Recycle Bin is not active, you cannot select an icon by pointing to it.

- **Select** the My Submenu and Shortcut to Mspaint icons (review, Exercise 71, step 2).

  ...end about here. 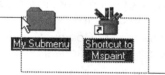 Start here and...

  The My Submenu folder and Shortcut to Mspaint are highlighted.

- **Click** File, then **click** Restore.

  The icons are moved to the desktop and the Recycle Bin is empty.

- **Close** the Recycle Bin folder window.

6 **Empty the Recycle Bin using the File command:**

- **Move** My Submenu and Shortcut to Mspaint back into the Recycle Bin.
- **Open** the Recycle Bin.
- **Click** File, then **click** Empty Recycle Bin.

  The Confirm Multiple File Delete dialog box asks: Are you sure you want to delete these 2 items?

- **Click** [Yes].

  The Recycle Bin is empty; the items are not moved to the desktop.

- **Close** the Recycle Bin folder window.

  NOTE: The Undo Delete command (covered in Exercise 86) works only because "deleted" items are put in the Recycle Bin.

7 **Delete an item without putting it in the Recycle Bin:**

- **Click** an empty space on the desktop.
- **Point** to the WordPad shortcut icon to select it.
- **Hold down** Shift while you **drag and drop** the WordPad shortcut icon onto the Recycle Bin.

  The Confirm File Delete dialog box asks, "Are you sure you want to delete 'WordPad'?"—not, "Are you sure you want to send 'WordPad' to the Recycle Bin," as it does when you don't hold down the Shift key.

  NOTE: If you hold down the Shift key when you delete, objects do not go to the Recycle Bin and you cannot undo the deletion.

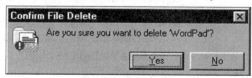

- **Click** [Yes].

  The WordPad shortcut icon is deleted from the desktop; the Recycle Bin remains empty.

- **Right-click** the desktop to display the desktop shortcut menu.

  There is no menu item that offers the opportunity to Undo Delete; you cannot undelete the WordPad shortcut.

- **Close** the shortcut menu.

 Terms and Notes

WARNING: When you delete objects on drive A:, they do not go to the Recycle Bin so you cannot undo the deletion.

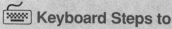 **Keyboard Steps to**

Put an Object in the Recycle Bin

1. **Select** an object *(see Exercise 35 or 86)*.
2. **Press** `Del`.
3. **Press** `Y` (Yes).

Delete an Object Without Putting it in the Recycle Bin

1. **Select** an object *(see Exercise 35 or 86)*.
2. **Hold down** `Shift` while you press `Del`.
3. **Press** `Y` (Yes).

Restore an Object from the Recycle Bin

1. **Press** `Ctrl` + `Esc`, `Esc`.
2. **Press** `Tab` three times (or until the desktop is selected).
3. **Press** `↑↓` (arrow keys) to select the Recycle Bin.
4. **Press** `Enter` to open the Recycle Bin folder window.
5. **Press** `Tab` until the workspace is selected.
6. **Press** `↑↓` (arrow keys) to select the desired object.
7. **Press** `Shift` + `F10` (shortcut menu).
   OR
   Press (the Application key).
8. **Press** `E` (Restore).

Empty the Recycle Bin

1. **Press** `Ctrl` + `Esc`, `Esc`.
2. **Press** `Tab` three times (or until the desktop is selected).
3. **Press** `↑↓` (arrow keys) to select the Recycle Bin.
4. **Press** `Shift` + `F10` (shortcut menu).
   OR
   Press (the Application key).
5. **Press** `B` (Empty Recycle Bin).
6. **Press** `Y` (Yes).

More Desktop

Tasks Reviewed:
- Turn the Active Desktop Off and On
- Work Offline
- Create a Web-Page Object
- Add a Web-Page Object to the Desktop
- Select an HTML Desktop Background
- Add a Submenu to the Programs Menu
- Add Programs to a Menu
- Move Items Within a Menu
- Remove Items from a Menu
- Put Items on the Quick Launch Toolbar
- Capture the Screen
- Capture a Window
- Undo an Action
- Use the Recycle Bin

Begin with the Active Desktop displayed and no taskbar buttons on the taskbar. You will need DATA DISK 2 for this practice exercise.

1
- **Turn off** the Active Desktop (i.e., return to the standard desktop).
- **Turn on** the Active Desktop.

2
- **Select** the Work Offline option (make sure you are working offline):
  - **Open** My Computer, then **click** File.
  - IF Work Offline is not selected, **click** it; otherwise, **click** outside the menu to close it.
  - **Close** the My Computer folder window.
- **Click** the View Channels button on the Quick Launch toolbar, then **click** Stay Offline .
- **Point** to the left side of the screen, then **click** the push pin to secure the Channel bar.
- **Click** the push pin again to release the Channel bar.
- **Display** the Channel bar, then **hide** the Channel bar.
- **Display** the taskbar, then **hide** the taskbar.
- **Turn off** the Full Screen mode.
- **Maximize** Internet Explorer.
- **Turn on** Full Screen mode, then **close** Internet Explorer.

3
- **Start** Notepad, then **type:** HTML documents end with the filename extension .htm or .html.
- **Save** the document on the desktop and **name** it mynote
- **Save** the document on the desktop with a different name using the Save As command; **name** it mypage.htm
- **Exit** Notepad.
- **Open** mynote, then **exit** Notepad.
- **Open** mypage, then **close** Internet Explorer.

4
- **Access** the Web tab in the Display Properties dialog box:
  - **Right-click** the desktop.
  - **Point** to Active Desktop, then **click** Customize my Desktop.
- **Add** mypage.htm to the list of Web-page objects in the Web tab:
  - **Click** New... , then **click** Browse... .
  - **Select** Desktop in the Look in drop-down list box.
  - **Click** mypage, **click** Open , then **click** OK in the New Active Desktop Item dialog box.
- **Put** the new Web-page object on the desktop:
  - **Click** OK in the Display Properties dialog box.
- **Close** the new Web-page object.
- **Put** the new Web-page object back on the desktop.
- **Delete** mypage from the Web tab of the Desktop Properties dialog box.
- **Insert** DATA DISK 2, then **open** the Floppy (A:) folder window.
- **Cut** mynote and mypage from the desktop and **paste** them into the Floppy (A:) folder window.

- **Arrange** the Floppy (A:) folder window icons by name. (Right-click the Floppy (A:) workspace, point to Arrange Icons, then click by Name.)
- **Close** the Floppy (A:) folder window.

5
- **Change** to the HTML wallpaper, *Windows98*.
- **Change** back to the original wallpaper or *(None)*.

6
- **Open** the Programs folder window.
- **Create** a new folder in the Programs folder; **name** it My Sub.
- **Close** the Programs folder window.
- **Look** at the new Programs submenu.

7
- **Open** the Taskbar Properties dialog box and **click** the Start Menu Programs tab.
- **Add** Notepad (in the Windows folder) to the My Sub folder.
- **Open** the My Sub menu (using the Start button), and **look** at Notepad.
- **Add** Calculator (in the Windows folder) to the My Sub folder.
- **Add** WordPad (in the Accessories folder) to the My Sub folder.
- **Close** the Taskbar Properties dialog box.
- **Open** the My Sub menu and **look** at the three new programs.

8
- **Open** the Programs menu, then **open** the My Sub menu.
- **Move** Calculator below WordPad.
- **Move** My Sub to its correct alphabetical position on the Programs menu.

9
- **Open** the Taskbar Properties dialog box.
- **Remove** Notepad from the My Sub folder.
- **Close** the Taskbar Properties dialog box.
- **Open** the My Sub menu and **delete** Calculator.
- **Open** the My Sub menu and **drag** WordPad onto the desktop.
- **Open** the Programs menu and **drag** My Sub onto the desktop.

10
- **Drag** the WordPad shortcut onto the taskbar, to the right end of the Quick Launch toolbar.
- **Drag** the My Sub folder to the right end of the Quick Launch toolbar.
- **Open** My Computer, **open** (C:), **open** Program Files, then **open** Accessories.
- **Drag** Mspaint to the right end of the Quick Launch toolbar.
- **Close** the Accessories folder window.
- **Size** the Quick Launch toolbar to show all of its icons.
- **Open** and then **exit** WordPad and Paint.
- **Close** the My Sub folder.
- **Drag** Paint from the Quick Launch toolbar to the desktop.
- **Delete** WordPad and the My Sub folder from the Quick Launch toolbar.
- **Size** the Quick Launch toolbar to show only its default icons (with no extra space).

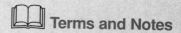
Terms and Notes

NOTES: In this exercise, you create My Sub as a folder (in the Programs folder). However, it also appears as a submenu of the Programs menu (that you open using the Start button). Although it may seem confusing, My Sub is both a menu and a folder (in fact, it is a special folder—a group folder). This explains why My Sub is sometimes referred to as a folder and other times referred to as a menu in this exercise.

Mspaint is the Paint program's file name; thus, when you open the Mspaint file (or the Shortcut to Mspaint), you are opening the Paint program.

Continued on the next page

Continued from the previous page

- **Drag** the WordPad shortcut icon, the Shortcut to Mspaint icon, and the My Sub folder next to the top-left side of the Channel bar.
- **Line up** the icons.
- **Capture** an image of the screen.
- **Start** WordPad and **paste** the screen capture in WordPad.
- **Print** the screen capture, then **exit** WordPad without saving.

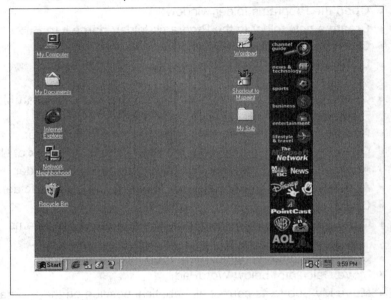

- **Open** the Floppy (A:) folder window.
- **Capture** an image of the Floppy (A:) folder window, then **close** the Floppy (A:) folder window.
- **Start** WordPad and **paste** the window capture in WordPad.
- **Print** the window capture, then **exit** WordPad without saving.

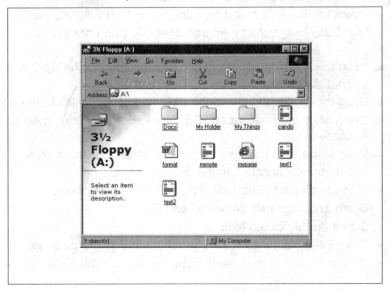

- **Remove** DATA DISK 2.

13 • **Rename** the Shortcut to Mspaint icon as Paint, then **undo** the rename.

• **Rename** the Shortcut to Mspaint icon as Paintbrush.

• **Drag and drop** the Paintbrush shortcut icon onto the My Sub folder.

• **Right-click** the WordPad shortcut icon, **click** Delete, then **click** [Yes] (to send the item to the Recycle Bin).

• **Undo** the last three changes.

• **Drag** the Shortcut to Mspaint icon and the WordPad shortcut icon back to where they were on the desktop.

14 • **Empty** the Recycle Bin.

• **Drag and drop** the WordPad shortcut icon and the My Sub folder onto the Recycle Bin icon, and **click** [Yes] (to send the items to the Recycle Bin).

• **Right-click** the Shortcut to Mspaint icon, **click** Delete, then **click** [Yes] (to send the item to the Recycle Bin).

• **Open** the Recycle Bin.

• **Restore** the WordPad shortcut. (Select WordPad, click File, then click Restore.)

• **Empty** the Recycle Bin (the My Sub folder and Shortcut to Mspaint icon).

• **Close** the Recycle Bin folder window.

• **Right-click** the WordPad shortcut icon, then **hold down** [Shift] while you **click** Delete.

• **Click** [Yes] (to delete the WordPad shortcut icon).

• **Try to undo** the delete to the WordPad shortcut icon.

Because you held down the Shift key when you deleted the WordPad shortcut icon, it did not go into the Recycle Bin, so you cannot undo the delete.

Lesson Seven Worksheet (8) is on page 308.

NEXT
LESSON

Lesson Eight

Windows Explorer

Table of Contents

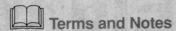
TOPIC 22 • Windows Explorer

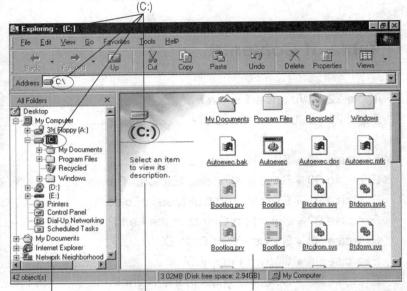

Terms and Notes

folder window
A window that displays the contents of a folder (or certain other objects, such as disk drives). Folder windows offer many of the same folder-managing features as Windows Explorer. Click a folder (if Web-style browsing is enabled) to open its window and see what is in it.

hierarchy
A system of things (or people) ranked one above the other. With regard to computers, the term *hierarchy* describes the multilevel structure of folders and subfolders on a disk. In the case of Windows 98, it further describes the multilevel structure of objects on the entire computer system. This structure is also referred to as a *tree*.

Windows Explorer
The Windows 98 program that you can use to look at and manage objects in your computer system, including remote computers if your system is networked. The left pane displays *All Folders* (a hierarchy of folders); the right pane displays the contents of the folder that is selected in the left pane.

NOTE: Don't confuse Windows Explorer (the file-managing program) with Internet Explorer (the Web-browsing program). Windows Explorer is often called simply Explorer.

A Look at Your Computer's Resources

Windows Explorer lets you see where your computer's resources are located. The Explorer window is divided into two panes. The **left pane** displays the Windows hierarchy; it is labeled *All Folders*. The **right pane** displays the objects within the folder (or object) selected in the left pane. The title bar displays the name of the folder (or object) selected in the left pane, as does the Address bar and the Web View icon.

Left pane (All Folders)   Web Page view   Right pane (contents of the folder selected in the left pane)

Windows Explorer is similar to a **folder window**; its right pane, in particular, resembles a folder window workspace. *(See Topic 12, Folder Windows.)*

Listed below are some of the similarities between folder windows and Windows Explorer:

- Both have the File, Edit, View, Go, Favorites, and Help menus.
- Both have the same bars and toolbars available.
- Both have the same shortcut (right-click) menus.
- Both let you start programs.
- Both let you open documents.
- Both let you create, move, copy, and delete files and folders.
- Both let you customize the folder window.
- Both have the View, as Web Page option.
- Both let you view objects in any of the four View modes.
- Both let you arrange (sort) icons as desired.
- Both let you use Quick View—if it is installed.
- Both let you format and copy disks.

Listed below are some of the differences between folder windows and Windows Explorer:

- Windows Explorer has a Tools menu.
- Windows Explorer has a left pane that displays the Windows 98 hierarchy.

Lesson Eight emphasizes the Windows Explorer features that folder windows do not share, and it provides a review of some of the features covered in Lessons Four and Five.

The Left Pane of Windows Explorer Shows the Computer's Structure

Because you often use shortcuts to quickly access folders and files, you may not think about the natural structure of your computer with its many levels of folders and files.

Windows Explorer helps you see how your computer system is structured. The illustration on the right shows how Windows Explorer displays the computer's structure in the **All Folders pane** (the left pane).

Notice that the desktop is the top-level folder on your computer system (i.e., level one). The desktop links you to: your local computer via My Computer, to network computers—if you're connected to remote computers—via Network Neighborhood, and to the Internet via your Web browser (e.g., Internet Explorer).

Because the desktop is also a folder, you can store objects, such as shortcuts, folders, and files there. Folders within the Desktop folder are second-level folders. Folders within second-level folders are third-level folders, and so forth, as shown in the illustration.

A plus sign (+) beside a folder means that the folder is **collapsed** (closed), so you can't see the subfolders it contains. Click a folder's plus sign to **expand** (open) the folder and show its subfolders.

A minus sign (-) beside a folder means that the folder has been **expanded** (opened) to show its subfolders. Click a folder's minus sign to **collapse** (close) it and hide its subfolders.

The illustration on the right shows some expanded folders and a lot of collapsed folders.

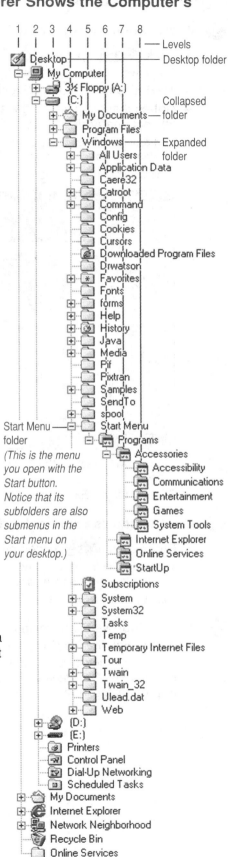

 Terms and Notes

All Folders pane
The left pane of Windows Explorer that displays the hierarchical structure on your computer system, including remote computers if your system is networked.

collapse ⊟
To hide the folders contained in an object. Objects that can be collapsed have a minus sign (-) beside them. It may help to think of collapse as "close."

collapsed
The state of a folder that has a plus sign (+) beside it. A *collapsed* folder has folders within it that are not visible. It may help to think of collapsed as "closed."

expand ⊞
To display the unseen folders contained in an object. Objects that can be expanded have a plus sign (+) beside them. It may help to think of expand as "open."

expanded
The state of a folder that has a minus sign (-) beside it. The folders within an *expanded* folder are displayed immediately below it. It may help to think of expanded as "opened."

subfolder
A folder contained within another folder.

EXERCISE 89 • Start Windows Explorer

To use three methods to open Windows Explorer.

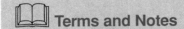 **Terms and Notes**

NOTES: Right-clicking the Start button or the My Computer icon is a quick way to start Windows Explorer. You can easily change the selected folder and browse once you are in Windows Explorer.

When you start Windows Explorer by right-clicking a folder, Explorer opens with that folder selected. When you open Windows Explorer from the Programs menu, Explorer opens with drive C: selected. When you start Windows Explorer by right-clicking the Start button, Explorer opens with the Start Menu folder selected.

Keyboard Steps to

Start Windows Explorer

—USING THE START MENU—

1. **Press** `Ctrl` + `Esc` (Start menu).

   OR

   Press `⊞` (the Windows key).

2. **Press** `P` (Programs).

3. **Press** `W` (Windows Explorer).
   NOTE: If Windows Explorer does not open, press the W key until Windows Explorer is highlighted; then press the Enter key.

—USING THE SHORTCUT MENU—

1. **Press** `Ctrl` + `Esc`, `Esc`.

2. **Press** `Tab` three times (or until the desktop is selected).

3. **Press** `↑↓` (arrow keys) to select one of the following:
   • My Computer
   • Recycle Bin
   • Network Neighborhood
   • My Document

4. **Press** `Shift` + `F10` to open the shortcut menu.

   OR

   Press `▤` (the Application key).

5. **Press** `E` (Explore).

Begin with the desktop displayed and with no taskbar buttons on the taskbar.

1 Start Windows Explorer using the Programs menu:

• **Click** `Start`, **point** to `Programs ▶`, then **click** `Windows Explorer`.
  Windows Explorer opens with (C:) in the title bar.
• **Maximize** the Windows Explorer window.
• **Notice** that the name of the selected object, *(C:)*, is displayed in the title bar, the Address bar, and the Web-Page view area.
  Windows Explorer looks something like the illustration below; the contents of your Windows Explorer window may be different.

Explorer's title bar   (C:)

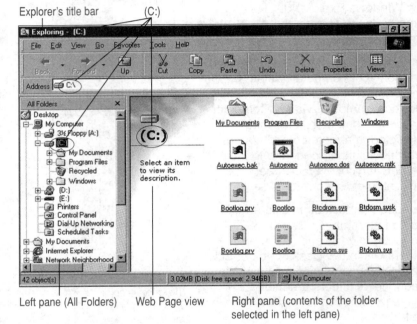

Left pane (All Folders)   Web Page view   Right pane (contents of the folder selected in the left pane)

• **Exit** Windows Explorer.

2 Start Windows Explorer by right-clicking the Start button:

• **Right-click** `Start`, then **click** Explore.
  Windows Explorer opens with Start Menu *in the title bar, the Address bar, and the Web-Page view area.*
• **Exit** Windows Explorer.

3 Start Windows Explorer by right-clicking the My Computer icon:

• **Right-click** the My Computer icon, then **click** Explore.
  Windows Explorer opens with My Computer *in the title bar, the Address bar, and the Web-Page view area.*
• **Exit** Windows Explorer.

Begin with the desktop displayed and with no taskbar buttons on the taskbar.

1 **Resize Windows Explorer panes:**

- **Start** and **maximize** Windows Explorer.
- **Move** the arrow pointer on the bar between the panes until the arrow pointer becomes a sizing pointer.

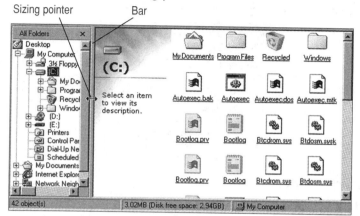

- **Drag** the bar until the left pane is about one inch wide.

  A very small scroll bar appears at the bottom of the left pane.

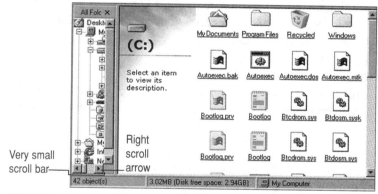

- **Click** the right scroll arrow on the bottom scroll bar continuously to scroll through the width of the left pane and view folder names.
- **Drag** the bar right until there is no scroll bar at the bottom of the left pane.

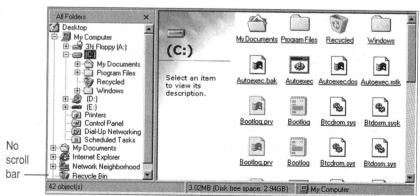

- **Drag** the bar until the left pane is about its original width.

2 - **Exit** Windows Explorer.

To move the bar between the left and right panes of the Windows Explorer window.

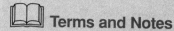 **Terms and Notes**

bar
The term *bar* is used to define the barrier between window panes (e.g., the bar that separates the two panes in Windows Explorer).

sizing pointer ⟷
The arrow pointer becomes a double-headed arrow when you point to a sizing handle or certain borders. The sizing pointer is used to size a window or the taskbar.

EXERCISE 91 • Expand and Collapse a Folder

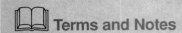
Begin with the desktop displayed and with no taskbar buttons on the taskbar.

① Open Windows Explorer with My Computer selected:
- **Right-click** the My Computer icon, **click** Explore, then **maximize** Windows Explorer.

  Windows Explorer opens with My Computer *in the title bar, the Address bar, and the Web-Page view area.*

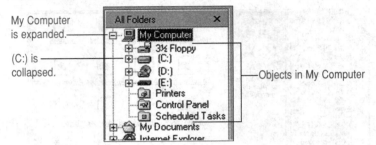

② Expand a folder:
- **Click** ➕ (the plus sign) beside 💾 (C:) to expand it.

  The folders on drive C: are displayed under (C:) in the left pane.
- **Scroll** through the drive C: subfolders until the Windows folder appears.
- **Click** ➕ (the plus sign) beside 📁 Windows to expand it.

  The folders in the Windows folder appear in the left pane.
- **Expand** the Start Menu folder.
- **Expand** the Programs folder.
- **Expand** the Accessories folder.

  The plus sign next to each folder becomes a minus sign showing that each folder is expanded and can now be collapsed, if desired.

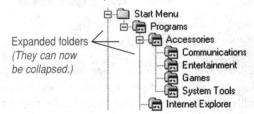

③ Collapse a folder:
- **Click** 🗕 (the minus sign) beside 📁 Accessories to collapse it.

  The Accessories folder is now collapsed.
- **Click** 🗕 (the minus sign) beside 📁 Programs to collapse it.

  The Programs folder is now collapsed.
- **Collapse** the Start Menu folder.
- **Collapse** the Windows folder.
- **Collapse** the (C:) folder.
- **Collapse** the My Computer folder.

  The minus sign by each folder becomes a plus sign, showing that each folder is collapsed and can now be expanded, if desired. The Windows 98 structure is now entirely collapsed.

④
- **Restore** Windows Explorer, then **exit** Windows Explorer.

Begin with the desktop displayed and with no taskbar buttons on the taskbar.

1 **Open Windows Explorer with the Start menu selected:**

- **Right-click** 🏁**Start**, then **click** Explore.
- **Expand** the Programs folder, then **expand** the Accessories folder (review, Exercise 91).
- **Size** the Windows Explorer left pane until there is no scroll bar at the bottom of the Explorer screen (review, Exercise 90).

2 **Select a folder in the left pane:**

NOTE: In the left pane of Windows Explorer, you must click an object to select it. In the right pane, you can simply point to an item to select it.

- **Scroll** up to find the Start Menu folder.
- **Click** the Start Menu folder, if it is not already selected.

The folder opens, the contents of the folder appear in the right pane, and the number of items in the folder appears on the left end of the status bar. The Web-Page view area may be reduced to the selected folder's title.

Selected folder
(Notice that the icon is an open folder.)

Web-Page view area
(It may be reduced to the title of the selected folder.)

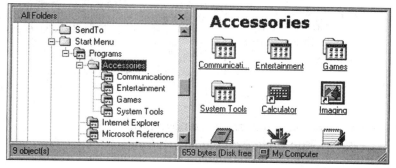

Number of objects in the selected folder   Contents of the selected folder

- **Click** the right pane workspace. (Don't click an icon.)
  The highlighting disappears from the Start Menu folder, but the folder icon itself remains open.
- **Click** the Programs folder (in left pane) to select it.
  The Programs folder icon opens.
- **Click** the Accessories folder (in left pane) to select it.
  The Accessories folder icon opens. Your screen appears something like the illustration below.

3 - **Exit** Windows Explorer or **go on** to Exercise 93.

To open a folder in the left Windows Explorer pane, causing that folder's contents to be displayed in the right pane.

⌨️ **Keyboard Steps to**

Select an Object in the Left Pane

—FROM THE EXPLORER WINDOW—

1. **Press** `Tab` until a folder in the left pane is selected.
2. **Use** the following cursor movements to select desired folder:

MOVE	PRESS
Up one line	↑
Down one line	↓
Up one screen	Page Up
Down one screen	Page Down
Top of the structure	Home
Bottom of the structure	End

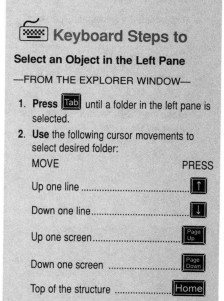

EXERCISE 93 • Browse Your Data Disk

To move through the folders stored on DATA DISK 1 and examine the files in the right pane of Windows Explorer.

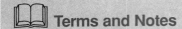 **Terms and Notes**

NOTE: Because drive C: holds many important files, people sometimes become protective of it. They fear—not unreasonably—that information might be inadvertently deleted or "lost." In Windows 98, rearranging the folder on a disk is as easy as dragging the pointer over them (purposely or accidentally). Therefore, this book lets you practice moving and copying with folders and files on your floppy data disk rather than those on drive C:.

IMPORTANT: You can create an accurate data disk for the exercises in Lessons Eight and Nine from the CD-ROM included with this book by following the directions below:

- **Insert** the CD-ROM that came with this book into the CD-ROM drive.

- **Insert** a blank, formatted disk in drive A:.

- **Open** My Computer, then **open** the CD-ROM drive.

- **Select** everything in the workspace.

- **Right-click** one of the selected icons, then **click** Copy.

- **Click** the Address bar drop-down arrow, then **click** Floppy (A:).

- **Right-click** the workspace, then **click** Paste.

- **Close** Floppy (A:).

- **Remove** the disk in drive A: and **label** it DATA DISK 1.

- **Close** the CD-ROM drive window, then **close** My Computer.

DATA DISK 1 Should Be Accurate for Lesson Eight

Since the file-managing exercises in Lesson Eight use DATA DISK 1, it is important that DATA DISK 1 has all the necessary folders and files on it.

Begin with the desktop displayed and with no taskbar buttons on the taskbar.

1
- **Start** Windows Explorer and **insert** DATA DISK 1 into drive A:.
- **Turn off** Web Page view in Windows Explorer. (Click <u>V</u>iew, then deselect *as <u>W</u>eb Page*.)
- **View** objects in a list. (Click <u>V</u>iew, then click <u>L</u>ist.)
- **Select** the Floppy (A:) folder (review, Exercise 92).
- **Expand** the Floppy (A:) folder (review, Exercise 91).
- Do you have the same folders and files in the right pane as those in the illustration?

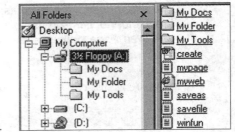

NOTE: The icons that represent WordPad documents may be different from those shown in these illustrations.

2
- **Select** the My Docs folder in the left pane.
- Do you have the same files in the right pane as those in the illustration?

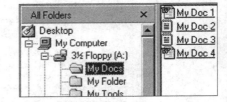

3
- **Select** the My Folder folder.
- Do you have the same files in the right pane as those in the illustration?

4
- **Select** the My Tools folder.
- Do you have the same files in the right pane as those in the illustration?

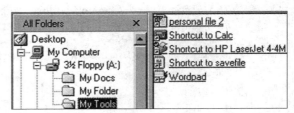

NOTE: Your printer shortcut may have a different name.

5
- **Exit** Windows Explorer and **remove** DATA DISK 1, or **go on** to Exercise 94.

Copying Your Data Disk

The Copy Disk procedure must be done using two disks of the same size and density. The disk you are copying is called the *source disk* (or *Copy from disk*) and the disk you are copying to is called the *destination disk* (or *Copy to disk*).

To complete this exercise, you will need a disk that matches DATA DISK 1 in **floppy disk size** and **floppy disk density**. This destination disk must either be blank and formatted *(see Exercise 107, Format a Floppy Disk, for more information)* or have unimportant data on it that you do not mind overwriting (losing). We will refer to this disk as DUPLICATE DATA DISK 1 because it will be an exact copy of DATA DISK 1. You will use DUPLICATE DATA DISK 1 in the exercises that follow. If you make errors in the procedures, you can copy DATA DISK 1 again and start the exercises over.

Begin with the desktop displayed and with no taskbar buttons on the taskbar.

1 Copy from DATA DISK 1:
- **Label** your blank, formatted disk: DUPLICATE DATA DISK 1.
- **Write protect** DATA DISK 1. (Slide the tab on the top-left corner of the back of the disk so the hole is open.)
- **Insert** DATA DISK 1 (the source disk) into drive A:.
- **Start** Windows Explorer.
- **Right-click** Floppy (A:), then **click** Copy Disk.
  The Copy Disk dialog box opens:

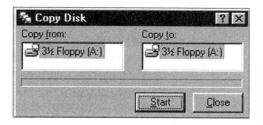

- **Click** Start.
  The Copy Disk dialog box says Reading source disk *and reports its progress.*

2 Copy to DUPLICATE DATA DISK 1:
- **Remove** DATA DISK 1 (the source disk) when prompted.
- **Insert** DUPLICATE DATA DISK 1 (the destination disk).
  WARNING: Any existing data on this disk will be destroyed when the information from the source disk is copied to it.
- **Click** OK.
  The Copy Disk dialog box says Writing to destination disk *and reports its progress.*
  In a short time, the Copy Disk dialog box reports Copy completed successfully.

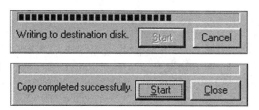

- **Click** Close.

3
- **Exit** Windows Explorer and **remove** DUPLICATE DATA DISK 1, or **go on** to Exercise 95.

To copy the entire contents of a floppy disk to another floppy disk of the same size and density.

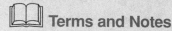 **Terms and Notes**

floppy disk density
Density refers to the surface coating on a floppy disk; the closer together the particles on the disk, the higher the disk capacity. Typically, 3½" floppy disks come in two densities:
- DD (double density)—720 Kb
- HD (high density)—1.44 Mb

floppy disk size
The physical size of floppy disks; typically, they are 3½". In the past, 5¼" was a common size for floppy disks.

byte (B)
The size of computer memory and storage units is measured in bytes. A *byte* is the amount of space needed to hold one character.
byte	= One character
kilobyte	= About 1,000 bytes (characters)
megabyte	= About 1,000,000 bytes (characters)
gigabyte	= About 1,000,000,000 bytes (characters)

WARNING: Do not remove your disk from drive A: when its light is on.

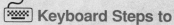 **Keyboard Steps to**

Copy a Floppy Disk
—FROM THE EXPLORER WINDOW—

1. Press Tab until a folder in the left pane is selected.
2. Press ↑↓ (up or down arrow) until Floppy (A:) is selected.
3. Press Shift+F10 (desktop shortcut menu). OR
   Press (the Application key).
4. Press Y (Copy Disk).
   The Copy Disk dialog box appears.
5. Insert the source disk into drive A:.
6. Press Enter to start the disk copy.
   A dialog box reports the progress.
7. Remove the source disk when prompted.
8. Insert the destination disk into drive A:.
9. Press Enter to complete the disk copy.
   A dialog box reports the progress.
10. Press C (Close) to close the Copy Disk dialog box.
11. Remove the duplicate disk.

To highlight one object, multiple adjoining objects, or multiple separate objects. Once objects are selected, you can copy, move, or delete them as a group.

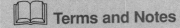

Terms and Notes

WARNING: You need to be careful when selecting multiple objects by pointing to them. It is easy to accidentally point to an object and undo all the selections you made previously.

Keyboard Steps to

Select an Object in the Right Pane

—FROM THE EXPLORER WINDOW—

1. **Press** `Tab` until an object in the right pane is selected.

2. **Press** `↑↓` (up or down arrow) until you select the desired object.

Select Multiple Adjoining Objects

—FROM THE EXPLORER WINDOW—

1. **Press** `Tab` until an object in the right pane is selected.

2. **Press** `↕↔` (arrow keys) until you reach the first object you want to select.

3. **Press** `Shift` + `↕↔` (arrow keys) until you reach the last object you want to select.

Select Multiple Separate Objects

—FROM THE EXPLORER WINDOW—

1. **Press** `Tab` until an object in the right pane is selected.

2. **Press** `↕↔` (arrow keys) until you reach the first object you want to select.

3. **Press and hold** `Ctrl` while you:

   a. **Press** `↕↔` (arrow keys) until you reach the next object you want to select.

   b. **Press** `Space` to select the object.

   c. **Repeat** steps a and b until all the desired objects are selected.

Begin with the desktop displayed and with no taskbar buttons on the taskbar.

1
- **Start** Windows Explorer.
- **View** objects in a list.
- **Turn off** Web Page view in Windows Explorer, if it's not already off.
- **With** DUPLICATE DATA DISK 1 inserted, **select** the Floppy (A:) folder.

  A screen similar to the illustration below appears:

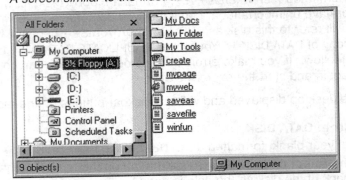

2 **Select a single object in the right pane:**

- **Point** to ⬜ My Docs in the right pane.

  The My Docs folder is selected (highlighted):

- **Point** to 📄 saveas.

  Saveas is selected and the My Docs folder is deselected:

My Docs (deselected)

Saveas (selected)

NOTE: When one object is selected and you point to another object, the new object is selected and the original object is deselected automatically.

3 **Select adjoining objects:**

- **Point** to ⬜ My Folder.

  My Folder is selected.

- **Press** `Shift` while you **point** to 📄 savefile.

  All the objects between (and including) My Folder and savefile are selected.

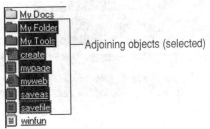

Adjoining objects (selected)

4 **Deselect all objects:**

- **Click** the right pane workspace to deselect the objects.

  The highlighting disappears from the objects. The last object that was selected has a dotted line around it.

(5) **Select non-adjoining objects:**

- **Point** to 📁 My Docs in the right pane.
  The My Docs folder is selected.

- **Press** `Ctrl` while you **point** to 📁 My Tools .

- **Press** `Ctrl` while you **point** to 📄 mypage .
  The non-adjoining objects are all selected.

(6) **Deselect a non-adjoining object:**

WARNING: As you may have noticed by now, you need to be careful when selecting multiple objects by pointing to them; it is easy to accidentally point to an object and deselect all the selections you made previously.

- **Press** `Ctrl` while you **point** to 📁 My Tools .
  The My Tools folder is deselected; however, the other objects remain selected.

- **Point** to 📄 winfun .
  Winfun is selected, and the My Docs folder and mypage are deselected.

- **Click** outside 📄 winfun to deselect it.

(7) **Select adjoining objects by dragging:**

HINT: When you select a group of objects, start with the pointer outside the objects rather than on an object. (If you start too close to an object, you may move or open it.) If you accidentally move, copy, or delete an object or objects, remember that you can undo the action by using the Undo command (see Exercise 86, Undo an Action).

- **Drag** the arrow pointer to select 📁 My Tools through 🌐 myweb .

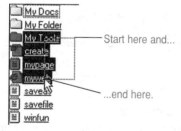

Start here and...

...end here.

- **Release** the mouse button.
  The My Tools folder, create, mypage, and myweb are selected.

- **Press** `Ctrl` while you **point** to 📁 My Tools .
  The My Tools folder is deselected.

- **Press** `Ctrl` while you **point** to 📄 mypage .
  Mypage is deselected. Create and myweb remain selected.

(8)
- **Click** outside the objects to deselect them.
- **Exit** Windows Explorer and **remove** DUPLICATE DATA DISK 1, or **go on** to Exercise 96.

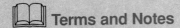 **EXERCISE 96** • **Invert Selection**

To reverse which objects are selected and which are not.

 Terms and Notes

NOTE: This feature is useful when you want to select all but a few objects within a large group of objects. Simply select the few objects you do not want selected, then invert the selection.

Begin with the desktop displayed and with no taskbar buttons on the taskbar.

1
- **Start** Windows Explorer.
- **View** objects in a list.
- **Turn off** Web Page view in Windows Explorer, if it's not already off.
- **With** DUPLICATE DATA DISK 1 inserted, **select** the Floppy (A:) folder.
- **Select** 🗐 mypage and 🗐 savefile .
  The two objects are selected as illustrated below:

2 **Invert the selection:**
- **Click** Edit, then **click** Invert Selection.
  The selected objects and deselected objects are reversed:

 ——Savefile

NOTE: There is a dotted line around savefile because it was the last object that was selected.

3 **Invert the selection again:**
- **Click** Edit, then **click** Invert Selection again.
  The selected and deselected objects return to their previous states:

4
- **Click** outside the objects to deselect them.
- **Exit** Windows Explorer and **remove** DUPLICATE DATA DISK 1, or **go on** to Exercise 97.

📧 **Keyboard Steps to**

Invert Selection

—FROM THE EXPLORER WINDOW—

1. **Select** objects you do *not* want selected. *(See Keyboard Steps, Exercise 95.)*

2. **Press** Alt + E (Edit).

3. **Press** I (Invert Selection).

Begin with the desktop displayed and with no taskbar buttons on the taskbar.

1
- **Start** Windows Explorer.
- **View** objects in a list.
- **Turn off** Web Page view in Windows Explorer, if it's not already off.
- **With** DUPLICATE DATA DISK 1 inserted, **select** the Floppy (A:) folder.
  The objects on drive A: are displayed in the right pane:

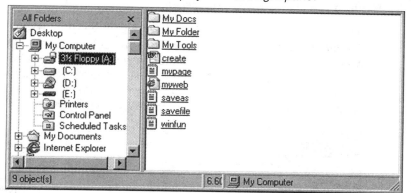

2 **Select all objects:**
- **Click** Edit, then **click** Select All.
  All of the objects in the right pane are selected:

3 **Deselect individual objects when all objects are selected:**
- **Press** [Ctrl] while you **point** to 📄 mypage .
- **Press** [Ctrl] while you **point** to 📄 savefile .
  The two files are deselected:

4
- **Click** outside the objects to deselect them.
- **Exit** Windows Explorer and **remove** DUPLICATE DATA DISK 1, or **go on** to Exercise 98.

To highlight all the objects in a folder.

 Terms and Notes

NOTE: This feature is useful when you want to select all the files in a folder, or when you want to select all but a few objects in a folder.

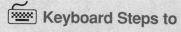 **Keyboard Steps to**

Select All Objects

SHORTCUT: [Ctrl] + [A]

—FROM THE EXPLORER WINDOW—

1. **Press** [Alt] + [E] (Edit).
2. **Press** [A] (Select All).

Deselect Objects

—WITH ALL OBJECTS SELECTED—

- **Press and hold** [Ctrl] while you:
  a. **Press** [↑↓] (arrow keys) until you reach an object you want to deselect. *NOTE: A dotted line around an object means that it is selected.*
  b. **Press** [Space] to deselect the object.
  c. **Repeat** steps a and b until all the desired objects are deselected.

To transfer an object from one location to another, removing the object from its original location.

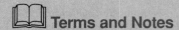 **Terms and Notes**

Ways to Move Objects

Move works the same way in any of the View modes. There are many other variables when moving, however, for example, you can:

- Move single or multiple objects.

  NOTE: *Single objects are used in this exercise, but you can also select multiple objects and then use the procedures shown in this exercise to move them.*

- Move a folder and its contents.
- Move a file using the drag-and-drop method—within the same disk drive only.

  NOTE: *You cannot use the drag-and-drop method to move files from one disk drive to another one. Dragging and dropping files from one disk to another copies the files to the new location; it does not move them.*

- Move a file using the cut-and-paste method with the shortcut menu.
- Move a file using the cut-and-paste method with the Edit menu.
- Undo a Move procedure.

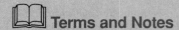 **Keyboard Steps to**

Move Objects

—FROM THE EXPLORER WINDOW—

1. **Select** the object(s) you want to move. *(See Keyboard Steps, Exercise 95.)*

2. **Press** Ctrl + X (Cut).

3. **Select** the object into which you want to move the cut object(s).

4. **Press** Ctrl + V (Paste).

Undo Move

—FROM THE EXPLORER WINDOW—

Press Ctrl + Z (Undo).

Begin with the desktop displayed and with no taskbar buttons on the taskbar.

1
- **Start** Windows Explorer.
- **View** objects in a list, then **turn off** Web Page view.
- **With** DUPLICATE DATA DISK 1 inserted, **select** the Floppy (A:) folder, then **expand** it.

2 Move a file using drag and drop:

- **Drag and drop** 📄 winfun onto 📁 My Folder in the right pane.

  The arrow pointer turns into a hand when you point to winfun. Then, the unavailable pointer appears in the area in which winfun is unable to perform an action. Finally, the arrow pointer appears when winfun reaches a folder. In a few moments, winfun disappears from the right pane.

  NOTE: *Be sure that My Folder is selected before you drop winfun onto it.*

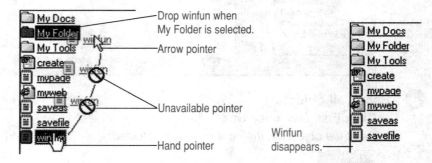

3 View winfun in My Folder:

- **Select** 📁 My Folder in the left pane.

  My Folder opens and winfun is among the files displayed in the right pane.

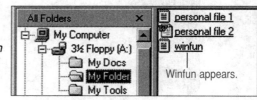

4 Move a file by dragging it onto an object in the left pane:

- **Drag and drop** 📄 winfun from the right pane onto Floppy (A:) in the left pane.

  Winfun disappears from the right pane.

- **Select** Floppy (A:).

  Winfun is back where it started, in Floppy (A:), and not in My Folder.

5 Move a file using cut and paste:

- **Right-click** 📄 saveas , then **click** Cut.

  The saveas icon is dimmed.

- **Right-click** 📁 My Folder in the left pane, then **click** Paste.

  Saveas disappears from the right pane.

- **Select** 📁 My Folder in the left pane.

  Saveas appears with the other objects in the right pane.

6 **Undo the Move procedure:**
- **Select** the Floppy (A:) folder.
- **Right-click** the right pane workspace, then **click** <u>U</u>ndo Move.
  Saveas reappears at the bottom of the list in the right pane.
- **Arrange** the icons in the right pane by name.
  Saveas is placed alphabetically in the list.

7 **Move a folder and its contents:**
NOTE: You can use several methods to perform this action. You can:
— Drag a folder in the left pane to another folder in the left pane.
— Drag a folder in the right pane to another folder in the right pane.
— Drag a folder in the right pane to a folder in the left pane.
— Use the cut-and-paste method to move a folder and its contents.
In this step, however, you are instructed use only the second method.

- **Drag and drop** 📁 <u>My Folder</u> in the right pane onto 📁 <u>My Docs</u> in the left pane.

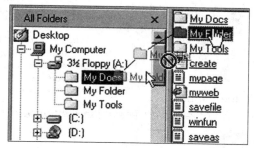

My Docs appears with a plus sign (+) beside it since it now contains a folder.

Plus sign

- **Expand** 📁 <u>My Docs</u>.
  My Folder is a subfolder of the My Docs folder:

My Folder, a subfolder of My Docs.

My Folder disappears.

- **Select** 📁 <u>My Folder</u>.
  The documents in My Folder appear in the right pane:

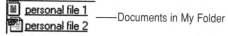
—Documents in My Folder

- **Right-click** the right pane workspace, then **click** <u>U</u>ndo Move.
  The objects in My Folder are still displayed in the right pane.
- **Select** the Floppy (A:) folder.
  The objects in the top level of drive A: are displayed in the right pane. (See Topic 23, A Look at Structure.)

8
- **Exit** Windows Explorer and **remove** DUPLICATE DATA DISK 1, or **go on** to Exercise 99.

EXERCISE 99 • Copy Objects

To transfer a copy of an object from one location to another, leaving the original object intact in its original location.

📖 Terms and Notes

Ways to Copy Objects

Copy works the same in any of the View modes. There are many other variables when copying, however, for example, you can:

- Copy single or multiple objects.
- Copy a folder and its contents.
- Copy a file using the drag-and-drop method while pressing the Ctrl key.
- Copy a file using the copy-and-paste method with the shortcut menu.
- Copy a file using the copy-and-paste method with the Edit menu.
- Copy a file or folder using the Send To feature.
- Undo a Copy procedure.

⌨ Keyboard Steps to

Copy Objects
—FROM THE EXPLORER WINDOW—

1. **Select** the object(s) you want to copy. *(See Keyboard Steps, Exercise 95.)*

2. **Press** `Ctrl` + `C` (Copy).

3. **Select** the object into which you want to paste the copied object(s).

4. **Press** `Ctrl` + `V` (Paste).

Copy Objects to Drive A: (Send To)
—FROM THE EXPLORER WINDOW—

1. **Select** the object(s) to copy that are not on drive A:. *(See Keyboard Steps, Exercise 95.)*

2. **Press** `Alt` + `F` (File).

3. **Press** `T` (Send To).

4. **Press** `↕↔` (arrow keys) to select Floppy (A:).

5. **Press** `Enter`.

Undo Copy
—FROM THE EXPLORER WINDOW—

1. **Press** `Alt` + `E` (Edit).

2. **Press** `U` (Undo Copy).

3. **Press** `Y` (Yes).
OR

Press `Ctrl` + `Z` (Undo).

Begin with the desktop displayed and with no taskbar buttons on the taskbar.

1
- **Start** Windows Explorer.
- **View** objects in a list, then **turn off** Web Page view.
- **With** DUPLICATE DATA DISK 1 inserted, **select** the Floppy (A:) folder, then **expand** it.

2 Copy multiple files using drag and drop:
- **Select** both 📄 saveas and 📄 winfun .
- **Press** `Ctrl` while you **drag and drop** one of the selected files onto 📁 My Folder in the right pane. (The other file will follow.)

The Copying dialog box appears briefly and shows the files flying into My Folder. Notice that the original files also remain in the right pane.

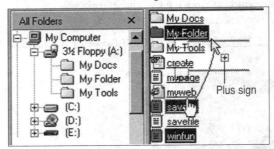

NOTES: *As soon as My Folder is highlighted, you can release the mouse button—be sure, however, to release the mouse button before you release the Ctrl key.*

When you copy, a plus sign (+) appears along with the arrow pointer to indicate that you are copying rather than moving the objects.

- **Select** 📁 My Folder in the left pane.

My Folder opens, displaying the copied files in the right pane:

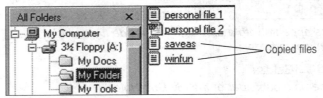

- **Select** the Floppy (A:) folder.

The files also remain intact in their original locations.

3 Copy a file by dragging it onto a folder in the left pane:
- **Press** `Ctrl` while you **drag and drop** 📄 winfun onto 📁 My Docs in the left pane.

The Copying dialog box appears briefly and shows winfun flying into the My Docs folder. Winfun also remains in the right pane.

- **Select** 📁 My Docs in the left pane.

Winfun appears at the bottom of the list in the right pane:

④ Copy a file using copy and paste:
- **Select** the Floppy (A:) folder.
- **Right-click** 📄 mypage , then **click** Copy.
  Nothing appears to happen, and mypage remains in the right pane.
- **Right-click** 📁 My Folder (in either pane), then **click** Paste.
- **Select** 📁 My Folder in the left pane.
  Mypage appears in the list of files in the right pane.

⑤ Undo the Copy procedure:
- **Right-click** the right pane workspace, then **click** Undo Copy.
  The Confirm File Delete dialog box appears.
- **Click** Yes .
  Mypage disappears from the right pane.
- **Select** the Floppy (A:) folder.
  Mypage remains in its original location.

⑥ Copy a folder and its contents:
NOTE: You can use several methods to perform this action. You can:
— Drag a folder in the left pane to another folder in the left pane while pressing Ctrl.
— Drag a folder in the right pane to another folder in the right pane while pressing Ctrl.
— Drag a folder in the right pane to a folder in the left pane while pressing Ctrl.
— Use the copy-and-paste procedure to copy the folder and its contents.
In this step, however, you are instructed to use only the third method.

- **Press** Ctrl while you **drag and drop** 📁 My Docs in the right pane
  onto 📁 My Folder in the left pane.
  My Folder appears with a plus sign (+) beside it since it now contains a folder. The original My Docs folder remains in the right pane.

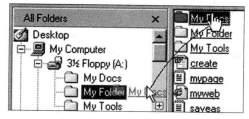

- **Expand** 📁 My Folder .
  My Docs is displayed under My Folder.
- **Select** the My Docs subfolder of My Folder.
  The documents in the My Docs subfolder appear in the right pane.

- **Select** the Floppy (A:) folder.
  The objects in the top level of drive A: are displayed in the right pane. (See Topic 23, A Look at Structure.)
- **Collapse** the Floppy (A:) folder.

Continued on the next page

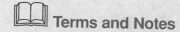

Terms and Notes

NOTES: When copying, always be sure to release the mouse button before you release the Ctrl key.

If you make a mistake when copying, remember that you can undo the last action by right-clicking the workspace and clicking Undo (Move, Copy, or Delete).

Continued from the previous page

7 **Copy a file to a different drive:**
- **Maximize** Windows Explorer, and **expand** the (C:) folder.
- **Scroll** the left pane, if necessary, until the Windows folder is visible.
- **Select** the Windows folder.
- **Scroll** the right pane until you find Triangles .

  NOTE: If you cannot find Triangles, use any other file with a bitmap icon .
- **Right-click** Triangles , then **click** Copy.
- **Scroll** the left pane, if necessary, until the Floppy (A:) folder is visible, but do not select it.
- **Right-click** the Floppy (A:) folder, then **click** Paste.

  The Copying dialog box appears briefly while Triangles is copied to the floppy disk in drive A:.
- **Select** the Floppy (A:) folder.

  Triangles appears in the list of files on drive A: in the right pane.

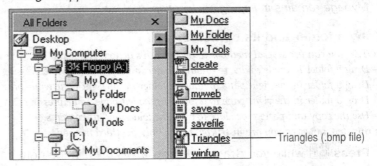
Triangles (.bmp file)

8 **Copy a file using the Send To command:**
- **Select** the Windows folder in the left pane. (You may need to scroll to find it.)
- **Right-click** Waves in the right pane.

  NOTE: If you cannot find Waves, use any other file with a bitmap icon .
- **Point** to Send To, then **click** 3½ Floppy (A:).

  The Copying dialog box appears briefly while Waves is copied to the floppy disk in drive A:. If the file is small, the Copying dialog box may not appear.
- **Select** the Floppy (A:) folder.

  Waves appears in the list of files on drive A: in the right pane.

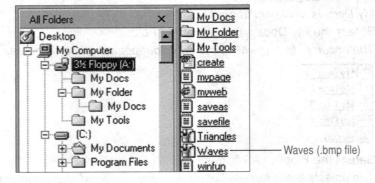
Waves (.bmp file)

9
- **Restore** Windows Explorer.
- **Exit** Windows Explorer.
- **Remove** DUPLICATE DATA DISK 1 or **go on** to Exercise 100.

Begin with the desktop displayed and with no taskbar buttons on the taskbar.

1
- **Start** Windows Explorer.
- **View** objects in a list, then **turn off** Web Page view.
- **With** DUPLICATE DATA DISK 1 inserted, **select** the Floppy (A:) folder, then **expand** it.
- **Expand** 📁 My Folder.

  The screen is similar to the illustration at the bottom of the previous page.

2 **Delete multiple files using the Delete key:**
- **Select** both 🎵 Triangles and 🎵 Waves in the right pane.

  NOTE: If you had to select files other than Triangles and Waves in steps and 7 and 8 on the previous page, select those files again here.
- **Press** Del.

  The Confirm Multiple File Delete dialog box appears:

- **Click** Yes.

  The Deleting dialog box appears briefly, and the two files are deleted.

3 **Delete a file using the shortcut menu:**
- **Select** 📁 My Docs immediately under Floppy (A:) in the left pane.
- **Right-click** 📄 winfun, **click** Delete, then **click** Yes.

  Winfun disappears from the right pane.

4 **Delete a folder and its contents:**
- **Right-click** 📁 My Docs which is a subfolder of 📁 My Folder (not the one in the right pane or the one that is a subfolder of Floppy [A:]).
- **Click** Delete, then **click** Yes.

  The folder and its contents are deleted. My Folder no longer has a plus sign (+) beside it.

5 **Delete multiple files using the shortcut menu:**
- **Select** 📁 My Folder in the left pane.
- **Select** both 📄 saveas and 📄 winfun in the right pane.
- **Right-click** one of the selected files, **click** Delete, then **click** Yes.

  The Deleting dialog box appears briefly, and the two files are deleted.
- **Select** the Floppy (A:) folder.

  A screen similar to the illustration below appears.

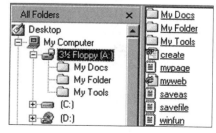

6
- **Exit** Windows Explorer.
- **Remove** DUPLICATE DATA DISK 1 or **go on** to Exercise 101.

To remove a file or folder from a disk.

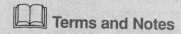 **Terms and Notes**

NOTE: When you delete objects on a floppy disk drive, they do not automatically go into the Recycle Bin as they do when you "delete" objects on the desktop or on the hard disk (see Exercise 87—Use the Recycle Bin). Because of this, you cannot use the Undo feature to restore deleted files on a floppy disk (see Exercise 86—Undo an Action).

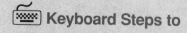 **Keyboard Steps to**

Delete Objects

—FROM THE EXPLORER WINDOW—

1. **Select** the object(s) you want to delete. *(See Keyboard Steps, Exercise 95.)*
2. **Press** Delete.
   The Confirm File (or Folder) Delete dialog box appears.
3. **Press** Enter.

Windows Explorer

Tasks Reviewed:
- Start Windows Explorer
- Resize Windows Explorer Panes
- Expand and Collapse a Folder
- Select an Object in the Left Pane
- Browse Your Data Disk
- Copy a Floppy Disk
- Select Objects in the Right Pane
- Invert Selection
- Select All Objects
- Move Objects
- Copy Objects
- Delete Objects

NOTE: You may need to scroll to locate objects in this exercise.

Begin with the desktop displayed and with no taskbar buttons on the taskbar.

In this exercise, you will need DATA DISK 2 and a blank, formatted disk that matches DATA DISK 2 in size and density.

1
- **Start** Windows Explorer by right-clicking the Start button, then **exit** Windows Explorer.
- **Start** Windows Explorer by right-clicking the My Computer icon, then **exit** Windows Explorer.
- **Start** Windows Explorer using the Programs menu.

2
- **Resize** Explorer's left pane to about one inch wide.
- **Resize** Explorer's left pane until the bottom scroll bar disappears.
- **Resize** Explorer's left pane to about its original width.
- **Exit** Windows Explorer.

3
- **Start** Windows Explorer by right-clicking the My Computer icon.
- **Maximize** the Windows Explorer window, then **turn off** Web Page view.
- **Expand** the C: folder.
- **Expand** the Windows folder.
- **Expand** the Start Menu folder.
- **Expand** the Programs folder.
- **Expand** the Accessories folder.
- **Collapse** the Accessories folder.
- **Collapse** the Programs folder.

4
- **View** objects in the right pane as large icons.
- **Select** the Start Menu folder, then **collapse** it.
- **Select** the Windows folder, then **collapse** it.
- **Select** the (C:) folder, then **collapse** it.
- **Restore** and then **exit** Windows Explorer.

5
- **Start** Windows Explorer by right-clicking the My Computer icon.
- **Insert** DATA DISK 2 in drive A:.
- **View** objects in the right pane in a list.
- **Expand** the Floppy (A:) folder.
- **Select** the Floppy (A:) folder and **notice** the contents of Floppy (A:) in the right pane.

The remainder of this exercise may not work as designed if the folders and files on your DATA DISK 2 do not match those in the following illustrations.

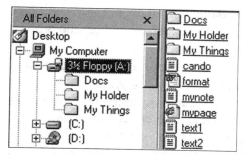

- **Select** the Docs folder in the left pane and **notice** its contents in the right pane:

- **Select** the My Holder folder in the left pane and **notice** its contents in the right pane:

- **Select** the My Things folder in the left pane and **notice** its contents in the right pane:

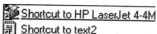

6
- **Label** your blank, formatted disk: DUPLICATE DATA DISK 2.
- **Write protect** DATA DISK 2.
- **Copy** DATA DISK 2 to DUPLICATE DATA DISK 2.
- **Close** the Copy Disk dialog box, then **exit** Windows Explorer.
- **Leave** DUPLICATE DATA DISK 2 in drive A:.

7
- **Start** Windows Explorer by right-clicking the My Computer icon.
- **Select** the Floppy (A:) folder, then **expand** it.
- **View** objects in the right pane in a list.
- **Select** text1, then **click** the workspace to deselect it.
- **Select** adjoining objects, My Things through text1.
- **Deselect** the objects by clicking the workspace.
- **Select** non-adjoining objects, the Docs folder, cando, and mynote.
- **Deselect** the objects.
- **Drag** the pointer to select any adjoining objects.
- **Deselect** the objects.

8
- **Select** non-adjoining objects, format and text2.
- **Invert** the selection, then **deselect** the objects.

9
- **Select** all objects.
- **Deselect** only the My Holder folder and mypage.
- **Deselect** the remaining objects.

Continued on the next page

- **Move** <u>cando</u> to the My Holder folder in the right pane using drag and drop.
- **Select** the My Holder folder in the left pane.
- **Move** <u>cando</u> to the Floppy (A:) folder using drag and drop.
- **Select** the Floppy (A:) folder.
- **Move** <u>mypage</u> to the My Holder folder using cut and paste.
- **Undo** the move, then **arrange** the icons by name.
- **Move** the Docs folder in the right pane to the My Holder folder in the left pane using either drag and drop *or* cut and paste.
- **Expand** the My Holder folder in the left pane.
- **Select** the Docs folder in the left pane, then **select** the Floppy (A:) folder.
- **Undo** the move, then **arrange** the icons by name.

NOTE: *Remember to press the Ctrl key when you use drag and drop to copy.*
- **Select** <u>mynote</u> and <u>text1</u>.
- **Copy** the selected files to the My Holder folder using drag and drop.
- **Select** the My Holder folder in the left pane to **view** the copied files.
- **Select** the Floppy (A:) folder.
- **Copy** <u>mypage</u> to the Docs folder using drag and drop.
- **Select** the Docs folder and **view** the copied file.
- **Select** the Floppy (A:) folder.
- **Undo** the copy in the right pane.
- **Copy** the Docs folder to the My Holder folder using copy and paste.
- **Expand** the My Holder folder, then **select** the Docs folder and **view** the files.
- **Select** the Floppy (A:) folder.
- **Maximize** Windows Explorer, **expand** the (C:) folder, then **select** the Windows folder.
- **Copy** *Tiles* to the Floppy (A:) folder using the Send To command.
- **Copy** *Pinstripe* to the Floppy (A:) folder using copy and paste.
- **Collapse** the (C:) folder.
- **Select** the Floppy (A:) folder.

- **Select** *Pinstripe* and *Tiles* in the right pane.
- **Delete** the selected files using the Delete key.
- **Using** the shortcut menu, **delete** the Docs folder which is a subfolder of My Holder (not the Docs folder that is in the right pane or the one that is a subfolder of Floppy [A:]).
- **Select** the My Holder folder in the left pane.
- **Select** <u>mynote</u> and <u>text1</u>.
- **Delete** the selected files using the shortcut menu.
- **Select** the Floppy (A:) folder.
  DUPLICATE DATA DISK 2 should contain the same folders and files that it did at the beginning of this exercise.

- **Exit** Windows Explorer and **remove** DUPLICATE DATA DISK 2.

Lessons Eight–Eleven Worksheet (9) is on page 309.

Lesson Nine
More Windows Explorer

Table of Contents

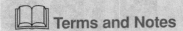

📖 Terms and Notes

associated file
A file that has been identified as belonging to a certain program, such as .txt with Notepad, .bmp with Paint, or .doc with Microsoft Word. When you open an associated file, the program related to that file opens automatically.

filename extension
The period and, usually but not always, three characters at the end of a filename (for example, .doc, .txt, .gif). Also called *file extension*.

Two File Options Produce Notable Changes

There are two advanced file options that change the way files and folders are viewed. One, *Hide file extension for known file types*, is discussed below; the other, *Hidden files*, is discussed on the next page. Changing these options has the potential to cause serious problems. The View tab of the Folders Options dialog box is where you change them.

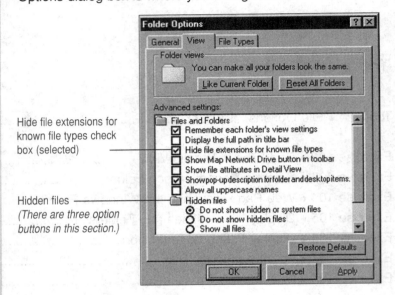

Hide file extensions for known file types check box (selected)

Hidden files
(There are three option buttons in this section.)

Hide File Extensions for Known File Types

When selected, the *Hide file extensions for known file types* check box hides most filename extensions. (This is the default setting.)

As discussed in Topic 10—Program File Types, filename extensions associate a document file with a specific program. While the computer system must use filename extensions to identify document types, you may prefer to use program icons to identify document types. Some users like to display filename extensions; others feel filename extensions just add clutter.

This is how the filename appears when filename extensions are hidden.

📄 winfun——No filename extension

This is how the filename appears when filename extensions are not hidden.

📄 winfun.txt——filename extension

Deselecting the *Hide file extensions for known file types* check box can affect the results of the exercises in this book where you rename files. If you rename a file when this option is selected, Windows 98 automatically adds the correct filename extension. If, however, this check box is deselected, you must provide the filename extension for the renamed file. If you do not provide the filename extension (or if you change it), a dialog box warns you that the file may become unusable.

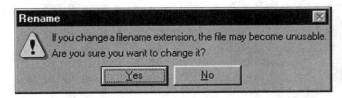

Hidden Files

The **Hidden files** feature is located in the View tab of the Folder Options dialog box. One of the following Hidden files option buttons must be selected:

- Do not show hidden or system files
  Keeps you from accidentally changing or deleting system files and folders. Reduces clutter in your folder windows and in Windows Explorer.
- Do not show hidden files
  Very similar to the option above because most hidden files are system files. However, this option may show some system files, and it allows you to hide files that you apply the Hidden attribute to.
- Show all files
  Specifies that all files and folders, even hidden and system files, appear in your folder windows and in Windows Explorer.

The default for hidden files is the *Do not show hidden or system files* option button.

Certain folders that are shipped with Windows 98 come with the Hidden attribute selected. These folders, which are used by Windows 98, are best left hidden. When displayed, hidden and system files are exposed to the possibility of being deleted accidentally.

Hidden folders and files will not appear in folder windows or in Windows Explorer unless you select the *Show all files* option button. To show all files:

- Click the Start button, point to Settings, then click Folder Options.
- Click the View tab, select Show all files, then click the OK button.

You can easily identify files and folders that have the Hidden attribute selected because their icons appear dimmed.

You may want to use the Hidden attribute for some of your personal folders and/or files. To change the Hidden attribute:

- Right-click a file or folder, click Properties, then click the General tab.
- Click the Hidden check box to select or deselect the option as desired.
- Click the OK button.

Below is the Spool Properties dialog box with the Hidden check box selected.

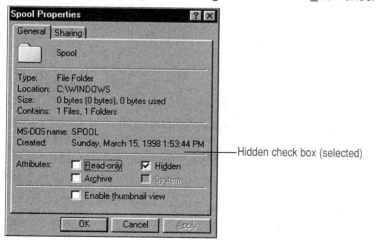

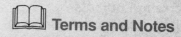
attribute
A characteristic (such as read-only, archive, hidden, or system) that changes how a file or folder can be used or displayed.

hidden files
Files and/or folders to which the Hidden attribute has been applied.

To arrange objects by clicking column headings in Details view. To adjust column widths.

 Terms and Notes

sort

When you arrange icons using the Uiew menu or the shortcut menu, you can sort files only from A-Z or 0-9 (ascending). When you arrange icons using column headings, however, you can sort files from Z-A or 9-0 (descending) as well as in ascending order.

NOTE: See Exercise 46, Arrange Icons, to sort objects using other methods (a shortcut menu or the Uiew menu).

Begin with the desktop displayed and with no taskbar buttons on the taskbar.

1
- **Start** Windows Explorer using the My Computer icon, then **maximize** the Explorer window.
- **Insert** DUPLICATE DATA DISK 1 into drive A:, and **select** the Floppy (A:) folder.
- **Turn off** Web Page view, if it's not already off (review, Exercise 41).
- **View** objects in Details view.
  The top of the left and right panes should look similar to this:

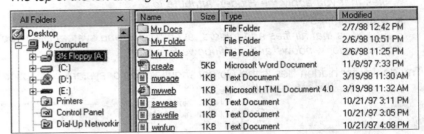

All Folders	X		Name	Size	Type	Modified
Desktop			My Docs		File Folder	2/7/98 12:42 PM
My Computer			My Folder		File Folder	2/6/98 10:51 PM
3½ Floppy (A:)			My Tools		File Folder	2/6/98 11:25 PM
(C:)			create	5KB	Microsoft Word Document	11/8/97 7:33 PM
(D:)			mypage	1KB	Text Document	3/19/98 11:30 AM
(E:)			myweb	1KB	Microsoft HTML Document 4.0	3/19/98 11:32 AM
Printers			saveas	1KB	Text Document	10/21/97 3:11 PM
Control Panel			savefile	1KB	Text Document	10/21/97 3:05 PM
Dial-Up Networkir			winfun	1KB	Text Document	10/21/97 4:08 PM

2 **Sort files by filename in descending order (Z to A):**
- **Click** Name two or three times.
- **Stop** when <u>winfun</u> is at the top of the list of objects.

Name	Size	Type	Modified
winfun	1KB	Text Document	10/21/97 4:08 PM
savefile	1KB	Text Document	10/21/97 3:05 PM
saveas	1KB	Text Document	10/21/97 3:11 PM
myweb	1KB	Microsoft HTML Doc...	3/19/98 11:32 AM
mypage	1KB	Text Document	3/19/98 11:30 AM
create	5KB	Microsoft Word Docu...	11/8/97 7:33 PM
My Tools		File Folder	2/6/98 11:25 PM
My Folder		File Folder	2/6/98 10:51 PM
My Docs		File Folder	2/7/98 12:42 PM

NOTE: Folders are grouped separately from files. Folders are shown together either at the top or at the bottom of the list of objects.

3 **Sort files by type in ascending order (A to Z):**
- **Click** Type two or three times.
- **Stop** when the folders are at the top of the list of objects.

Name	Size	Type	Modified
My Docs		File Folder	2/7/98 12:42 PM
My Folder		File Folder	2/6/98 10:51 PM
My Tools		File Folder	2/6/98 11:25 PM
myweb	1KB	Microsoft HTML Doc...	3/19/98 11:32 AM
create	5KB	Microsoft Word Docu...	11/8/97 7:33 PM
mypage	1KB	Text Document	3/19/98 11:30 AM
saveas	1KB	Text Document	10/21/97 3:11 PM
savefile	1KB	Text Document	10/21/97 3:05 PM
winfun	1KB	Text Document	10/21/97 4:08 PM

4 **Sort files by date modified in descending order (oldest to newest):**
- **Click** Modified two or three times.
- **Stop** when the oldest modified date is at the top.

5 **Sort files by filename in ascending order (A to Z):**
- **Click** Name until the files are sorted from A to Z by name.

6 **Resize columns:**

- **Point** to the border between *Name* and *Size* in the column headings until the arrow pointer becomes a sizing pointer.

- **Drag** the sizing pointer until only the Name column heading is visible.

Name	Size	Type	Modified	
📁 M...		File Folder	2/7/98 12:42 PM	
📁 M...		File Folder	2/6/98 10:51 PM	
📁 M...		File Folder	2/6/98 11:25 PM	
📄 cr...	5KB	Microsoft Word Docu...	11/8/97 7:33 PM	
📄 m...	1KB	Text Document	3/19/98 11:30 AM	
📄 m...	1KB	Microsoft HTML Doc...	3/19/98 11:32 AM	

- **Drag** the border back until the Name column heading is about its previous size.

Name		Size	Type	Modified
📁 My Docs			File Folder	2/7/98 12:42 PM
📁 My Folder			File Folder	2/6/98 10:51 PM
📁 My Tools			File Folder	2/6/98 11:25 PM
📄 create		5KB	Microsoft Word Docu...	11/8/97 7:33 PM
📄 mypage		1KB	Text Document	3/19/98 11:30 AM

7 **Adjust columns to fit the widest column entry:**

- **Point** to the border between *Name* and *Size* in the column headings until the arrow pointer becomes a sizing pointer.

- **Double-click** the border to adjust the column to fit the widest column entry.

The Name column adjusts to fit the widest column entry.

WITH THE SIZING POINTER VISIBLE:

- **Double-click** the right border of the Size heading.

The Size column adjusts to fit the widest column entry.

- **Double-click** the right border of the Type heading.

The Type column adjusts to fit the widest column entry.

- **Double-click** the right border of the Modified heading.

All of the columns are adjusted to fit their widest column entries.

Name	Size	Type	Modified
📁 My Docs		File Folder	2/7/98 12:42 PM
📁 My Folder		File Folder	2/6/98 10:51 PM
📁 My Tools		File Folder	2/6/98 11:25 PM
📄 create	5KB	Microsoft Word Document	11/8/97 7:33 PM
📄 mypage	1KB	Text Document	3/19/98 11:30 AM
📄 myweb	1KB	Microsoft HTML Document 4.0	3/19/98 11:32 AM
📄 saveas	1KB	Text Document	10/21/97 3:11 PM
📄 savefile	1KB	Text Document	10/21/97 3:05 PM
📄 winfun	1KB	Text Document	10/21/97 4:08 PM

8
- **Exit** Windows Explorer and **remove** DUPLICATE DATA DISK 1, or **go on** to Exercise 103.

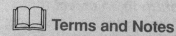
Terms and Notes

sizing pointer
The arrow pointer becomes a double-headed arrow when you point to a sizing handle or certain borders. The sizing pointer is used to size a window or the taskbar.

EXERCISE 103 • Select a Recently Used Folder

To return to an object that has been selected since you last opened Windows Explorer.

 Terms and Notes

NOTES: See Exercise 36, Use Back, Forward, and Up Buttons. These buttons are also available in Windows Explorer.

Also, the File menu in folder windows displays a list of recently selected folders just as it does in Windows Explorer.

Begin with the desktop displayed and with no taskbar buttons on the taskbar.

1
- **Start** Windows Explorer using the My Computer icon, then **maximize** the Explorer window.
- **Insert** DUPLICATE DATA DISK 1 into drive A:.
- **View** objects as large icons, then **turn off** Web Page view.

2 **Look at the recently used folder list on the File menu:**
- **Click** File, **look** at the menu, then **close** it.
  The recently used folder list on the File menu shows that My Computer *is selected:*

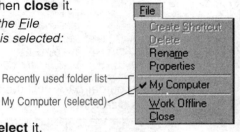

Recently used folder list
My Computer (selected)

- **Expand** the (C:) folder, then **select** it.
- **Click** File, **look** at the menu, then **close** it.
  The recently used folder list on the File menu shows that (C:) is selected. My Computer remains on the File menu.

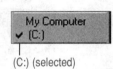

(C:) (selected)

- **Expand** the Windows folder, then **select** it.
- **Expand** the Start Menu folder, then **select** it.
- **Scroll** to the top of the left pane.
- **Expand** and **select** the Floppy (A:) folder.
- **Select** the My Docs folder.
- **Click** File, **look** at the menu, then **close** it.
  The recently used folder list on the File menu displays a list of the objects you have selected since you opened Windows Explorer.

My Docs (selected)

3 **Select a recently used folder (or object) from the File menu:**
- **Click** Start Menu (on the recently used folder list on the File menu).
  The left pane displays the Start Menu folder; it is selected (it may not be highlighted, but notice that the folder is open) and the right pane displays the contents of the Start Menu folder.
- **Click** File, then **click** My Docs.
  My Docs is selected and its contents are displayed in the right pane.
- **Click** File, then **click** Windows.
  Windows is selected and its contents are displayed in the right pane.

4 **Clear the recently used folder list on the File menu:**
- **Exit** Windows Explorer, then **start** Windows Explorer using the My Computer desktop icon.
- **Click** File.
  My Computer is the only item in the recently used folder list on the File menu, and it is selected.

5
- **Exit** Windows Explorer and **remove** DUPLICATE DATA DISK 1, or **go on** to Exercise 104.

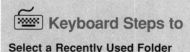 **Keyboard Steps to**

Select a Recently Used Folder

—FROM THE EXPLORER WINDOW—

1. **Press** `Alt` + `F` (File).

2. **Press** `↓` (down arrow) until you select the desired folder listed in the recently used folder list on the File menu.

3. **Press** `Enter`.

Begin with the desktop displayed and with no taskbar buttons on the taskbar.

1
- **Start** Windows Explorer using the My Computer icon, then **maximize** the Explorer window.
- **With** DUPLICATE DATA DISK 1 inserted, **select** Floppy (A:).
- **View** objects in a list.

2 **Turn on Web Page view:**
- **Click** View.
- IF *as Web Page* is selected, **click** outside the menu to close it; otherwise, **click** *as Web Page* to select it.

  Windows Explorer displays Web Page view with the selected object's name, a picture of the object, and clouds in the top-left corner of the right pane.

3 **Display selected object in Web Page view as only a name:**
- **Restore** Windows Explorer.
- IF Web Page view still displays the clouds, **size** the Explorer window smaller until the clouds disappear.

  Web Page view displays only the name of the selected object.

4 **Select the Windows folder:**
- **Expand** the (C:) folder, then **select** the Windows folder.

  A warning appears in the right pane instead of the contents of the Windows folder.

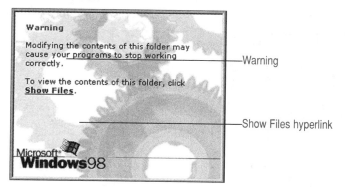

Warning

Show Files hyperlink

- **Click** **Show Files**.

  The contents of the Windows folder are now displayed in the right pane.
- **Collapse** the (C:) folder.
- **Click** View, then **click** *as Web Page* (to deselect it).
- **Expand** the (C:) folder, then **select** the Windows folder.

  The contents of the Windows folder are displayed in the right pane without a warning box. In addition, you are not required to click the Show Files hyperlink.

5
- **Exit** Windows Explorer and **remove** DUPLICATE DATA DISK 1.

To turn Web Page view on and off in Windows Explorer. To notice what happens when you select the Windows folder when Web Page view is enabled or disabled.

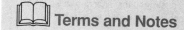

Terms and Notes

Web Page view
A Windows 98 feature in folder windows (and Windows Explorer) that displays:
- a picture of the selected item in the top-left corner of the workspace
- the selected item's name
- information about the selected item along the left side of the workspace

While this feature is turned on automatically in the Web-style mode, it can be used in Classic-style mode as well.

NOTES: If you select the Windows folder when Web Page view is turned on (not to be confused with the Web-style folder option), you get a warning about the danger of modifying the contents of the Windows folder rather than seeing the actual contents of the Windows folder. To see the contents of the Windows folder, click the blue underlined hyperlink, Show Files.

If you are using Windows 95 with Internet Explorer 4 installed, the Windows folder may open without first displaying the warning window with the Show Files hyperlink when you are in the Web Page view.

EXERCISE 105 • Display Hidden Files and Folders

To show files and folders that have the Hidden attribute selected.

 Terms and Notes

NOTE: See Topic 24, File Options.

attribute
A characteristic (such as read-only, archive, hidden, or system) that changes how a file or folder can be used or displayed.

hidden files
Files and/or folders to which the Hidden attribute has been applied.

NOTE: The default is to hide files and folders that have the Hidden attribute applied.

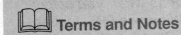 **Keyboard Steps to**

Show All Files

—FROM THE EXPLORER WINDOW—

1. Press **Alt** + **V** (View).
2. Press **O** (Folder Options).
3. Press **Ctrl** + **Tab** to display the View tab.
4. Press **Tab**, **Tab**.
   Files and Folders is highlighted.
5. Press **↓** (down arrow) until the *Show all files* option button is highlighted.
6. Press **Space** to select the *Show all files* option button.
7. Press **Tab**, **Tab** to select the OK button.
8. Press **Enter** to accept it.

Hide Hidden and System Files

—FROM THE EXPLORER WINDOW—

1. Press **Alt** + **V** (View).
2. Press **O** (Folder Options).
3. Press **Ctrl** + **Tab** to display the View tab.
4. Press **Tab**, **Tab**.
   Files and Folders is highlighted.
5. Press **↓** (down arrow) until the *Do not show hidden or system files* option button is highlighted.
6. Press **Space** to select the *Do not show hidden or system files* option button.
7. Press **Tab**, **Tab** to select the OK button.
8. Press **Enter** to accept it.

Begin with the desktop displayed and with no taskbar buttons on the taskbar.

1
- **Start** Windows Explorer using the My Computer icon, then **maximize** the Explorer window.
- **View** objects in a list, then **turn off** Web Page view.
- **Expand** the (C:) folder, then **expand** the Windows folder.
- **Select** the Windows folder.
- **Click** the right scroll arrow in the right pane once.
  A screen similar to the illustration below is displayed.

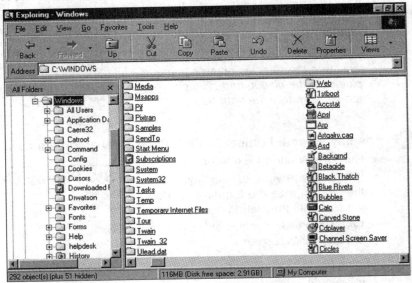

2 Display hidden and system folders and files:
- **Click** View, **click** Folder Options, then **click** the View tab.
  The Folder Options dialog box is displayed with the View tab selected.

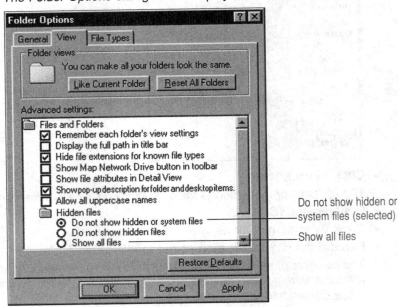

Do not show hidden or system files (selected)

Show all files

- **Click** the *Show all files* option button (to select it).
- **Click** [OK].

- IF the Refresh in Offline Mode dialog box appears, **click** 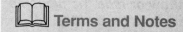.

  Explorer is "refreshed" and the previously hidden objects (system files and folders and files with the Hidden attribute selected) are now displayed. You may have to scroll the right pane to see the hidden and system files.

  Hidden files and folders, and system files and folders, are circled in the illustration below.

📖 **Terms and Notes**

NOTE: Once you choose to display all files and folders (as you do in step 2 of this exercise), you can easily identify hidden files and folders in the right pane of Explorer because their icons are dimmed.

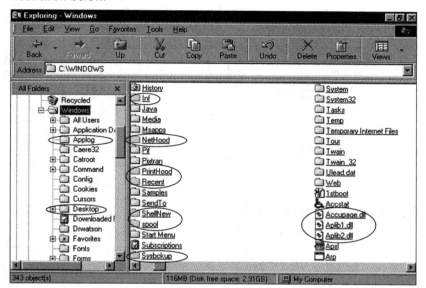

3 Open a folder with the Hidden attribute selected:
- **Click** the dimmed Inf folder in the right pane. (You may need to scroll to find it.)

  The Inf folder opens, and its files are displayed in the right pane.

- **Click** **Up** (the Up button) on the Standard toolbar to return to the Windows folder.

4 Look at **properties of a folder with the Hidden attribute selected:**
- **Right-click** the dimmed Inf folder in the right pane, then **click** P**r**operties.

  The Inf Properties dialog box opens. The Attributes section shows that the Hidden attribute is selected.

— Hidden check box (selected)

- **Close** the Inf Properties dialog box.

5 Do not show hidden or system files:
- **Click** **V**iew, **click** Folder **O**ptions, then **click** the View tab.
- **Click** the *Do not show hidden or system files* option button (to select it).

- **Click** OK .

  Windows Explorer is refreshed and appears without hidden objects. (See the top illustration on the previous page.)

- **Exit** Windows Explorer.

EXERCISE 106 • Display Filename Extensions

To show or hide the filename extensions for all files.

 Terms and Notes

NOTE: See Topic 14, Files and Filenames, and Topic 24, File Options.

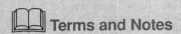 **Keyboard Steps to**

Display or Hide Filename Extensions

—FROM THE EXPLORER WINDOW—

1. **Press** `Alt` + `V` (View).

2. **Press** `O` (Folder Options).

3. **Press** `Ctrl` + `Tab` to display the View tab.

4. **Press** `Tab`, `Tab`.
   Files and Folders is highlighted.

5. **Press** `↓` (down arrow) until the *Hide file extensions for known file types* check box is highlighted.

6. **Complete** one of the following procedures:

   Display all filename extensions
   - IF the check box has a check mark in it,
     press `Space` to deselect the *Hide file extensions for known file types* check box; otherwise, **press** `Esc` to cancel the Folder Options dialog box.

   Hide filename extensions for known file types
   - IF the check box does not have a check mark in it, **press** `Space` to select the *Hide file extensions for known file types* check box; otherwise, **press** `Esc` to cancel the Folder Options dialog box.

7. **Press** `Tab`, `Tab` to select the OK button.

8. **Press** `Enter` to accept it.

Begin with the desktop displayed and with no taskbar buttons on the taskbar.

1
- **Start** Windows Explorer using the My Computer icon, then **maximize** the Explorer window.
- **Insert** DUPLICATE DATA DISK 1 into drive A: and **select** the Floppy (A:) folder.
- **View** objects as large icons, then **turn off** Web Page view.
  A screen similar to the illustration below appears.

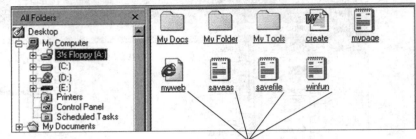

No filename extensions

2 **Display all filename extensions:**
- **Click** View, **click** Folder Options, then **click** the View tab.
  The Folder Options dialog box is displayed with the View tab selected.
- **Click** the *Hide file extensions for known file types* check box (to deselect it).
- **Click** OK .
  Windows Explorer is refreshed and the filename extensions are now displayed.

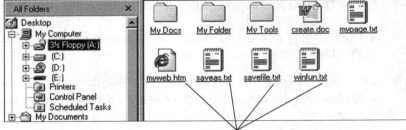

Filename extensions

3 **Hide filename extensions for known file types:**
- **Click** View, **click** Folder Options, then **click** the View tab.
- **Click** the *Hide file extensions for known file types* check box (to select it).
- **Click** OK .
  Windows Explorer is "refreshed" and appears without filename extensions for the known file types (see top illustration).
- **Exit** Windows Explorer and **remove** DUPLICATE DATA DISK 1.

Formatting a Floppy Disk

In this exercise, you will format DUPLICATE DATA DISK 1. Later, you can use the same procedure to format other disks. Before you format a disk, however, you need to identify the size and density of that disk. The most common disk size and density used for drive A: in computers today is 3½" HD (1.44 Mb). However, you may run across double-density disks and, perhaps, extra high-density disks.

3½" disks come in two standard densities:
- DD (double density)—720 Kb
- HD (high density)—1.44 Mb

Typically, 3½" disks that can be formatted to 1.44 Mb have two holes at the top while those that can be formatted to 720 Kb have only one hole.

Begin with the desktop displayed and with no taskbar buttons on the taskbar.

1
- **Start** Windows Explorer.
- **Turn on** Web Page view, if it's not already on.
- **Insert** DUPLICATE DATA DISK 1 into drive A:.

2 **Choose a format capacity for your drive A: disk:**
- **Right-click** the Floppy (A:) folder, then **click** For<u>m</u>at.
  The Format - 3½ Floppy (A:) *dialog box opens.*

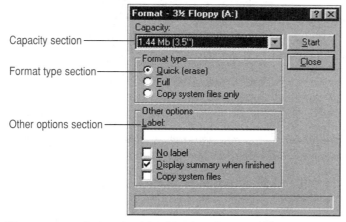

Capacity section

Format type section

Other options section

- IF you are using a double-density disk (720 Kb) (you probably are not), **click** the Ca<u>p</u>acity drop-down list box, then **click** 720 Kb (3.5").

3 **Select a format type:**

There are three format types. Below are explanations of what each one does:

—<u>Q</u>uick (erase)
*Removes all the files from a previously formatted disk. You should use this option only if you are sure that your disk is not damaged since this procedure does not scan the disk for **bad sectors**. This is the default setting.*

—<u>F</u>ull
Prepares a disk to store information, and scans the disk for bad sectors. Any files on the disk will be removed.

—Copy system files <u>o</u>nly
*Copies system files to a disk that is already formatted. This procedure does not erase the files already on the disk. Use this option to prepare a disk that can be used as a **startup disk** on drive A:.*

Continued on the next page

To prepare a floppy disk so that you can store data on it.

 Terms and Notes

bad sectors
Damaged areas on a disk that are marked as unusable when the disk is formatted. A few bad sectors do not necessarily make the entire disk unusable. However, a disk with bad sectors should not be used as a destination disk when copying a disk—nor should it be used to store important files.

floppy disk density
Density refers to the surface coating on a floppy disk; the closer together the particles on the disk, the higher the disk capacity. Typically, 3½" floppy disks come in two densities: DD (double density)—720 Kb and HD (high density)—1.44 Mb

startup disk
A disk that contains certain system files that create a system disk. It is a good safeguard to have a startup disk for drive A:. If the hard disk should have a problem, you can boot the computer using this floppy system disk. This is also known as a *bootable disk*.

Continued from the previous page

- **Click** the <u>F</u>ull option button (to select it).

Full —————
option button
(selected)

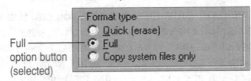

4 **Select desired Other options:**

There are three Other options. Below are explanations of what each one does:

—<u>N</u>o label

Specifies that you do not want to name the disk. If you do not check this box, you can name your disk in the <u>L</u>abel text box.

—<u>D</u>isplay summary when finished

Displays information about the disk after formatting is finished.

—Copy s<u>y</u>stem files

Copies system files to the disk after it is formatted.

- **Click** the <u>L</u>abel text box, then **type:** MY DISK #1
- **Click** the <u>D</u>isplay summary when finished check box (to select it).

The <u>D</u>isplay summary when finished check box should be the only option selected.

Label text box ————

Display summary
when finished check——
box (selected)

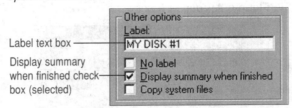

NOTES: You do not need to label your data disk. Many people prefer to select the <u>N</u>o label check box.

You can see a disk's label by looking at its Properties dialog box. Right-click the Floppy (A:) folder and click P<u>r</u>operties. (You can also change the disk's label in the Properties dialog box.)

5 **Start the Format procedure:**

- **Click** [Start] .

The formatting process begins; the bottom of the dialog box reports the computer's status and progress:

Status ————
Progress ————

When the format is complete, the Format Results - 3½ Floppy (A:) *dialog box appears:*

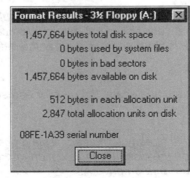

Keyboard Steps to

Format a Disk

—FROM THE EXPLORER WINDOW—

1. **Select** Floppy (A:). *(See Keyboard Steps for Exercise 92.)*

2. **Press** `Shift` + `F10` (shortcut menu).

    OR

    Press `▤` (the Application key).

3. **Press** `M` (For<u>m</u>at).
    The Format - 3½ Floppy (A:) dialog box opens.

4. **Select** desired capacity, if necessary:

    - **Press** `Alt` + `P` (Ca<u>p</u>acity).
    - **Press** `▲▼` (up or down arrow) to select the desired capacity.

5. **Select** desired format type from the following:

    - **Press** `Alt` + `Q` (<u>Q</u>uick [erase]).
    - **Press** `Alt` + `F` (<u>F</u>ull).
    - **Press** `Alt` + `O` (Copy system files <u>o</u>nly).

6. **Enter** a disk label, if desired:

    - **Press** `Alt` + `L` (<u>L</u>abel).
    - **Type** the desired label.

7. **Select** other options as desired:

    - **Press** `Alt` + `N` (<u>N</u>o label).
    - **Press** `Alt` + `D` (<u>D</u>isplay summary when finished).
    - **Press** `Alt` + `Y` (Copy s<u>y</u>stem files).

8. **Press** `Alt` + `S` (<u>S</u>tart).
    The dialog box reports the computer's status and progress.

9. **Press** `Enter` to activate the Close command button.

10. **Press** `Esc` to close the *Format Results - 3½ Floppy (A:)* dialog box.

6 **Complete the Format procedure:**

- **Click** [Close] (the Close button) in the Format Results - 3½ Floppy (A:) dialog box.
- **Click** [Close] (the Close button) in the Format - 3½ Floppy (A:) dialog box.
- **Select** the Floppy (A:) folder.
- **Notice** the contents of the Floppy (A:) folder in the right pane.

  Nothing appears in the right pane because all the files on the disk were erased when the disk was formatted.

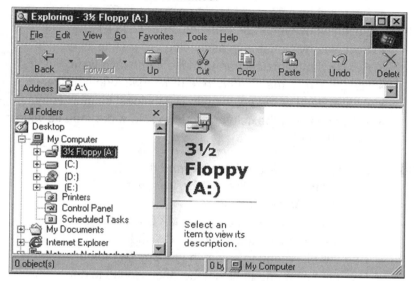

7 **Copy a floppy disk:**

- **Copy** DATA DISK 1 to DUPLICATE DATA DISK 1 (review, Exercise 94).

  The disk Copy procedure ends up with DUPLICATE DATA DISK 1 in drive A:.
- **Close** the Copy Disk dialog box.
- **View** objects as large icons.
- **Select** the Floppy (A:) folder.

  The contents of DATA DISK 1 have been copied to DUPLICATE DATA DISK 1 and are displayed in the right pane.

8 • **Exit** Windows Explorer and **remove** DUPLICATE DATA DISK 1.

More Windows Explorer

Tasks Reviewed:
- Sort Files in Details View
- Select a Recently Used Folder
- Web Page View and the Windows Folder
- Display Hidden Files and Folders
- Display Filename Extensions
- Format a Floppy Disk

Begin with the desktop displayed and with no taskbar buttons on the taskbar.

You will need DUPLICATE DATA DISK 2 (created in Exercise 101, Lesson Eight Practice) for this practice exercise.

- **Start** and **maximize** Windows Explorer using the My Computer icon.
- **Insert** DUPLICATE DATA DISK 2 into drive A:, and **select** the Floppy (A:) folder.
- **View** objects in Details view.
- **Sort** files by filename in descending order (Z to A).
- **Sort** files by date modified in descending order (oldest to newest).
- **Sort** files by type in ascending order (A to Z).
- **Sort** files by type in descending order (Z to A).
- **Sort** files by filename in ascending order (A to Z).
- **Resize** the Name column to make it one inch wide.
- **Resize** the Name column to return it to its original size.
- **Adjust** each of the columns to fit its widest column entry.
- **Adjust** each of the columns to be a little wider than its widest column entry.

- **Select** the (C:) folder, then **expand** it.
- **Select** the Program Files folder, then **expand** it.
- **Select** the Accessories folder.
- **Use** the File menu to select the My Computer folder.
- **Use** the File menu to select the (C:) folder.
- **Use** the File menu to select the Floppy (A:) folder.
- **Use** the File menu to select the Accessories folder.
- **Exit** Windows Explorer, then **start** Windows Explorer using the My Computer icon.
- **Click** File, and **look** at its recently used folder list.
  Only My Computer *appears in the recently used folder list on the File menu.*

- **Turn on** Web Page view, if necessary.
- **Select** and **expand** the (C:) folder, then **select** the Windows folder.
- **Click** the Show Files hyperlink, if necessary.
- **Turn off** Web Page view.
- **Select** the (C:) folder, then **select** the Windows folder.
- **Notice** that the right pane displays the folders and files in the Windows folder without first giving you a warning message.

- **View** objects in the right pane as a list.
- **Click** the right scroll arrow in the right pane once.
- **Expand** the Windows folder.
- **Notice** the folders and files.
- **Access** the View tab of the Folder Options dialog box.
- **Select** the *Show all files* option button.
- **Click** No .

- **Open** the Folder Options dialog box, **click** the View tab, **select** the *Do not show hidden or system files* option button, then **click** OK .
- **Notice** that some of the folders and files previously displayed are now hidden.

5
- **Select** the Floppy (A:) folder.
- **View** objects in the right pane as large icons.
- **Open** the Folder Options dialog box, **click** the View tab, **deselect** the *Hide file extensions for known file types* check box, then **click** OK .
- **Notice** the filename extensions that now appear in the right pane.
- **Open** the Folder Options dialog box, **click** the View tab, **select** the *Hide file extensions for known file types* check box, then **click** OK .
- **Notice** that the filename extensions have disappeared.

6
- **Format** DUPLICATE DATA DISK 2 using the *Full* format type. Using the Label text box, **label** your disk: My Disk #2
- **Close** the two dialog boxes when the format is complete.
- **Select** the Floppy (A:) folder and **notice** that there are no files visible in the right pane.
- **Restore** Windows Explorer.

7
- **Remove** DUPLICATE DATA DISK 2 and **insert** DATA DISK 2.
- **Select** the Floppy (A:) folder, and **notice** the files displayed.
- **Copy** DATA DISK 2 to the disk you just formatted, DUPLICATE DATA DISK 2.
- **Select** the Floppy (A:) folder, and **notice** the files displayed.
- **Exit** Windows Explorer and **remove** DUPLICATE DATA DISK 2.

Lessons Eight–Eleven Worksheet (9) is on page 309.

NEXT
LESSON

Lesson Ten
Finding Files

Table of Contents

TOPIC 25 • **Find Files and Folders**

📖 **Terms and Notes**

Find
A program that helps you locate files and
folders by using *search criteria* that you specify
for the files you want to find.

search criteria
Guidelines you define that tell the Find program
what file and folder characteristics to look for
when searching. For example, you can search
for all the files that contain the .doc filename
extension or all the files that were created in the
last month.

The Find Program

The **Find** program helps you locate files and folders; that is, it finds the folder (including the path to it) where the files and/or folders you are looking for reside. You can access Find in any of the following ways:

- on the Start menu
- on Windows Explorer's Tools menu
- by right-clicking the Start button, My Computer, or most other folder icons

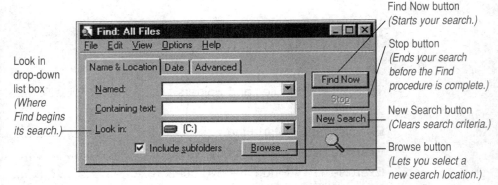

Look in
drop-down
list box
*(Where
Find begins
its search.)*

Find Now button
(Starts your search.)

Stop button
*(Ends your search
before the Find
procedure is complete.)*

New Search button
(Clears search criteria.)

Browse button
*(Lets you select a
new search location.)*

When you search for files, you will use **search criteria** (or a combination of several search criteria). When searching for files and folders, you can use any of the following as search criteria:

- filename (or partial filename), file location, or file contents
- date of file creation or last modification
- file type or file size

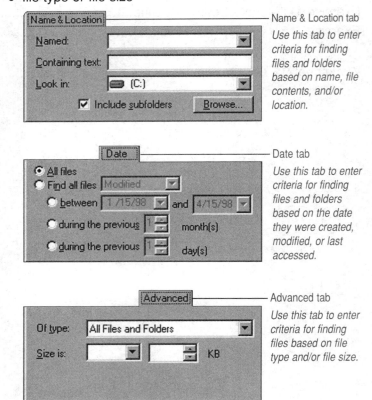

Name & Location tab
*Use this tab to enter
criteria for finding
files and folders
based on name, file
contents, and/or
location.*

Date tab
*Use this tab to enter
criteria for finding
files and folders
based on the date
they were created,
modified, or last
accessed.*

Advanced tab
*Use this tab to enter
criteria for finding
files based on file
type and/or file size.*

Browse for a Folder

Click the Browse button on the Name & Location tab to find the folder in which you want to begin your search. The Browse for Folder dialog box is organized like the left pane of Windows Explorer—you can expand and collapse folders to find the one you want. Select a folder and click the OK button to put that folder in the Find program's Look in drop-down list box.

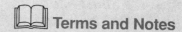

Terms and Notes

browse
To look at files, folders, disks, printers, programs, documents, and other objects on your computer system.

search results
The files and/or folders that meet the *search criteria* you specified. The search results appear in the workspace at the bottom of the Find program after you click the F̲ind Now command button.

Using Search Criteria

Finding a file can be as simple as typing a filename (or a partial filename) in the N̲amed text box and clicking the F̲ind Now button on the Name & Location tab. Or, it can be as complex as using one or more search criteria from each of the Find tabs shown on the previous page.

The illustration below displays the **search results** (files and folders) that you would find on DUPLICATE DATA DISK 1 in drive A: if you typed *my* in the N̲amed text box and then clicked the F̲ind Now button.

Search criteria

Named
(*My is part of a filename.*)

Look in
(*Tells Find to search on drive A:.*)

Search results
(*All files and folders meet the search criteria, that is, all contain* my *and all are located on drive A:.*)

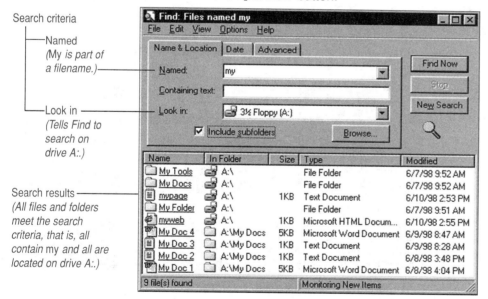

Once files and folders have been found, you can perform any of the basic file-management tasks shown in Topic 20, Documents. You can save search criteria and the results of a search.

To open the Find feature using different methods.

Begin with the desktop displayed and with no taskbar buttons on the taskbar.

1 **Start Find from the Start menu:**

- **Click** **Start**, **point** to Find, then **click** Files or Folders.
  The Find program opens.

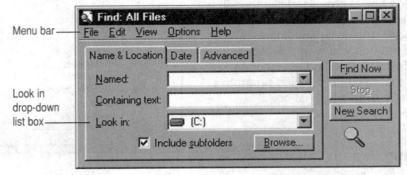

Menu bar

Look in drop-down list box

- **Exit** Find.

2 **Start Find from Windows Explorer:**

- **Click** **Start**, **point** to Programs, then **click** Windows Explorer.
- **Click** Tools, **point** to Find, then **click** Files or Folders.
  The Find program opens.

3 **Look at the Find menus:**

- **Click** the File menu to open it.
- **Point** to the remaining menus, examining each as it opens.

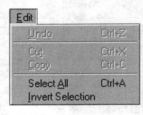

NOTE: When there is a results section, the File menu will have different options available, depending upon the selected object in the search results.

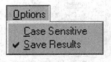

- **Exit** Find, then **exit** Windows Explorer.

4 **Start Find by right-clicking the Start button:**

- **Right-click** **Start**, then **click** Find.
  The Find program opens with C:\WINDOWS\Start Menu in the Look in drop-down list box.

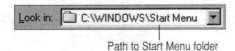

Path to Start Menu folder

NOTE: The last folder in the path (in this case, Start Menu) is the folder that Find searches.

Keyboard Steps to

Start Find

SHORTCUT: F3

—USING THE START MENU—

1. **Press** Ctrl + Esc (Start menu).

   OR

   Press ⊞ (the Windows key).

2. **Press** F (Find).

3. **Press** F (Files or Folders).

—USING THE START BUTTON—

1. **Press** Ctrl + Esc , Esc .

2. **Press** Shift + F10 .

   OR

   Press 🗒 (the Application key).

3. **Press** F (Find).

—FROM WINDOWS EXPLORER—

1. **Press** Alt + T (Tools).

2. **Press** F (Find).

3. **Press** F (Files or Folders).

—USING MY COMPUTER—

1. **Press** Ctrl + Esc , Esc .

2. **Press** Shift + Tab .

3. **Press** ◄► (arrow keys) to select My Computer.

4. **Press** Shift + F10 .

   OR

   Press 🗒 (the Application key).

5. **Press** F (Find).

⑤ Change the <u>L</u>ook in drop-down list box to (C:):
- **Click** the <u>L</u>ook in drop-down arrow.

  The drop-down list box opens.

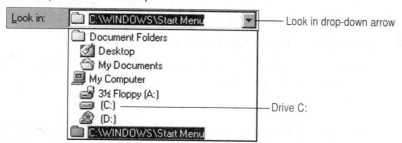
— Look in drop-down arrow

— Drive C:

- **Click** 🖴 (C:) .

  (C:) *now appears in the <u>L</u>ook in drop-down list box:*

- **Exit** Find.

⑥ Start Find by right-clicking My Computer:
- **Right-click** the My Computer icon, then **click** <u>F</u>ind.

  The Find program opens with My Computer *in the <u>L</u>ook in drop-down list box.*

- **Exit** Find.

⑦ Start Find by right-clicking a folder:
- **Start** Windows Explorer, then **expand** (C:).
- **Scroll** until you locate the Windows folder icon.
- **Right-click** the Windows folder icon, then **click** <u>F</u>ind.

  The Find program opens with the Windows folder in the <u>L</u>ook in drop-down list box.

  NOTE: When you start Find from a folder, your search will automatically begin with the selected folder.

- **Do not exit** Find.

⑧ Start Find by pressing the F3 key:
- **Switch** to Windows Explorer. (Click the Explorer window or its taskbar button.)
- **Select** the Program Files folder in the left column by clicking it.
- **Press** ▦ .

  The Find program opens with Program Files *in the <u>L</u>ook in drop-down list box. Two Find taskbar buttons now appear on the taskbar.*

⑨
- **Exit** Find, **exit** Windows Explorer, then **exit** the remaining Find program.

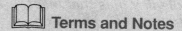
Terms and Notes

NOTE: You can have more than one Find program open at the same time.

EXERCISE 110 • Find Files by Name

To display files that meet search criteria based on filenames or partial filenames.

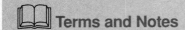 **Terms and Notes**

NOTE: *Folders are treated as files in the search results. Notice that the Find program status bar also includes folders in the number of "file(s) found."*

Begin with the desktop displayed and with no taskbar buttons on the taskbar.

1
- **Open** My Computer, **right-click** (C:), then **click** Find.
  The Find program opens with the cursor blinking in the Named text box and (C:) in the Look in drop-down list box.

2 **Use a filename as search criteria:**
- **Type:** Triangles in the Named drop-down list box, then **click** Find Now .
  The magnifying glass icon rotates as Find searches drive C:.

  The results of your search are displayed in the list box at the bottom of the Find program. Find locates the folder in which the file named Triangles is stored; it lists the file's approximate size, its file type, and the date last modified, as well as the number of file(s) found that contain Triangles in their name(s).

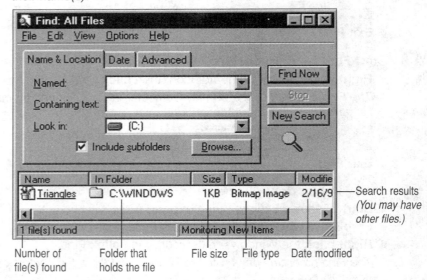

Search results *(You may have other files.)*

Number of file(s) found · Folder that holds the file · File size · File type · Date modified

- IF *Triangles* does not appear in the search results, **repeat** step 2, this time typing Pinstripe or Stitches instead of *Triangles*.
- **Exit** Find, but **leave** the My Computer folder window open.

3 **Search without search criteria:**
- **Insert** DUPLICATE DATA DISK 1 into drive A:.
- **Right-click** the Floppy (A:) icon in the My Computer folder window, then **click** Find.
  Find opens with Floppy (A:) in the Look in drop-down list box.
- **Click** Find Now , then **maximize** Find.
  Find displays all the files (and folders) on DUPLICATE DATA DISK 1 in the search results. The left end of the status bar informs you that 20 file(s) were found.
- **Adjust** the column widths so you can see all the search results (review, Exercise 102, steps 6 and 7).
- **Scroll** through the files and **notice** all the files on your disk.

4 **Use part of a filename as search criteria:**
- **Click** the Named drop-down list box.
- **Type:** my then **click** Find Now .

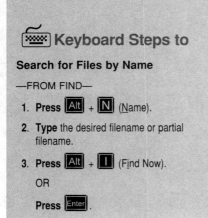 **Keyboard Steps to**

Search for Files by Name

—FROM FIND—

1. **Press** Alt + N (Name).
2. **Type** the desired filename or partial filename.
3. **Press** Alt + I (Find Now).
   OR
   Press Enter .

Nine files are displayed.

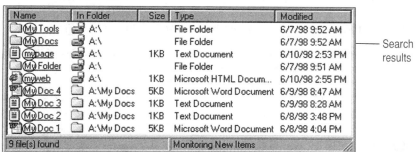

— Search results

5 **Change the search criteria:**

- **Click** the Named drop-down list box, **type:** doc then **click** [Find Now].
  The search results show that seven files meet the search criteria. Of these, five files contain the letters doc *in their names (circled below), while the remaining two files do not.*

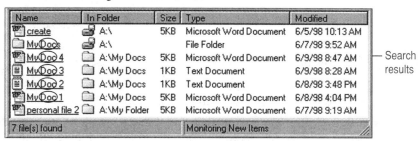

— Search results

- **Why** are there two filenames without *doc* in them?
  The two filenames really do have doc in them. Remember that WordPad automatically puts the .doc extension on all files you save. Find recognizes filename extensions even though they are probably hidden. (See Exercise 106, Display Filename Extensions.)

6 **Search for a specific file:**

- **Click** the Named drop-down list box, **type:** myweb and **click** [Find Now].
  The search results display the myweb file.

- **Click** the Named list box, **type:** my doc 4 and **click** [Find Now].
  The seach results display 12 files.
  NOTE: *If the search criteria contains one or more space(s), Find searches for all files that contain any one part of the search criteria. You must use quotation marks around long filenames in order for Find to see it as a single filename.*

7 **Use a long filename as search criteria:**

- **Click** the Named list box, **type:** "my doc 4" then **click** [Find Now].
  A message in the search results says: There are no items to show in this view. *When you enclose a long filename in quotation marks, you must include its filename extension.*

- **Click** the Named list box, **type:** "my doc 4.doc" then **click** [Find Now].
  My Doc 4 is displayed in the search results:

Name	In Folder	Size	Type	Modified
My Doc 4	A:\My Docs	5KB	Microsoft Word Document	2/3/98 11:39 PM

8 - **Exit** Find, then **close** the My Computer folder window.
- **Remove** DUPLICATE DATA DISK 1 or **go on** to Exercise 111.

EXERCISE 111 • Find Files by Location

To display files that meet search criteria based on the location of those files.

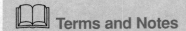 **Terms and Notes**

NOTE: To ensure a successful search, the location in the Look in drop-down list box must include the folder containing the file you are looking for.

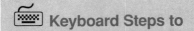 **Keyboard Steps to**

Change the Search Location

—FROM FIND—

Change the drive or folder:

1. Press **Alt** + **L** (Look in).

2. Press **Alt** + **↓** (down arrow) to open the list box.

3. Press **↑↓** (up or down arrow) to highlight the desired location.

4. Press **Enter**.

Browse for a folder to search:

1. Press **Alt** + **B** (Browse).

2. Press **↑↓** (up or down arrow) to highlight the desired folder.

   • Press **→** (right arrow) to expand a folder.

   • Press **←** (left arrow) to collapse a folder.

3. **Continue** step 2 until you select the desired folder to search.

4. Press **Enter**.

Do not search subfolders:

Press **Alt** + **S** (Include subfolders) to deselect the check box.

Start a new search (reset Find to its defaults):

1. Press **Alt** + **W** (New Search).

2. Press **Enter**.

Begin with the desktop displayed and with no taskbar buttons on the taskbar.

1
• **Open** My Computer, **right-click** (C:), then **click** Find.

• **Type:** Triangles in the Named drop-down list box, then **click** Find Now.
  NOTE: IF Triangles did not appear in the search results for Exercise 110, type Pinstripe *or* Stitches *again instead of* Triangles.

• **Notice** the amount of time it takes for Find to search all of drive C: for files that contain all or part of the word *Triangles* in their names.

2 **Browse for a new location:**

• **Click** Browse... .
  The Browse for Folder dialog box opens:

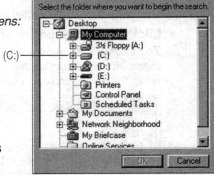

(C:) ──

• **Expand** (C:), **select** the Windows folder, then **click** OK .
  C:\WINDOWS *appears in the Look in drop-down list box.*

• **Click** Find Now and **notice** that it takes less time for Find to search since the program is searching only in the Windows folder.

3 **Change the Look in drop-down list box to Floppy (A:):**
• **With** DUPLICATE DATA DISK 1 inserted, **click** the Look in drop-down arrow.
  The drop-down list box opens:

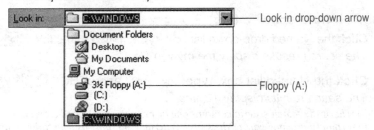

— Look in drop-down arrow

— Floppy (A:)

• **Click** 3½ Floppy (A:) , then **click** Find Now .
  Because you told Find to look in a location that does not contain Triangles, *a message in the search results says:* There are no items to show in this view.

4 **Search for files in Floppy (A:) and its subfolders:**
NOTE: When you start Find, the Include subfolders *check box in the Name & Location tab is selected by default. Therefore, Find automatically searches the folder or drive in the Look in drop-down list box as well as all the subfolders of that folder or drive.*

• **Click** the Named drop-down list box, **type:** my and **press** Enter.
  Nine files are displayed. (See the illustration at the top of the previous page.)

- **Maximize** Find and **look** at the files.

5 Search without including subfolders:

- **Click** the Include subfolders check box (located under the Look in drop-down list box) to deselect it.

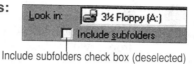

Include subfolders check box (deselected)

- **Click** `Find Now`.

Now only five files are displayed since no subfolders are searched.

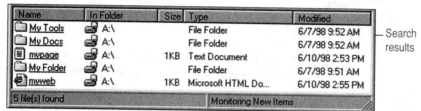

— Search results

Name	In Folder	Size	Type	Modified
My Tools	A:\		File Folder	6/7/98 9:52 AM
My Docs	A:\		File Folder	6/7/98 9:52 AM
mypage	A:\	1KB	Text Document	6/10/98 2:53 PM
My Folder	A:\		File Folder	6/7/98 9:51 AM
myweb	A:\	1KB	Microsoft HTML Do...	6/10/98 2:55 PM

5 file(s) found   Monitoring New Items

- **Restore** Find.

6 Start a new search (reset Find to its defaults):

- **Click** `New Search`.

The following dialog box appears:

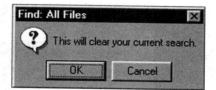

Find: All Files

This will clear your current search.

OK   Cancel

- **Click** `OK`.

The Find program is cleared. Find now appears without a search results workspace, with Document Folders displayed in the Look in drop-down list box, and with the Include subfolders check box selected.

Named drop-down list box (cleared)

Document Folders

Include subfolders check box (selected)

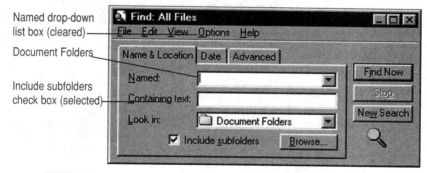

Find: All Files

File Edit View Options Help

Name & Location | Date | Advanced

Named: [   ]   Find Now

Containing text: [   ]   Stop

Look in: [Document Folders]   New Search

☑ Include subfolders   Browse...

- **Click** `Find Now`.
- **Maximize** Find, then **double-click** the right border of the *In Folder* column heading to adjust the column to fit the widest column entry.
- **Scroll** through the files.

7 Use previous Find settings:

- **Click** the Look in drop-down arrow, then **click** Floppy (A:).
- **Click** the Named drop-down arrow, **click** my then **click** `Find Now`.
Nine files are displayed.

8
- **Exit** Find, then **close** the My Computer folder window.
- **Remove** DUPLICATE DATA DISK 1 or **go on** Exercise 112.

EXERCISE 112 • Find Files by File Contents

To display files that meet search criteria based on text that appears within those files.

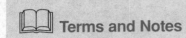

Terms and Notes

case sensitive
A feature that tells a program (e.g., Find) to recognize the difference between upper- and lowercase letters when it is searching for text.

Keyboard Steps to

Find Files by File Contents

—FROM FIND—

1. **Press** `Ctrl` + `Tab` until the Name & Location tab moves to the front.

2. **Press** `Alt` + `O` (Options).

3. **Complete** one of the following procedures:
   Prepare criteria that is not case sensitive
   - IF Case Sensitive has a check mark,
     press `C` (Case Sensitive) to deselect it; otherwise, **press** `Alt` to close the menu.
   - **Press** `Alt` + `C` (Containing text).
   - **Type** the *text to search for* without regard to upper- or lowercase letters.

   Prepare case-sensitive criteria
   - IF Case Sensitive has a check mark,
     press `Alt` to close the menu; otherwise,
     press `C` (Case Sensitive) to select it.
   - **Press** `Alt` + `C` (Containing text).
   - **Type** the *text to search for* using the letter case(s) as desired.

4. **Press** `Alt` + `I` (Find Now).

Begin with the desktop displayed and with no taskbar buttons on the taskbar.

1
- **Start** Find.
- **With** DUPLICATE DATA DISK 1 inserted, **change** the Look in drop-down list box to *Floppy (A:)* (review, Exercise 111, step 3).
- **Click** the Options menu.
  The Options menu opens:

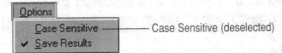

- IF Case Sensitive has a check mark beside it, **click** Case Sensitive to deselect it; otherwise, **click** outside the Options menu to close it.

2 **Find all files that contain the word, *Notepad*:**
- **Click** the *Containing text* text box.
- **Type:** Notepad and **click** Find Now .
- **Size** the Find program window so you can see all the search results.
  Five files are found that contain the text, Notepad, within them.

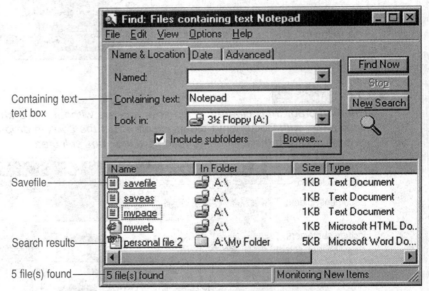

- **Click** savefile to open it, then **locate** the word *Notepad*.
  The very first word is Notepad.
- **Exit** Notepad.

3 **Find all files that contain the word, *click*:**
- **Click** the *Containing text* text box, then **delete** the text in it.
- **Type:** click and **click** Find Now .
  Find searches for all instances of click. *Two files are found.*

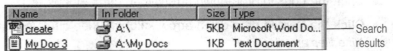

NOTE: Find is searching for both upper- and lowercase instances of the word, click.
- **Open** My Doc 3, then **locate** the word *click*.
  Click *is in the middle line.*
- **Exit** Notepad.

4 Find all files that contain the uppercase word, *CLICK:*
- **Click** the _Containing text_ text box, then **delete** the text in it.
- **Type:** CLICK and **click** [Find Now].
  The same two files are displayed that were found in step 3.
  NOTE: *Find is still searching for both upper- and lowercase instances of* click.
- **Click** the _Options_ menu, then **click** _Case Sensitive (to select it)._
- **Click** [Find Now].
  Find searches only for uppercase instances of CLICK. Now just one file is found:

Name	In Folder	Size	Type
create	A:\	5KB	Microsoft Word Do...

- **Open** create, then **locate** the uppercase word, *CLICK.*
  The word, CLICK, is in the last line. You may need to scroll to find it.
- **Exit** the program that opened create.

5 Find all files that contain the lowercase word, *click:*
- **Click** the _Containing text_ text box, then **delete** the text in it.
- **Type:** click and **click** [Find Now].
  Find searches only for lowercase instances of click. *One file is found:*

Name	In Folder	Size	Type
My Doc 3	A:\My Docs	1KB	Text Document

- **Open** My Doc 3, then **locate** the lowercase word, *click.*
  The word, click, is in the middle line.
- **Exit** Notepad.
- **Click** _Options_, then **click** _Case Sensitive (to deselect it)._
- **Click** [Find Now].
  Find searches for all instances of click *on the A: drive, and, since the _Case Sensitive_ option is deselected, two files are found this time.*

6 Find all files that contain the word, *friendly:*
- **Click** the _Containing text_ text box, then **delete** the text in it.
- **Type:** friendly and **click** [Find Now].
  One file is found:

Name	In Folder	Size	Type
winfun	A:\	1KB	Text Document

- **Open** winfun.
  Notepad opens winfun; friendly *is easy to find.*
- **Exit** Notepad.

7 Close Find, then reopen it:
- **Exit** Find.
- **Click** [Start], **point** to _Find_, then **click** _Files or Folders._
  Find opens with the last location used (Floppy [A:]) displayed in the _Look in_ drop-down list box. Any other search criteria in Find are reset to their defaults; for example, there is no text in the _Containing text_ text box.

8
- **Exit** Find.
- **Remove** DUPLICATE DATA DISK 1 or **go on** to Exercise 113.

To display files that meet search criteria based on the date those files were created, modified, or last accessed.

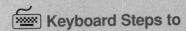 **Keyboard Steps to**

Find Files by Date Modified
—FROM FIND—

1. **Press** `Ctrl` + `Tab` until the Date tab moves to the front.

2. **Press** `Alt` + `N` (Fi_n_d all files).

3. **Press** `Tab`.

4. **Press** `↑↓` (up or down arrow) to select files that were:
   - Created
   - Modified
   - (last) Accessed

5. **Choose** one of the following search by options:

   Between [date] and [date]
   - **Press** `Alt` + `B` (_b_etween [date] and [date]).
   - **Press** `Tab` to move to the first date text box.
   - **Type** the beginning search date.
   - **Press** `Tab` to move to the second date text box.
   - **Type** the ending search date.

   During the previous [number] months
   - **Press** `Alt` + `S` (during the previou_s_ month[s]).
   - **Press** `Tab` to move to the month(s) spin box.
   - **Type** the number of months.

   During the previous [number] days
   - **Press** `Alt` + `D` (_d_uring the previous day[s]).
   - **Press** `Tab` to move to the day(s) spin box.
   - **Type** the number of days.

6. **Press** `Alt` + `I` (Fi_n_d Now).

Find Files by the Date They Were Created, Modified, or Last Accessed

You can use the Date tab in the Find program to locate files that were created, modified, or last accessed within a specific time frame.

First, select the Fi_n_d all files option button on the Date tab.

Next, click the Fi_n_d all files drop-down arrow and choose the desired date category: *Created, Modified,* or *Accessed.*

- **Created** is the most restrictive date category:
  - only files that have been created (but not those that have been opened *or* changed since they were created) on the specified date.
- **Modified** is a less restrictive date category:
  - files that have not been opened since created.
  - files that have been opened *and* modified since created (but not those that have been opened and *not* changed).
- **Accessed** is the least restrictive date category:
  - files that have not been opened since created.
  - files that have been opened since created, but not modified.
  - files that have been opened and modified.

Finally, select one of the three time intervals listed below to search for files that have been created, modified, or accessed:

- _b_etween [date] and [date]
- during the previou_s_ [number] month(s)
- _d_uring the previous [number] day(s)

Begin with the desktop displayed and with no taskbar buttons on the taskbar.

1 **Look at a file's date properties:**
- **Start** Find.
- **With** DUPLICATE DATA DISK 1 inserted, **change** in the Look in drop-down list box to *Floppy (A:)* (review, Exercise 111, step 3), then **click** `Find Now`.
  The 20 files and folders on DUPLICATE DATA DISK 1 are displayed.
- **Right-click** save_file_, then **click** P_r_operties.
  The third section of the savefile Properties dialog box displays information about when savefile was created, modified, and last accessed.

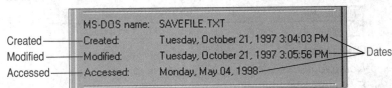

- **Close** the savefile Properties dialog box.

2 **Find all files modified yesterday:**
- **Change** the Look in drop-down list box to (*C:*).
- **Click** the Date tab, then **click** the *Find all* files option button (to select it).
- **Leave** *Modified* as the selection in the drop-down list box.
- **Click** the *during the previous [1] day(s)* option button (to select it).
- **Click** `Find Now` and **notice** the number of files found.

The results are displayed; there are system files included. The displayed files were modified in the last day (24 hours).

Find all files
option button
(Modified) ——

During the
previous
[number] day(s)
option button
(selected) ——

*NOTE: Your
files may be
different.*

File(s) found ——

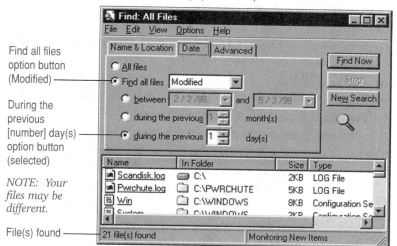

3 **Find all files created yesterday:**
- **Click** the Find all files drop-down arrow.

  The Find all files drop-down list box opens.

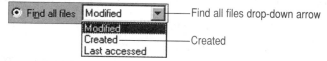

Find all files drop-down arrow

Created

- **Click** Created.
- **Click** Find Now and **notice** the number of files found.

  The displayed files were created in the last day (24 hours). There were fewer files created in the past 24 hours than were modified.

4 **Find all files accessed yesterday:**
- **Click** the Find all files drop-down arrow, then **click** Last accessed.
- **Click** Find Now and **notice** the number of files found.

  The displayed files were opened in the last day (24 hours).
- **Maximize** Find, **sort** by Modified, and **scroll** through the files.

  There were more files accessed in the past 24 hours than were modified.

5 **Find all files modified during the previous two days:**
- **Click** the Find all files drop-down arrow, then **click** Modified.
- **Change** during the previous [1] day(s) to *2* using the spin box up arrow.

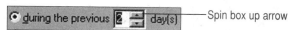

Spin box up arrow

- **Click** Find Now and **notice** the number of files found.

6 - **Exit** Find.
- **Remove** DUPLICATE DATA DISK 1 or **go on** to Exercise 114.

To display files that meet search criteria based on file size.

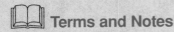 **Terms and Notes**

NOTE: Your file sizes may may be different than the results shown in this exercise.

byte (B)
The size of computer memory and storage units is measured in bytes. A byte is the amount of space needed to hold one character.

byte	=One character
kilobyte	=About 1,000 bytes (characters)
megabyte	=About 1,000,000 bytes (characters)
gigabyte	=About 1,000,000,000 bytes (characters)

A Few Facts About File Size

There are a few facts about file size and hard disk use that are helpful in understanding how disk space is assigned and how the Find program measures file size.

- The exact number of bytes in a kilobyte is 1,024. The number is rounded to 1,000 to make it easier to estimate.
- Floppy disk space is divided into units of one-half kilobyte (or 512 bytes). If a file has fewer than 512 bytes, the full 512 bytes is still allocated for that file. When any file flows into another unit of disk space, even if only 1 byte of it is needed, the entire one-half kilobyte unit is used.
- The files you create using this book are very small; however, because most document files are fairly large, the Find program measures files in kilobytes instead of bytes.

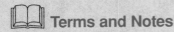 **Keyboard Steps to**

Find Files by Size

—FROM FIND—

1. **Press** Ctrl + Tab until the Advanced tab is selected.
2. **Press** Alt + S (Size is).
3. **Press** Alt + ↓ (down arrow) to open the drop-down list box.
4. **Press** ↑↓ (up or down arrow) to highlight the desired size option:
   - [none]
   - At least
   - At most
5. **Press** Tab.
6. **Type** the desired number of Kb.
7. **Press** Alt + I (Find Now).

Begin with the desktop displayed and with no taskbar buttons on the taskbar.

1 **Look at a file's size properties:**
- **Start** Find.
- **With** DUPLICATE DATA DISK 1 inserted, **change** the Look in drop-down list box to *Floppy (A:)*.
- **Click** Find Now.
  The 20 files and folders on DUPLICATE DATA DISK 1 are displayed.
- **Right-click** winfun, then **click** Properties.
  The winfun Properties dialog box opens.

File size is 35 bytes... 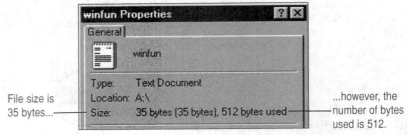 ...however, the number of bytes used is 512.

- **Notice** the difference between the file size and the bytes used.
  NOTE: Because disk space is divided into storage units of one-half kilobyte (or 512 bytes), even though a file has fewer than 512 bytes, the full 512 bytes must be allocated to the file.
- **Close** the winfun Properties dialog box.
- **Right-click** savefile, then **click** Properties.
  Savefile is 638 bytes. (Your file size should be close to that.) The amount of space used on the disk is 1024 bytes (or 1 kilobyte):

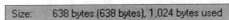

- **Close** the savefile Properties dialog box.
- **Right-click** create, then **click** Properties.
  Create is 5 kilobytes (or 5,000 bytes):

Size: 5.00KB (5,120 bytes), 5,120 bytes used

NOTE: While the create file has only about 100 more characters in it than savefile does, its much larger size is attributed mainly to the formatting codes found in WordPad.
- **Close** the create Properties dialog box.

2 **Find all files that are at most 1 Kb:**
- **Click** the Advanced tab in the Find program, then **click** the *Size is* drop-down arrow.
  The drop-down list box displays three options: [none], At least, and At most.

At most 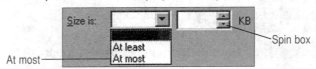 Spin box

- **Click** At most.
  NOTE: The At most option ensures that every file will be equal to or less than the number of Kb shown in the spin box.
- **Change** the KB spin box setting to *1* using the spin box up arrow.

- **Click** `Find Now`.

  There are 16 files on drive A: that are At most 1 KB; that is, 1 Kb or less.
- **Notice** that all of your files are listed as 1 Kb.

  NOTE: Because most document files are fairly large (more than 1 kilobyte), Find rounds all files up to the nearest kilobyte; Find does not show the exact number of bytes in each file.

3 Find all files that are at least 1 Kb:

- **Click** the *Size is* drop-down arrow, then **click** At least.
- **Click** `Find Now`.

  Four files are found that are at least 1 Kb.
- **Where** are all the 1 Kb files?

  The 16 files that met the At most 1 KB criteria are all less than 1 Kb so they will not meet the criteria of At least 1 KB.

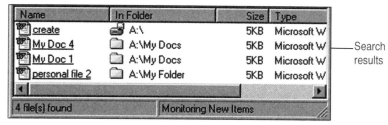
Search results

4 Find all files that are at least 1,000 Kb (1 megabyte):

- **Click** the Name & Location tab, then **change** the Look in drop-down list box to *(C:)*.
- **Click** the Advanced tab.
- **Click** the *Size is* drop-down arrow, then **click** At least, if necessary.
- **Type:** 1000 in the KB text box, then **click** `Find Now`.

  Close to 100 or, perhaps, several hundred files appear.
- **Maximize** Find.
- **Click** in the center of the Size column heading.

  The files are sorted from the smallest to the largest.
- **Double-click** the right border of the Size column heading to adjust it to fit the widest column entry.
- **Click** in the center of the Size column heading again.

  The files are now sorted from largest to smallest.
- **Double-click** the right border of the Size column heading to readjust the Size column.
- **Notice** the size of the largest files on your computer system.

  The largest file on your computer system is at the top of the list of files.

5
- **Exit** Find.
- **Click** `Start`, **point** to Find, and **click** Files or Folders.

  Find opens and the size criteria are returned to their original states.
- **Click** the Advanced tab and **notice** that your size settings are gone.
- **Exit** Find.
- **Remove** DUPLICATE DATA DISK 1 or **go on** to Exercise 115.

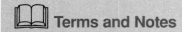

EXERCISE 115 • Find Files by File Type

To display files that meet search criteria based on file type.

📖 Terms and Notes

NOTE: *Folders are treated as files in the search results. Notice that the Find program status bar also includes folders in the number of "file(s) found."*

Begin with the desktop displayed and with no taskbar buttons on the taskbar.

1
- **Start** and **maximize** Find.
- **With** DUPLICATE DATA DISK 1 inserted, **change** the Look in drop-down list box to *Floppy (A:)*.
- **Click** the Advanced tab.
  The Of type drop-down list box displays All Files and Folders.

2 Find all files and folders:
- **Click** `Find Now` and **notice** the number of files found.
  The results section displays all the files and folders on your disk—20 file(s) are found.
- **Scroll** through the files and folders.
  The files and folders below should all be displayed. Your results may be slightly different, and you may have to scroll through the window to view all the files.

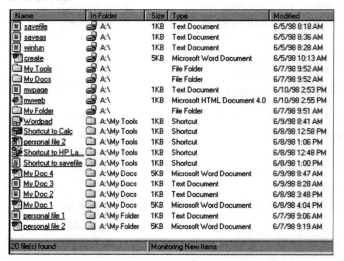

3 Find one type of file (Microsoft Word Document):
- **Click** the Of type drop-down arrow.
  The Of type drop-down list opens:

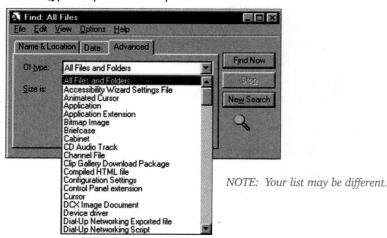

NOTE: Your list may be different.

⌨ Keyboard Steps to

Find Files by Type

—FROM FIND—

1. Press `Ctrl` + `Tab` until the Advanced tab moves to the front.

2. Press `Alt` + `T` (Of type).

3. Press `Alt` + `↓` (down arrow) to open the drop-down list box.

4. Press `Page Down`, `Page Up`, or `↑↓` (up or down arrow) to highlight the desired file type.

5. Press `Enter`.

6. Press `Alt` + `I` (Find Now).

- **Scroll** through the drop-down list until you find *Microsoft Word Document*.
- **Click** Microsoft Word Document.
- **Click** Find Now .

  The Microsoft Word Documents on your disk are listed in the results section of Find.

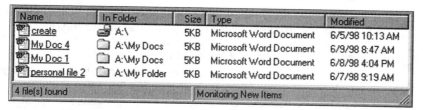

Name	In Folder	Size	Type	Modified
create	A:\	5KB	Microsoft Word Document	6/5/98 10:13 AM
My Doc 4	A:\My Docs	5KB	Microsoft Word Document	6/9/98 8:47 AM
My Doc 1	A:\My Docs	5KB	Microsoft Word Document	6/8/98 4:04 PM
personal file 2	A:\My Folder	5KB	Microsoft Word Document	6/7/98 9:19 AM
4 file(s) found			Monitoring New Items	

4 **Find one type of file (Text Document):**
- **Click** the Of type drop-down arrow.
- **Scroll** through the drop-down list until you find *Text Document*.
- **Click** Text Document.
- **Click** Find Now .

  The Text Documents on your disk are listed in the results section of Find.

Name	In Folder	Size	Type	Modified
savefile	A:\	1KB	Text Document	6/5/98 8:18 AM
winfun	A:\	1KB	Text Document	6/5/98 8:28 AM
saveas	A:\	1KB	Text Document	6/5/98 8:36 AM
mypage	A:\	1KB	Text Document	6/10/98 2:53 PM
My Doc 3	A:\My Docs	1KB	Text Document	6/9/98 8:28 AM
My Doc 2	A:\My Docs	1KB	Text Document	6/8/98 3:48 PM
personal file 1	A:\My Folder	1KB	Text Document	6/7/98 9:06 AM
7 file(s) found			Monitoring New Items	

5 **Find all folders:**
- **Click** the Of type drop-down arrow.
- **Scroll** through the drop-down list until you find *Folder*.
- **Click** Folder.
- **Click** Find Now .

  The folders on your disk are listed in the results section of Find.

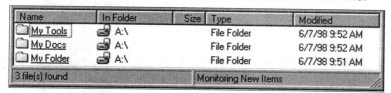

Name	In Folder	Size	Type	Modified
My Tools	A:\		File Folder	6/7/98 9:52 AM
My Docs	A:\		File Folder	6/7/98 9:52 AM
My Folder	A:\		File Folder	6/7/98 9:51 AM
3 file(s) found			Monitoring New Items	

6
- **Exit** Find.
- **Remove** DUPLICATE DATA DISK 1 or **go on** to Exercise 116.

EXERCISE 116 • Save Search Criteria

To save a file that contains search criteria you entered in the Find program.

Begin with the desktop displayed and with no taskbar buttons on the taskbar.

1
- **Start** and **maximize** Find.
- **With** DUPLICATE DATA DISK 1 inserted, **change** the Look in drop-down list box to *Floppy (A:)*.
- **Click** the Options menu.
- IF Save Results does not have a check mark beside it, **close** the Options menu; otherwise, **click** Save Results to deselect it.

2 **Create search criteria with several variables:**
- **Find** all the files that contain the word, *document* (review, Exercise 112).
  Find displays 11 files that contain the word, document.

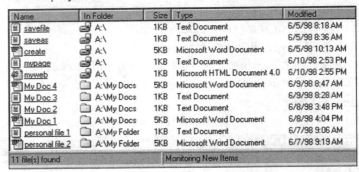

- **Find** all the files that are Text Documents (review, Exercise 115). Keep the word *document* in the *Containing text* text box.
  Six files are found that contain the word, document, *and are Text Documents.*

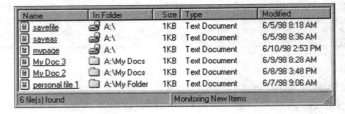

3 **Save the search criteria:**
- **Click** File, then **click** Save Search, then **exit** Find.
  The search icon is saved in the next available space on the desktop.
- **Point** to the search icon. (You may need to click the desktop to select it before the icon will be selected when you point to it.)
  The full icon title appears:
- **Click** the search icon.
  Find opens with its previous criteria. The Containing text *text box still displays* document.
- **Click** the Advanced tab.
  The Of type drop-down list box still displays Text Document.
- **Click** Find Now .
  The results are the same as the last result in step 2, 6 file(s) found.
- **Go on** to Exercise 117 without stopping.

—Search icon

—Search icon (selected)

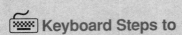 **Keyboard Steps to**

Save a Search Without Results

—FROM FIND—

1. **Create** the desired search criteria. *(See Keyboard Steps for Exercises 110-115.)*

2. **Press** `Alt` + `O` (Options).
   - IF Save Results has a check mark:
     press `S` (Save Results) to deselect it;
     otherwise, **press** `Alt` to close the menu.

3. **Press** `Alt` + `F` (File).

4. **Press** `A` (Save Search).

Open Saved Search Criteria

1. **Press** `Alt` + `F` (File).

2. **Press** `C` (Close) to close the Find program.
   - IF the desired icon on the desktop is *not* selected: **press** `Ctrl` + `Esc`,
     `Esc`, `Tab`, `Tab`, `Tab`.

3. **Press** 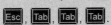 (arrow keys) to select the search icon.

4. **Press** `Enter` to open Find with the saved criteria.

Continue from Exercise 116 without stopping.

1 **Save the search criteria and its results:**
- **Click** Options, then **click** Save Results to select it.
- **Click** File, then **click** Save Search.
- **Exit** Find.

   The search icon is saved in the first available space on the desktop; it has (2) at the end of its name to differentiate it from the first search icon.

- **Point** to the new search icon. (You may need to click the desktop first.)

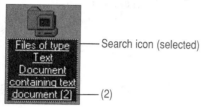

— Search icon (selected)

— (2)

- **Click** the search icon that ends with *(2)*.

   Find opens with all the criteria you entered previously, and this time the search results have also been saved.

2 **Print the Find window:**
- **Click** the Advanced tab.
- **Size** the Find window to show all the files in the results section.
- **Capture** the Find window by pressing [Alt] + [Print Scrn] (review, Exercise 85).
- **Print** the Find window. (Open WordPad, paste the capture into WordPad, print the WordPad file, and exit WordPad without saving.)

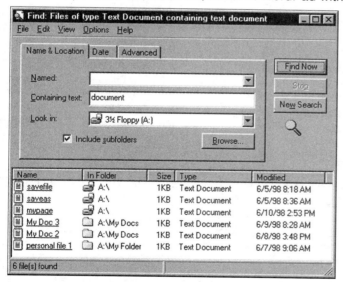

3
- **Click** Options, then **click** Save Results to deselect it.
- **Exit** Find.
- **Drag and drop** the two search icons onto the Recycle Bin.
- **Empty** the Recycle Bin.
- **Remove** DUPLICATE DATA DISK 1 or **go on** to Exercise 118.

To save a file that contains the search criteria you entered in the Find program along with the results of that search.

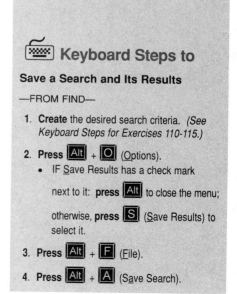

⌨ **Keyboard Steps to**

Save a Search and Its Results

—FROM FIND—

1. **Create** the desired search criteria. *(See Keyboard Steps for Exercises 110-115.)*

2. **Press** [Alt] + [O] (Options).
   - IF Save Results has a check mark next to it: **press** [Alt] to close the menu; otherwise, **press** [S] (Save Results) to select it.

3. **Press** [Alt] + [F] (File).

4. **Press** [Alt] + [A] (Save Search).

EXERCISE 118 • Lesson Ten Practice

Finding Files

Tasks Reviewed:
- Start Find
- Find Files by Name
- Find Files by Location
- Find Files by File Contents
- Find Files by Date Modified
- Find Files by File Size
- Find Files by File Type
- Save Search Criteria
- Save Search Results

Begin with the desktop displayed and with no taskbar buttons on the taskbar.

You will need DUPLICATE DATA DISK 2 for this practice exercise.

- **Start** Find from the Start menu, then **exit** Find.
- **Start** Find by right-clicking the Start button, then **exit** Find.
- **Start** Find by right-clicking the My Computer desktop icon, then **exit** Find.
- **Start** Windows Explorer, **start** Find using the Tools menu, then **exit** Find.
- **Expand** (C:), then **start** Find by right-clicking any folder.
  When Find opens, the path to the folder you right-clicked is in the Look in drop-down list box.
- **Exit** Find and **exit** Windows Explorer.

- **Start** Find from the Start menu, then **maximize** the Find window.
- **Change** the Look in drop-down list box to *(C:)*.
- **Find** all files named *Pinstripe*.

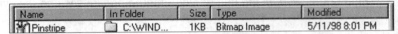

- **Insert** DUPLICATE DATA DISK 2 in drive A:.
- **Change** the Look in drop-down list box to *Floppy (A:)*.
- **Delete** *Pinstripe* from the Named drop-down list box.
- **Find** all the files on your disk (click the Find Now button) and **compare** your files to the ones shown in the illustration below.
  Find lists all the files on DUPLICATE DATA DISK 2. You may have to scroll to see all of your files. Your files may be in a different order.

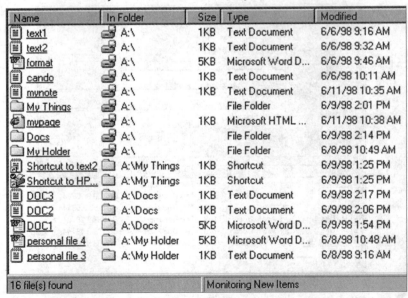

- **Find** all files named (or partially named) *text*.

Name	In Folder	Size	Type	Modified
text1	A:\	1KB	Text Document	6/6/98 9:16 AM
text2	A:\	1KB	Text Document	6/6/98 9:32 AM
Shortcut to text2	A:\My Things	1KB	Shortcut	6/9/98 1:25 PM

3 file(s) found   Monitoring New Items

- **Find** all files named (or partially named) *2.*

Name	In Folder	Size	Type	Modified
text2	A:\	1KB	Text Document	6/6/98 9:32 AM
Shortcut to text2	A:\My Thi...	1KB	Shortcut	6/9/98 1:25 PM
DOC2	A:\Docs	1KB	Text Document	6/9/98 2:06 PM

3 file(s) found — Monitoring New Items

- **Deselect** the Include <u>s</u>ubfolders check box in the Name & Location tab.
- **Open** the <u>N</u>amed drop-down list box, and **select** *text.*
- **Find** all files named (or partially named) *text* that are not in subfolders.

Name	In Folder	Size	Type	Modified
text1	A:\	1KB	Text Document	6/6/98 9:16 AM
text2	A:\	1KB	Text Document	6/6/98 9:32 AM

2 file(s) found — Monitoring New Items

- **Select** the Include <u>s</u>ubfolders check box in the Name & Location tab.

3
- **Browse** folders, then **select** the My Things folder on Floppy (A:).
- **Find** all files named (or partially named) *text* in the My Things folder.

Name	In Folder	Size	Type	Modified
Shortcut to text2	A:\My Things	1KB	Shortcut	6/9/98 1:25 PM

- **Change** the <u>L</u>ook in drop-down list box to *(C:).*
- **Find** all files named (or partially named) *text.*
  Find displays quite a few files that have text *in their names.*
- **Start** a new search. (Click the Ne<u>w</u> Search button, then click the OK button.)

4
- **Change** the <u>L</u>ook in drop-down list box to *Floppy (A:).*
- **Click** the <u>O</u>ptions menu and, if <u>C</u>ase Sensitive is selected, deselect it.
- **Find** all files that contain the word, *whether,* using the <u>C</u>ontaining text text box.
  Find searches for all instances of whether, *regardless of case.*

Name	In Folder	Size	Type	Modified
cando	A:\	1KB	Text Document	6/6/98 10:11 AM

- **Open** <u>cando</u>, **locate** *whether,* then **exit** Notepad.
- **Find** all files that contain the text, *document.*
  Find searches for all instances of document, *regardless of case.*

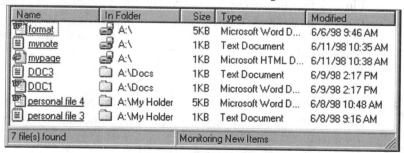

Name	In Folder	Size	Type	Modified
format	A:\	5KB	Microsoft Word D...	6/6/98 9:46 AM
mynote	A:\	1KB	Text Document	6/11/98 10:35 AM
mypage	A:\	1KB	Microsoft HTML D...	6/11/98 10:38 AM
DOC3	A:\Docs	1KB	Text Document	6/9/98 2:17 PM
DOC1	A:\Docs	1KB	Microsoft Word D...	6/9/98 2:17 PM
personal file 4	A:\My Holder	5KB	Microsoft Word D...	6/8/98 10:48 AM
personal file 3	A:\My Holder	1KB	Text Document	6/8/98 9:16 AM

7 file(s) found — Monitoring New Items

- **Restore** the Find window, then **size** the Find window as desired.
- **Select** the <u>C</u>ase Sensitive option.

Continued on the next page

Continued from the previous page

- **Find** all files that contain the case-sensitive text, *document*.

  Find searches only for lowercase instances of document.

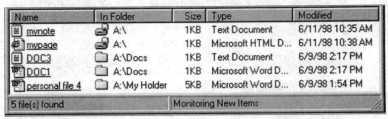

Name	In Folder	Size	Type	Modified
mynote	A:\	1KB	Text Document	6/11/98 10:35 AM
mypage	A:\	1KB	Microsoft HTML D...	6/11/98 10:38 AM
DOC3	A:\Docs	1KB	Text Document	6/9/98 2:17 PM
DOC1	A:\Docs	1KB	Microsoft Word D...	6/9/98 2:17 PM
personal file 4	A:\My Holder	5KB	Microsoft Word D...	6/9/98 1:54 PM
5 file(s) found			Monitoring New Items	

- **Open** DOC3, **locate** *document*, then **exit** Notepad.
- **Find** all files that contain the case-sensitive text, *Document*. (Change the lowercase *d* in the <u>C</u>ontaining text text box to an uppercase *D*.)

  Find searches only for instances of Document *with an initial capital letter. There are four files that meet the search criteria. One file, personal file 4, also meets the search criteria for the previous search.*

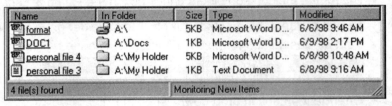

Name	In Folder	Size	Type	Modified
format	A:\	5KB	Microsoft Word D...	6/6/98 9:46 AM
DOC1	A:\Docs	1KB	Microsoft Word D...	6/9/98 2:17 PM
personal file 4	A:\My Holder	5KB	Microsoft Word D...	6/8/98 10:48 AM
personal file 3	A:\My Holder	1KB	Text Document	6/8/98 9:16 AM
4 file(s) found			Monitoring New Items	

- **Open** personal file 4, **locate** *Document* and *document*, then **exit** the program that opened.
- **Open** personal file 3, **locate** *Document*, then **exit** Notepad.

  The search found a file with the word, Documents, *which contains the search text,* Document.

- **Deselect** the <u>C</u>ase Sensitive option.
- **Exit** Find.

5
- **Start** Find from the Start menu, then **maximize** the Find window.
- **Change** the <u>L</u>ook in drop-down list box to *(C:)*.
- **Access** the Date tab.
- **Find** all files modified during the previous two months and **notice** the number of files found.
- **Find** all files modified during the previous three days and **notice** the number of files found.
- **Find** all files last accessed during the previous three days and **notice** the number of files found.

  There will probably be many more files that were accessed in the preceding three days than were modified during the previous three days.

- **Exit** Find.

6
- **Start** Find from the Start menu, then **maximize** the Find window.
- **Change** the <u>L</u>ook in drop-down list to *(C:)*, if necessary, then **click** the Advanced tab.
- **Find** all files that are at least 1,000 Kb.
- **Click** the Size column heading twice to sort in descending order.

  The files are sorted from largest to smallest. The largest file on drive C: is at the top of the list of files.

- **Scroll** through the list of files and **notice** which files on drive C: are very large.
- **Find** all files that are at most 1 Kb.

  There are probably 2,000 to 5,000 files of this size.
- **Exit** Find.

- **Start** and **maximize** Find.
- **Change** the Look in drop-down list box to *(C:)*, if necessary.
- **Access** the Advanced tab, then **change** Of type to *Text Document.*
- **Find** all Text Document files.
- **Access** the Name & Location tab.
- **Change** the Look in drop-down list box to *Floppy (A:).*
- **Find** all Text Document files.

Name	In Folder	Size	Type	Modified
text1	A:\	1KB	Text Document	6/6/98 9:16 AM
text2	A:\	1KB	Text Document	6/6/98 9:32 AM
cando	A:\	1KB	Text Document	6/6/98 10:11 AM
mynote	A:\	1KB	Text Document	6/11/98 10:35 AM
DOC3	A:\Docs	1KB	Text Document	6/9/98 2:17 PM
DOC2	A:\Docs	1KB	Text Document	6/9/98 2:06 PM
personal file 3	A:\My Holder	1KB	Text Document	6/8/98 9:16 AM
7 file(s) found		Monitoring New Items		

- **Access** the Advanced tab, then **change** Of type to *Shortcut.*
- **Find** all Shortcut files.

Name	In Folder	Size	Type	Modified
Shortcut to text2	A:\My Things	1KB	Shortcut	6/9/98 1:25 PM
Shortcut to HP ...	A:\My Things	1KB	Shortcut	6/9/98 1:25 PM
2 file(s) found		Monitoring New Items		

- **Exit** Find.

- **Start** Find.
- **Change** the Look in drop-down list box to *Floppy (A:)*, if necessary.
- **Access** the Advanced tab, then **change** Of type to *Text Document.*
- **Click** the Options menu and, if Save Results is selected, deselect it.
- **Access** the Name & Location tab.
- **Type:** create in the *Containing text* text box.
- **Find** all Text Document files that contain the word, *create.*

  Three files meet the criteria:

Name	In Folder	Size	Type	Modified
text1	A:\	1KB	Text Document	6/6/98 9:16 AM
text2	A:\	1KB	Text Document	6/6/98 9:32 AM
DOC3	A:\Docs	1KB	Text Document	6/9/98 2:17 PM
3 file(s) found		Monitoring New Items		

- **Save** the search criteria.

  The search icon is saved on the desktop.
- **Exit** Find.
- **Click** the desktop to select it, then **click** the search icon to open the saved search criteria.

Continued on the next page

Continued from the previous page

 9

- **Click** Find Now .
- **Select** the <u>S</u>ave Results option.
- **Save** the search criteria and its results.
- **Exit** Find.
- **Click** the desktop to select it.

    The search icon is saved on the desktop with a (2) at the end of the filename. The filename is so long, however, that you must point to it to select it and see the (2) at the bottom.

- **Open** the search criteria and its results.
- **Size** the Find window to show all the files in the results section.
- **Print** the Find window.

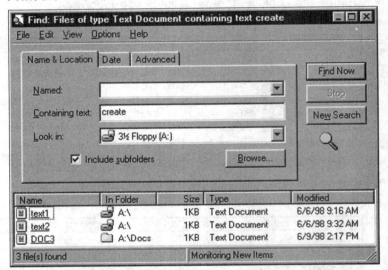

- **Deselect** the <u>S</u>ave Results option.
- **Exit** Find.
- **Drag and drop** the two search icons onto the Recycle Bin.
- **Empty** the Recycle Bin.
- **Remove** DUPLICATE DATA DISK 2.

Lessons Eight–Eleven Worksheet (9) is on page 309.

Lesson Eleven

Other Features

Table of Contents

EXERCISE 119 • Use the MS-DOS Prompt

 Terms and Notes

directory
Another name for a folder.

long filename
A filename that is up to 255 characters long and can contain spaces and most symbols. *(See also Topic 14, Files and Filenames.)*

MS-DOS (Microsoft Disk Operating System)
The main operating system used before Windows was developed.

MS-DOS–based application
A program that is designed to run under the MS-DOS operating system rather than the Windows operating system.

MS-DOS prompt
The signal that MS-DOS is ready for you to tell it what to do. The default MS-DOS prompt displays the path to the current folder followed by the greater than sign (>) and a blinking underline. For example, if you are in Windows, the MS-DOS prompt will look like this: C:\Windows>_

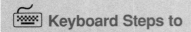 **Keyboard Steps to**

Use the MS-DOS Prompt Window

1. Press `Ctrl` + `Esc` (Start menu).

2. Press `P` (Programs).

3. Press `M` until *MS-DOS Prompt* is selected.

4. Press `Enter`.

Switch Between MS-DOS Prompt Window and MS-DOS Full-Screen Display

Press `Alt` + `Enter`.

Exit the MS-DOS Prompt Window

1. **Type:** exit

2. Press `Enter`.

The MS-DOS Prompt

MS-DOS (Microsoft Disk Operating System) is the operating system that was used before Windows was developed. MS-DOS is still needed to bridge the gap between **MS-DOS–based applications** and Windows 98, however. There have been some important changes to MS-DOS to make it blend with Windows 98. One of the most important features is the ability of MS-DOS to recognize long filenames. The Windows 98 version of MS-DOS also has improved support for running MS-DOS–based programs, which you may or may not have on your computer.

You do not need to know how to use MS-DOS in order to use Windows 98; but those who are familiar with MS-DOS can still perform most MS-DOS commands in Windows 98—although some commands are no longer available.

Begin with the desktop displayed and with no taskbar buttons on the taskbar.

1 **Open the MS-DOS Prompt window:**

• **Click** [Start], **point** to Programs, then **click** [MS-DOS Prompt].
The MS-DOS Prompt window opens with the Windows folder current, as indicated by the prompt.

• IF your MS-DOS Prompt window does not have borders (i.e., if it fills the screen), **press** `Alt` + `Enter`.

2 **Switch the MS-DOS Prompt window to a full-screen display:**

• **Press** `Alt` + `Enter`.
The MS-DOS Prompt window becomes a full screen, losing its borders, title bar, and toolbar.

3 **Perform the MS-DOS command, CD (Change Directory):**

• **Type:** CD\ then **press** `Enter`.
MS-DOS changes to the root directory (i.e., the top-level folder.)
`C:\>`

• **Type:** CD WINDOWS then **press** `Enter`.
MS-DOS changes to the Windows folder.
`C:\WINDOWS>`

• **Type:** CD\ then **press** `Enter`.
MS-DOS changes back to the root directory.
`C:\>`

• **Type:** CD "PROGRAM FILES\ACCESSORIES" then **press** `Enter`.
REMINDER: Since the name of the folder, Program Files, is a long filename, the path must be enclosed in quotes for MS-DOS to recognize it.
MS-DOS changes to the Accessories folder, a subfolder of Program Files.
`C:\Program Files\Accessories>`

④ **Perform the MS-DOS command, DIR (Directory):**

- **Type:** DIR then **press** [Enter].

  MS-DOS lists the files in the Accessories folder.

```
C:\WINDOWS>CD\

C:\>CD "PROGRAM FILES\ACCESSORIES"

C:\Program Files\Accessories>DIR

 Volume in drive C has no label
 Volume Serial Number is 461B-0909
 Directory of C:\Program Files\Accessories

.               <DIR>         09-21-97  9:47a .
..              <DIR>         09-21-97  9:47a ..
BACKUP          <DIR>         03-07-98  7:37p BACKUP
MSPAINT   EXE     344,064     05-11-98  8:01p MSPAINT.EXE
PPPMENU   SCP       2,815     05-11-98  8:01p PPPMENU.SCP
SLIP      SCP       2,375     05-11-98  8:01p SLIP.SCP
SLIPMENU  SCP       2,813     05-11-98  8:01p SLIPMENU.SCP
WORDPAD   EXE     204,800     05-11-98  8:01p WORDPAD.EXE
CIS       SCP         733     05-11-98  8:01p CIS.SCP
HYPERT~1        <DIR>         09-21-97  9:48a HyperTerminal
WORDPAD   ZIP      77,253     06-08-98 11:36a Wordpad.zip
         7 file(s)        634,853 bytes
         4 dir(s)   1,212,981,248 bytes free

C:\Program Files\Accessories>
```

- **Type:** DIR/V then **press** [Enter].

  NOTE: V is for verbose.

  MS-DOS lists the files in the Accessories folder showing additional detail.

```
..
BACKUP          <DIR>                     03-07-98  7:37p  03-07-98   D
BACKUP
MSPAINT   EXE     344,064     344,064     05-11-98  8:01p  06-11-98   A
MSPAINT.EXE
PPPMENU   SCP       2,815       4,096     05-11-98  8:01p  05-29-98   A
PPPMENU.SCP
SLIP      SCP       2,375       4,096     05-11-98  8:01p  05-29-98   A
SLIP.SCP
SLIPMENU  SCP       2,813       4,096     05-11-98  8:01p  05-29-98   A
SLIPMENU.SCP
WORDPAD   EXE     204,800     204,800     05-11-98  8:01p  06-15-98   A
WORDPAD.EXE
CIS       SCP         733       4,096     05-11-98  8:01p  05-29-98   A
CIS.SCP
HYPERT~1        <DIR>                     09-21-97  9:48a  09-21-97   D
HyperTerminal
WORDPAD   ZIP      77,253      77,824     06-08-98 11:36a  06-08-98   A
Wordpad.zip
         7 file(s)        634,853 bytes
         4 dir(s)         643,072 bytes allocated
                   1,212,981,248 bytes free
                   2,550,669,312 bytes total disk space,  52% in use

C:\Program Files\Accessories>
```

⑤ **Return to the desktop:**

- **Press** [Alt]+[Tab].

  Windows switches to the desktop.

- **Press** [Alt]+[Tab].

- **Type:** CD.. (be sure to include the two periods), then **press** [Enter].

  MS-DOS changes to the folder immediately above the current folder, Program Files.

- **Press** [Alt]+[Enter].

  MS-DOS switches back to the window format.

⑥ **Exit the MS-DOS Prompt window:**

- **Type:** EXIT then **press** [Enter].

  OR

  Click the Close button.

  The MS-DOS Prompt window closes and you are returned to the desktop.

EXERCISE 120 • Use the Run Command

To start programs and open documents and folders using the Run command.

📖 Terms and Notes

path
The route to an object; it consists of the disk drive, folder, subfolders (if any), and the filename (if the path is to a file). For example, C:\WINDOWS\CALC is the path to the Calculator program. If long filenames are used in a path, the path must be enclosed in quotes ("). For example, "A:\MY DOCS\MY DOC 1.DOC" is the path to the Microsoft Word file, mydoc1, on drive A:.

A full path includes the following:
- the disk drive (followed by a colon [:] and a backslash [\]).
- all the folders needed to find the desired document or folder (each followed by a backslash).
- the filename (including its filename extension) or the final folder.

Example of a path to the Media folder:
C:\WINDOWS\MEDIA

Example of a path to the CHIMES.WAV file in the media folder:
C:\WINDOWS\MEDIA\CHIMES.WAV

NOTE: The paths have been written here using uppercase letters for clarity. You can also use lowercase letters or mixed upper- and lowercase letters.

Begin with the desktop displayed and with no taskbar buttons on the taskbar.

1 **Start the Run command:**

- **Click** 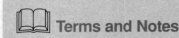 **Start**, then **click**  **Run...**.
  The Run command opens.
- IF there is something highlighted in the Open drop-down list box, **press** Del.

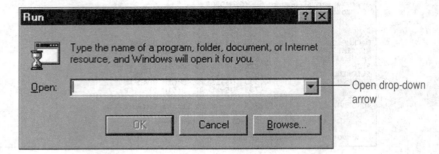

Open drop-down arrow

2 **Start programs from the Run command:**

NOTE: You can start many programs simply by typing their names in the Open drop-down list box and pressing Enter. In some cases, however, you need to use the program's filename rather than its standard name.

- **Type:** notepad in the Open drop-down list box, then **press** Enter.
  Notepad opens.
- **Exit** Notepad.
- **Start** Run, **type:** paint in the Open drop-down list box, then **press** Enter.
  A message box appears saying that it cannot find 'paint' (or one of its components).
- **Click** OK.
- **Type:** mspaint in the Open drop-down list box, then **press** Enter.
  Paint opens when you use its actual filename, mspaint, rather than its standard name.
- **Exit** Paint.
- **Start** Run, **type:** wordpad in the Open drop-down list box, then **press** Enter.
  WordPad opens.
- **Exit** WordPad.
- **Start** Run, **type:** calc in the Open drop-down list box, then **press** Enter.
  Calculator opens.
- **Exit** Calculator.

3 **Use a previous command in Run:**
- **Start** Run.
- **Click** the Open drop-down arrow.
  A menu appears with up to 26 of the commands you used last.

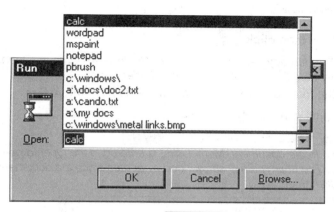

- **Click** notepad, then **click** [OK].

  Notepad opens.

- **Exit** Notepad.

4 **Open a document using the Browse button in Run:**

- **Start** Run.

  Run opens with the last command entered in the Open drop-down list box.

- **Click** [Browse...].

  The Browse dialog box opens.

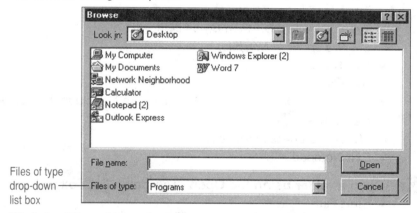

Files of type drop-down list box

- **Click** the Files of type drop-down arrow, then **click** All Files .

  NOTE: The Browse dialog box that opens from Run defaults to Programs *for Files of type. Since you are going to open a document, you must change Files of type to* All Files.

- **Open** My Computer, **open** the (C:) folder, then **open** the Windows folder.

- **Scroll** until you find [ ] Forest .

- **Click** [ ] Forest , then **click** [Open].

  The Browse dialog box closes and the path to the document, Forest, is entered in the Open drop-down list box. The path does not include a long filename, so it is not enclosed in quotes.

- **Click** [OK].

  The document, Forest, opens in Paint.

- **Exit** Paint.

Continued on the next page

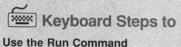 **Keyboard Steps to**

Use the Run Command

1. **Press** Ctrl + Esc .

2. **Press** R (Run).

3. **Type** the program's filename.
   OR
   Type the entire path to the desired program, folder, or document.

4. **Press** Enter .

Open a Document or Program Using the Browse Button in Run

1. **Press** Ctrl + Esc .

2. **Press** R (Run).

3. **Press** Alt + B (Browse).

4. **Use** the actions below, as needed, to select a document or program:

   Change drives (or other object) in the Look in drop-down list box

   - **Press** Alt + I (Look in).

   - **Press** I (down arrow) to open the list.

   - **Press** [up/down] (up or down arrow) to highlight the desired location.

   - **Press** Enter .

   Change files of type

   - **Press** Alt + T (Files of type).

   - **Press** I (down arrow) to open the list.

   - **Press** [up/down] (up or down arrow) to select *All Files* or *Programs*.

   - **Press** Enter .

   Go up or down one folder level within the Browse dialog box

   - **Press** Tab until an item in the workspace is selected.

   - **Press** [arrows] (arrow keys) to select the desired folder.

   - **Press** Enter to go down a level.

   - **Press** Backspace to go up a level.

   Select a program or file
   —FROM THE DESIRED FOLDER—

   - **Press** [arrows] (arrow keys) to select desired file.

5. **Press** Enter , Enter .

Continued from the previous page

5 • **Start** Run, then **click** Browse... .

Since Run already has the path to the Windows folder in its Open drop-down list box, Browse opens with that folder open.

• **Click** the Files of type drop-down arrow, then **click** All Files.

• **Scroll** until you find Metal Links .

• **Click** Metal Links , then **click** Open .

The path to the document, Metal Links, is entered in the Open drop-down list box. The entire path is surrounded by quotes since the document has a long filename.

Open: "C:\WINDOWS\Metal Links.bmp"

• **Click** OK .

The document, Metal Links, opens in Paint.

• **Exit** Paint.

6 **Open a document using the Open drop-down list box in Run:**

• **Insert** DUPLICATE DATA DISK 1 into drive A:.

• **Start** Run.

NOTE: You can use upper- or lowercase letters, or a combination of both, when typing the path.

• **Type:** A:\SAVEFILE.TXT then **press** Enter .

Savefile opens in Notepad.

• **Exit** Notepad.

• **Start** Run.

• **Type:** "A:\MY DOCS\MY DOC 3.TXT" (be sure to include the two periods), then **press** Enter .

MY DOC 3 opens in Notepad.

• **Exit** Notepad.

7 **Open a folder using the Open drop-down list box in Run:**

• **Start** Run.

• **Type:** C:\WINDOWS then **press** Enter .

The Windows folder opens.

• **Close** the Windows folder window.

• **Start** Run.

• **Type:** C:\PROGRAM FILES\ACCESSORIES then **press** Enter .

The Accessories folder opens.

• **Close** the Accessories folder window.

• **Start** Run.

• **Type:** A:\MY DOCS then **press** Enter .

The My Docs folder opens.

• **Close** the My Docs folder window and **remove** DUPLICATE DATA DISK 1.

Begin with the desktop displayed and with no taskbar buttons on the taskbar.

1 Open the StartUp folder:

- **Right-click** 🟦**Start**, then **click** Open.
- **Open** Programs, then **open** StartUp.
  The StartUp folder is empty unless someone has already put program shortcuts into it.

2 Create a shortcut to Notepad in the StartUp folder:

- **Right-click** the workspace, **point** to New, then **click** Shortcut.
  The Create Shortcut dialog box opens.
- **Click** Browse... , then **double-click** the Windows folder to open it.
- **Scroll** until you find 📄Notepad .
- **Click** 📄Notepad , then **click** Open .
- **Click** Next > , then **click** Finish .
  The Notepad shortcut appears in the StartUp folder window.

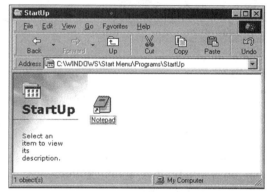

3 Look at the StartUp menu:

- **Close** the StartUp folder window.
- **Click** 🟦**Start**, **point** to Programs, then **point** to StartUp.
  The StartUp menu displays: 📄Notepad .
- **Click** 📄Notepad .
  Notepad opens.
- **Exit** Notepad.

4 Use StartUp to start programs when Windows opens:

- **Click** 🟦**Start**, **click** Shut Down, **click** the Restart option button
  (to select it), then **click** OK .
- **Log on** as you normally do.
  When Windows opens, Notepad is also opened.
- **Exit** Notepad.

5 Create a shortcut to Calculator in the StartUp folder:

NOTE: Below, a different method is used to create a shortcut than those used in step 2.

- **Right-click** the Start button, then **click** Explore.
  Windows Explorer opens with the Start Menu in the title bar and its contents in the right pane.
- **Expand** the Programs folder and **locate** the StartUp folder in the left pane. (You will use it later.) *Continued on the next page*

To place program shortcuts in the StartUp menu so the programs start automatically when you turn on the computer.

⌨ **Keyboard Steps to**

Open the StartUp Folder

1. **Press** Ctrl + Esc , Esc .
2. **Press** Shift + F10 .
3. **Press** O (Open).
4. **Press** Tab until an item in the workspace is selected.
5. **Press** ↑↓ (arrow keys) to select Programs.
6. **Press** Enter .
7. **Press** ↑↓ (arrow keys) to select Startup.
8. **Press** Enter .

Create a Shortcut for a Program in the StartUp Folder

1. **Press** Alt + F (File).
2. **Press** N (New).
3. **Press** S (Shortcut).
4. **Press** Alt + R (Browse).
5. **Press** Tab until an item in the workspace is selected.
6. **Press** ↑↓ (arrow keys) to select the Windows folder.
7. **Press** Enter .
8. **Press** ↑↓ (arrow keys) to select the desired program.
9. **Press** Alt + O (Open).
10. **Press** Enter to activate the Next button.
11. **Press** Enter to activate the Finish button.
12. **Press** Alt + F (File).
13. **Press** C (Close).

Look at the StartUp Menu

1. **Press** Ctrl + Esc .
2. **Press** P (Programs).
3. **Press** S until StartUp is highlighted.
4. **Press** Enter .

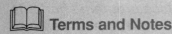

Continued from the previous page

- **Scroll** up in the left pane to find the Windows folder, then **select** it.
- **Click** <u>Show Files</u> in the right pane, if necessary.
- **Scroll** down in the right pane, **right-click** Calc, then **click** Create <u>S</u>hortcut.

  Shortcut to Calc appears, selected, at the end of the files in the right pane.
- **Scroll** down through the left pane until the StartUp folder is visible.
- **Drag** Shortcut to Calc onto the StartUp folder.
- **Exit** Windows Explorer.

⑥ Change a shortcut so the program starts minimized:

- **Right-click** 🏁 **Start**, then **click** <u>O</u>pen.
- **Open** Programs, then **open** Startup.

  Your Notepad and Calculator shortcuts appear in the StartUp folder window.

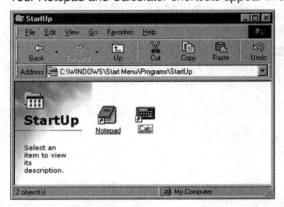

- **Right-click** the Notepad shortcut, then **click** P<u>r</u>operties.

  The Notepad Properties dialog box opens.
- **Click** the Shortcut tab, then **click** the <u>R</u>un drop-down arrow.

  The <u>R</u>un drop-down list box opens.

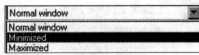

- **Click** Minimized, then **click** ⬜ OK ⬜.
- **Close** the StartUp folder window.

⑦ Use StartUp to start programs minimized:

- **Click** 🏁 **Start**, **click** Sh<u>u</u>t Down, **click** the <u>R</u>estart option button (to select it), then **click** ⬜ OK ⬜.
- **Log on** as you normally do.

  When Windows opens, Notepad is minimized (i.e., a button on the taskbar) and Calculator is open.
- **Click** the Notepad taskbar button, then **exit** Notepad.
- **Exit** Calculator.

⑧ Remove the program shortcuts from the StartUp folder:

- **Right-click** 🏁 **Start**, then **click** <u>O</u>pen.
- **Open** Programs, then **open** StartUp.
- **Delete** the Notepad and Calculator shortcuts.
- **Close** the StartUp folder window.
- **Empty** the Recycle Bin.

📖 Terms and Notes

NOTE: It is handy to have Windows 98 open with several of your most frequently used programs appearing as taskbar buttons.

⌨ Keyboard Steps to

Change Shortcuts to Open Minimized

—FROM THE STARTUP FOLDER—

1. **Select** the shortcut icon you want to change.
2. **Press** |Shift| + |F10|.
3. **Press** |R| (Properties).
4. **Press** |Ctrl| + |Tab| to select the Shortcut tab, if necessary.
5. **Press** |Alt| + |R| (Run).
6. **Press** |↑↓| (up or down arrow) until *Minimized* appears in the drop-down list box.
7. **Press** |Enter|.
8. **Press** |Alt| + |F4| to close the StartUp folder window.

Start Programs Using Startup

1. **Press** |Ctrl| + |Esc|.
2. **Press** |U| (Sh<u>u</u>t Down).
3. **Press** |R| (<u>R</u>estart).
4. **Press** |Enter|.
5. **Log on** as usual.

   The program(s) in the StartUp menu open automatically.

Begin with the desktop displayed and no taskbar buttons on the taskbar.

1 **Open the Control Panel:**

- **Click** 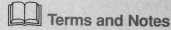, **point** to Settings, then **click** Control Panel.

  The Control Panel folder window opens:

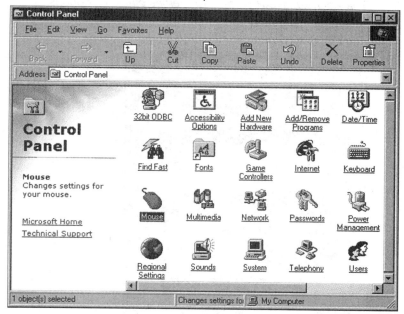

2 **Look at the New Hardware Wizard:**

- **Click** Add New Hardware.

  The Add New Hardware Wizard dialog box opens:

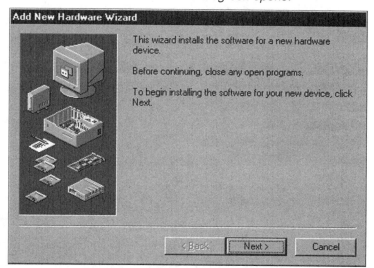

- **Click** Cancel to close the dialog box without making any changes.

To access dialog boxes and programs that let you change settings in Windows 98.

Terms and Notes

Control Panel
A folder that contains all command, control, and configuration functions for Windows 98 in one place.

NOTE: Since many of the controls and configurations in the Control Panel are sensitive, you are instructed to simply look at some of the features and then cancel out of the dialog box without making any changes.

Keyboard Steps to

Open the Control Panel

1. Press `Ctrl` + `Esc`.
2. Press `S` (Settings).
3. Press `C` (Control Panel).

Open a Control Panel Object

1. Press `Tab` until an item in the workspace is selected.
2. Press arrow keys to select the desired object.
3. Press `Enter` to open the desired object.

Continued on the next page

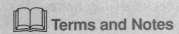 Terms and Notes

Below are most of the Control Panel objects and a short description of what they do.

Accessibility Options
Set accessibility options for your keyboard, sound, display, and mouse.

Add New Hardware
Install software for a new hardware device.

Add/Remove Programs
Install and uninstall components and software.

Date/Time
Set the date, time, and time zone.

Desktop Themes
Personalize your computer's appearance and sounds.

Display
Customize your display properties.

Fonts
Add, remove, and view fonts.

Game Controllers
Add, remove, and configure game controllers.

Internet
Change your Internet settings.

Keyboard
Set your keyboard properties.

Modems
Add, remove, and configure modems.

Mouse
Change settings for your mouse.

Multimedia
Customize multimedia devices.

Network
Configure network hardware and software.

Passwords
Change Windows passwords and set security options.

Power Management
Set power scheme for your computer.

Printers
Add, remove, and configure printers.

Regional Settings
Set options for numbers, currencies, dates, and times.

Sounds
Customize system and program sounds.

System
Obtain system information and change advanced settings.

Users
Set up accounts for multiple users on your computer.

Continued from the previous page

3 **Look at Add/Remove Programs Properties:**

- **Right-click** , then **click** Open.

  The Add/Remove Programs Properties dialog box opens.

- **Click** the Windows Setup tab.

  The Windows Setup tab moves to the front:

- **Click** Cancel to close the dialog box without making any changes.

4 **Look at Date/Time Properties:**

- **Click** Date/Time .

  The Date/Time Properties dialog box opens:

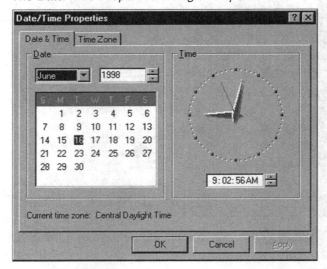

- **Click** Cancel to close the dialog box without making any changes.

⑤ Look at Regional Settings Properties:

- **Click** Regional Settings .

  The Regional Settings Properties dialog box opens:

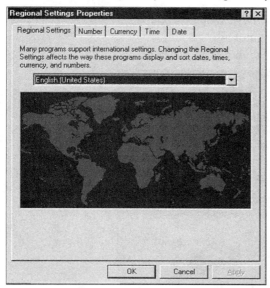

- **Click** [Cancel] to close the dialog box without making any changes.

⑥ Look at System Properties:

- **Click** System .

  The System Properties dialog box opens:

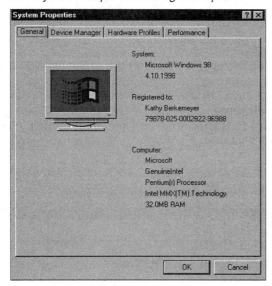

- **Click** [Cancel] to close the dialog box without making any changes.
- **Close** the Control Panel folder window.

EXERCISE 123 • Change Screen Colors

To make changes to the screen display using the Appearance tab in the Display Properties dialog box.

Begin with the desktop displayed and with no taskbar buttons on the taskbar.

1 **Open the Display Properties dialog box:**
- **Open** the Control Panel (review, Exercise 122, step 1).

- **Click** Display .
  The Display Properties dialog box opens.
- **Click** the Appearance tab.
  The Appearance tab moves to the front:

2 **View color schemes:**
- **Click** the Scheme drop-down list box.
- **Press** Page Up until you reach the top scheme, Brick.
  The preview area displays the Brick color scheme.
- **Press** ↓ (down arrow).
  The preview area displays the Desert color scheme.
- **Press** ↓ (down arrow) to scroll through the entire list and **notice** the changes to the preview area.

3 **Change the color scheme:**
- **Scroll** until you find a color scheme you like, then **click** it.
- **Click** Apply .
  The screen changes to the new color scheme.

4 **Change the color scheme to Windows Standard:**
- **With** the Appearance tab of Display Properties still open, **click** the Scheme drop-down list box.
- **Scroll** to the bottom of the list.
- **Click** the Windows Standard color scheme.
- **Click** Apply .
  NOTE: If you previously chose a large or extra large color scheme, you may not be able to see the Apply button now.

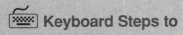 **Keyboard Steps to**

View Color Schemes

1. **Open** the Control Panel *(see Exercise 122)*.
2. **Press** Tab until an item in the workspace is selected.
3. **Press** ⬍ (arrow keys) to select the Display icon.
4. **Press** Enter to open the Display Properties dialog box.
5. **Press** Ctrl + Tab until the Appearance tab moves to the front.
6. **Press** Alt + S (Scheme).
7. **Press** Alt + ↓ (down arrow) to open the drop-down list box.
8. **Press** ⬍ (up or down arrow) and watch as the color schemes change in the preview area.

Change Color Schemes

—FROM THE SCHEME DROP-DOWN LIST BOX—

1. **Press** ⬍ (up or down arrow) until the desired color scheme is selected.
2. **Press** Enter .
3. **Press** Alt + A (Apply).
4. **Press** Enter to close the Display Properties dialog box.

Change to the Windows Standard Color Scheme

- **Follow** the procedure above, selecting *Windows Standard* in step 1.

Continued on the page 234

- IF you cannot see the Apply button, **press** ⎇ Alt + Ⓐ.
- IF the taskbar has increased in size to two layers, **point** to the upper edge of the taskbar until the arrow pointer becomes a sizing pointer, then **drag** the sizing pointer down until the taskbar returns to one layer. Each window element that can be changed is named here.

5 **Design a color scheme:**

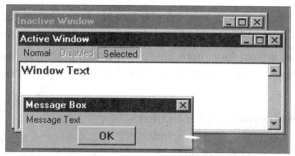

- **With** the Appearance tab of Display Properties still open, **click** the Item drop-down list box.
- **Scroll** until you find *Active Title Bar*, then **click** it.
- **Notice** that the size is 18 and the color is dark blue.
- **Click** the up arrow in the (item) Size spin box until you reach 30. **Notice** that the title bars in the preview area increase in size every time you click the up arrow.
- **Click** the (item) Color drop-down list box (not the [font] Color box).
  The color palette opens with 20 colors to choose from.

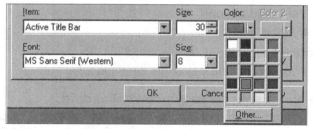

- **Click** the desired color.
  The two active title bars in the preview area change to the selected color.

6 **Change a window element's font:**

- **With** the Appearance tab of Display Properties dialog box still open and **with** *Active Title Bar* still in the Item drop-down list box, **click** the Font drop-down arrow.
  The Font drop-down list box opens:

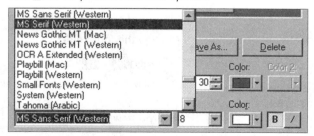

Continued on the next page

 Terms and Notes

COLOR SCHEMES
Brick
Desert
Eggplant
High Contrast #1
High Contrast #1 (extra large)
High Contrast #1 (large)
High Contrast #2
High Contrast #2 (extra large)
High Contrast #2 (large)
High Contrast Black
High Contrast Black (extra large)
High Contrast Black (large)
High Contrast White
High Contrast White (extra large)
High Contrast White (large)
Lilac
Lilac (large)
Maple
Marine (high color)
Plum (high color)
Pumpkin (large)
Rainy Day
Red, White, and Blue (VGA)
Rose
Rose (large)
Slate
Spruce
Storm (VGA)
Teal (VGA)
Wheat
Windows Standard
Windows Standard (extra large)
Windows Standard (large)

WINDOW ITEMS
3D Objects
Active Title Bar
Active Window Border
Application Background
Caption Buttons
Desktop
Icon
Icon Spacing (Horizontal)
Icon Spacing (Vertical)
Inactive Title Bar
Inactive Window Border
Menu
Message Box
Palette Title
Scrollbar
Selected Items
ToolTip
Window

NOTE: Some items are not shown in the color scheme preview area.

Continued from page 232

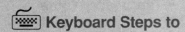 **Keyboard Steps to**

Design a Color Scheme

—FROM THE APPEARANCE TAB OF DISPLAY PROPERTIES—

Select window element to change:

1. Press **Alt** + **I** (Item).

2. Press **Alt** + **↓** (down arrow) to open the drop-down list box.

3. Press **↑↓** (arrow keys) to select desired item.

4. Press **Enter**.

Change window element size:

1. Press **Alt** + **Z** (Size).

2. Press **↑↓** (up or down arrow) to select desired item size.

Change window element color:

1. Press **Alt** + **L** (Color).

2. Press **Ctrl** + **Space**.

3. Press **Alt** + **O** (Other).
   The current Basic color is selected.

4. Press **↑↓** (arrow keys) to select desired item color.

5. Press **Space** to apply desired color.

6. Press **Enter** to return to the Appearance tab.
   The selected color is displayed in the preview area.

Change the font:

1. Press **Alt** + **F** (Font).

2. Press **Alt** + **↓** (down arrow) to open the drop-down list box.

3. Press **↑↓** (arrow keys) to select desired font face.

4. Press **Enter**.

Continued from the previous page

- **Click** MS Serif (Western).
  The font style changes on the title bars. The title bars return to their original sizes.

7 **Change a window element's font size:**

- **Click** the (font) Si**z**e drop-down arrow.
  The Size drop-down list box opens with 8 highlighted.

- **Press** **↓** (down arrow) to select *10*. **Notice** that the size of the font in the title bars increases.

- **Press** **↓** (down arrow) four more times. **Notice** the size of the font in the title bars gets larger each time you press the down arrow key.

- **Click** 14.

8 **Change a window element's font color:**

- **Click** the (font) Colo**r** drop-down arrow.
  The Color drop-down list box opens.

- **Click** a color other than the title bar color.
  The active title bar's font color changes from white to the color you chose.

9 **Change a window element's font type:**

- **Click** **B** (the Bold button).
  The title bar font becomes smaller since it loses its bold attribute.

- **Click** **/** (the Italic button).
  The title bar font is italicized (slanted).

- **Click** **B** (the Bold button).
  The title bar font is bold.

- **Click** **/** (the Italic button).
  The title bar font is straight; it loses its italic attribute.

10 **Change the color scheme to Windows Standard:**

- **With** the Appearance tab of Display Properties still open, **click** the **S**cheme drop-down list box, then **scroll** to the bottom of the list.

- **Click** the Windows Standard color scheme.

- **Click** **Apply**.

- **Close** the Display Properties dialog box.

- **Close** the Control Panel folder window.

Change the font size:

1. Press **Alt** + **E** (Si**z**e).

2. Press **Alt** + **↓** (down arrow) to open the drop-down list box.

3. Press **↑↓** (up or down arrow) to select desired font size.

4. Press **Enter**.

Change the font type:

1. Press **Tab** to move forward or
   Shift + **Tab** to move backward until a faint, dotted box appears on the Bold or Italic button.
   NOTE: If the button is selected, you will not see a faint, dotted box.

2. Press **Space** to toggle between selecting and deselecting the button.

Change the font color:

1. Press **Alt** + **R** (Colo**r**).

2. **Follow** steps 2-6, **Change window element color**.

Apply a new color scheme:

1. Press **Alt** + **A** (**A**pply).

2. Press **Enter**.

Begin with the desktop displayed and with no taskbar buttons on the taskbar.

1 **Open the Mouse Properties dialog box:**
- **Open** the Control Panel (review, Exercise 122, step 1).

- **Click** Mouse .

The Mouse Properties dialog box opens:

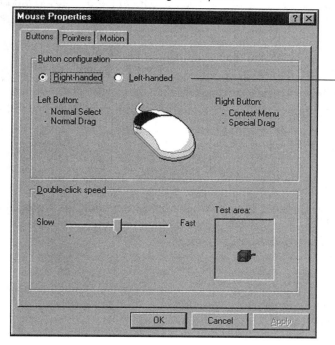

Right-handed
option button
(selected)
*This is the default
setting.*

2 **Change the mouse button configuration:**
- **Notice** the Left Button and Right Button functions.
- **Click** the Left-handed option button (to select it).
  The Left Button and Right Button functions switch.
- **Click** the Right-handed option button (to select it).
  The Left Button and Right Button functions switch back.

3 **Change and test the mouse button double-click speed:**
- **Double-click** the Test area box. Try until the box opens.
  A jack-in-the-box pops up.

- **Drag** the *Double-click speed* slider toward the Slow end.
- **Double-click** the Test area box. Is it easy to open (or close) the box?
- **Drag** the *Double-click speed* slider closer to the Fast end.
- **Double-click** the Test area box. Is it hard to open (or close) the box?
- **Drag** the *Double-click speed* slider as far right as possible.
- **Double-click** the Test area box. Can you open (or close) the box?
- **Drag** the *Double-click speed* slider to about the middle of the scale.
- **Double-click** the Test area box until it is closed.

Continued on the next page

***To access the Mouse
Properties dialog box and
change or look at the
various mouse controls.***

Keyboard Steps to

Access Mouse Properties

1. **Open** the Control Panel.
2. **Press** `Tab` until an item in the workspace is selected.
3. **Press** `↑↓` (arrow keys) to select the Mouse icon.
4. **Press** `Enter`.
5. **Press** `Ctrl` + `Tab` until the desired tab moves to the front.

Adjust Mouse Button Configuration

—FROM THE BUTTONS TAB—

Press `Alt` + `R` (Right-handed).
OR
Press `Alt` + `L` (Left-handed).

Look at the Mouse Pointers

—FROM THE POINTERS TAB—
With Scheme drop-down list box selected:

1. **Press** `Tab` two (or three) times until OK is selected but without dotted lines within it.
2. **Press** `↑↓` (up or down arrow), `Page Up` or `Page Down` to scroll through the pointers.

Change Mouse Pointer Size

—FROM THE POINTERS TAB—

1. **Press** `Alt` + `S` (Scheme).
2. **Press** `Alt` + `↓` (down arrow) to open the drop-down list box.
3. **Press** `↑↓` (up or down arrow) to select desired item:
   - Windows Standard
   - Windows Standard (large)
   - Windows Standard (extra large)

Toggle Mouse Pointer Trails

—FROM THE MOTION TAB—

Press `Alt` + `O` (Show pointer trails).

Apply New Mouse Properties

1. **Press** `Alt` + `A` (Apply).
2. **Press** `Enter`.

Terms and Notes

Pointer Shape

NAME	MOUSE POINTER
Normal Select	
Help Select	
Working in Background	
Busy	
Precision Select	
Text Select	
Handwriting	
Unavailable	
Vertical Resize	
Horizontal Resize	
Diagonal Resize 1	
Diagonal Resize 2	
Move	
Alternate Select	
Link Select	

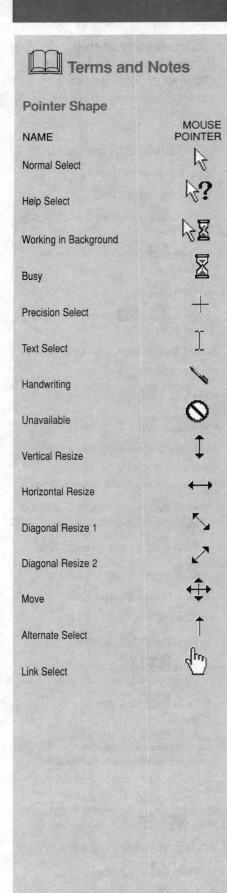

4 **Look at the mouse pointers:**
- **Click** the Pointers tab.
  The Pointers tab moves to the front.
- **Scroll** through the mouse pointers.
- **Click** the Normal Select pointer (at the top of the list), if it is not already selected.
  The Normal Select pointer shape appears in the box above the list of pointers and to the right.

5 **Change the mouse pointer size:**
- **Click** the Scheme drop-down list box, then **click** Windows Standard (large).
  The pointers become larger.

- **Click** the Scheme drop-down list box, then **click** Windows Standard (extra large).
  The pointers become even larger.

- **Click** the Scheme drop-down list box, then **click** (None).
  The pointers return to their original sizes.

6 **Look at mouse pointer trails:**
- **Click** the Motion tab.
  The Motion tab moves to the front.

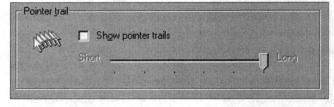

- **Click** the Show pointer trails check box (to select it).
- **Move** the mouse around and **watch** the pointer trails that follow the pointer.
- **Drag** the *Pointer trail* slider toward the Short end.
- **Move** the mouse around and **watch** the pointer trails that follow the pointer.
- **Drag** the *Pointer trail* slider all the way to the Long end.
- **Click** the Show pointer trails check box (to deselect it).
- **Close** the Mouse Properties dialog box using the Close button.
- **Close** the Control Panel folder window.

Begin with the desktop displayed and with no taskbar buttons on the taskbar.

1 **Open the Fonts folder window:**
- **Open** the Control Panel.
- **Click** Fonts .
  The Fonts folder window opens.
- **Click** List (the List button).
  The fonts are displayed in List view; some of your fonts may differ from those illustrated below.

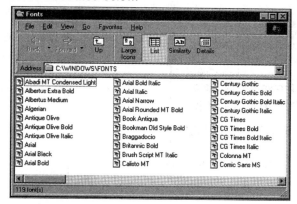

2 **View fonts by similarity:**
- **Click** Similarity (the Similarity button).
  The Fonts folder icon view changes.

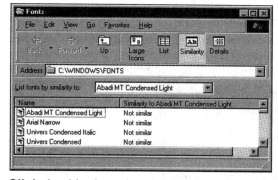

- **Click** the *List fonts by similarity to* drop-down list box.
- **Scroll** until you find Times New Roman, then **click** it.
  The order of the fonts changes with the most similar fonts at the top and the least similar fonts at the bottom.
- **Click** the *List fonts by similarity to* drop-down list box again.
- **Scroll** up until you find Arial, then **click** it.
- **Click** List (the List button).

3 **Hide font variations:**
- **Click** View, then **click** Hide Variations (Bold, Italic, etc.) to select it.
  Duplicate font names (those representing variations of a font) disappear.
- **Click** View, then **click** Hide Variations (Bold, Italic, etc.) to deselect it.

Continued on the next page

To access the Fonts folder and view the fonts that are available on your system.

📖 **Terms and Notes**

sans serif
A font design that has no cross-strokes at the top and bottom of the characters; it is straight.

For example: T

serif
A font design that has small cross-strokes at the top and bottom of the characters.

For example: T

TrueType font
Scalable fonts that are shipped with Windows 98: Arial, Courier New, Lucida Console, Symbol, Times New Roman, and Wingdings.

Continued from the previous page

Keyboard Steps to

Open the Fonts Folder

1. **Open** the Control Panel.

2. **Press** `Tab` until an item in the workspace is selected.

3. **Press** `↑↓` (arrow keys) to select the Fonts icon.

4. **Press** `Enter`.

View Fonts by Similarity

1. **Press** `Alt` + `V` (View).

2. **Press** `S`, `S` (List Fonts By Similarity).

3. **Press** `Enter`.

View Fonts in List View

1. **Press** `Alt` + `V` (View).

2. **Press** `L` (List).

Hide Font Variations

1. **Press** `Alt` + `V` (View).

2. **Press** `H` (Hide Variations [Bold, Italic, etc.]) to select or deselect option.

View and Print a Font

1. **Press** `↑↓` (arrow keys) to select the desired font.

2. **Press** `Alt` + `F` (File).

3. **Press** `O` (Open).

To print the font:

- Make sure your printer is turned on and ready to receive data.

- **Press** `Alt` + `P` (Print).
  The Print dialog box opens.

- **Press** `Enter`.
  The font prints.

4. **Press** `Alt` + `D` (Done).

   OR

   Press `Alt` + `F4`.

---

4 **View a font:**

- **Double-click** Arial.

  OR

  Right-click Arial, then **click** Open.
  The Arial (TrueType) dialog box opens:

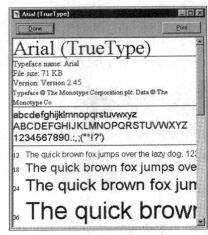

- **Scroll** through the document to examine it.

5 **Print a font:**

- **Click** [Print], then **click** [OK].
  The Arial font description and examples are printed.

- **Click** [Done].
  The Arial (TrueType) dialog box closes.

6 **View a symbol font (Wingdings):**

NOTE: *When the Wingdings font is selected, typing keyboard letters produces simple pictures.*

The Wingdings (TrueType) dialog box opens:

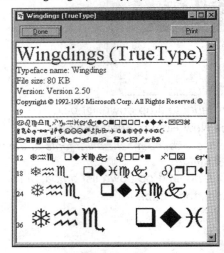

- **Print** the Wingdings font (review, step 5).
  The Wingdings font description and examples are printed.
- **Close** the Wingdings (TrueType) dialog box.
- **Close** the Fonts folder window.
- **Close** the Control Panel folder window.

Begin with the desktop displayed and with no taskbar buttons on the taskbar. You will need DUPLICATE DATA DISK 2 for this practice exercise.

1
- **Open** the MS-DOS Prompt window.
- **Switch** from the MS-DOS Prompt window to a full-screen display.
- **Return** to the desktop.
- **Switch** back to the MS-DOS full-screen display.
- **Switch** the MS-DOS full-screen display back to a window.
- **Exit** the MS-DOS Prompt window.

2
- **Start** the Run command.
- **Start** Notepad using the Run command.
- **Exit** Notepad.
- **Start** Calculator using the Run command.
  REMINDER: Calculator's filename is Calc.
- **Exit** Calculator.
- **Start** the Run command.
- **Start** Notepad using the Open drop-down list box.
- **Exit** Notepad.
- **Start** the Run command.
- **Locate** and **open** the CLOUDS file in the Windows folder using the Browse command. (Remember to change Files of type to *All Files* in the Browse dialog box.)
- **Exit** Paint.
- **Start** the Run command.
- **Insert** DUPLICATE DATA DISK 2 in drive A:.
- **Type** the path to CANDO.TXT (A:\cando.txt).
- **Open** CANDO.
- **Exit** Notepad.
- **Start** the Run command.
- **Type** the path to DOC2.TXT in the Docs folder (A:\DOCS\DOC2.TXT).
- **Open** DOC2.
- **Exit** Notepad.
- **Start** the Run command.
- **Type** the path to the Windows folder (C:\WINDOWS).
- **Open** the Windows folder.
- **Close** the Windows folder window.
- **Remove** DUPLICATE DATA DISK 2.

3
- **Open** the StartUp folder.
- **Create** a Notepad shortcut in the StartUp folder.
- **Change** the Notepad shortcut so Notepad starts minimized.
- **Close** the StartUp folder window.
- **Look** at the StartUp menu. Is Notepad in it?
- **Close** the menus.
- **Shut down** Windows 98 and **restart** your computer.
- **Log on** to Windows 98 as you normally do. Is Notepad minimized on the taskbar?

Continued on the next page

Tasks Reviewed:
- Use the MS-DOS Prompt
- Use the Run Command
- Use StartUp
- Use the Control Panel
- Change Screen Colors
- Change Mouse Settings
- Look at Fonts

Continued from the previous page

- **Click** the Notepad taskbar button to maximize its window.
- **Exit** Notepad.
- **Open** the StartUp folder, **delete** the Notepad shortcut, then **close** the StartUp folder window.
- **Empty** the Recycle Bin.

4
- **Open** the Control Panel.
- **Open** the Date/Time Properties dialog box.
- **Cancel** the Date/Time Properties dialog box without making changes.
- **Open** the Printers folder.
- **Close** the Printers folder window without making changes.
- **Close** the Control Panel folder window.

5
- **Open** the Control Panel.
- **Open** the Display Properties dialog box.
- **Change** to the color scheme of your choice.
- **Apply** the color change.
- **Change** the color scheme to Windows Standard.
- **Apply** the scheme change.
- **Select** *Menu* from the Item drop-down list box.
- **Change** the size of the menu bar.
- **Change** the color of the menu bar.
- **Change** the menu bar font to MS Serif (Western).
- **Change** the menu bar font size to 12.
- **Change** the menu bar font color.
- **Change** the menu bar font type to bold and italic.
- **Apply** the menu bar changes.
- **Return** the color scheme to Windows Standard.
- **Apply** the scheme change.
- **Close** the Display Properties dialog box.
- **Close** the Control Panel folder window.

6
- **Open** the Control Panel.
- **Open** the Mouse Properties dialog box.
- **Test** the mouse double-click speed.
- **Increase** and **test** the mouse double-click speed.
- **Decrease** and **test** the mouse double-click speed.
- **Change** the mouse double-click speed to a medium speed (i.e., the middle of the slider scale).
- **Look** at the mouse pointers.
- **Change** the mouse pointer size to Windows Standard (extra large).
- **Change** the mouse pointer size to Windows Standard.
- **Turn on** mouse pointer trails.
- **Drag** the mouse around and **look** at the mouse pointer trails.
- **Turn off** mouse pointer trails.
- **Close** the Mouse Properties dialog box using the Close button.
- **Close** the Control Panel folder window.

7
- **Open** the Control Panel.
- **Open** the Fonts folder window.
- **View** fonts in List view.
- **View** fonts by Similarity.
- **View** fonts in List view again.
- **Hide** font variations.
- **View** all font variations.
- **View** the Times New Roman font.

- **Print** the Times New Roman font.
- **Close** the Times New Roman (TrueType) dialog box.
- **Close** the Fonts folder window.
- **Close** the Control Panel folder window.

Lessons Eight–Eleven Worksheet (9) is on page 309.

NEXT
LESSON

Lesson Twelve

Internet Explorer

Table of Contents

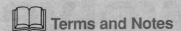
Terms and Notes

communications protocol
A set of rules (or standards) that lets computers connect with one another and exchange information with as little chance of error as possible. Also called *protocol*.

e-mail (electronic mail)
A global communication system for exchanging messages and attached files; this is probably the most widely used feature on the Internet. Many Web browsers include an e-mail program—Internet Explorer uses Outlook Express for e-mail.

FTP (File Transfer Protocol)
A method of remotely transferring files from one computer to another over a network (or across the *Internet*) using special communication software.

Gopher
A browsing system for Internet resources that predates the *World Wide Web*. Gopher works much like a directory, listing Internet sites in a hierarchical menu of files.

HTTP (Hypertext Transfer Protocol)
The protocol (standardized set of rules) that allows computers to communicate across the *World Wide Web* and connects Web pages to each other via *hyperlinks*.

hyperlink
Text or graphics that, when clicked, connect(s) to one of the following:
- another place on the same Web page.
- another Web page on the same Web site.
- another Web page on a different Web site.
Also called a *link*.

Internet
A global collection of computers that communicate with one another using common communication protocols (e.g., HTTP).

network
Two or more computers that are linked together to share programs, data, and certain hardware components, for example, a printer.

Telnet
A program that lets one computer log onto a remote computer. Telnet is often used to search libraries and databases.

Usenet
A global system of discussion groups called *newsgroups*. Many Web browsers include a newsreader program to access the newsgroups—Internet Explorer uses Outlook Express to access Usenet.

World Wide Web
The graphical part of the *Internet* that uses hypertext to link Web pages on Web sites around the world. Also called *Web*, *W3*, or *www*.

The Internet and the World Wide Web

The **Internet** is a global collection of computer **networks** that communicate with each other using common **communications protocols**. The Internet was developed by the U.S. Department of Defense in 1969 to support communications in the event of a nuclear attack. Before long, other networks connected to the Internet, enlarging its scope. In 1989, the **World Wide Web** was created, and today it makes up the largest part of the Internet.

The World Wide Web is the graphical part of the Internet. In its early days, the Internet was a text-based communication system; connecting with other sites meant typing long, cryptic addresses with 100 percent accuracy. Then, World Wide Web technology came along. The ability to include images on Web sites suddenly made the information on the Web more interesting—and easier to digest. Also, **HTTP (Hypertext Transfer Protocol)**, allowed Web pages to connect to each other via **hyperlinks**, making it easy to jump between Web sites located in opposite corners of the world.

Although the terms *Internet* and *World Wide Web* are often used interchangeably, it is important to remember that the Web is only one of many components that make up the Internet. Other components include **e-mail**, **FTP**, **Gopher**, **Telnet**, and **Usenet**. This book instructs you only on working with the World Wide Web part of the Internet.

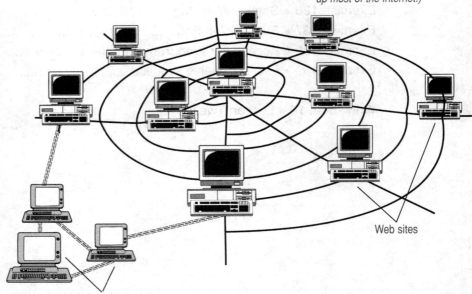

The Internet

World Wide Web
(Represented in this illustration as the computers that touch the web. Today, the World Wide Web makes up most of the Internet.)

Web sites

These are parts of the Internet that are not considered parts of the World Wide Web: e-mail, FTP, Gopher, Telnet, and Usenet.

What are Web Sites?

The Web is made up of millions of Web sites. **Web sites** are groups of **Web pages** posted on the Web by an individual or an organization. A typical Web site has many Web pages, starting with a **home page**, which outlines what the site has to offer. A typical Web site also contains hyperlinks to other Web pages within the site and to other Web sites as well. A Web site can be as small as a single Web page created by an individual or as large as several hundred Web pages created by an organization. Every Web page has a unique Internet address called a **URL (Uniform Resource Locator)**.

Web sites are created using **HTML (Hypertext Markup Language)**. HTML is a programming language that allows any computer connected to the Web to access and view Web pages and to navigate through them using hyperlinks. Web sites are posted on the Web by computers called **Web servers**. A server is a computer that can be accessed by other computers, or clients, on a network. A server usually shares files with (or provides other services to) the client computers that log onto it. Web servers use HTTP server software to serve up HTML documents when requested by a client connected to the Web, such as a Web browser. As you will see on the following page, a Web browser is a software program that allows you to locate, call up, and display documents posted on the World Wide Web. The Internet Explorer browser program comes as a component of Windows 98.

Getting Connected to the Internet

You must have a connection to access the Internet. There are several methods of connecting to the Internet, and new, faster methods are under development all the time. The three most common ways to connect to the Internet today are: online services, Internet service providers (ISP), and direct access.

An **online service** is a business, such as AOL, CompuServe, or Microsoft Network (MSN), that offers many communication services—among them, access to the Internet. When you use an online service, you must use their connection program to log on to their service, then once connected, you can use Internet Explorer. Online services have monthly fees that cover their many services, and additional hourly Internet access fees can add up fast.

An **Internet service provider** is a smaller, more specialized company that offers fewer options than an online service. ISPs offer Internet access at either an hourly rate for a lower fee, or unlimited access at a higher fee. They also provide you with an e-mail account. In the past, Internet access through an ISP has been less expensive than access through an online service.

Direct access to the Internet is available through many educational institutions and large organizations. Rather than using a modem, these groups have a dedicated line that provides a continuous connection to the Internet.

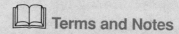
Terms and Notes

dial-up access
A widely used method of accessing the Internet in which you use a modem and telephone line to connect to the Internet through an *Internet service provider* or *online service*. Dial-up access is said to be "temporary" as opposed to "dedicated." See *direct access*, below.

direct access
A convenient method of accessing the Internet that is used by large organizations and some schools in which a dedicated line provides a continuous connection to the Internet. Direct access is said to be "dedicated" as opposed to "temporary." See *dial-up access*, above.

home page
1. The first page of a *Web site*. The home page usually outlines what the site has to offer, somewhat like a book's table of contents.
2. The first page you see when you open Internet Explorer (or another Web browser). Click the Home button in Internet Explorer to return to the home page.
Also called the *start page*.

HTML (Hypertext Markup Language)
The programming language used to create Web pages so that they can be viewed, read, and accessed by any computer running on any type of operating system.

Internet service provider (ISP)
A company (often local) that provides you with a connection to the Internet for a fee. An example of *dial-up access*.

online service
A business, such as AOL, CompuServe, or Microsoft Network (MSN), that offers access to the Internet (along with other services) for a fee. An example of *dial-up access*.

URL (Uniform Resource Locator)
The unique address assigned to each page on the Web. Your Web browser uses URLs to locate and retrieve Web pages. Also called *address* or *Web address*.

Web page
A document created using *HTML* that can be posted on the World Wide Web by a *Web server*.

Web server
A server that uses HTTP server software to serve up *HTML* documents when requested by a Web client, such as a Web browser.

Web site
A group of related *Web pages* served up by a *Web server* on the World Wide Web. A typical Web site has a *home page* and includes hyperlinks to other Web pages on the site.

Continued on the next page

Continued from the previous page

Internet Explorer
The Windows 98, Web-browsing program with a built-in interface to the Active Desktop and with many easy-to-use features that open the door to the world of information on the Internet.

Web browser
A program that lets you access the Web and view Web pages. Also called *browser*.

Some Internet Activities

- Send and receive e-mail
- Entertainment
- Order products
- Find information
- Retrieve files
- Chat with others
- Subscribe to Web pages
- Join newsgroups
- Go on virtual field trips
- Make travel arrangements
- Do video conferencing
- Obtain stock quotes
- Promote your business
- Do banking tasks
- Publish on the Web
- Do on-line tutorials
- Take classes
- Find phone numbers
- Get weather reports
- Get current news
- Track packages

Web Browsers

Web browsers are programs for viewing the Web. They are simply vehicles for accessing the information and many features on the Web. Web browsers work in conjunction with your Internet connection, and they offer their own set of handy features such as:

- Keeping a history of Web pages you have opened.
- Providing a way to save your favorite Web-page addresses.
- Providing toolbar buttons that let you:
  —easily go backward and forward between Web pages opened during the current Internet session.
  —return to the home page.
  —interrupt a Web-page download.

The Windows 98 Web browser, Internet Explorer, is the browser used in this book.

Warnings

Be careful not to believe everything you see on the Internet. Anyone can publish information, and since there is no Internet editor or monitor, some information may be false. All information found on the World Wide Web should be checked through reputable sources for accuracy.

Be careful when sending confidential information to anyone over the Internet. Much of what you send is easily accessible to others, and computer hackers can find ways to access information that is "protected," including e-mail.

The Internet is a fun and exciting place, but there are some frustrations associated with its use. Expect to run into occasional glitches, get disconnected from time to time, and experience difficulties locating certain Web sites.

Your computer can also get computer viruses from the Internet. These small, frequently destructive, computer programs hide inside innocent-looking programs.

For a more detailed look at the Internet, you may want to go through DDC's *Learning the Internet, 2nd Edition*.

Internet-Related Features Already Covered

Since Windows 98 combines its user interface with its Web browser, **Internet Explorer**, many earlier exercises in this book have included Internet-related features:

- Exercise 36—Use Back, Forward, and Up Buttons
- Exercise 39—Manage Toolbars
- Exercise 40—Use the Address Bar to Find Folders
- Exercise 44—View Explorer Bars
- Exercise 57—Use Favorites
- Exercise 74—Turn the Active Desktop Off and On
- Exercise 75—Work Offline
- Exercise 76—Create a Web-Page Object
- Exercise 77—Add a Web-Page Object to the Desktop
- Exercise 78—Select an HTML Desktop Background

Where the features in the above exercises are covered again in Lessons 12 and 13, the directions will be repeated in most cases.

Begin with the desktop displayed and with no taskbar buttons on the taskbar.

1 **Start Internet Explorer and connect to the Internet:**
  • IF you are using an online service, **follow** their instructions to connect to the service, then **minimize** the online service window.

  • **Click** (the Internet Explorer icon) on the desktop.
  • IF the Refresh in Offline Mode dialog box appears, **click** `Connect`.
  • IF you are using an ISP connection, your modem will automatically begin connecting to the Internet, or the Dial-up Connection dialog box may open. If the dialog box opens:
    —**Type** your user name in the User name text box, if necessary.
    —**Type** your password in the Password text box, if necessary.
    —**Click** the Save password check box (to select it), if desired.

    —**Click** `Connect`.
  • IF you have direct access to the Internet through a dedicated line, you are already connected to the Internet. **Skip** to Exercise 128.
    Internet Explorer opens, and the Internet icon on the right end of the menu bar starts to rotate: Internet icon (animated)

    The status bar displays the loading progress of the home page:

    Loading progress

    > Opening page http://

    The home page is displayed in the workspace. The illustration below shows the default home page, home.microsoft.com.

Web-page name   Menu bar

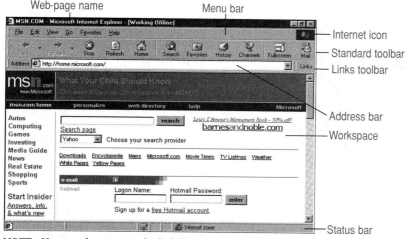

Internet icon
Standard toolbar
Links toolbar
Address bar
Workspace

Status bar

NOTE: Your workspace may look different since Microsoft makes frequent changes to its home page. Your home page may also have been changed to a different Web site.

2 • **Go on** to Exercise 128 without stopping.

To start Internet Explorer and connect to the Internet.

📖 **Terms and Notes**

ASSUMPTION: It is assumed that you have an established connection to the Internet through one of the following:
  • *an online service, such as AOL or CompuServe.*
  • *an Internet service provider.*
  • *direct access that is provided by large organizations and some schools.*

WARNING: Since you are working live on the Internet, we cannot guarantee that Web pages will appear as indicated in this book. Web pages are updated regularly so entries and hyperlinks may be different. Web pages may also be completely redesigned or even removed from the Web.

home page
  1. The first page of a Web site. The home page usually outlines what the site has to offer, somewhat like a book's table of contents.
  2. The first page you see when you open Internet Explorer (or another Web browser). Click the Home button in Internet Explorer to return to the home page.
Also called the *start page.*

Internet service provider (ISP)
A company (often local) that provides you with a connection to the Internet for a fee.

⌨ **Keyboard Steps to**

Start Internet Explorer
  1. **Press** `Ctrl` + `Esc`.
  2. **Press** `P` (Programs).
  3. **Press** `↑↓` to highlight the Internet Explorer group folder.
  4. **Press** `→` to open the cascading menu.
  5. **Press** `↑↓` to highlight Internet Explorer.
  6. **Press** `Enter`.

Connect to the Internet Using an Internet Service Provider
—WITH DIAL-UP CONNECTION OPEN—
  1. **Type:** *[your user name],* if necessary.
  2. **Press** `Tab`.
  3. **Type:** *[your password],* if necessary.
  4. **Press** `Tab`.
  5. **Press** `Space` to select the Save password check box, if necessary.
  6. **Press** `Enter`.

EXERCISE 128 • Exit Internet Explorer

Continue from Exercise 127 without stopping.

① Exit Internet Explorer:

- **Click** **X** (the Internet Explorer Close button).
  Internet Explorer closes.

② Disconnect from the Internet:

- IF you have direct access to the Internet through a dedicated line, you do not need to disconnect. **Skip** to step 3.
- IF you are using an online service, **follow** their instructions to disconnect from the service.
- IF you are using a dial-up connection through an ISP, the Disconnect dialog box may appear. If it does, **click** [Yes].
  Your Internet connection closes.
- IF you are using a dial-up connection through an ISP, and the Disconnect dialog box does not appear, and the Connected Modem icon is still displayed in the taskbar system tray:

  —**Double-click** (the Connected Modem icon) to open its dialog box.
  The Connected to [your Internet service provider] *dialog box appears.*

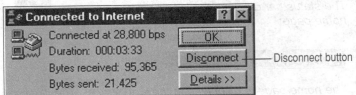

Disconnect button

  —**Click** [Disconnect]
  Your Internet connection closes, and the Connected Modem icon disappears from the system tray.

③ Start Internet Explorer from the taskbar:

- IF you are using an online service, **follow** their instructions to connect to the service, then **minimize** the online service window.
- **Point** to the Launch Internet Explorer Browser icon on the Quick Launch toolbar that resides, by default, on the left end of the taskbar.
  The Launch Internet Explorer Browser icon raises to become a button, and a ToolTip appears with the button's name:

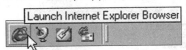

- **Click** (the Launch Internet Explorer Browser button).
- IF you are using an ISP connection and the Dial-up Connection dialog box opens, **enter** your user information, then **click** [Connect].

④
- **Go on** to Exercise 129 without stopping.

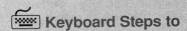

Continue from Exercise 128 without stopping.

1 **Look at the Internet Explorer menus:**
- **Click** the File menu to open it, then **point** to the remaining menu items, examining each menu as it opens.

  Each menu drops down.

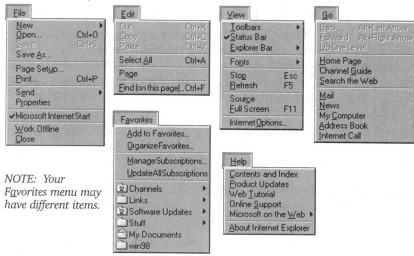

  NOTE: Your Favorites menu may have different items.

- **Click** outside the menus to close them.

2 **Hide and display Standard toolbar text labels:**

NOTE: If the Standard toolbar displays text labels (the default), the Print and Edit buttons may not show on the right end of the toolbar.

- **Click** View, then **point** to Toolbars.

  The Toolbars menu opens.

- IF Text Labels is selected, **click** Text Labels (to deselect it); otherwise, **click** outside the menu to close it.

  The Standard toolbar displays its buttons without text labels. Also shown below are the Address bar and the Links toolbar.

- **Click** View, **point** to Toolbars, then **click** Text Labels (to select it).

  The Standard toolbar displays text labels with its buttons.

3 - **Exit** Internet Explorer and **disconnect** from the Internet (review, Exercise 128), or **go on** to Exercise 130.

  NOTE: If you are connecting to the Internet using direct access, please disregard any instruction to connect to or disconnect from the Internet.

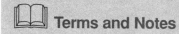

To retrieve a Web page by typing a URL in the Address bar.

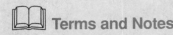 **Terms and Notes**

communications protocol
A set of rules (or standards) that lets computers connect with one another and exchange information with as little chance of error as possible.

domain name
The unique name that identifies an Internet site. A domain name has two or more parts separated by periods (often called *dots*):
- The part on the left of the final dot is the unique part of the Web-site name. It is called the *second-level domain name*.
- The part on the right of the final dot is the type of Web publisher, for example, .com (commercial) or .gov (government). It is called the *top-level domain name.*

While www is a common part of the domain name of Web sites, it is not always an essential part (and it is certainly not a unique part) of a domain name. Many Web sites today can be reached with or without www as part of the address. However, in this book, you will be instructed to use the www if it is part of the domain name.

HTTP (Hypertext Transfer Protocol)
The protocol (standardized set of rules) that allows computers to communicate across the World Wide Web and connects *Web pages* to each other via hyperlinks.

URL (Uniform Resource Locator)
The unique address assigned to each page on the Web. Your Web browser uses URLs to locate and retrieve Web pages. Also called *address* or *Web address.*

Web page
A document created using HTML that can be posted on the World Wide Web by a *Web server.*

Web server
A server that uses HTTP server software to serve up HTML documents when requested by a Web client, such as a Web browser.

Web site
A group of related Web pages served up by a Web server on the World Wide Web. A typical Web site has a home page and includes hyperlinks to other Web pages on the site.

What is a URL?

Protocol   Domain name

Example of a URL: **http://www.ddcpub.com**

A **URL (Uniform Resource Locator)** is the entire address for a Web site or Web page. Every URL has at least two parts. The first part of the URL in the example above, *http:*, is the **communications protocol** used to access a **Web site**. (The two slashes are a network code.)

The second part of the URL in the example above, *www.ddcpub.com*, is the unique name for the Web site, called a **domain name**. The part of the domain name which follows the final dot, *.com*, is called the *top-level domain name*; it refers to the type of Web publisher (or the Web site's country of origin). Some common types of Web publishers are listed below:

DOMAIN	TYPE	DOMAIN	TYPE
.com	commercial/business	.org	various organizations
.gov	government	.mil	military
.edu	educational	.net	network resources

The part of the domain name that comes before the final dot, *www.ddcpub*, is called the *second-level domain name*, and it names the entity that posts the Web page.

Some URLs have a third part—the path to a **Web page** within a Web site. In this URL, *http://www.ddcpub.com/learn*, the additional part, */learn,* names the Web page, *Learn the Net with DDC.* (The single slashes that occur in URLs after the domain name separate folder names and filenames on the Web site's computer.)

Begin with the desktop displayed and with no taskbar buttons on the taskbar.

1
- **Start** Internet Explorer and **connect** to the Internet, if necessary (review, Exercise 127).

2
   Go to a Web site using the Address bar:
- **Click** the Address bar.
   The URL is highlighted:

NOTE: You may have a different URL in your Address bar.

- **Type:** www.ddcpub.com then **press** .
   NOTE: Internet Explorer automatically enters the Web protocol and two slashes (http://) in the Address bar so that you do not have to type them when accessing a site.
   The DDC Publishing Web site is loaded into Internet Explorer. The Internet icon is animated, indicating that the Internet connection is active.

Web-page name

Internet icon

DDC Publishing's URL

NOTE: Your workspace may look different because DDC Publishing may have changed its home page.

3 **Go to a Web page in the current site using the Address bar:**
- **Click** the Address bar text box.

  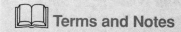

  The URL is highlighted. Notice that Internet Explorer added a slash at the end of the domain name you entered in step 2.
- **Press** `End` to move the cursor to the end of the URL.
- **Type:** learn then press `Enter`.

  The Learn the Net with DDC Web page is loaded into Internet Explorer.

4 **Go to Internet Explorer's home page using the Address bar:**
- **Click** the Address bar text box.
- **Type:** home.microsoft.com/ then **press** `Enter`.

  The Internet Explorer home page is loaded.

5 **Return to DDC's home page using the Address bar:**
- **Click** the Address bar drop-down arrow.

  The Address bar drop-down list opens.

  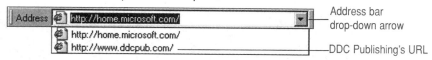

  Address bar drop-down arrow

  DDC Publishing's URL
- **Click** DDC Publishing's URL.

  The DDC Publishing home page moves quickly into the workspace without the Internet icon rotating and with very little, if any, loading progress in the status bar.

  NOTE: Internet Explorer stores Web pages that you load and can quickly reload them from memory instead of loading them from scratch through your Internet connection.

6 **Use the Address bar AutoComplete feature:**
- **Click** the Address bar text box, then **type:** hom

  The AutoComplete feature suggests a match as you type and highlights that match in the Address bar.

  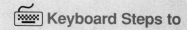
- **Press** `Enter` to load the suggested match, the MSN.com home page.

7 **Access Web sites using business URLs:**

  NOTE: This method of loading a company's Web site doesn't always work because the company's URL may not match its name. Often though it's worth a try.
- **Click** the Address bar text box.
- **Type:** www.burgerking.com then **press** `Enter`.

  The Burger King Web site is loaded into Internet Explorer.
- **Click** the Address bar text box.
- **Type:** www.historychannel.com then **press** `Enter`.

  The History Channel *Web site is loaded into Internet Explorer.*
- **Click** the Address bar text box.
- **Type:** www. and **type** the company name of your choice, **type:** .com and then **press** `Enter`.
- IF a dialog box appears saying that Internet Explorer cannot open the site you used, **click** `OK` and try another company.

8
- **Exit** Internet Explorer and **disconnect** from the Internet (review, Exercise 128), or **go on** to Exercise 131.

📖 Terms and Notes

AutoComplete
A feature in the Address bar that automatically completes an address when you begin to enter a previously typed address.

Web-page name
A descriptive title given to a Web page; not its URL. The name of the loaded Web page appears in the Internet Explorer title bar.

NOTE: The letter cases (i.e., upper- or lowercase) used in URLs are not usually important; however, occasionally they do matter.

⌨ Keyboard Steps to

Go to a Web Site Using the Address Bar

—WITH INTERNET EXPLORER OPEN—

1. **Press** `F4`.

   OR

   Press `Ctrl` + `O` (Open).
2. **Type** the desired URL.
3. **Press** `Enter`.

Access a URL in the Address Bar Drop-Down List Box

—WITH INTERNET EXPLORER OPEN—

1. **Press** `F4` to open the Address bar drop-down list box.
2. **Press** `↑↓` (up or down arrow) to select the desired item.
3. **Press** `Enter`.

To load Web pages and move to different locations within a Web site using hyperlinks.

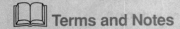 **Terms and Notes**

hyperlink
Text or graphics that, when clicked, connect(s) to one of the following:
- another place on the same Web page.
- another Web page on the same Web site.
- another Web page on a different Web site.

In Windows 98, hyperlinks are also used to connect one location to another within your computer system. When you point to a hyperlink, the arrow pointer becomes a hand. Also called a *link*.

Begin with the desktop displayed and with no taskbar buttons on the taskbar.

1
- **Start** Internet Explorer and **connect** to the Internet, if necessary (review, Exercise 127).
- IF the URL in the Address bar is not *home.microsoft.com/*, **click** the Address bar, **type:** home.microsoft.com/ and **press** Enter.
  The MSN.COM *Web page is loaded into Internet Explorer.*
- **Scroll** to the bottom of the Web page, **view** the Web-page contents, then **scroll** back to the top of the Web page.

2 Select hyperlinks:
- **Move** the arrow pointer around on the Web page and **notice** when the arrow pointer changes to a hand:
  NOTE: Any element that turns the arrow pointer into a hand is a hyperlink.
- **Notice** the topics on the black bar displayed near the top of the Web page.
  The first four topics take you to Web pages within the MSN.COM *Web site.*

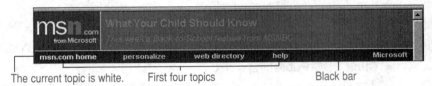

The current topic is white.   First four topics   Black bar

3 Link to a different Web page in the same Web site:
- Point to the second topic, *personalize*.
  The hand pointer appears.
- Point to the third topic, *web directory*.
  The hand pointer appears:

- **Click** web directory.
  The web directory Web page is loaded. Notice the first four topics across the black bar near the top of the Web page. Because it is the current Web page, web directory *is now white.*
- **Notice** the current Web-page name is displayed in the title bar and the current URL is displayed in the Address bar.

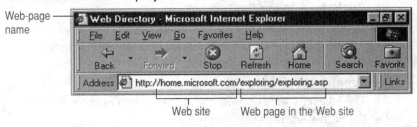

Web-page name

Web site   Web page in the Web site

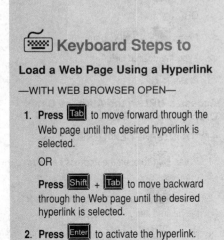 **Keyboard Steps to**

Load a Web Page Using a Hyperlink

—WITH WEB BROWSER OPEN—

1. **Press** Tab to move forward through the Web page until the desired hyperlink is selected.

   OR

   Press Shift + Tab to move backward through the Web page until the desired hyperlink is selected.

2. **Press** Enter to activate the hyperlink.

④ Link to another area on the same Web page:

- **Move** the arrow pointer around in the Web page and **notice** when the arrow pointer changes to a hand.
- **Scroll** to the bottom of the Web page.

  The bottom of the Web page has a link back to the top of the Web page.

  NOTE: *It is fairly common to see these convenient links at the bottom of Web pages; they allow you to return directly to the top of the Web page without using the scroll bar.*

- **Click** Back to top.

  The hyperlink takes you to the top of the Web page.

- **Click** ⬅ Back (the Back button) on the Standard toolbar.

  The bottom of the page jumps back into view. This is the screen you last saw and the location of the hyperlink you last used.

- **Click** ➡ Forward (the Forward button) on the Standard toolbar.

  The top of the screen jumps into view.

⑤ Link to a Web page on a different Web site:

- **Click** Microsoft (the *Welcome to Microsoft's Homepage* Web page hyperlink) on the right end of the black bar near the top of the Web page.

  The Welcome to Microsoft's Homepage *Web page is loaded. Its URL is: www.microsoft.com/ie40.htm.*

- **Click** Microsoft Network (the Microsoft Network hyperlink), located on the black bar near the top of the Web page.

  The Microsoft Network *Web site is loaded.*

  —IF Microsoft Network does not appear on the black bar near the top of the Web page, **click** ▶ Business (the Business hyperlink), then **skip** to step 6.

- **Notice** that the URL for *The Microsoft Network* Web page now appears in the Address bar.

    Web site   Web page in the Web site

- **Scroll** through the Web page and **notice** the hyperlinks leading to different topics of interest.

- **Click** one of the following: sidewalk.com or **Sidewalk City Guides** (the Sidewalk hyperlinks).

  The welcome to sidewalk *Web site is loaded, displaying hyperlinks to some large cities.*

- **Click** the File menu and **notice** the list of recently used Web sites.

  A check mark appears next to the current Web page, welcome to sidewalk.

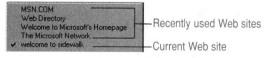

    —Recently used Web sites
    —Current Web site

⑥
- **Exit** Internet Explorer and **disconnect** from the Internet (review, Exercise 128), or **go on** to Exercise 132.

Keyboard Shortcuts

Scroll Within a Web Page

ACTION	PRESS
Line up	↑
Line down	↓
Screen up	Page Up
Screen down	Page Down
Beginning of Web page	Home
End of Web page	End

EXERCISE 132 • Change the Home Page

To change the home page and then change back to the default home page.

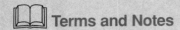 **Terms and Notes**

WARNING: Your home page is probably already set to http://home.microsoft.com, as the default. However, even if it is not, you will set this Web page as your default home page in this exercise and then leave this change in place for the rest of the exercises in this book. If you currently have a home page that is not the default shown above, you should write down its URL so you can reset it as the home page after you complete this book.

home page

1. The first page of a Web site. The home page usually outlines what the site has to offer, somewhat like a book's table of contents.
2. The first page you see when you open Internet Explorer (or another Web browser). Click the Home button in Internet Explorer to return to the home page.

Also called the *start page*.

⌨ **Keyboard Steps to**

Change to the Default Home Page

—WITH INTERNET EXPLORER OPEN—

1. Press **Alt** + **V** (View).
2. Press **O** (Internet Options).
3. Press **Tab** twice to select the Use Default button.
4. Press **Enter**.
5. Press **Tab** until the OK button is selected.
6. Press **Enter**.

Change the Home Page to the Currently Displayed Web Page

—FROM THE DESIRED WEB PAGE—

1. Press **Alt** + **V** (View).
2. Press **O** (Internet Options).
3. Press **Tab** to select the Use Current button.
4. Press **Enter**.
5. Press **Tab** until the OK button is selected.
6. Press **Enter**.

Begin with the desktop displayed and with no taskbar buttons on the taskbar.

1 **Load the Web page that you want to set as your new home page:**
   - **Start** Internet Explorer and **connect** to the Internet, if necessary (review, Exercise 127).
   - **Click** the Address bar, **type:** www.ddcpub.com then **press** Enter.
     The DDC Publishing Web site is loaded into Internet Explorer.
   - **Click** 🏠 Home (the Home button).
     The Home button takes you back to your home page.
   - **Click** ↩ Back (the Back button).
     Internet Explorer goes back to the DDC Publishing Web site.

2 **Change the home page to the currently displayed Web page:**
   - **Click** View, then **click** Internet Options.
     The Internet Options dialog box opens with the General tab selected. The Home page section is at the top of the dialog box.

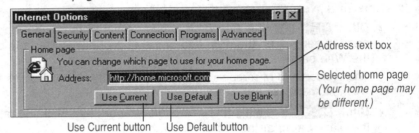

Address text box — Selected home page *(Your home page may be different.)*

Use Current button   Use Default button

   - IF the home page in the Address text box is not the default, *http://home.microsoft.com/*, **write** down its address so you can reset it as the home page later, if you desire.
   - **Click** Use Current, then **click** OK.
     The home page was changed to: http://www.ddcpub.com/

3 **Return to the home page using the Home button:**
   - **Click** the Back button.
     Internet Explorer goes back to the previous Web page.
   - **Click** the Home button.
     The Home button takes you to the new home page: http://www.ddcpub.com/

4 **Change to the default home page:**
   - **Click** View, then **click** Internet Options.
   - **Click** Use Default, then **click** OK.
     The home page has changed to the default Internet Explorer home page: http://home.microsoft.com/
   - **Click** 🏠 Home (the Home button).
     The Home button takes you to the default home page: http://home.microsoft.com/
     NOTE: The rest of the exercises in this book will use the Microsoft Internet Start page as the home page.

5
   - **Exit** Internet Explorer and **disconnect** from the Internet (review, Exercise 128), or **go on** to Exercise 133.

Stop a Web Page from Loading • EXERCISE 133

Begin with the desktop displayed and with no taskbar buttons on the taskbar.

1 • **Start** Internet Explorer and **connect** to the Internet, if necessary (review, Exercise 127).

2 **Stop the loading of a Web page:**

• **Locate**  (the Stop button) on the Standard toolbar and **be ready** to click the Stop button shortly after you click the Microsoft hyperlink.

• **Click** **Microsoft** (the Welcome to Microsoft's Homepage hyperlink), located in the black bar across the top of the Web page; then, after a few

moments—but before the page is fully loaded, **click** [Stop].
The Welcome to Microsoft's Homepage *Web page stops loading.*

• **Notice** the picture icons that indicate unloaded graphics. The number of icons will depend on how soon you interrupted the loading process.

Picture icon

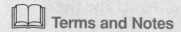
Microsoft Corporation

• IF the Web page loaded completely before you clicked the Stop button, don't worry about it and **skip** to step 4.

3 **Restart a stopped Web page:**

• **Click** [Refresh] (the Refresh button) on the Standard toolbar.
The Web page restarts its loading.

4 **Stop and restart the loading of another Web page:**

NOTE: Keep in mind that since you have a live connection to the Internet, it is possible that some sites, including the one below, may not be available at this time. If this occurs, replace the URL with that of another available site.

• **Click** the Address bar text box.

• **Type:** www.pepsi.com then press [Enter].

OR

Type: www.makeawish.org then press [Enter].

• **Click** [Stop] (the Stop button) before the Web page is fully loaded.
Internet Explorer stops loading the Web page.

• **Click** [Refresh] (the Refresh button) and let the Web page load completely.
Internet Explorer restarts and completes loading the Web page.

5 • **Exit** Internet Explorer and **disconnect** from the Internet (review, Exercise 128).

To interrupt the loading of a Web page by clicking the Stop button on the Standard toolbar.

Terms and Notes

Why Stop a Web Page from Loading?

There are two main reasons to stop a Web page from loading:

• to stop a very large Web page because it is taking longer to load than you want to wait.
• to regain control of your Web browser when it continues trying to load a Web page which, for some reason, won't load.

NOTE: Since we cannot predict when a Web page will quit loading on its own, preventing you from accessing Internet Explorer, we cannot walk you through this type of event. However, this exercise shows you how to stop the loading of a Web page before the load is complete.

Keyboard Steps to

Stop a Web Page from Loading
SHORTCUT: [Esc]
—WITH INTERNET EXPLORER OPEN—
1. **Press** [Alt] + [V] (*V*iew).
2. **Press** [P] (Sto*p*).

Restart a Web Page Loading
—WITH DESIRED URL IN ADDRESS BAR—
Press [F5] (Refresh).

Terms and Notes

dimmed command
A command or button that cannot be used in the current situation. It is displayed in gray instead of in black or in color.

Begin with the desktop displayed and with no taskbar buttons on the taskbar.

1
- **Start** Internet Explorer and **connect** to the Internet (review, Exercise 127).
  The MSN.COM *Web page is loaded into Internet Explorer because you set it as your home page in Exercise 132.*

2 **Load some Web pages:**
- **Click** the Address bar, **type:** www.ddcpub.com then **press** Enter.
  The DDC Publishing Home Page *Web page is loaded.*
- **Click** [Learn the Net] (the Learn the Net button). You may have to scroll to find it.
  The DDC Publishing Learn the Net *Web page is loaded.*
- **Click** Lesson 2: Internet Explorer, Exercise 2 "White House"
  An old version of the Welcome To The White House *Web page, stored on the DDC Publishing Web site, is loaded.*

3 **Move back and forth one Web page at a time:**
- **Notice** that the Back button is available, and that the Forward button is dimmed, because there is nothing to go forward to:

- **Point** to [Back] (the Back button).
  A ToolTip tells you where the Back button will take you:

- **Click** [Back] (the Back button).
  Internet Explorer moves back to the previous Web page, and the Forward button is now available.
- **Click** [Forward] (the Forward button).
  Internet Explorer moves "forward" to the previous Web page, and the Forward button is dimmed again.
- **Click** [Back] (the Back button).
  Internet Explorer goes back to the previous Web page, DDC Publishing Learn the Net.
- **Click** [Back] (the Back button) again.
  Internet Explorer goes back to the next previous Web page, DDC Publishing Home Page.
- **Click** [Back] (the Back button) once again.
  Internet Explorer goes back to the home Web page, MSN.COM, *and the Back button is dimmed.*

Keyboard Steps to

Move Back and Forth One Web Page at a Time

BACK:  OR 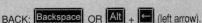 (left arrow).

FORWARD: +  OR

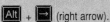 (right arrow).

—WITH INTERNET EXPLORER OPEN—

1. **Press** Alt + G (Go).
2. **Press** B (Back) to go backward.
   OR
   Press F (Forward) to go forward.

Move to a Specific Web Page

—WITH INTERNET EXPLORER OPEN—

1. **Press** Alt + F (File).
2. **Press** ↑↓ (up or down arrow) to select desired recently used Web page.
3. **Press** Enter to load desired Web page.

---

④ Move back and forth to/from a specific Web page:

- **Click** the Forward button drop-down arrow.

  A list of Web pages that you can return to appears:

—Forward button drop-down arrow

- **Click** *Welcome To The White House.*

  The Welcome To The White House *Web page is loaded.*

- **Click** the File menu.

  The recently used Web-page section lists the available Web pages and displays a check mark beside the current Web page.

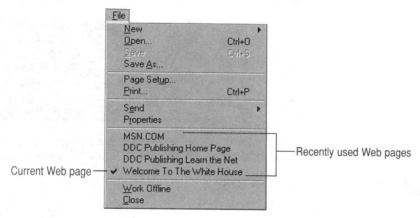

Current Web page—

—Recently used Web pages

- **Click** *MSN.COM* on the File menu.

  The MSN.COM *Web page is loaded.*

- **Click** the File menu, then **click** *DDC Publishing Learn the Net.*

  The DDC Publishing Learn the Net *Web page is loaded.*

- **Click** (the Home button) to return to the MSN.COM Web page.

⑤ - **Exit** Internet Explorer and **disconnect** from the Internet, or **go on** to Exercise 135.

EXERCISE 135 • Use Favorites with the Internet

To view, open, add, rename, and organize Web sites in the Favorites folder.

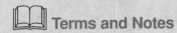

Terms and Notes

Favorites menu
A list of frequently used Web sites and/or folders that you can easily access from the Start menu, all folder windows, Windows Explorer, or Internet Explorer.

Add a Web Site to Favorites

—FROM INTERNET EXPLORER—

1. **Load** the desired Web page. *(See Keyboard Steps for Exercise 130).*

2. **Press** `Alt` + `A` (F<u>a</u>vorites).

3. **Press** `Enter` to accept the preselected <u>A</u>dd to Favorites option.
   The Add Favorite dialog box opens.
   —IF you want to change the name of the Web page:
   - **Press** `Tab`.
   - **Type** the desired new name.

4. **Press** `Enter` to add the current Web page to your Favorites.

Open a Favorite with the Start Menu

1. **Press** `Ctrl` + `Esc` OR `⊞` (the Windows key).

2. **Press** `A` (F<u>a</u>vorites).

3. **Press** `↕` (arrow keys) to select the favorite item you want to open.

4. **Press** `Enter`.

Open the Favorites Explorer Bar

—FROM INTERNET EXPLORER—

1. **Press** `Alt` + `V` (<u>V</u>iew).

2. **Press** `E` (<u>E</u>xplorer Bar).

3. **Press** `F` (<u>F</u>avorites).

Close the Favorites Explorer Bar

—WITH THE FAVORITES EXPLORER BAR OPEN—

1. **Press** `Alt` + `V` (<u>V</u>iew).

2. **Press** `E` (<u>E</u>xplorer Bar).

3. **Press** `N` (<u>N</u>one).

Begin with the desktop displayed and with no taskbar buttons on the taskbar.

1 **Look at favorites:**

- **Start** Internet Explorer and **connect** to the Internet, if necessary.

- **Click** [Favorites] (the Favorites button) on the Standard toolbar.
  The Favorites Explorer bar opens on the left side of the browser window (see Exercise 44, View Explorer Bars).

- **Point** to [Links] (the Links folder icon) on the Favorites Explorer bar.
  Links becomes a raised button.

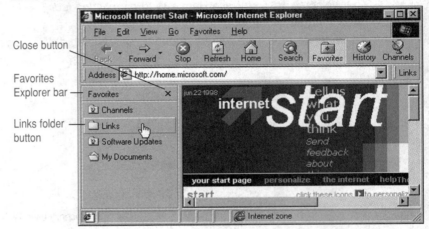

2 **Open a favorite Web site:**

- **Click** [Links] (the Links folder button) in the Explorer bar.
  The Links folder opens, displaying the favorites stored in it.

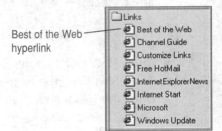

- **Click** [Best of the Web] (the Best of the Web hyperlink).
  The Web Directory Web page opens in the right pane. It contains hyperlinks to many interesting Web sites.

- **Close** the Favorites Explorer bar by clicking its Close button.

3 **Add a Web page to the Favorites folder:**

- **Load** the DDC Publishing Web site. Its URL is: *www.ddcpub.com* (review, Exercise 130).

- **Click** the F<u>a</u>vorites menu, then **click** <u>A</u>dd to Favorites.
  The Add Favorite dialog box appears:

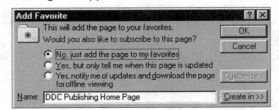

- **Click** [OK] to add the Web page to the Favorites folder without subscribing to it.

- **Load** the History Channel site: *www.historychannel.com* (review, Exercise 130).
- **Click** the F<u>a</u>vorites menu.

  The F<u>a</u>vorites menu drops down, displaying the same folders at the bottom of the menu as were in the Favorites Explorer bar. The DDC Publishing Home Page has been added to the list.

  NOTE: Your F<u>a</u>vorites menu may have other items on it.

  New favorite

4 **Add a favorite and change its name:**
- **Click** <u>A</u>dd to Favorites.

  The Add Favorite dialog box opens.
- **Click** the <u>N</u>ame text box, **delete:** The then **click** [OK].
- **Click** the F<u>a</u>vorites menu and **notice** the new favorite, *History Channel*, at the bottom.
- **Press** Esc to close the F<u>a</u>vorites menu.

5 **Create a subfolder in the Favorites folder:**
- **Click** the F<u>a</u>vorites menu, then **click** <u>O</u>rganize Favorites.

  The Organize Favorites dialog box opens.
- **Click** 📁 (the Create New Folder button) in the Organize Favorites dialog box.
- **Type:** [your three initials] over the highlighted, *New Folder* text, for example, mmb; then **press** Enter.

  NOTE: If you are in a classroom or another setting in which more than one person uses a computer, using initials as folder names individualizes the folders and makes them easy to identify.

  The Organize Favorites dialog box reappears.

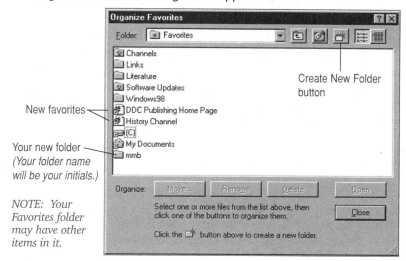

New favorites

Your new folder *(Your folder name will be your initials.)*

NOTE: Your Favorites folder may have other items in it.

6 **Organize your favorites:**
- **Drag** the DDC Publishing Home Page favorite onto your new folder.
- **Drag** the History Channel favorite onto your folder.
- **Close** the Organize Favorites dialog box.

 **Keyboard Steps to**

Organize Your Favorites

—FROM INTERNET EXPLORER—

1. **Press** Alt + A (F<u>a</u>vorites).
2. **Press** O (<u>O</u>rganize Favorites).

   The Organize Favorites dialog box opens.
3. **Choose** from the following options:

   Create a new folder
   - **Press** Tab until an item in the workspace is selected.
   - **Press** Shift + F10 (shortcut menu).
   - **Press** N (<u>N</u>ew).
   - **Press** Enter to accept the preselected option, *Folder*.

   Rename a favorites folder
   - **Press** ↕ (arrow keys) to select the item you want to rename.
   - **Press** Alt + M (Rena<u>m</u>e).
   - **Type** the desired folder name.
   - **Press** Enter.

   Move a favorite into a folder
   - **Press** Tab until an item in the workspace is selected.
   - **Press** ↕ (arrow keys) to select the item you want to move.
   - **Press** Alt + V (Mo<u>v</u>e).

     The Browse for Folder dialog box opens.
   - **Press** ↕ (up or down arrow) to select the destination folder.
   - **Press** Enter.

   Delete an item
   - **Press** Tab until an item in the workspace is selected.
   - **Press** ↕ (arrow keys) to select the item you want to delete.
   - **Press** Alt + D (<u>D</u>elete).
   - **Press** Enter to confirm deletion.
4. **Press** Alt + C (<u>C</u>lose) to close the Organize Favorites dialog box.

Continued on the next page

Continued from the previous page

7 **Open a favorite Web page from the Start menu:**

• **Exit** Internet Explorer, but do *not* disconnect from the Internet.
  Internet Explorer closes and the desktop appears.

• **Click** , **point** to F<u>a</u>vorites, then **point** to the folder you created in step 5.
  The favorites that you added in steps 3 and 4 appear in the folder you created.

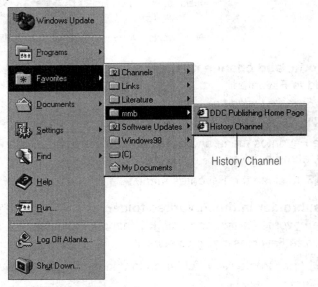

History Channel

• **Click** History Channel.
  Internet Explorer starts and loads The History Channel Web page.
  NOTE: *You can also open a favorite from any folder window by clicking the F<u>a</u>vorites menu and then clicking the desired favorite.*

8 **Delete a favorite from the Favorites folder:**

• **Click** the F<u>a</u>vorites menu, then **click** <u>O</u>rganize Favorites.
  The Organize Favorites dialog box opens.

• **Open** the folder you created in step 5 by double-clicking it.
  The folder opens and reveals the two favorites you dragged onto it in step 6.

• **Click** DDC Publishing Home Page, then **click** | <u>D</u>elete |.
  The Confirm File Delete dialog box opens.

• **Click** | <u>Y</u>es | (you do want to delete the favorite).

9 **Delete a folder from the Favorites folder:**

• **Click** [↑] (the Up One Level button) in the Organize Favorites dialog box.
  The Favorites folder workspace is displayed.

• **Click** the folder you created in step 5, then click | <u>D</u>elete |.
  The Confirm Folder Delete dialog box opens.

• **Click** | <u>Y</u>es | (you do *not* want to delete the folder and the favorite in it).

• **Close** the Organize Favorites dialog box.

10 • **Exit** Internet Explorer and **disconnect** from the Internet, or **go on** to Exercise 136.

Begin with the desktop displayed and with no taskbar buttons on the taskbar.

1 • **Start** Internet Explorer and **connect** to the Internet, if necessary.
   • **Load** the following web page: *www.ddcpub.com/learn*

2 **Save a Web page as an HTML document:**
   • **Click** <u>F</u>ile, then **click** Save <u>A</u>s.
   The Save HTML Document dialog box opens.
   • **Click** 🔼 (the Up One Level button) until *Desktop* appears in the Save <u>i</u>n drop-down list box.
   • **Delete** the text in the File <u>n</u>ame text box, then **type:** Learn
   • **Notice** that *HTML File* appears in the Save as <u>t</u>ype drop-down list box.
   • **Click** [<u>S</u>ave].
   The Web page is saved as an HTML document; that is, in the same format as it appears in Internet Explorer.

3 **Save a Web page as a text document:**
   • **Click** <u>F</u>ile, **click** Save <u>A</u>s, then **type:** Learn
   The new text replaces the highlighted text in the File <u>n</u>ame text box. Desktop remains in the Save <u>i</u>n drop-down list box.
   • **Click** the Save as <u>t</u>ype drop-down arrow, then **click** Text File (*.txt).
   • **Click** [<u>S</u>ave].
   The Web page is saved as a plain text document; that is, it does not contain graphics, hyperlinks, or other HTML formatting.

4 **Open an HTML document:**
   • **Click** ✍ (the Show Desktop button) on the taskbar.
   The two files appear as icons on the desktop:

HTML document ⸺[Learn]   Text document ⸺[Learn]

   • **Open** the HTML document icon, <u>Learn</u>.
   The HTML document opens in Internet Explorer. The graphics are not loaded, but their positions are indicated by the picture icons.

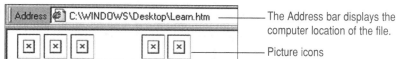

| Address | 🔄 C:\WINDOWS\Desktop\Learn.htm | ⸺ The Address bar displays the computer location of the file. |

☒ ☒ ☒   ☒ ☒ ⸺ Picture icons

   NOTE: Hyperlinks that appear in a saved Web page are not active.
   • **Exit** Internet Explorer.

5 **Open a text document:**
   • **Open** the text document icon, <u>Learn</u>.
   • **Exit** Notepad.

6 • **Put** both <u>Learn</u> documents in the Recycle Bin.
   • **Empty** the Recycle Bin.
   • **Click** the Internet Explorer taskbar button.

7 • **Exit** Internet Explorer and **disconnect** from the Internet, or **go on** to Exercise 136.

To save a Web page on your desktop as an HTML document and as a text document. To open those documents once they are saved.

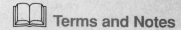 **Terms and Notes**

NOTE: When you save a Web page, all of the graphics that appeared on the Web page are replaced by picture icons in the saved version. The images are not saved because most Web-page images are actually stored in separate Web files, each with its own URL.

HTML (Hypertext Markup Language)
The programming language used to create Web pages so that they can be viewed, read, and accessed by any computer running on any type of operating system.

⌨ **Keyboard Steps to**

Save a Web Page

—WITH INTERNET EXPLORER OPEN—

1. **Load** the desired Web page. *(See Keyboard Steps for Exercise 130).*
2. **Press** [Alt] + [F] (<u>F</u>ile).
3. **Press** [A] (Save <u>A</u>s).
4. **Change** the following options as desired:
   Save in location
   • **Press** [Alt] + [I] (Save <u>i</u>n).
   • **Press** [↓] (down arrow) to open the drop-down list.
   • **Press** [↑↓] (up or down arrow) to select the desired location.
   • **Press** [Enter].
   Save as type
   • **Press** [Alt] + [T] (Save as <u>t</u>ype).
   • **Press** [↓] (down arrow) to open the drop-down list.
   • **Press** [↑↓] (up or down arrow) to select *HTML File* or *Text File*.
5. **Press** [Alt] + [N] (File <u>N</u>ame).
6. **Type** the desired filename.
7. **Press** [Enter].

EXERCISE 137 • Print a Web Page

To print the following: a hard copy of a Web page, the first page of a Web page, and a Web page with its table of links.

 Terms and Notes

WARNINGS: There is nothing in a Web page to indicate its precise length. Before you start to print a Web page, however, take a look at the size of its scroll box. If the scroll box is very small, it may take a lot of printed pages to print the Web page—maybe 15, 20, 30, or even 100. As you gain experience printing, you can estimate the number of pages that will print—the larger the scroll box, the fewer the number of printed pages in a Web page. If you just want to print a specific section of a Web page, you can either tell the printer to print a specific page number or you can select the text to print (you may also need to choose the Selection option button in the Print dialog box). However, except for the first and second printed page, it's hard to predict which printed page number will print a specific section of the Web page.

Since you are working live on the Internet, we cannot guarantee that Web pages will appear as indicated in this book. Web pages are updated regularly so entries and hyperlinks may be different. Web pages may also be completely redesigned or even removed from the Web.

Begin with the desktop displayed and with no taskbar buttons on the taskbar.

1
- **Start** Internet Explorer and **connect** to the Internet, if necessary.
- **Type:** www.ddcpub.com/lesson2.2/nasa/ in the Address bar, then **press** .
  An old version of The NASA Homepage is loaded from the DDC Web site.
- **Hide** the text labels on the Standard toolbar (review, Exercise 129).
  The entire Standard toolbar is displayed. (This is for those users whose screen resolution does not permit the entire toolbar to show when text labels are displayed.)

2 **Print a Web page:**
- **Make** sure your printer is turned on and ready to receive data.
- **Click** 🖨 (the Print button) on the Standard toolbar.
  The current Web page is sent to the printer without opening the Print dialog box. The top-right corner of each page shows the page number and the total number of pages printed. Your hard copy may not match the one below.

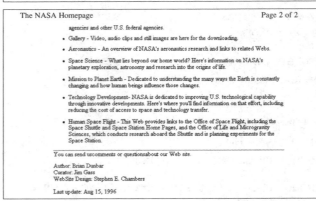

- **Display** the text labels on the Standard toolbar.

3 **Print only the first page of a Web page:**
- **Click** <u>F</u>ile, then **click** <u>P</u>rint.

The Print dialog box opens.
- **Click** the Pa<u>g</u>es option button (to select it).
The 1 in the <u>f</u>rom text box is highlighted.
- **Click** [OK].
Only the first printed page of the Web page prints.

Print range
section — from text box

All option
button —
(selected)

┌─Print range────────────────────┐
│ ⦿ <u>A</u>ll   │
│ ○ Pages <u>f</u>rom: [1] <u>t</u>o: [1]   │
│ ○ <u>S</u>election   │
└────────────────────────────────┘

Pages option button

4 **Print a Web page and its table of links:**
- **Load** the DDC Publishing Web site. Its URL is: *www.ddcpub.com*
- **Click** <u>F</u>ile, then **click** <u>P</u>rint.
The Print dialog box opens.
- **Click** the <u>A</u>ll option button (to select it).

Print table of links check box

Bottom section of the —
Print dialog box

┌──┐
│ ☐ Print all lin<u>k</u>ed documents   ☐ Print ta<u>b</u>le of links │
│   [OK] [Cancel] │
└──┘

- **Click** the *Print ta<u>b</u>le of links* check box (to select it), then **click** [OK].
The last page prints a table of all the hyperlinks on the Web page. The table of links looks something like the illustration below:

DDC Publishing Home Page   Page 3 of 3

This document contains the following shortcuts:

Shortcut Text	Internet Address
	http://www.ddcpub.com/html/order.html
	http://www.ddcpub.com/html/products.html
	http://www.ddcpub.com/html/custserv.html
	http://www.ddcpub.com/html/modules.html
	http://www.ddcpub.com/html/contact.html
	http://www.ddcpub.com/html/learn_the_internet.html
	http://www.ddcpub.com/html/tips.html
	http://www.ddcpub.com/html/updates.html
Amazon.com	http://www.amazon.com/exec/obidos/redirect-home/ddcpublishing
here	http://www.ddcpub.com/html/amazon2.html
Learning the Internet for Kids	http://www.ddcpub.com/html/products/z25.html
here	http://www.ddcpub.com/#monique
	http://www.ddcpub.com/html/lt_tix.html
Word	http://www.ddcpub.com/WORD97/HOME.html
Excel	http://www.ddcpub.com/EXCEL97/HOME.html
PowerPoint	http://www.ddcpub.com/POWERPOINT97/HOME.html
Access	http://www.ddcpub.com/ACCESS97/HOME.html
Outlook	http://www.ddcpub.com/OUTLOOK97/HOME.html
	http://www.ddcpub.com/html/inhour1.html
Interactive Catalog	http://www.ddcpub.com/catalog/catalog.zip
Customer Service	mailto:ddcpub@aol.com
Technical Support	mailto:techsupp@ddcpub.com
Webmaster	mailto:webmaster@ddcpub.com

---

5 • **Exit** Internet Explorer and **disconnect** from the Internet, or **go on** to Exercise 138.

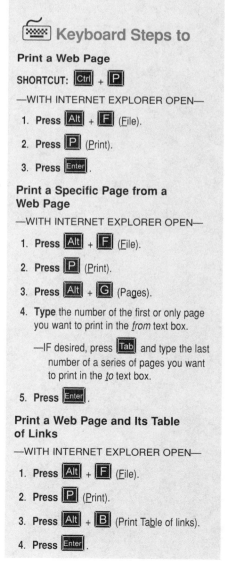

⌨ **Keyboard Steps to**

Print a Web Page
SHORTCUT: [Ctrl] + [P]
—WITH INTERNET EXPLORER OPEN—
1. **Press** [Alt] + [F] (<u>F</u>ile).
2. **Press** [P] (<u>P</u>rint).
3. **Press** [Enter].

Print a Specific Page from a Web Page
—WITH INTERNET EXPLORER OPEN—
1. **Press** [Alt] + [F] (<u>F</u>ile).
2. **Press** [P] (<u>P</u>rint).
3. **Press** [Alt] + [G] (Pa<u>g</u>es).
4. **Type** the number of the first or only page you want to print in the *from* text box.
   —IF desired, press [Tab] and type the last number of a series of pages you want to print in the *to* text box.
5. **Press** [Enter].

Print a Web Page and Its Table of Links
—WITH INTERNET EXPLORER OPEN—
1. **Press** [Alt] + [F] (<u>F</u>ile).
2. **Press** [P] (<u>P</u>rint).
3. **Press** [Alt] + [B] (Print Ta<u>b</u>le of links).
4. **Press** [Enter].

To start Internet Explorer within a folder window using four methods.

📖 Terms and Notes

Internet icon
The button at the right end of the menu bar, illustrated with a Windows flag, that accesses the Internet when clicked.

Begin with the desktop displayed and with no taskbar buttons on the taskbar.

1 **Start Internet Explorer using the Internet button:**
- IF you are using an online service, **follow** their instructions to connect to the service, then **minimize** the online service window.
- **Open** My Computer.
- **Click** 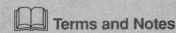 (the Internet button) on the right end of the menu bar and **connect** to the Internet as you usually do, if necessary.

  The Internet icon starts to rotate and Internet Explorer opens into the My Computer folder window. If you are using a modem to connect to the Internet, the Connected Modem icon appears in the taskbar system tray.
- **Click** the Back button.

  Internet Explorer disappears and My Computer reappears in the folder window.
- **Click** the Internet button again, then **click** the Back button again.

2 **Start Internet Explorer using the Address bar:**
- **Click** the Address bar, **type:** www.ddcpub.com then **press** [Enter].

  Internet Explorer opens in the folder window and loads the DDC Publishing Home Page.
- **Click** the Back button.

  Internet Explorer disappears and My Computer reappears in the folder window.

3 **Start Internet Explorer using the Go menu:**
- **Click** Go, then **click** Search the Web.

  Internet Explorer opens in the folder window, loads a search engine, and offers five search engines to pick from on the left side of the folder window.

- **Click** the Home button.

  The Internet Explorer home page loads.
- **Click** the Back button twice to return to the My Computer folder window.

4 **Start Internet Explorer using the Links toolbar:**
- **Double-click** [Links] (the Links title) to slide the Links toolbar open.
- **Click** [🔗] Best of the Web (the Best of the Web hyperlink).

  Internet Explorer opens in the folder window and loads the Best of the Web *Web page.*
- **Click** the Back button to return to the My Computer folder window.
- **Double-click** [Links] (the Links title) to slide the Links toolbar closed.
- **Close** the My Computer folder window and **disconnect** from the Internet.

Begin with the desktop displayed and with no taskbar buttons on the taskbar.

1
- **Start** Internet Explorer using the desktop Internet Explorer icon and **connect** to the Internet.

2
- **Exit** Internet Explorer but do *not* disconnect from the Internet.
- **Start** Internet Explorer using the Launch Internet Explorer Browser button on the taskbar.

3
- **Look** at each Internet Explorer menu: File, Edit, View, Go, Favorites, and Help and **examine** the menu items in each menu.
- **Hide** the Standard toolbar text labels.
- **Display** the Standard toolbar text labels.

4
- **Go** to the following Web site using the Address bar: www.cnn.com
- **Scroll** through the *CNN Interactive* Web site and look at the hyperlinks.
- **Go** to the following Web page using the Address bar: www.msnbc.com/news/default.asp
- IF the Security Warning dialog box appears, click No
- **Scroll** through the *MSNBC Cover Page* Web page.
- **Go** to Internet Explorer's home page using the Address bar and **complete** the following URL using AutoComplete: home.microsoft.com

5
- **Click** web directory on the black bar, then **click** the Health hyperlink in the *best of the web* index.

6
- **Click** File, **click** Open, **type:** www.ddcpub.com/lesson2.2/nasa and **press** Enter.
  The NASA Homepage is loaded.
- **Change** the home page to the current Web page, The NASA Homepage.
- **Click** the Back button, then **click** the Home button.
  The NASA Homepage is loaded.
- **Change** to the default home page.
- **Click** the Home button to return to the *MSN.COM* Web page.

7
- **Click** Microsoft on the black bar and, when the page starts to load, **click** the Stop button.
- **Scroll** through the stopped Web page and **notice** the picture icons that represent unloaded graphics.
- **Restart** the stopped Web page.
- **Exit** Internet Explorer, but do not disconnect from the Internet. (IF asked to disconnect, click the No button.)

8
- **Start** Internet Explorer.
- **Click** Microsoft, then click Microsoft Network (the Microsoft Network hyperlink) located on the black bar.
- **Scroll** until you find the Sidewalk hyperlink.

Continued on the next page

Internet Explorer

Tasks Reviewed:
- Start Internet Explorer
- Exit Internet Explorer
- Examine Internet Explorer
- Use the Address Bar to Access a Web Site
- Use Hyperlinks
- Change the Home Page
- Stop a Web Page from Loading
- Move Through Web Pages
- Use Favorites
- Save a Web Page
- Print a Web Page

Continued from the previous page

- **Click** <u>Sidewalk City Guides</u> or (one of the Sidewalk hyperlinks).

  The welcome to sidewalk *Web page is loaded.*
- **Click** **seattle** (the Seattle hyperlink).
- **Go back** to the *welcome to sidewalk* Web page.
- **Go forward** to the *today: seattle.sidewalk* Web page.
- **Go back** to the *MSN.COM* Web page using the Back button drop-down arrow.
- **Go forward** to the *today: seattle.sidewalk* Web page using the Forward button drop-down arrow.
- **Go to** the *welcome to sidewalk* Web page using the recently used Web-page section of the <u>F</u>ile menu.
- **Click** **houston** (the Houston hyperlink).

9
- **Click** the Favorites button to open the Favorites Explorer bar.
- **Click** the Links folder, then **click** the Best of the Web hyperlink to load the site.
- **Close** the Favorites Explorer bar.

  The Web Directory *Web page expands to fill the workspace.*
- **Add** the current page, Best of the Web, to the F<u>a</u>vorites menu and **change** the name of the Web page to BOW.
- After you complete the process of adding the BOW Web page to the F<u>a</u>vorites menu, **click** the F<u>a</u>vorites menu and **notice** the added Web page at the bottom of the menu.
- **Open** the Organize Favorites dialog box.
- **Create** a new folder; **name** it Practice.
- **Move** the BOW Web page into the Practice folder, then **close** the Organize Favorites dialog box.
- **Exit** Internet Explorer, but do *not* disconnect from the Internet.
- **Open** the BOW Web page from the Start menu.

  Internet Explorer opens, displaying the BOW Web page.
- **Open** the Organize Favorites dialog box, **delete** the Practice folder (with the BOW Web page in it), then **close** the Organize Favorites dialog box.

10
- **Press** [Ctrl] + [O] (Open), **type:** www.ddcpub.com/learn and **press** [Enter].

  The DDC Publishing Learn the Net *Web page opens.*
- **Save** the Web page on the desktop as an HTML File; **name** it Net1.
- **Save** the Web page on the desktop as a Text File; **name** it Net2.
- **Access** the desktop using the Show Desktop button on the taskbar.
- **Open** <u>Net1</u>, then **exit** Internet Explorer.
- **Open** <u>Net2</u>, then **exit** Notepad.
- **Click** the *Internet Explorer* taskbar button to activate it.

⑪ • **Print** the first page of the current Web page.

DDC Publishing Learning the Net   Page 1 of 1

Home
Products
Customer Service
Office 97 Modules
Order Form
Contact
Learn the Net
Online Tips
Book Updates

Learn the Net

The exercises on this page are intended to work with our book *Learning the Internet*. If you do not have a copy of this book, you may contact us to order one.

Users of *Learning the Internet*: Click here for important update information.

Lesson 1: Netscape Navigator, Exercise 2 "White House"
Lesson 1: Netscape Navigator, Exercise 2 "Smithsonian"

Lesson 2: Internet Explorer, Exercise 2 "White House"
Lesson 2: Internet Explorer, Exercise 2 "NASA"
Lesson 2: Internet Explorer, Exercise 5 "Smithsonian"

Lesson 3: Search Engines, Exercise 1 "Yahoo"
Lesson 3: Search Engines, Exercise 2 "Yahoo"
Lesson 3: Search Engines, Exercise 2 "MetaCrawler"
Lesson 3: Search Engines, Exercise 3 "Lycos"
Lesson 3: Search Engines, Exercise 4 "Alta Vista"
Lesson 3: Search Engines, Exercise 5 "Lycos"
Lesson 3: Search Engines, Exercise 6 "Excite"
Lesson 3: Search Engines, Exercise 7 "AltaVista"
Lesson 3: Search Engines, Exercise 8 "Yahoo"
Lesson 3: Search Engines, Exercise 9 "AltaVista"

Home | Products | Customer Service | Office 97 Modules | Order Form | Contact | Learn the Net | Online Tips | Book Updates

Contact our Customer Service department if you have questions about books, pricing, or orders.
Contact our Technical Support staff with questions about software and CD-ROM problems.
Contact our Webmaster if you have any problems, comments, or questions about our Web site.

http://www.ddcpub.com/learn/   9/20/98

• **Exit** Internet Explorer and **disconnect** from the Internet.
• **Put** Net1 and Net2 in the Recycle Bin.
• **Empty** the Recycle Bin.

Lesson Twelve Worksheet (10) is on page 310.

NEXT
LESSON

Lesson Thirteen
More Internet Explorer

Table of Contents

To locate text on a Web page using the Find (on this page) command.

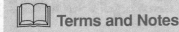

Terms and Notes

NOTES: If you are connecting to the Internet using direct access, please disregard any instruction to connect to or disconnect from the Internet.

Sometimes Web pages can be quite long. If you are searching for something specific, the Find (on this page) command is an important tool that can relieve a lot of frustration.

Begin with the desktop displayed and with no taskbar buttons on the taskbar.

1 **Load a Web page using the Open command:**
- **Start** Internet Explorer and **connect** to the Internet.
- **Click** File, then **click** Open.

  The Open dialog box appears with the insertion point in the Open text box.

  Open text box

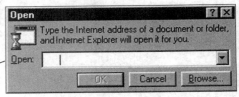

- **Type** the URL: www.ddcpub.com/lesson2.2/nasa then **click** OK.

  NOTE: When AutoComplete takes over, you can press the End key and continue as necessary to complete the URL, or you can type the entire URL and ignore AutoComplete.

  An old version of The NASA Homepage, is loaded from the DDC Publishing Web site.

2 **Find text on a Web page:**
- **Press** Ctrl + F (Find [on this page]).
  OR
  Click Edit, then **click** Find (on this page).

  The Find dialog box opens with the insertion point in the Find what text box and the Down option button selected.

  Find what text box

  Match whole word only check box

  Match case check box

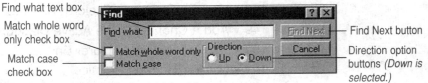

  Find Next button

  Direction option buttons *(Down is selected.)*

- **Type:** nasa in the Find what text box.
- **Press** Enter to activate the preselected Find Next button.
  OR
  Click Find Next.

  The first occurrence of the word NASA is selected.

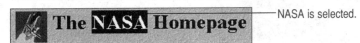
  NASA is selected.

- Continue **pressing** Enter or **clicking** Find Next until no more occurrences of the word *nasa* are found.

  NOTE: When you can't see the selected text, NASA, it is probably behind the Find dialog box. You can move the dialog box to see the selected text, if you wish.

  The Microsoft Internet Explorer dialog box appears. The last occurrence of the word NASA is selected at the bottom of the screen.

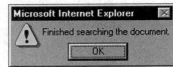

- **Click** OK.

  The Microsoft Internet Explorer dialog box disappears and the Find dialog box remains.

3 **Start a search where the previous one left off:**
- **Type:** web in the Find what text box, then **press** Enter.

  Find searches down from the last occurrence of the word NASA to find the next occurrence of the word web on the Web page.

- IF Find won't search for *web*, **skip** to step 5.
- **Press** [Enter] until the you reach the last occurrence of the word *web* and the Microsoft Internet Explorer dialog box reappears.
- **Click** [OK] to close the dialog box, then **click** [Cancel]. *The Find dialog box closes.*
- **Press** [Ctrl] + [F] (Find [on this page]).
- **Click** [Find Next]. *The Microsoft Internet Explorer dialog box reappears.*

4 Start a search from the top of a Web page:

- **Click** [OK], then **click** [Cancel].
- **Click** the workspace to deselect the text, *web*.
- **Press** [Ctrl] + [F] (Find [on this page]), then **click** [Find Next]. *Find searches from the top of the Web page and selects the first occurrence of the word* web *on the Web page.*
- **Click** [Find Next] until Find is finished searching the Web page. *Seven occurrences of the word,* web, *were found.*

5 Find whole word only:

- **Click** [OK], **click** [Cancel], **click** the workspace, then **open** the Find dialog box.
- **Click** the *Match whole word only* check box (to select it).
- **Click** [Find Next] until Find is finished searching the Web page. *Five occurrences of the whole word,* web, *were found.*

6 Find text that matches the case you enter:

- **Click** [OK], **click** [Cancel], **click** the workspace, then **open** the Find dialog box.
- **Type:** space in the Find what text box, then **click** [Find Next] until Find is finished searching the Web page. *Eleven occurrences of the word,* space, *were found.*
- **Click** [OK], **click** [Cancel], **click** the workspace, then **open** the Find dialog box.
- **Click** the Match case check box (to select it), then **click** [Find Next] until Find is finished searching the Web page. *Three occurrences of the lowercase word,* space, *were found.*

7 Search up a Web page for text:

- **Click** [OK], then **type:** page in the Find what text box.
- **Click** the Match case check box (to deselect it), then **click** the Up option button (to select it).
- **Click** [Find Next] until Find is finished searching the Web page. *Four occurrences of the word,* page, *were found.*
- **Click** [OK], then **click** [Cancel].

8
- **Exit** Internet Explorer and **disconnect** from the Internet, or **go on** to Exercise 141.

EXERCISE 141 • Copy Text from a Web Page to a Document

To copy Web-page text and paste it into a WordPad document.

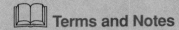 **Terms and Notes**

WARNING: It's easy to copy material from the Web, but it's not always legal. Before you copy text or graphic images to your own Web page or use them in other ways, make sure you have permission from the author or artist.

Begin with the desktop displayed and with no taskbar buttons on the taskbar.

1
- **Start** Internet Explorer and **connect** to the Internet, if necessary.
- **Load** the Web page with this URL: www.ddcpub.com/lesson2.2/nasa
- **Start** and **maximize** WordPad.
- **Switch** back to Internet Explorer. (Click its taskbar button.)
- **Scroll** down one screen on the Web page. (Click below the scroll box.)

2 Copy Web-page text:
- **Move** the arrow pointer around and **notice** that, when it is over text, the arrow pointer turns into an I-beam.
- **Point** to the beginning of the title so the arrow pointer turns into an I-beam pointer.

I-beam pointer

- **Drag** the I-beam pointer over the title to select it.

 —Selected text

- **Press** Ctrl + C (Copy).

Nothing seems to happen, but the text is copied.

3 Paste Web-page text into WordPad:
- **Switch** to WordPad. (Click its taskbar button.)
- **Press** Ctrl + V (Paste).

The title is copied into WordPad. The font is not as large as it was in the Web page.

NOTE: If you were to paste text into a more sophisticated word-processing program, the text formatting would match that on the Web page.

- **Switch** back to Internet Explorer.
- **Select** the first paragraph, then **right-click** the selected text.

NOTE: If you accidentally deselect the text, repeat the step above.

A shortcut menu appears:

Copy   Shortcut menu

> Welcome - This is a good place to begin your journey. Start by reading a letter from NASA Administrator, Dan Goldin, [Copy / Select All / Print] ategic Plan. Check out the User Tips page to find the helper applications you [ ] the most out of what we have to offer. If you're looking for something specific, [ ]rch engine for the top-level NASA pages.

- **Click** Copy, then **switch** to WordPad.
- **Right-click** the workspace, then **click** Paste.

The paragraph is pasted into WordPad.

NOTE: This text would have a bullet if it were pasted into a more sophisticated word-processing program.

- **Copy** the second paragraph from the Web page, **paste** it into WordPad, then **press** Enter.

4 Copy a URL:
- **Switch** back to Internet Explorer.
- **Click** the Address bar.
  The URL is selected.
- **Copy** the URL using the method you prefer.
- **Switch** to WordPad, **paste** the URL into WordPad, then **press** Enter .

5 Print a WordPad document:
- **Print** the document, then **start** a new document without saving the current document. (Click ☐ [the New button], click OK , then click No .)
  The document is printed.

> The NASA Homepage
>
> Welcome - This is a good place to begin your journey. Start by reading a letter from NASA Administrator, Dan Goldin, or NASA's Strategic Plan. Check out the User Tips page to find the helper applications you will need to get the most out of what we have to offer. If you're looking for something specific, there's a search engine for the top-level NASA pages.
>
> Today@NASA - If you've read about NASA recently or seen something on TV, this is place to go for links to more details about breaking news. You can find the most recent Hubble Space Telescope Images, links to the Shuttle Web and the latest news releases. [This site is extremely busy, please be patient.]
>
> http://www.ddcpub.com/lesson2.2/nasa/

6 • **Exit** Internet Explorer and **disconnect** from the Internet, or **go on** to Exercise 142.

EXERCISE 142 • Copy and Paste an Image into a Document

To copy a Web-page image and paste it into a WordPad document.

Begin with the desktop displayed and with no taskbar buttons on the taskbar.

1
- **Start** Internet Explorer and **connect** to the Internet, if necessary.
- **Load** the Web page with this URL: www.ddcpub.com/lesson2.2/whitehouse
- **Start** and **maximize** WordPad.
- **Switch** to Internet Explorer. (Click its taskbar button.)

2 Copy a Web-page image:
- **Right-click** the Good Afternoon image at the top of the page, then **click** <u>C</u>opy.
  Nothing seems to happen, but the image was copied.

3 Paste a Web-page image into WordPad:
- **Switch** to WordPad. (Click its taskbar button.)
- **Press** Ctrl + V (Paste).
  The Good Afternoon image was pasted into WordPad; it has a line around it with small squares indicating that it is selected.
- **Press** End to deselect the image, then **press** Enter.
  The insertion point moves to the right of the image when you press the End key. It moves below the image when you press the Enter key.
- **Switch** back to Internet Explorer.
- **Right-click** the White House image between the two flags, then **click** <u>C</u>opy.
- **Switch** to WordPad.
- **Right-click** the workspace, **click** <u>P</u>aste, then **press** End to deselect the image.
- **Press** Enter to move the insertion point below the image.

4 Paste a row of Web-page images:
- **Switch** back to Internet Explorer, **right-click** one of the flags, then **click** <u>C</u>opy.
- **Switch** to WordPad, then **paste** the flag into WordPad.
- **Click** to the right of the flag, then **paste** the flag again.
- **Paste** the flag into WordPad three more times, one after the other.
- IF the flag didn't copy the first time (because you caught it at the wrong time while it was waving), **copy** it again.
- After the flag is copied five times and the last flag is deselected, **press** Enter.
  A row of five flags appears across the page.

5 Combine copied Web-page text and images in WordPad:
- **Switch** to Internet Explorer, then **scroll** until you find the eagle image:

- **Copy** the eagle image, **switch** to WordPad, then **paste** the image beneath the flags.
- **Deselect** the image, then **press** Enter.

- **Switch** back to Internet Explorer, then **select** the text to the right of the eagle, including the heading, *Interactive Citizens' Handbook:* (review, Exercise 141).
- **Copy** the selected text, then **paste** it into WordPad.

6 **Copy one more image and print the WordPad document:**
- **Switch** back to Internet Explorer, **scroll** to the bottom of the Web page, then **copy** the image of the red, white, and blue pencil.
- **Paste** the image into WordPad.
- **Print** the document, then **exit** WordPad without saving.

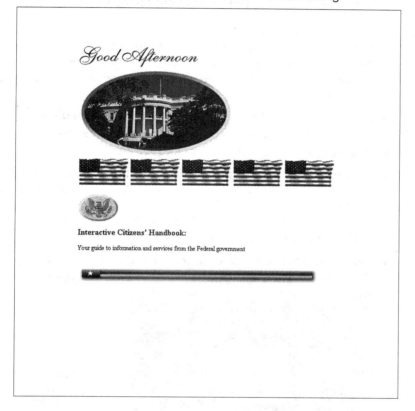

7 • **Exit** Internet Explorer and **disconnect** from the Internet, or **go on** to Exercise 143.

EXERCISE 143 • Use a Web-Page Image for Wallpaper

To set a Web-page image as wallpaper and change the way the wallpaper is displayed. To rename an Internet Explorer Wallpaper file and then delete the renamed file.

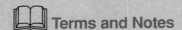 **Terms and Notes**

Quick Launch toolbar
A toolbar that appears next to the Start button on the taskbar (by default) and contains buttons for the following frequently used features: Internet Explorer, Outlook Express, desktop, and channels.

Begin with the desktop displayed and with no taskbar buttons on the taskbar.

1
- **Start** Internet Explorer and **connect** to the Internet, if necessary.
- **Load** the Web page with this URL: www.ddcpub.com/lesson2.5/si

2 Set a Web-page image as wallpaper:
- **Scroll** down one screen so the birthday cake image is visible.
- **Right-click** the birthday cake, then **click** Set as Wallpaper.
  The birthday cake image appears on the desktop.
- **Click** 🖉 (the Show Desktop button) on the taskbar.

3 Change the wallpaper display:
- **Right-click** the desktop, then **click** Properties.
  The Display Properties dialog box opens with the birthday cake image in the screen display preview and Internet Explorer Wallpaper selected in the Wallpaper list box.
- **Click** the Display drop-down arrow, **click** Tile, then **click** `OK`.
  The birthday cake image is repeated over the entire desktop.
- **Right-click** the desktop, then **click** Properties.
- **Click** the Display drop-down arrow, **click** Stretch, then **click** `OK`.
  NOTE: If you are using Windows 95 with Internet Explorer 4 installed, you may not have the Stretch option in your Display drop-down list box.
  The birthday cake image is stretched to fill the entire desktop.
- **Right-click** the desktop, then **click** Properties.
- **Click** the Display drop-down arrow, **click** Center, then **click** `OK`.
  The birthday cake image appears in the center of the desktop.

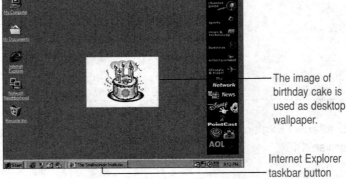

The image of birthday cake is used as desktop wallpaper.

Internet Explorer taskbar button

4 Change the Internet Explorer Wallpaper:
NOTE: Every time you set a new Web-page image as wallpaper, the new image replaces the previous one set as wallpaper.
- **Click** the Internet Explorer taskbar button.
- **Scroll** to the top of the Web page.
- **Right-click** the Smithsonian image, then **click** Set as Wallpaper.
- **Click** the Show Desktop button on the taskbar.
  The Smithsonian image has replaced the birthday cake image as the desktop wallpaper.
- **Right-click** the desktop, then **click** Properties.
  The Display Properties dialog box opens with the Smithsonian image in the screen display preview and Internet Explorer Wallpaper selected in the Wallpaper list box.
- **Close** the Display Properties dialog box.

5 **Rename Internet Explorer Wallpaper:**

NOTE: If you want to keep the current image as a wallpaper option, you can rename it before setting a new image as wallpaper. That way, the new image won't replace the existing one.

- **Click** My Computer, **open** (C:), **open** the Windows folder. (Remember to click <u>Show Files</u> if you are in Web Page view.)
- **Maximize** the Windows folder window, then **view** objects in Details view.
- **Sort** files by date modified in ascending order (newest to oldest).
- **Scroll** past the folders and **look** for the Internet Explorer Wallpaper file with its bitmap icon, <u>Internet Explor...</u> . (Its entire name may not be visible.)

  The Internet Explorer Wallpaper file is one of the first five files after the folders.

- **Point** to <u>Internet Explorer Wallpaper</u>.

  Web Page view displays the Smithsonian image on the left side.

- **Right-click** <u>Internet Explorer Wallpaper</u>, then **click** Rena<u>m</u>e.

  The filename is highlighted.

- **Type:** Smithsonian then **press** [Enter].

  The filename changes to Smithsonian.

- **Close** the Windows folder window.

6 **View the new wallpaper name:**

- **Right-click** the desktop, then **click** P<u>r</u>operties.
- **Notice** that the Internet Explorer Wallpaper file has returned to the default, blank desktop.

  The Display Properties dialog box opens with a blank screen display preview and Internet Explorer Wallpaper selected in the Wallpaper list box.

- **Press** [↑] (up arrow) until the Smithsonian wallpaper is selected.
- **Press** [↑] (up arrow) until you get to the top of the Wallpaper list box.

  (None) *is selected; the screen display preview is blank.*

- **Click** [OK].

  The desktop appears without wallpaper.

7 **Delete the renamed wallpaper:**

- **Click** My Computer, **open** (C:), **open** the Windows folder.
- **Maximize** the Windows folder window, then **view** objects as large icons.
- **Arrange** icons by name. (Right-click the workspace, point to Arrange <u>I</u>cons, then click *by <u>N</u>ame*.)
- **Scroll** until you find <u>Smithsonian</u>, then **point** to it (to select it).
- **Hold down** [Shift] while you **press** [Del], then **press** [Enter] to accept the <u>Y</u>es button.

  The Smithsonian file is deleted without being sent to the Recycle Bin.

- **Close** the Windows folder window.

8

- **Exit** Internet Explorer and **disconnect** from the Internet, or **go on** to Exercise 144.

 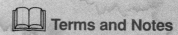

EXERCISE 144 • Save a Web-Page Image

To save a Web-page image on your desktop in two graphic file formats. To delete both versions of the file.

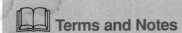 **Terms and Notes**

bitmap
A format for image files used by the Paint program (among others), which handles an image as a set of dots rather than as a mathematical formula. The filename extension for bitmap images is *.bmp*.

NOTE: If you are using Windows 95 with Internet Explorer 4 installed, your bitmap icon may look like this:

GIF (Graphics Interchange Format)
A standard format for image files on the Web. The filename extension for GIF images is *.gif*.

Begin with the desktop displayed and with no taskbar buttons on the taskbar.

1
- **Start** Internet Explorer and **connect** to the Internet, if necessary.
- **Load** the Web page with this URL: www.ddcpub.com/lesson2.5/si

2 Save a Web-page image as a GIF file:
- **Scroll** down one screen so the birthday cake image is visible.
- **Right-click** the birthday cake image, then **click** Save Picture As.
  The Save Picture dialog box appears.
- **Click** 🔼 (the Up One Level button) until *Desktop* appears in the Save in drop-down list box.
- **Click** the Save as type drop-down arrow.
  The Save as type list box opens, revealing that you can save the image in one of two file formats: GIF or Bitmap.

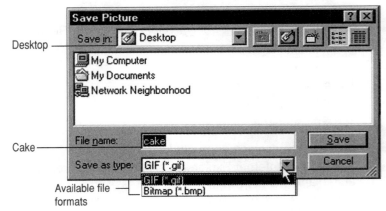

- **Click** GIF (*.gif).
- **Notice** that the File name text box contains the name, *cake*, by default.
- **Click** Save .
  The image was saved to the desktop as a GIF file.

3 Save a Web-page image as a bitmap file:
- **Right-click** the birthday cake image, then **click** Save Picture As.
  The Save Picture dialog box appears with Desktop *in the Save in drop-down list box and the name,* cake, *in the File name text box.*
- **Click** the Save as type drop-down arrow, then **click** Bitmap (*.bmp).
- **Click** Save .
  The image was saved to the desktop as a bitmap file.
- **Click** 🖌 (the Show Desktop button) on the taskbar.
  The Web-page image files appear as icons on the desktop:

GIF document · Bitmap document

4 Open a GIF image and a bitmap image:
- **Open** the <u>cake</u> GIF document.
  The birthday cake image opens in Internet Explorer.

- **Notice** the path in the title bar and in the Address bar.

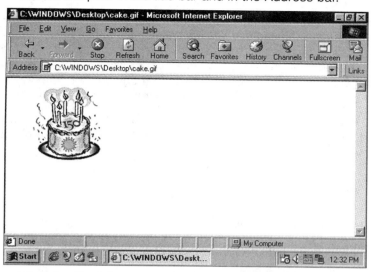

- **Click** the Back button on the Standard toolbar to return to the previous Web page.
- **Click** the Show Desktop button on the taskbar again.
- **Open** the <u>cake</u> bitmap document.

  The birthday cake image opens in Paint.

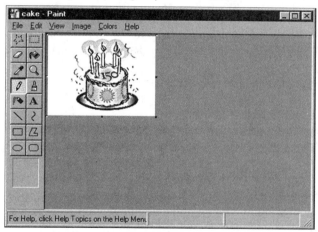

- **Exit** Paint.
- **Put** both <u>cake</u> files in the Recycle Bin.
- **Empty** the Recycle Bin.
- **Click** the Internet Explorer taskbar button.

5
- **Exit** Internet Explorer and **disconnect** from the Internet, or **go on** to Exercise 145.

To follow hyperlinks through a hierarchy of information, working your way from more general topics to specific ones.

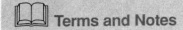 **Terms and Notes**

directory
A categorized and hierarchically organized listing of information on the World Wide Web.

NOTE: Since you are working live on the Internet, we cannot guarantee that Web pages will appear as indicated in this book. Web pages are updated regularly so entries and hyperlinks may be different. Web pages may also be completely redesigned or even removed from the Web.

Directories Have Many Names

There are several ways to find information on the Web. One way is to use a hierarchically structured **directory** of Web pages. Directories are organized into a few major categories that have subcategories beneath them and additional subcategories under those subcategories, and so forth. You can browse through a directory, working your way through very general topics at the top levels to more specific topics in the lower levels of the hierarchy.

As you gain experience with the Internet, you will see that directories have a variety of names, as well as a variety of labels, to define their hierarchical levels. Names and labels such as:

- Internet guides
- topical Web guides
- browse categories
- interest categories
- indexing systems
- indexes
- catalogs
- guides
- subjects
- topics
- categories
- subcategories

In this exercise, you will explore an example of a directory that is in the *Microsoft Internet Start* Web site.

Begin with the desktop displayed and with no taskbar buttons on the taskbar.

1
- **Start** Internet Explorer and **connect** to the Internet, if necessary.
- **Click** the Home button.
  The MSN.COM *Web page is loaded.*

2 **Examine a directory:**
- **Click** web directory on the black bar displayed near the top of the Web page.
  The Web Directory *Web page is loaded.*
  Microsoft calls this directory an index. *The top-level of its hierarchy is called* best of the web.
  NOTE: As you will soon see, the second-level items in this directory's hierarchy are called categories; *third-level items are called* subcategories; *and fourth-level items are called* subentries.

index
best of the web
Education & Reference

ms.com from Microsoft / directory web / VERIO — www.Your-Name.com GET YOUR OWN WEB ADDRESS! — Click Here / Click Here / VERIO

msn.com home | personalize | web directory | help | Microsoft

index
best of the web
Business
Computers & Internet
Education & Reference
Entertainment
Health
Home & Family
Lifestyles & Hobbies
News
Shopping

Now! — July 25
Click here to select a different time zone.
12:00 AM GMT - Oldies and Beach, 105.7 WGQR - Windows Media - Audio
On Demand - Microsoft finds bug in RealNetworks Beta G2 Player - Windows Media - Audio
4:45 PM GMT - 7/26/98 - Connected - the Internet's first call-in talkshow - Windows Media - Audio

Windows Media Technologies

Today's Link
Visit the Museum of Tolerance

The Chilling Fields
Follow a team of explorers as they trek across the

Internet zone

NOTE: Your workspace may look different since Microsoft makes frequent changes to its Web sites. The items listed in the Web directory's hierarchy may also differ.

3 Look at the categories available for a *best of the web* topic:

- **Click** Education & Reference in the *best of the web* column.

   The Education & Reference *Web page is loaded, and the Education & Reference categories appear to the right of the* best of the web *column.*

Earth and life sciences   Education & Reference categories

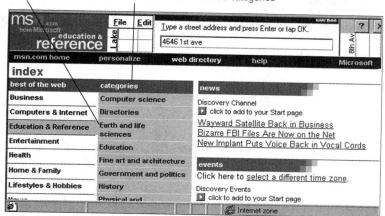

4 Look at the subcategories available for a category:

- **Click** *Earth and life sciences* in the *categories* column.

   Subcategories of Earth and life sciences *appear on the left side of the window.*

Earth and life sciences subcategories

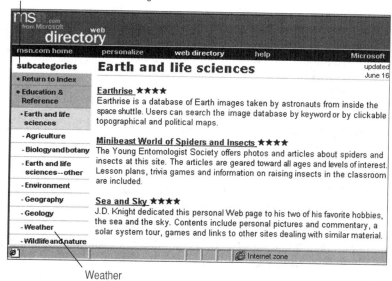

Weather

5 Look at a specific subcategory:

- **Scroll**, if necessary, to locate the Weather subcategory link, then **click** it.

   The Weather *subcategory page loads, displaying the first of several pages of Weather subentries. Each subentry takes you to the Web site that is described briefly under its hyperlink.*

Continued on the next page

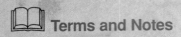

Terms and Notes

NOTE: Remember that since you are working live on the Internet, your Web pages may be different from those shown here; they may have been redesigned. In addition, Web pages are updated regularly so entries and hyperlinks may be different.

Continued from the previous page

subentries   page 1 of 5 pages of subentries about Weather   Date the Web page was last updated

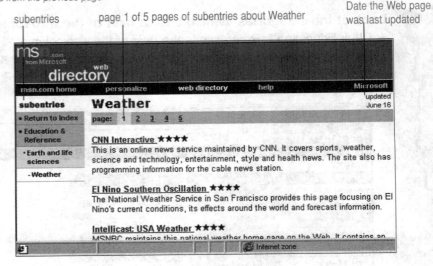

6 **Load a subentry:**
- **Scroll** through the Weather subentries.
- **Click** one of the Weather subentries that interests you.
  The Web page for the selected subentry loads.

7 **Return to the *index* Web page:**
- **Click** the Back button on the Standard toolbar.
  The Weather subcategories Web page is reloaded.

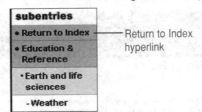

Return to Index hyperlink

- **Click** Return to Index in the upper-left corner of the Web page.
  The Web page, web directory, is reloaded.

8 **Browse other topics:**
- **Click** Entertainment in the *best of the web* column.
  The Entertainment categories are loaded.
- **Click** *TV and radio* in the *categories* column.
  Subcategories of TV and radio are loaded.
- **Click** Return to Index again.
- **Click** the topic of your choice, then **click** the category of your choice to reveal its subcategories.

9 - **Exit** Internet Explorer and **disconnect** from the Internet, or **go on** to Exercise 146.

Begin with the desktop displayed and with no taskbar buttons on the taskbar.

1 **Find information about a word:**

- **Start** Internet Explorer and **connect** to the Internet, if necessary.

- **Click** the Address bar, **type:** find giraffe then **press** Enter .

The AutoSearch feature loads a list of search results with hyperlinks to Web pages containing the word giraffe. *Every occurrence of the word* giraffe *on the page is bold so you can easily detect it. The Microsoft Internet Explorer AutoSearch logo is displayed at the top of the page.*

AutoSearch logo

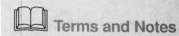

Giraffe is bold.

- **Click** one of the giraffe hyperlinks to load its Web page.
  The Web page containing the word, giraffe, *is displayed.*

- **Find** all occurrences of the word *giraffe* on this page (review, Exercise 140).

- **Close** Find.

2 **Find information about a phrase:**

- **Click** the Address bar, **type:** go white cat then **press** Enter .

- **Scroll** through the search results and **notice** where you see the bold words *white* and *cat* and possibly the bold phrase *white cat*.

The search results contain the word white *and the word* cat, *but they do not necessarily occur together.*

> - Cat Food: The Other White Meat - includes recipes.
> - Cat - learn all about this black and **white cat** who was discovered at Temple Beth-El in Jersey City, New Jersey.- *http://members.aol.com/BethElJC/cat.html*
> - Sammy the Cat for President in '96 - vote for Sammy, he's our man, if he can't do it, no one can; bring a furry belly into the **White** House, vote for Sammy the **cat**.
> - Socks The Cat Fan Club - full of news and views about life in the **White** House, from a **cat**'s eye view.

3 **Find information about an exact phrase:**

- **Click** the Address bar, **type:** go "white cat" then **press** Enter .

The search results contain the words white *and* cat, *and, because you placed quotation marks around the phrase, the two words always occur together.*

> - Cat - learn all about this black and **white cat** who was discovered at Temple Beth-El in Jersey City, New Jersey.- *http://members.aol.com/BethElJC/cat.html*
> - Martinez, Daniel - a tribute to the **White Cat**, travel photos, art and more.- *http://whitecat.com*
> - Kuro-Nyan - black and **white cat** living in Japan. In Japanese and English.

4 - **Exit** Internet Explorer and **disconnect** from the Internet, or **go on** to Exercise 147.

To find information about a word or phrase on the Internet using the AutoSearch feature.

📖 **Terms and Notes**

AutoSearch
A feature that uses a *search engine* to find information about the word or phrase you enter in the Address bar after typing *go*, *find*, or *?*.

AutoSearch is the quickest, simplest, and most convenient way to search for information on the Internet.

exact phrase
A phrase that has quotation marks around it so the words in the phrase will appear together, exactly as typed, in your search results.

phrase
A combination of letters and/or numbers with one or more space(s).

search engine
A program that searches Web pages for information you want to find (e.g., InfoSeek, Excite, Yahoo!, Lycos). Also called *search service*.

search results
The files, folders, or Web pages that meet the search criteria—or match the *search terms*—you specify.

search term
A *word*, *phrase*, or *exact phrase* that you type into a *search term box* to describe what you are looking for. Also called a *keyword*.

search term box
Within a search engine, the (usually) unnamed text box in which you enter your search term(s) when conducting an Internet search.

word
A combination of letters and/or numbers without a space.

⌨️ **Keyboard Steps to**

Use AutoSearch
—WITH INTERNET EXPLORER OPEN—

1. **Press** Ctrl + F4 , Ctrl + F4 .
   The Address bar is selected.

2. **Type** one of the following:
   - find
   - go
   - ?

3. **Press** Space .

4. **Type** the desired word or phrase.

5. **Press** Enter .

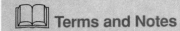

To open the Search Explorer bar and use a search engine to find information on the Internet.

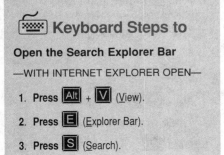

Terms and Notes

NOTE: This book covers search engines as they are presented in the Explorer bar. There are many useful search engine features and search techniques that are not addressed here. Further, there are many more search engines than those provided in the Search Explorer bar. For more practice using search engines, please see DDC's Learning the Internet, 2nd Edition.

directory
1. A categorized and hierarchically organized listing of information on the World Wide Web.
2. Another name for a *folder*.

search engine
A program that searches Web pages for information you want to find (e.g., InfoSeek, Excite, Yahoo!, Lycos). Also called *search service*.

NOTE: The search engines provided in the Search Explorer bar are simplified versions of those found on the search engines' own Web sites.

Search feature
A Windows 98 feature that uses the Explorer bar to present several popular Internet search engines so you can easily find information on the World Wide Web.

search term box
Within a search engine, the (usually) unnamed text box in which you enter your search term(s) when conducting an Internet search.

start-the-search button
The button in every search engine that starts your search when clicked. Different search engines have different terms on this button (e.g., Search, Go, Seek, Go Get It, Find!).

Keyboard Steps to

Open the Search Explorer Bar

—WITH INTERNET EXPLORER OPEN—

1. Press **Alt** + **V** (*V*iew).
2. Press **E** (*E*xplorer Bar).
3. Press **S** (*S*earch).

Search Explorer Bar

The Search Explorer bar offers quick access to **search engines** so you can easily find information. Search engine sites function a bit like a library—cataloging, classifying, and organizing the information available on the Internet to make it accessible. There are two main methods of finding information on the Web. One method is browsing **directories** *(see Exercise 145)*. The other method is using a search engine to find sites containing a particular word or phrase. Most search services now offer both directory and search engine features.

You tell a search engine to find what you're looking for by typing a search term (word, phrase, or exact phrase) in the **search term box** and clicking the **start-the-search button**. The search engine then lists all the Web pages it can find that match your search term. The most relevant content will appear at the top of these search results.

Begin with the desktop displayed and with no taskbar buttons on the taskbar.

1 **Open the Search Explorer bar:**
- **Start** Internet Explorer and **connect** to the Internet, if necessary.
- **Click** [Search] (the Search button) on the Standard toolbar.

  NOTE: Microsoft is offering an update to a new Internet Explorer, Search Explorer bar that has more search provider choices and more customization options. If your version of Windows 98 does not have this update, a message may appear under the Search bar that offers you the choice to update to the new Search bar.

  The Search Explorer bar opens on the left side of the window with a search engine in it. The top of your Search bar has either a Select provider *drop-down list box or a* Choose a Search Engine *drop-down arrow.*

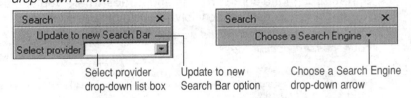

Select provider drop-down list box   Update to new Search Bar option   Choose a Search Engine drop-down arrow

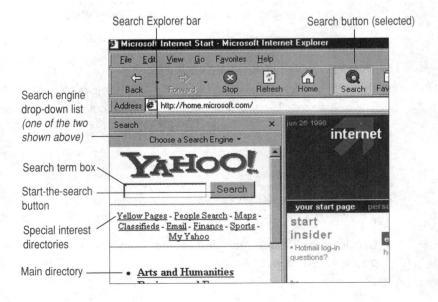

Search Explorer bar   Search button (selected)

Search engine drop-down list *(one of the two shown above)*

Search term box

Start-the-search button

Special interest directories

Main directory

2 **Change the search engine in the Search Explorer bar:**

- IF the drop-down list box in your Search Explorer bar is labeled *Select provider:*
  - **Click** the Select provider drop-down arrow.

    The list opens, displaying the names of five search engines and the Pick-of-the-day option.
  - **Click** Excite.

    The Excite search engine opens in the Explorer bar.

- IF the drop-down list box in your Search Explorer bar is labeled *Choose a Search Engine:*
  - **Click** the Choose a Search Engine drop-down arrow.

    The list opens, displaying one or more search engines and the List of all Search Engines *option.*
  - **Click** List of all Search Engines.

    The Microsoft Pick a Search Engine *Web page opens in the right pane with a complete list of Internet Explorer search engine providers.*

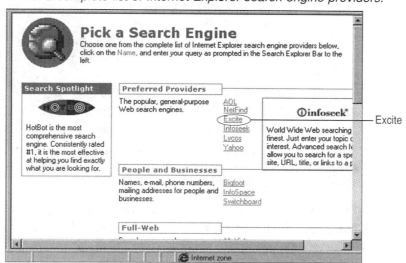

  - **Click** Excite.

    The Excite search engine opens in the Explorer bar.
- **Scroll** through the Excite Channels in the Explorer bar.

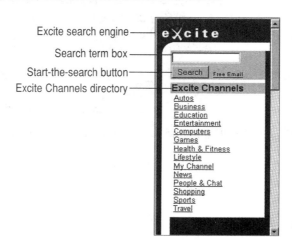

Excite search engine
Search term box
Start-the-search button
Excite Channels directory

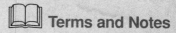 **Terms and Notes**

Search Engine Similarities

Typically, most search engines have the following items:
- search term box
- start-the-search button
- directory
- special-interest directories

Search Engine Differences

While all search engines have a start-the-search button, they have different names for it. And, while most search engines have a directory, they use different titles for that feature as well.

SEARCH ENGINE	SEARCH BUTTON	DIRECTORY NAME
AOL Netfind	Find!	Time Savers
Excite	Search	Excite Channels
Infoseek	seek	Topics
Lycos	Go Get It	Web Guides
Yahoo!	Search	Internet Guides

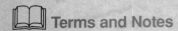
3 **Open and compare search engines in the Search Explorer bar:**

- **Change** the search engine in the Explorer bar to Infoseek (review, step 2).
- **Notice** the search term box, the start-the-search button, and the Topics (i.e., directory).
- **Scroll** through the Topics.
- **Change** the search engine to Lycos and **notice** the differences between Lycos and the previous search engines you have examined.
- **Change** the search engine to AOL Netfind and **notice** the differences between AOL NetFind and the previous search engines you have examined.

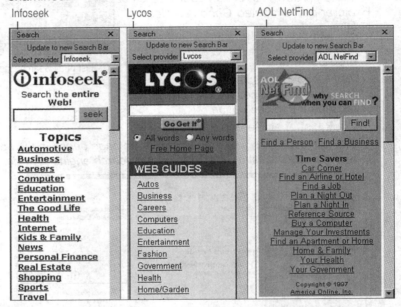

Infoseek   Lycos   AOL NetFind

- **Change** the search engine to Yahoo! and **notice** the differences between Yahoo! (see the step 1 illustration) and the previous search engines you have examined.

4 **Find information using a search engine special directory:**

- **Click** Yellow Pages just under the Search button in Yahoo!.
  The Yahoo! Yellow Pages directory opens in the right pane.
- **Click** the *Search a City for a Business* text box.
  - IF the *Search a City for a Business* text box does not appear, scroll to the right and **click** Change City. Then **click** the *Search a City for a Business* text box.
- **Type:** Crescent City, CA in the *Search a City for a Business* text box then **press** Enter .
  A list of business categories for Crescent City, CA, appears.
- IF the Security Alert dialog box appears, **click** Yes .

NOTE: The Security Alert dialog box appears because you are sending information from your computer about what you want the search engine to find. In this book, in order to complete Internet exercises, you must always click the Yes button when the Security Alert dialog box appears. You will not be instructed to do so in the future, however. You may wish to select the In the future do not show the warning for this zone check box before you click the Yes button so the dialog box does not keep appearing.

- **Scroll** until you find the following:

  - **Entertainment and Arts**
    Nightclubs, Movies, Music, ...

- **Click** Movies.

  The Movies and Film subcategory page for Crescent City, CA, opens.

- **Scroll** down until you see **Beyond Crescent City** then **click** it.

  The search results page lists theaters in the area beyond Crescent City.

5 Find information using a search engine's main directory:

- **Scroll** through the Yahoo! main directory in the Search Explorer bar until you find the Entertainment hyperlink, then **click** it.

  The Entertainment *Web page is loaded in the right pane.*

- **Scroll** through the Entertainment page in the right pane until you find the Movies and Film hyperlink, then **click** it.

  The Movies and Film *Web page is loaded.*

- **Scroll** until you find the Awards hyperlink, then **click** it.

  The Awards *Web page is loaded.*

- **Notice** the top-left corner of the Web page.

  The current category name appears in the top-left corner. Hyperlinks above the category name not only provide a quick way back to any of the previous categories in your journey, but also help you keep track of where you've been.

  Hyperlinks to previously visited categories ——
  Current categories ——

  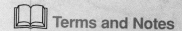

  YAHOO! Personalize

  Home : Entertainment : Movies and Film :
  Awards

- **Scroll** until you find Golden Raspberry Award Foundation, then **click** it.

  The Golden Raspberry Award Foundation *Web page is loaded.*

6 Find a person using a search engine:

- **Change** the search engine in the Search Explorer bar to AOL NetFind.

- **Click** Find a Person.

  The AOL White Pages Web page is loaded in the right pane, displaying a search form containing text boxes for you to enter the name of the person you want to find, as well as the city and state in which he/she lives.

- **Scroll** to the right to display the entire search form, if necessary.

- **Click** the First Name text box, then **type:** [your first name]

- **Click** the Last Name text box, then **type:** [your last name]

- **Click** the State text box, then **type:** [your state]

- **Click** Find!.

  The search results display the address(es) and phone number(s) listed for the name you entered along with hyperlinks on the right that let you send a card, flowers, or a gift.

- **Scroll** down to the right to display the entire search form.

- **Type** the first and last name of a person you want to find, as well as the state and city (if you know them) in which he/she lives, then

  click Find!.

  The search engine displays the search results.

7 **Find information in a search engine using search terms:**

- **Click** the search term box in the Search Explorer bar, **type:** anteater then **click** Find! .

  AOL NetFind displays the top ten matches in the Explorer bar.
- **Scroll** through the entries.
- **Click** Next 10 at the bottom of the Search Explorer bar to display the next ten matches.
- **Click** next to one of the hyperlinks to display its summary.

  The plus sign (+) turns into a minus sign (-) and information about the site is displayed below the hyperlink.
- **Click** one of the hyperlinks to load it.
- **Click** Search (the Search button) on the Standard toolbar to close the Explorer bar.

8 **Look at a search engine's home page:**

- **Type:** www.yahoo.com in the Address bar, then **press** Enter .

  The Yahoo! home page is loaded.
- **Scroll** through the home page and look at its hyperlinks and layout.
- **Print** the Web page (review, Exercise 137).

  Because of Web-page updates, your Yahoo! home page may look different.

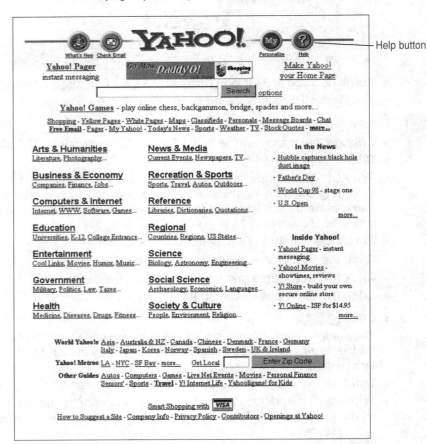

— Help button

9 **Exit** Internet Explorer and **disconnect** from the Internet, or **go on** to Exercise 148.

Channels

A **channel** is a Web site designed to deliver updated information to your computer automatically, without your having to load the Web site. To view the content of an entire channel and to enable automatic updates, you must **subscribe** to the channel.

Begin with the desktop displayed and with no taskbar buttons on the taskbar.

NOTE: This exercise instructs you to view the channel categories in the Channels Explorer bar and open a channel's cover page. The cover page allows you to preview a channel before subscribing to it. This exercise, however, does not cover subscriptions.

 Open the Channels Explorer bar:

- **Start** Internet Explorer and **connect** to the Internet, if necessary.

- **Click** Channels (the Channels button) on the Standard toolbar.

  The Channels Explorer bar opens on the left side of the the window with a list of channels in it.

  News and Technology channel

  Directional arrowhead

- **IF** the Internet Explorer window is maximized, **restore** it.

- **Click** the directional arrowhead at the bottom of the Channels Explorer bar until you get to the bottom of the Channels list.

  The Channels bar has directional arrowheads for scrolling rather than a scroll bar. As you scroll down, a directional arrowhead appears at the top of the Channels list.

- **Click** the directional arrowhead at the top of the Channels Explorer bar until you get to the top of the Channels list.

- **Maximize** the Internet Explorer window.

 Open a channel's cover page:

- **Click** News and Technology in the Channels Explorer bar.

  The news & technology channel category opens, displaying a list of channels related to news and/or technology.

  news & technology channel category (selected)

  The New York Times hyperlink

- **Click** ꆑ The New York Times in the Channels Explorer bar.

  The cover page for The New York Times channel opens in the right pane.

- **Scroll** through the Web site.

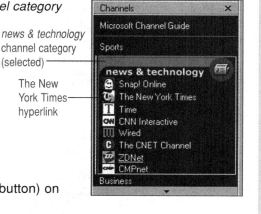

- **Click** Channels (the Channels button) on the Standard toolbar.

  The Channels Explorer bar closes.

3 • **Go on** to Exercise 149 without stopping.

To open the Channels Explorer bar, view the icons for Channel sites within a Channels category, and view a channel's preview cover page.

📖 Terms and Notes

channel
A Web site designed to deliver content to your computer automatically, without your having to go to the Web site. The channel provider specifies what content is available. See also *subscribe*, below.

push
A new technology that allows content providers to send information to you without your having to go to their Web sites. With push technology, you can schedule automatic downloads of updated channel content.

subscribe
To set up your Web browser to check a Web page for new content and then notify you that the site has been updated. You may also set up your browser to automatically download any updates. See also *channel*, above.

Four Ways to Access a List of Channels

Channel links are available from four locations on your computer:
- Active Desktop Channel bar
- Favorites folder
- Channels list in the Explorer bar
- View Channels button on the Quick Launch toolbar

To open a channel's preview cover page using the desktop Channel bar, subscribe to the channel by adding it to the Active Desktop, manually update the channel, and then delete the channel from the desktop.

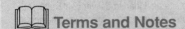

Terms and Notes

ticker
Information that cycles through a heading that can be updated manually or automatically. Stocks, sports scores, and news headlines are common types of information to use in a ticker.

NOTE: IF the Channel bar does not appear, complete the following steps:
- **Right-click** an empty space on the desktop.
- **Point** to Active Desktop.
- **Click** Customize my Desktop.
- **Click** the Internet Explorer Channel Bar check box (to select it).

Continue from Exercise 148 without stopping.

1 **Open a channel Web page from the Active Desktop Channel bar:**
- **Exit** Internet Explorer but **do not disconnect** from the Internet.
- **IF** the Active Desktop Channel bar is not on your desktop, see the side panel.
- **Click** [news & technology] (the *news & technology* channel button) on the Active Desktop Channel bar.

  The news & technology *Web page opens in Internet Explorer in Fullscreen view. Some channel icons appear on the black background. They represent the same channels that appeared when you selected the* News and Technology *channel in the Channels Explorer bar in the previous exercise.*

  New York Times channel link

- **Click** The New York Times channel link.

  The New York Times channel is loaded. The channel cover page appears in Fullscreen view, that is, with the title bar, menu bar, and Address bar hidden.

- **Point** to the ADD TO DESKTOP hyperlink.

  Two desktop options appear:

  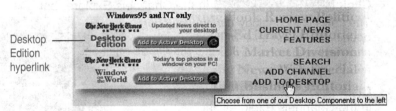

2 **Subscribe to a channel by adding it to your Active Desktop:**
- **Click** the ADD TO DESKTOP hyperlink.

  The Security Alert dialog box appears:

  Security Alert
  Do you want to add a desktop item to your active desktop?
  [Yes]   [No]

- **Click** [Yes].

The Add item to Active Desktop(TM) *dialog box appears:*

Customize
Subscription
button

- **Click** Customize Subscription... .

The Subscription Wizard opens:

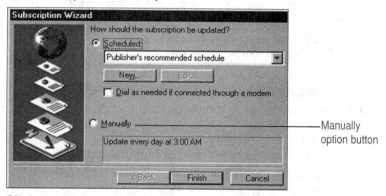

Manually
option button

- **Click** the Manually option button (to select it).

Information appears under the Manually option button.

NOTE: *In this exercise, you are directed to update your channel manually; however, you can use the Subscription Wizard to schedule automatic downloads—while you are away from the computer, for example.*

- **Click** Finish .

The Subscription Wizard closes and the Add item to Active Desktop(TM) *dialog box reappears.*

- **Click** OK *to close the* Add item to Active Desktop(TM) *dialog box.*

The Downloading Subscriptions dialog box reports the downloading progress:

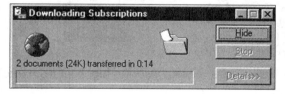

3 **Exit Fullscreen view and close the Channel bar:**

- **Click** 🔲 (the Fullscreen button) on the Standard toolbar.

The Internet Explorer window displays its title bar, menu bar, Links toolbar and status bar.

- **Click** Channels (the Channels button) on the Standard toolbar.

The Channels Explorer bar disappears.

4 **View the ticker on the Active Desktop:**

- **Minimize** Internet Explorer. (Click its Minimize button on the title bar.)

  The New York Times news ticker appears on the desktop with headlines scrolling across its banner and a hyperlink to The New York Times channel.

Click this hyperlink button to open The New York Times channel.

- **Click** the desktop, then **point** to the top of the news ticker until a gray border appears around it and the title bar appears (review, Exercise 77).

Title bar

- **Drag** the news ticker to a new location that is handy for you.

5 **Update your subscription:**

- **Click** the Internet Explorer taskbar button to open it.
- **Click** F̲avorites, then **click** U̲pdate All Subscriptions.

  The Downloading Subscriptions dialog box reports the downloading progress.

- **Minimize** Internet Explorer, then **look** at the fresh headlines in the news ticker.

  NOTE: *Because your update is so close to the time you downloaded the ticker, the news headlines may not change.*

6 **Delete an item from your Active Desktop:**

- **Right-click** the desktop, **point** to A̲ctive Desktop, then **click** C̲ustomize my Desktop.

  The Display Properties dialog box opens with the Web tab selected. The New York Times News Ticker appears in the list.

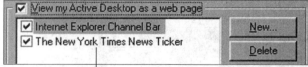

The New York Times News Ticker

- **Click** *The New York Times News Ticker* (to highlight it's name).
- **Click** [Delete].

  The Active Desktop Item dialog box appears.

- **Click** [Yes], then **click** [OK].

  The news ticker is deleted.

7
- **Click** the Internet Explorer taskbar button to open it.
- **Maximize** Internet Explorer.

8
- **Exit** Internet Explorer and **disconnect** from the Internet.

History

The History feature automatically stores Web pages that you visit and organizes their addresses into three time frames:

- Web pages you visited today
- Web pages you visited this week
- Web pages you visited before this week

You can quickly load any Web page you have visited for the past 20 days using the History Explorer bar. While Internet Explorer defaults to storing Web-page addresses for 20 days, you can change the number of days Web-page addresses are stored.

You can clear the History, but realize that clearing your History also clears your Address bar drop-down list.

When you clear the History, however, the recently used Web-page section on the File menu and the drop-down list boxes on the Back and Forward buttons retain their Web addresses (until you exit Internet Explorer).

Begin with the desktop displayed and with no taskbar buttons on the taskbar.

1
- **Start** Internet Explorer and **connect** to the Internet.
  The Microsoft Internet Start *Web page is loaded.*
- **Click** the Address bar drop-down arrow and **notice** the addresses that are displayed in the list.
- **Click** the Address bar drop-down arrow again to close the list box.
- **Click** (the History button) on the Standard toolbar.
  The History Explorer bar opens on the left side of the Internet Explorer window.
- **Notice** what is in the History Explorer bar.
- **Click** the History button on the Standard toolbar again to close the History Explorer bar.

2 **Clear your History:**
- **Click** View, then **click** Internet Options.
  The Internet Options dialog box opens with the General tab selected.

History section of the Internet Options dialog box

Clear History button

NOTE: You can change the number of days that History stores Web URLs in the Days to keep pages in history *spin box. If you are low on disk space, you may want to decrease the number of days you keep URLs.*

- **Click** Clear History .
  The Internet Properties dialog box appears:

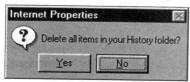

- **Click** Yes , then **click** OK to close the Internet Options dialog box.
  The History is cleared.

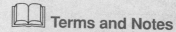 **Terms and Notes**

History
A list of previously visited Web sites that are stored by Internet Explorer automatically.

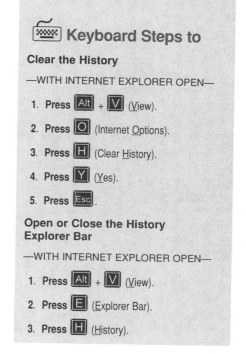 **Keyboard Steps to**

Clear the History

—WITH INTERNET EXPLORER OPEN—

1. **Press** `Alt` + `V` (View).
2. **Press** `O` (Internet Options).
3. **Press** `H` (Clear History).
4. **Press** `Y` (Yes).
5. **Press** `Esc`.

Open or Close the History Explorer Bar

—WITH INTERNET EXPLORER OPEN—

1. **Press** `Alt` + `V` (View).
2. **Press** `E` (Explorer Bar).
3. **Press** `H` (History).

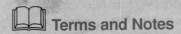
NOTE: Since you cleared your History, you have only the Today folder with its subfolders in your History folder. Below is an example of how the History Explorer bar might look if you had 20 days of Web-page visits in it.

- **Click** the Address bar drop-down arrow and **notice** that the drop-down list is empty.
- **Click** the Address bar drop-down arrow again to close the list box.
- **Click** the History button on the Standard toolbar to open the History Explorer bar.

A blank History Explorer bar opens.

History button (selected)

The History Explorer bar with no entries

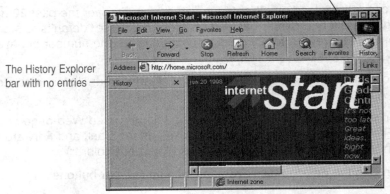

- **Click** the History button on the Standard toolbar again to close the History Explorer bar.

③ Create a History:
- **Load** the DDC Publishing Web site: www.ddcpub.com
- **Scroll** a little, if necessary, then **click** **Learn the Net** (the *Learn the Net* button).
- **Scroll** a little, if necessary, then **click** Lesson 2: Internet Explorer, Exercise 2 "NASA".

  A copy of the NASA home page opens from the DDC Web site.
- **Click** the Home button on the Standard toolbar.

  The MSN.COM Web page opens.
- **Click** **Microsoft** (the Microsoft hyperlink) located on the black bar displayed near the top of the Web page.
- **Click** the Home button on the Standard toolbar again to return to the *MSN.COM* Web page.

④ Examine the History Explorer bar:
- **Click** the History button on the Standard toolbar.

  The History Explorer bar opens with the current Web site opened and the current Web page, Microsoft Internet Start, *selected below the current Web site.*

  The Today folder holds a subfolder for each Web site you visited today.

  Each Web site folder holds the Web pages you visited in that site.

Today folder
Web-site subfolders

Web page in the *home.microsoft.com* folder (selected)

- **Point** to the selected Web page until its ToolTip appears.

  The ToolTip displays the Web-site name and URL:

- **Click** the *home.microsoft.com* folder (to select it).
- **Click** the *home.microsoft.com* folder again to close it.

  The folder remains selected:

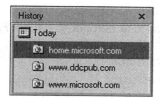

- **Click** the *home.microsoft.com* folder again to open it.
- **Click** the *home.microsoft.com* folder once again to close it.

5 Open a Web page using the History Explorer bar:

- **Click** ![www.ddcpub....] (the *www.ddcpub.com* folder) in the Explorer bar.

  The folder opens and displays three Web pages:

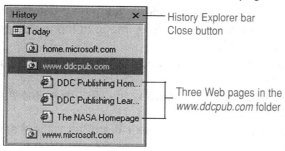

- **Point** to each of the Web pages in the *www.ddcpub.com* folder to display their ToolTips.
- **Click** on the *DDC Publishing Learn the Net* Web page.

  The DDC Publishing Learn the Net *Web page opens.*
- **Click** ![www.microsoft.com] (the *www.microsoft.com* folder) in the Explorer bar.
- **Click** the Web page displayed under the folder.

  The Welcome to Microsoft's Homepage *Web page opens.*
- **Click** ![X] (the History Explorer bar Close button).

  The History Explorer bar closes.

6 • **Exit** Internet Explorer and **disconnect** from the Internet.

More Internet Explorer

Tasks Reviewed:

- Find Text in a Web Page
- Copy Text from a Web Page to a Document
- Copy and Paste an Image into a Document
- Use a Web-Page Image for Wallpaper
- Save a Web-Page Image
- Browse the Web Using Directories
- Use AutoSearch
- Use the Search Explorer Bar
- Use the Channel Explorer Bar
- Add a Channel to the Active Desktop
- Use the History Explorer Bar

Begin with the Active Desktop displayed and no taskbar buttons on the taskbar.

- **Start** Internet Explorer and **connect** to the Internet.
- **Load** the Learn the Net with DDC Web page: www.ddcpub.com/learn
- **Click** Lesson 2: Internet Explorer, Exercise 2 "White House".
- **Click** White House Help Desk: at the bottom of the page.
- **Click** Frequently Asked Questions.
  The Frequently Asked Questions *Web page is loaded.*
- **Find** all occurrences of the word *socks*.
- **Find** all occurrences of the word *our*. (Remember to cancel Find and click the desktop between searches.)
- **Find** all occurrences of the whole word *our*.
- **Find** all occurrences of the word *People*.
- **Find** all occurrences that match the case of the word *People*.

- **Open** and **maximize** WordPad.
- **Switch** to Internet Explorer, then **click** the Back button.
- **Copy** the image at the top of the page and **paste** it into WordPad. (Remember to press the End key to deselect the image and then press the Enter key to go to the next line after you paste an image into WordPad.)
- **Switch** back to Internet Explorer, then **click** the Forward button.
- **Copy** the Frequently Asked Questions image at the top of the page and **paste** it into WordPad.
- **Switch** back to Internet Explorer, **copy** the first paragraph and **paste** it into WordPad.
- **Switch** back to Internet Explorer, **copy** the URL (from the Address bar) and **paste** it into WordPad.
- **Print** the WordPad document, then **exit** WordPad without saving the document.

White House Help Desk

Frequently Asked Questions

Welcome to the White House is a key access point to government information that is available on the Internet, a network of computer networks used by people in over 150 countries. Using a service on the Internet called the World Wide Web (WWW), people all over the world can locate documents that not only contain text but also include graphics, photos, sound, and video.

http://www.ddcpub.com/lesson2.2/whitehouse/faq.html

- **Scroll** to the bottom of the Web page.
- **Set** the question mark image as wallpaper.
- **Show** the desktop.
- **Open** the Display Properties dialog box. (Right-click the desktop, then click Properties.)

- **Set** the <u>D</u>isplay drop-down list box to *Tile*, then **click** [OK] .
- **Open** the Display Properties dialog box.

- **Set** the <u>D</u>isplay drop-down list box to *Center*, then **click** [OK] .
- **Open** the Display Properties dialog box.

- **Press** [Home] to move to the top of the wallpaper list and select (*None*).
- **Click** [OK] to set the wallpaper to (*None*).

4
- **Switch** back to Internet Explorer.
- **Save** the pencil image (located at the bottom of the Web page) on the *desktop* as a GIF file; **name** it Pencil 1
- **Save** the pencil image on the *desktop* as a bitmap image; **name** it Pencil 2
- **Show** the desktop.
- **Open** <u>Pencil 1</u>, then **exit** Internet Explorer.
- **Open** <u>Pencil 2</u>, then **exit** Paint.
- **Drag and drop** <u>Pencil 1</u> and <u>Pencil 2</u> onto the Recycle Bin.
- **Empty** the Recycle Bin.

5
- **Switch** back to Internet Explorer.
- **Click** the Home button on the Standard toolbar, then **click** **web directory** on the black bar near the top of the Web page.
- **Load** the categories for the Entertainment topic. (Click its hyperlink.)
- **Load** the subcategories for the *Books and publishing* category.
- **Load** the subentries for the *Comics and cartoons* subcategory.
- **Load** the subentry of your choice.

6
- **Find** Web pages that contain the word antelope using the AutoSearch feature.
- **Find** Web pages that contain the words antelope county (that may or may not occur next to each other) using the AutoSearch feature.
- **Find** Web pages in which the exact phrase antelope county appears (the words must appear next to each other) using the AutoSearch feature.

7
- **Open** the Search Explorer bar by clicking the Search button.
- **Change** the search engine in the Search Explorer bar to Lycos.
- **Change** the search engine in the Search Explorer bar to Yahoo.
- **Open** <u>Yellow Pages</u>.
- IF the *Enter a City, State Zip; OR a Zip code:* text box does not appear in the right pane, **scroll** to the right and **click** <u>Change City</u>.
- **Type:** Crescent City in the *Search a City for a Business* text box and **press** [Enter] .
- **Click** Crescent City, FL, in the search results, then **click** the *Go to Yellow Pages* button.
- **Click** the Computer Stores hyperlink (under Computers and Internet).

Continued on the next page

Continued from the previous page

- **Press** `Ctrl` + `F` (Find), **type:** ruby then **press** `Enter`.
- **Click** `Cancel`.
- **Click** Ruby's Computer Place.
  NOTE: If this hyperlink no longer exists, click another one.

8
- **Click** Reference in Yahoo! in the Search Explorer bar. (You may need to scroll to find the hyperlink.)
- **Click** Postal Information in the right pane.
- **Scroll** to the bottom of the Web page, then **click** Zip Find.
- **Type:** 02169 in the Zip 1 text box and 95503 in the Zip 2 text box.
- **Click** the Calculate Distance button.
  The result is displayed: Miles between Quincy, MA and Eureka, CA: 2709.
- **Close** the Search Explorer bar.

9
- **Open** the Channels Explorer bar. (Click the Channels button.)
- **Click** the *news & technology* channel category button in the Explorer bar to display its contents, then **click** the *Snap! Online* channel button from the Channels Explorer bar (left pane) to load its Web page.
- **Close** the Channels Explorer bar.
- **Click** the Fullscreen button to enter Fullscreen view.

10
- **Subscribe** to the channel by clicking the Add to Active Desktop button.
  The Security Alert dialog box appears.
- **Click** `Yes`.
  The Add item to Active Desktop(TM) dialog box appears.
- **Click** the Customize Subscription button.
- **Click** the Manually option button (to select it), then **click** `Finish`.
- **Click** `OK` in the Add item to Active Desktop(TM) dialog box.
  The Downloading Subscriptions dialog box shows the progress, then disappears.
- **Click** the Fullscreen button to exit Fullscreen view.
- **Show** the desktop.
  The Snap! search form is displayed on the desktop.

- **Move** the search form to a convenient desktop location. (Remember to point to the search form until a gray border appears around it and the title bar appears before you try to drag it.)
- **Update** your subscription. (Switch to Internet Explorer, click Favorites, then click Update All Subscriptions.)
- **Display** the Web tab in the Display Properties dialog box. (Right-click the desktop, point to Active Desktop, then click Customize my Desktop.)
- **Delete** the Snap! search form. (Click the Snap! Search name, click the Delete button, click the Yes button, then click the OK button.)

⑪
- **Switch** back to Internet Explorer.
- **Open** the Address bar drop-down list and **notice** the addresses.
- **Close** the Address bar drop-down list.
- **Click** the Home button on the Standard toolbar.
- **Open** the History Explorer bar and **notice** the History list.
- **Clear** the History. (Click View, click Internet Options, click Clear History, click the Yes button, then click the OK button.)
- **Close** the History Explorer bar.
- **Load** the DDC Publishing Web site: www.ddcpub.com
- **Click** the Learn the Net hyperlink button.
- **Click** Lesson 2: Internet Explorer, Exercise 2 "White House".
- **Click** White House Help Desk:.
- **Click** Frequently Asked Questions.
- **Click** link to all online resources.
- **Click** the Home button on the Standard toolbar.
- **Click** web directory on the black bar near the top of the page.
- **Open** the History Explorer bar.
- **Close** the *home.microsoft.com* folder in the History Explorer bar. (Click it twice.)
- **Open** the *www.ddcpub.com* folder in the History Explorer bar.
- **Open** the *Links to Government Agencies* Web page using the History Explorer bar.
- **Open** the *home.microsoft.com* folder in the History Explorer bar, then **open** the *Web Directory* Web page.
- **Exit** Internet Explorer and **disconnect** from the Internet.

Lesson Thirteen Worksheet (11) is on page 311.

WORKSHEETS

NAME_____ **SCORE**_____

DIRECTIONS: Use the following terms to fill in the blanks below.

Close button	menu bar	Start button	window title
desktop	Minimize button	status bar	workspace
graphical user interface (GUI)	object	title bar	
icon	program	window	
Maximize button	Restore button	window border	

1. A phrase that is commonly used to describe Microsoft Windows 98 and other operating sytems that use pictures to help you connect to the computer system's hardware and software in an easy-to-understand, intuitive way.

    1._____

2. A small picture that represents one of the many objects that you use when working with the computer system.

    2._____

3. The button in the middle of the three buttons located at the right end of the title bar on a maximized window; it returns a maximized window to its previous size.

    3._____

4. One of the many things that you use when working with the computer system—items such as: files, programs, folders, shortcuts, disk drives, Control Panel tools, My Computer, Network Neighborhood, the Recycle Bin, and My Briefcase.

    4._____

5. A rectangle that holds a dialog box, folder, program, or document.

    5._____

6. The opening screen in Windows 98 that contains a few objects, the Start button, and the taskbar.

    6._____

7. The button located at the left end of the taskbar that you click to open the Start menu.

    7._____

8. The button in the middle of the three buttons located at the right end of the title bar on a restored window; it enlarges a window to its greatest possible size.

    8._____

9. The bar at the bottom of a program or folder window that displays information about the program or folder.

    9._____

10. A button located at the right end of a document and/or program title bar that you can click to quit a window.

    10._____

11. The bar located under the title bar that lists the available menu items for the open program or folder.

    11._____

12. The button located on the right side of a menu bar and/or title bar that you can click to reduce a window to a taskbar button.

    12._____

13. The boundary that marks the edges of a window and can be used to size that window.

    13._____

14. A set of instructions that your computer follows to perform a specific task, such as word processing or creating a graphic.

    14._____

15. The name of a window, located just to the right of the Control menu button.

    15._____

16. The horizontal bar at the top of a window that provides the name of the open document and/or program.

    16._____

17. The inner part of a window where the work in a program or document is carried out.

    17._____

This page may be copied.

WORKSHEET 2 • Lesson One

NAME_____ SCORE_____

DIRECTIONS: Use the following terms to fill in the blanks below.

Accessories	dimmed command	menu	submenu
close	directional arrowhead	menu item	task
commands	keyboard shortcuts	password	taskbar button
control keys	launch	pointer	user name
dialog box	log on	pressed	

1. Instructions that you issue, causing an action to be carried out.

2. Supplemental, built-in programs that come with Windows 98, such as Notepad and Calculator.

3. Certain keys (Shift, Ctrl, and Alt) that are used in combination with other keys to issue commands.

4. Key combinations that are used to activate certain commands as an alternative to using the mouse.

5. The arrow-shaped cursor on the screen that moves with the mouse as you slide it over a flat surface.

6. A special kind of window that offers different controls for you to manipulate in order to change the performance or appearance of a document or program.

7. A command that lets you quit a window.

8. To identify yourself to your computer (with a user name and a password) and open the Windows desktop.

9. A combination of characters that you type, when prompted, in order to access Windows (or another feature).

10. A name given to a Windows user; it allows different people to use the same computer and to keep their work secure.

11. A small arrowhead that appears at the beginning and/or end of menus and toolbars to indicate that there are more items available than can be seen at the present time.

12. A drop-down or pop-up list of items from which you may choose only one at a time.

13. One of the choices on a menu.

14. A menu that cascades out from another menu.

15. An open, but not necessarily active, program.

16. A button located on the taskbar that represents an open program; it displays the program icon and its name.

17. A command, menu item, or button that is displayed in gray instead of in black (or in color), indicating that it cannot be used in the current situation.

18. A 3-D effect in which a button appears sunken, indicating it is selected (i.e., active).

19. To start a program.

1._____

2._____

3._____

4._____

5._____

6._____

7._____

8._____

9._____

10._____

11._____

12._____

13._____

14._____

15._____

16._____

17._____

18._____

19._____

This page may be copied.

NAME_____ **SCORE**_____

DIRECTIONS: Use the following terms to fill in the blanks below.

associated file	default	filename extension	Save
common commands	file	program file	Save As
common dialog boxes	file type	properties	tabs
controls	filename	Properties dialog box	toolbar

1. The name you give to data that is stored on a disk.

    1._____

2. A file containing a set of instructions that your computer follows to perform a task, such as word processing.

    2._____

3. Dialog boxes, such as Open, Save As, and Print, which are basically the same in many different programs and which make it easier for you to learn new programs.

    3._____

4. Data or program instructions that are saved on a disk as a named unit.

    4._____

5. The period and, usually but not always, three characters at the end of a filename (for example, .doc, .txt, .gif).

    5._____

6. The kind of file that is created by a particular program.

    6._____

7. The elements in a dialog box that ask for information from the user, for example, check boxes and text boxes.

    7._____

8. Characteristics of an object; for example, the color scheme on the desktop.

    8._____

9. A special kind of dialog box that groups the settings for a specific object's properties.

    9._____

10. The command that opens the Save As dialog box, letting you rename a previously saved document.

    10._____

11. Commands such as New, Save, and Print that work the same way in most Windows programs.

    11._____

12. A file type that has been identified as belonging to a certain program, such as *.txt* with Notepad, *.bmp* with Paint, or *.doc* with Microsoft Word.

    12._____

13. An automatic setting in a program.

    13._____

14. The "flaps" at the top of a series of separate groups of settings in dialog boxes.

    14._____

15. A row of buttons, usually along the top or bottom of the screen by default, that provides quick access to frequently used commands.

    15._____

16. The command that saves changes to a previously named document or opens the Save As dialog box so you can save a new document.

    16._____

This page may be copied.

WORKSHEET 4 • Lesson Three

NAME_____ SCORE_____

DIRECTIONS: Use the following terms to fill in the blanks below.

Address bar	Quick Launch Toolbar	system tray
flat	raised	taskbar
floating toolbar	sizing handle	ToolTip

1. A drop-down text box in Windows 98 folders and certain programs that lets you access a Web page or a location on your computer by typing or selecting an address or path.

   1._____

2. The area at the right end of the taskbar that displays system icons and offers easy access to those system features.

   2._____

3. A pop-up box that displays the name of, and/or information about, a button or an icon.

   3._____

4. A 3-D effect in which a toolbar icon that is normally flat is defined as a button when you point to it.

   4._____

5. An area in the bottom-right corner of windows that is used to size windows which can be sized.

   5._____

6. A toolbar that you have dragged from the taskbar to an unanchored position on your desktop.

   6._____

7. The smooth, level appearance of icons on many toolbars in Windows 98.

   7._____

8. The bar that appears by default at the bottom of the desktop and lets you start programs, switch between tasks, and access the tools (and toolbars) of your choice.

   8._____

9. A toolbar that appears next to the Start button on the taskbar (by default) and contains buttons for the following frequently used features: Internet Explorer, Outlook Express, desktop, and channels.

   9._____

This page may be copied.

NAME_____ SCORE_____

DIRECTIONS: Use the following terms to fill in the blanks below.

Active Desktop	Explorer bar	My Documents	Web style
Auto Arrange	folder	offline	wizard
AutoComplete	folder window	subfolder	work offline mode
Classic style	My Computer	Web Page view	

1. A window that displays the contents of a folder (or certain other objects, such as disk drives).

   1._____

2. A structure that holds files and/or subfolders that are stored on a disk.

   2._____

3. The approach to working with folders, icons, and the desktop that includes browsing windows using the same window, click-to-open browsing, and underlined icon titles.

   3._____

4. The Windows 98 desktop that consists of two layers: one on which you can display standard desktop objects, and another on which you can display HTML objects.

   4._____

5. The Windows 95 approach to working with folders, icons, and the desktop that includes browsing windows using separate windows, double-click-to-open browsing, and icon titles that are not underlined.

   5._____

6. A Windows 98 feature in folder windows and Windows Explorer that displays the name, picture, and information regarding the selected item along the left side of the workspace.

   6._____

7. A special folder on the desktop that gives you a quick route to the disk drives, folders, files, and other objects on your computer system.

   7._____

8. Not connected to the Internet.

   8._____

9. A feature in the Address bar that finishes an address when you begin to enter a previously typed address.

   9._____

10. A folder contained within another folder.

    10._____

11. A special folder that is designed to store your personal files.

    11._____

12. A tool that walks you through a complex task step by step.

    12._____

13. A command that prevents desktop and folder icons from being moved out of their aligned positions.

    13._____

14. A condition in which you can view Web pages (and Web-page objects) that are stored on the computer without being connected to the Internet.

    14._____

15. A way to browse through a list of Web links—such as those in Search, Favorites, History, and Channels.

    15._____

WORKSHEET 6 • Lesson Five

NAME_____ SCORE_____

DIRECTIONS: Use the following terms to fill in the blanks below.

browse	Favorites menu	long filename	short filename
clipboard	group folder	Network Neighborhood	Windows Explorer
cut	hierarchy	paste	

1. To look at files, programs, and other objects on your computer system.

    1._____

2. The multilevel structure of objects on the entire computer system, including the structure of folders and subfolders on a disk.

    2._____

3. A list of frequently used Web sites and/or folders that you can access from the Start menu, all folder windows, Windows Explorer, or your Web browser.

    3._____

4. A filename that is no longer than eight characters and does not contain spaces or certain symbols.

    4._____

5. A folder within the Start Menu folder that holds groups of program shortcuts and other folders.

    5._____

6. An object that lets you browse through other computers on your network if you are connected to a network.

    6._____

7. A filename that is up to 255 characters long and can contain spaces and most symbols.

    7._____

8. To copy information from the clipboard into a folder or document.

    8._____

9. A temporary storage area in the computer's memory used to hold information that is being cut/copied and pasted.

    9._____

10. To transfer information from its current location to the clipboard.

    10._____

11. The Windows 98 program that you can use to look at and manage objects in your computer system.

    11._____

NAME_____ SCORE_____

DIRECTIONS: Use the following terms to fill in the blanks below.

command line	document-centric	jump arrow	shortcut
document	Documents menu	path	target

1. An icon containing a direct route to a specific object and displaying a small jump arrow on its lower-left corner.

    1._____

2. The route to an object that may consist of a disk drive, a folder, subfolders, and a filename.

    2._____

3. A file that consists of data created in a program, such as a report typed in WordPad or a picture drawn in Paint.

    3._____

4. A system that focuses on documents and their contents rather than on the programs used to create those documents.

    4._____

5. A text box where you enter the path to the desired file or folder.

    5._____

6. A menu on the Start menu that holds the My Documents folder and up to 15 of your most recently used files.

    6._____

7. A small arrow that appears on the lower-left corner of shortcut icons, thereby distinguishing them from other icons.

    7._____

8. The object (including its path) to which a shortcut is pointing.

    8._____

WORKSHEET 8 • Lesson Seven

NAME_____ SCORE_____

DIRECTIONS: Use the following terms to fill in the blanks below.

channel	expand	HTML document	Recycle Bin
Channel bar	Full Screen view	Internet Explorer	standard desktop
collapse	HTML (Hypertext Markup Language)	Programs menu	View Channels button

1. A submenu of the Start menu that holds programs and submenus which contain groups of related programs.

    1._____

2. A place to put objects (such as icons for shortcuts, folders, and files) for quick and easy access.

    2._____

3. The Windows 98 Web-browsing program.

    3._____

4. A View menu option in Internet Explorer in which only one bar is displayed (at the top), leaving the entire screen available for Internet content.

    4._____

5. A button on the taskbar's Quick Launch toolbar that opens Internet Explorer in Full Screen view and displays the Channel bar.

    5._____

6. A special folder on the desktop that temporarily holds "deleted" files so you can restore them if you change your mind.

    6._____

7. A Web site designed to deliver content to your computer automatically, without your having to go to the Web site. The Web site provider specifies what Web content is available.

    7._____

8. An Active Desktop option that displays the channels installed on your computer.

    8._____

9. A document that can be viewed in a Web browser.

    9._____

10. The programming language used to create Web pages so that they can be viewed, read, and accessed by any computer running on any type of operating system.

    10._____

11. To display the unseen folders contained in an object that appears in the left pane of Windows Explorer.

    11._____

12. To hide the folders contained in an object that is displayed in the left pane of Windows Explorer.

    12._____

NAME_____ SCORE_____

DIRECTIONS: Use the following terms to fill in the blanks below.

attribute	Find	megabyte (Mb)	search criteria
byte (B)	gigabyte (Gb)	MS-DOS (Microsoft Disk Operating System)	search results
case sensitive	hidden files		sort
Control Panel	kilobyte (Kb)	MS-DOS–based application	TrueType font

1. The amount of space needed to hold one character in a computer's memory or storage area.

   1._____

2. Approximately 1,000,000,000 bytes.

   2._____

3. Approximately 1,000 bytes.

   3._____

4. Approximately 1,000,000 bytes.

   4._____

5. To arrange files in ascending or descending order.

   5._____

6. Files and/or folders to which the Hidden attribute has been applied.

   6._____

7. A characteristic (such as read-only, archive, hidden, or system) that changes how a file or folder can be used or displayed.

   7._____

8. A program that helps you locate files and folders using search criteria.

   8._____

9. A feature that tells a program to recognize the difference between upper- and lowercase letters when searching for text.

   9._____

10. The files, folders, or Web pages that meet the search criteria you specified.

    10._____

11. Guidelines you define that tell the Find program what file and folder characteristics to look for when searching.

    11._____

12. A folder that contains command, control, and configuration functions for Windows 98.

    12._____

13. A scalable font that is shipped with Windows 98, for example, Arial, Times New Roman, and Wingdings.

    13._____

14. A program that is designed to run under the MS-DOS operating system rather than the Windows operating system.

    14._____

15. The main operating system used before Windows was developed.

    15._____

This page may be copied.

NAME_____ SCORE_____

DIRECTIONS: Use the following terms to fill in the blanks below.

communications protocol	HTTP (Hypertext Transfer Protocol)	Internet Service Provider (ISP)	Web browser
dial-up access		Links toolbar	Web page
direct access	hyperlink	online service	Web server
home page	Internet	URL (Uniform Resource Locator)	Web site
	Internet icon		World Wide Web

1. Text or graphics that, when clicked, connect(s) to another Web page.

    1._____

2. A set of rules (or standards) that lets computers connect with one another and exchange information with as little chance of error as possible.

    2._____

3. A server that uses HTTP server software to serve up HTML documents when requested by a Web client, such as a Web browser.

    3._____

4. The protocol that allows computers to communicate across the Web and connects Web pages to each other via hyperlinks.

    4._____

5. The graphical part of the Internet that uses hypertext to link Web pages on Web sites around the world.

    5._____

6. A widely used method of accessing the Internet in which you use a modem and telephone line to connect to the Internet through an online service or Internet service provider.

    6._____

7. A business, such as AOL, CompuServe, or Microsoft Network (MSN), that offers access to the Internet (along with other services) for a fee.

    7._____

8. The first page of a Web site or the first page you see when you open Internet Explorer.

    8._____

9. A convenient method of accessing the Internet that is used by large organizations and some schools in which a dedicated line provides a continuous connection to the Internet.

    9._____

10. A company (often local) that provides you with a connection to the Internet for a fee.

    10._____

11. A document that is created using HTML that can be posted on the World Wide Web by a Web server.

    11._____

12. A global collection of computers that communicate with one another using common communication protocols (e.g., HTTP).

    12._____

13. The unique address assigned to each page on the Web.

    13._____

14. The button at the right end of the menu bar illustrated with a Windows flag that accesses the Internet when clicked.

    14._____

15. A program that lets you access the Web and view Web pages.

    15._____

16. A group of related Web pages that typically includes a home page and hyperlinks to other Web pages.

    16._____

17. The toolbar that provides quick access to commonly used Web sites.

    17._____

This page may be copied.

NAME_____ SCORE_____

DIRECTIONS: Use the following terms to fill in the blanks below.

AutoSearch	GIF (Graphics Interchange Format)	search engine	subscribe
bitmap		Search feature	ticker
directory	phrase	search term	
exact phrase	push	search term box	

1. A Windows 98 feature that uses the Explorer bar to present several popular Internet search engines so you can easily find information.

    1._____

2. A feature that uses a search engine to find information about the word or phrase you enter in the Address bar after first typing go, find, or ?.

    2._____

3. A standard format for image files on the Web.

    3._____

4. A format for image files used by the Paint program (among others). It handles an image as a set of dots rather than as a mathematical formula.

    4._____

5. A group of words that has quotation marks around it so the words will appear together, precisely as typed, in your search results.

    5._____

6. A combination of letters and/or numbers with one or more space(s).

    6._____

7. Information that cycles through a heading that can be updated manually or automatically.

    7._____

8. A program that searches Web pages for information you want to find (e.g., InfoSeek, Excite, Yahoo!, Lycos).

    8._____

9. A word, phrase, or exact phrase that you type into a search term box to describe what you are looking for.

    9._____

10. A new technology that allows content providers to send information to you without your having to go to their Web sites.

    10._____

11. Within a search engine, the (usually) unnamed text box in which you enter your search term(s) when conducting an Internet search.

    11._____

12. To set up your Web browser to check a Web page for new content and then notify you that the site has been updated.

    12._____

13. A categorized and hierarchically organized listing of information on the Web.

    13._____

SOLUTIONS

WORKSHEET 1
LESSON ONE

		Missed	Score
		0	100
1.	graphical user interface (GUI)	1	94
2.	icon	2	89
3.	Restore button	3	83
4.	object	4	77
5.	window	5	71
6.	desktop	6	65
7.	Start button	7	59
8.	Maximize button	8	53
9.	status bar	9	48
10.	Close button	10	42
11.	menu bar	11	36
12.	Minimize button	12	30
13.	window border	13	24
14.	program	14	18
15.	window title	15	12
16.	title bar	16	6
17.	workspace	17	0

WORKSHEET 2
LESSON ONE

		Missed	Score
		0	100
1.	commands	1	95
2.	Accessories	2	89
3.	control keys	3	84
4.	keyboard shortcuts	4	79
5.	pointer	5	74
6.	dialog box	6	68
7.	Close	7	63
8.	log on	8	58
9.	password	9	53
10.	user name	10	47
11.	directional arrowhead	11	42
12.	menu	12	37
13.	menu item	13	53
14.	submenu	14	26
15.	task	15	21
16.	taskbar button	16	16
17.	dimmed command	17	11
18.	pressed	18	5
19.	launch	19	0

WORKSHEET 3
LESSON TWO

		Missed	Score
		0	100
1.	filename	1	94
2.	program file	2	88
3.	common dialog boxes	3	82
4.	file	4	75
5.	filename extension	5	69
6.	file type	6	63
7.	controls	7	57
8.	properties	8	50
9.	Properties dialog box	9	44
10.	Save As	10	38
11.	common commands	11	32
12.	associated file	12	25
13.	default	13	19
14.	tabs	14	13
15.	toolbar	15	7
16.	Save	16	0

WORKSHEET 4
LESSON THREE

		Missed	Score
		0	100
1.	Address bar	1	89
2.	system tray	2	78
3.	ToolTip	3	67
4.	raised	4	56
5.	sizing handle	5	45
6.	floating toolbar	6	34
7.	flat	7	23
8.	taskbar	8	12
9.	Quick Launch toolbar	9	0

WORKSHEET 5
LESSON FOUR

		Missed	Score
		0	100
1.	folder window	1	93
2.	folder	2	87
3.	Web style	3	80
4.	Active Desktop	4	73
5.	Classic style	5	67
6.	Web Page view	6	60
7.	My Computer	7	53
8.	offline	8	47
9.	AutoComplete	9	40
10.	subfolder	10	33
11.	My Documents	11	27
12.	wizard	12	20
13.	Auto Arrange	13	13
14.	work offline mode	14	7
15.	Explorer bars	15	0

WORKSHEET SOLUTIONS

WORKSHEET 6
LESSON FIVE

	Missed	Score
	0	100
1. browse	1	91
2. hierarchy	2	82
3. Favorites menu	3	73
4. short filename	4	61
5. group folder	5	55
6. Network Neighborhood	6	46
7. long filename	7	37
8. paste	8	28
9. clipboard	9	19
10. cut	10	10
11. Windows Explorer	11	0

WORKSHEET 7
LESSON SIX

	Missed	Score
	0	100
1. shortcut	1	88
2. path	2	75
3. document	3	63
4. document-centric	4	50
5. command line	5	38
6. Documents menu	6	25
7. jump arrow	7	13
8. target	8	0

WORKSHEET 8
LESSON SEVEN

	Missed	Score
	0	100
1. Programs menu	1	92
2. standard desktop	2	84
3. Internet Explorer	3	76
4. Full Screen view	4	48
5. View Channels button	5	60
6. Recycle Bin	6	52
7. channel	7	44
8. Channel bar	8	36
9. HTML document	9	28
10. HTML (Hypertext Markup Language)	10	20
11. expand	11	12
12. collapse	12	0

WORKSHEET 9
LESSONS EIGHT—ELEVEN

	Missed	Score
	0	100
1. byte (B)	1	93
2. gigabyte (Gb)	2	87
3. kilobyte (Kb)	3	80
4. megabyte (Mb)	4	73
5. sort	5	67
6. hidden files	6	60
7. attribute	7	53
8. Find	8	47
9. case sensitive	9	40
10. search results	10	33
11. search criteria	11	27
12. Control Panel	12	20
13. TrueType font	13	13
14. MS-DOS (Microsoft Disk Operating System)	14	7
15. MS-DOS–based application	15	0

WORKSHEET 10
LESSON TWELVE

	Missed	Score
	0	100
1. hyperlink	1	94
2. communications protocol	2	89
3. Web server	3	83
4. HTTP (Hypertext Transfer Protocol)	4	77
5. World Wide Web	5	71
6. dial-up access	6	65
7. online service	7	59
8. home page	8	53
9. direct access	9	48
10. Internet service provider (ISP)	10	42
11. Web page	11	36
12. Internet	12	30
13. URL (Uniform Resource Locator)	13	24
14. Internet icon	14	18
15. Web browser	15	12
16. Web site	16	6
17. Links toolbar	17	0

WORKSHEET 11
LESSON THIRTEEN

	Missed	Score
	0	100
1. Search feature	1	93
2. AutoSearch	2	85
3. GIF (Graphics Interchange Format)	3	77
4. bitmap	4	70
5. exact phrase	5	62
6. phrase	6	55
7. ticker	7	47
8. search engine	8	40
9. search term	9	32
10. push	10	24
11. search term box	11	17
12. subscribe	12	9
13. directory	13	0

GLOSSARY

accessories
Supplemental, built-in programs that come with Windows 98. These programs include the following: games, general use, multimedia, Internet, system tools, and telecommunications.

Active Desktop
The Windows 98 desktop that consists of two layers: one layer on which you can display standard desktop objects, and a second layer on which you can display HTML objects.

active window
The window whose title bar is highlighted (i.e., in color—not gray), indicating that it is currently in use.

Address bar
In Windows 98 folders and programs, a drop-down text box that lets you access a Web page or a location on your computer by typing or selecting an address or path.

alignment
The horizontal placement of paragraphs or lines of text. One can align the text to the left, center, or right. Also called *justification*.

All Folders pane
The left pane of Windows Explorer that displays the hierarchical structure on your computer system, including remote computers if your system is networked.

application software
See *program*.

arrow pointer
See *pointer*.

associated file
A file that has been identified as belonging to a certain program, such as .txt with Notepad, .bmp with Paint, or .doc with Microsoft Word. When you open an associated file, the program related to that file also opens automatically. See also *file type*.

attribute
A characteristic (such as read-only, archive, hidden, or system) that changes how a file or folder can be used or displayed.

Auto Arrange
A command that prevents desktop and folder icons from being moved out of their aligned positions.

AutoComplete
A feature in the Address bar that automatically completes an address when you begin to enter a previously typed address.

AutoSearch
A feature that uses a search engine to find information about the word or phrase you enter in the Address bar after typing *go*, *find*, or *?*. AutoSearch is the quickest, simplest, and most convenient way to search for information on the Internet.

Back button
Moves back to a previous view when navigating through folder windows or Web pages.

bad sectors
Damaged areas on a disk that are marked as unusable when the disk is formatted. A few bad sectors do not necessarily make the entire disk unusable. However, a disk with bad sectors should not be used as a destination disk when copying a disk—nor should it be used to store important files.

bar
The term *bar* is used several ways:
- to define window stripes (e.g., the title bar, menu bar, and status bar).
- to define the barrier between window panes (e.g., the bar that separates the two panes in Windows Explorer).
- to define certain features (e.g., the Explorer bar, Channel bar, and Address bar). While the Address bar is included in the Toolbars menu as a toolbar that you can hide or display, it is not, strictly speaking, considered a toolbar.

bitmap
A format for image files used by the Paint program (among others), which handles an image as a set of dots rather than as a mathematical formula. The filename extension for bitmap images is *.bmp*.

browse
To look at files, folders, disks, printers, programs, and other objects on your computer system.

button
A graphic element found in dialog boxes, on toolbars, and in certain other places that, when activated, performs a specific function.

byte (b)
The size of computer memory and storage units is measured in bytes. A *byte* is the amount of space needed to hold one character.

byte	= One character
kilobyte	= About 1,000 bytes (characters)
megabyte	= About 1,000,000 bytes (characters)
gigabyte	= About 1,000,000,000 bytes (characters)

cascade
To resize and layer windows on the desktop so that the title bar of each window is visible.

case sensitive
A feature that tells a program (e.g., Find) to recognize the difference between upper- and lowercase letters when it is searching for text.

CD-ROM (Compact Disk Read-Only Memory)
A removable, read-only optical disk that can store relatively (when compared to 3½"' floppy disks) large amounts of data.

CD-ROM drive
A hardware component of your computer system. A drive that retrieves information from CD-ROMS.

central processing unit
See *CPU (central processing unit)*.

channel
A Web site designed to deliver content to your computer automatically, without your having to go to the Web site. The channel provider specifies what Web content is available. See also *subscribe*.

Channel bar
An Active Desktop option (also an Internet Explorer and a folder window Explorer bar option) that displays the channels installed on your computer.

check box
In dialog boxes, the square boxes next to items in a list from which you may select as many as desired. Selected check boxes contain a check mark.

Classic style
The Windows 95 approach to working with folders, icons, and the desktop. It includes:
- browsing windows using separate windows
- click-to-select/double-click-to-open browsing
- icon titles that are *not* underlined

See also *Web style*.

click
A mouse action in which you press and quickly release the left mouse button.

client
See *server*.

clipboard
A temporary storage area in the computer's memory used to hold information that is being cut/copied and pasted.

Close
A command that lets you quit a window. *Close* means essentially the same thing as *exit*; however, traditionally the term *exit* refers to quitting a program, while the term *close* refers to quitting everything except a program, for example, a dialog box, a document, or a folder window. The Close command is found in the Control menu and in a folder window's File menu.

Close button
A button located at the right end of a document and/or program title bar that you can click to close a window.

collapse
To hide the folders contained in an object. Objects that can be collapsed have a minus sign (-) beside them. See also *expand*.

command button
A rectangular button in a dialog box which appears with its function name visible, for example, OK, Yes, No, Cancel, Save, Open, etc.

command line
A text box where you enter the path to the desired file or folder.

commands
Instructions that you issue, causing an action to be carried out.

common commands
Commands such as New, Save, and Print that work the same way in most Windows programs.

common dialog boxes
Dialog boxes, such as Open, Save As, and Print, which are basically the same in many different programs. Common dialog boxes make it easier for you to learn new programs.

communications protocol
A set of rules (or standards) that lets computers connect with one another and exchange information with as little chance of error as possible. Also called *protocol*.

computer
An electronic device that performs complex tasks at a high speed and with great accuracy. There are two main parts of a computer—the processor and the memory.

control keys
Certain keys (Shift, Ctrl, and Alt) that are used in combination with other keys to issue commands. Also called *modifier keys*.

Control menu
A menu with items that you use to manipulate a program or folder window (e.g., Restore, Move, Size, Minimize, Maximize, and Close). The control menu is opened by clicking the Control menu button or by right-clicking the desired program's taskbar button.

Control menu button
An icon on the left side of the title bar that opens the Control menu. The icon for the Control menu button matches the file type icon. (For folder windows, the icon is a folder.)

Control Panel
A folder that contains all command, control, and configuration functions for Windows 98 in one place.

controls
The elements in a dialog box that ask for information from the user in order for the command to be complete. Such elements include check boxes, command buttons, drop-down list boxes, list boxes, option buttons, sliders, spin boxes, tabs, and text boxes.

CPU (central processing unit)
The part of the computer that processes the instructions in the memory.

cut
To transfer information (a file or a section of highlighted text) from its current location to the clipboard where it remains until it is pasted or replaced when another item is cut or copied.

data file
See *document*.

default
An automatic setting in a program, preset by the software manufacturer.

desktop
The opening screen in Windows 98 that contains a few objects, the Start button, and the taskbar.

destination disk
A floppy disk to copy data files to. See also *source disk*.

dialog box
A special kind of window that offers controls for you to manipulate in order to change the performance or appearance of a document or program.

dial-up access
A widely used method of accessing the Internet in which you use a modem and telephone line to connect to the Internet through an Internet service provider or online service. Dial-up access is said to be "temporary" as opposed to "dedicated." See also *direct access*.

dimmed command

A command or button that cannot be used in the current situation. It is displayed in gray instead of in black or in color.

direct access

A convenient method of accessing the Internet that is used by large organizations and some schools in which a dedicated line provides a continuous connection to the Internet. Direct access is said to be "dedicated" as opposed to "temporary." See also *dial-up access*.

directional arrowhead

A small arrowhead that appears at the beginning and/or end of menus and toolbars to indicate that there are more items than you can presently see on the menu or toolbar. Point to the arrowhead to scroll through the menu or toolbar items. See also *submenu*.

directory

1. Another name for a folder. See also *folder*.
2. A categorized and hierarchically organized listing of information on the World Wide Web.

disk

Media on which information is stored and retrieved in named units called *files*.

disk drive

A hardware component of your computer system used to transfer information back and forth between the computer's memory and a disk.

document

A file that consists of data created in a program, such as a letter typed in WordPad or a picture drawn in Paint. Also called *data file*.

document-centric

A system that focuses on documents and their contents rather than on the programs used to create those documents.

Documents menu

A menu on the Start menu that holds the My Documents folder and up to 15 of the documents you have used most recently.

domain name

The unique name that identifies an Internet site. A domain name has two or more parts separated by periods (often called *dots*):

- The part on the left of the final dot is the unique part of the Web-site name. It is called the **second-level domain name**.
- The part on the right of the final dot is the type of Web publisher, for example, .com (commercial) or .gov (government). It is called the **top-level domain name**.

double-click

A mouse action in which you press and quickly release the left mouse button twice.

download

To copy data files (e-mail, software, documents, etc.) from a remote computer to your own computer so that you may view the files offline and/or save them for future reference. See also *upload*.

drag

A mouse action in which you complete the following steps:

- Point to the item to move.
- Hold down the left mouse button.
- Slide the arrow pointer to the desired location.
- Release the mouse button.

drag and drop

A procedure in which you drag an object and drop it onto another object to perform a task, for example, to move, copy, delete, or print a document. See also *drag*.

drop-down list box

In a dialog box, similar to a list box except that a drop-down list box must first be opened by clicking it or its drop-down arrow. Drop-down list boxes are usually found in small or crowded dialog boxes.

e-mail (electronic mail)

A global communication system for exchanging messages and attached files; this is probably the most widely used feature on the Internet. Many Web browsers include an e-mail program—Internet Explorer uses Outlook Express for e-mail.

exact phrase

A phrase that has quotation marks around it so the words in the phrase will appear together, exactly as typed, in your search results.

Exit

A command that lets you quit a Windows program. The Exit command is found in a program's File menu. See also *Close*.

expand

To display the unseen folders contained in an object. Objects that can be expanded have a plus sign (+) beside them. See also *collapse*.

Explorer bars

A way to browse through a list of Web links—such as those in Search, Favorites, History, and Channels.

Favorites menu

A list of frequently used Web sites and/or folders that you can easily access from the Start menu, all folder windows, Windows Explorer, or Internet Explorer.

file

Data or program instructions that are saved on a disk as a named unit.

filename

The name you give to data that is stored on a disk.

filename extension

The period and, usually but not always, three characters at the end of a filename (for example, .doc, .txt, .gif). Also called *file extension*.

file type

The kind of file that is created by a particular program. Files are defined by the programs they are created in. Every file type has an icon associated with it; occasionally, a file type has more than one icon associated with it. See also *associated file*.

Find

A program that helps you locate files and folders by using search criteria that you specify for the file(s) you want to find.

firmware
A kind of system software. More specifically, *firmware* is instructions that are built into the computer on ROM chips.

flat
The smooth, level appearance of icons on many toolbars in Windows 98. When you point to a flat toolbar icon (i.e., dimmed command), it is "raised" and becomes an active button. See also *raised*.

floating toolbar
A toolbar that you have dragged from the taskbar to an unanchored position on your desktop.

floppy disk
A removable, magnetically coated diskette on/from which information can be stored and retrieved.

floppy disk density
Density refers to the surface coating on a floppy disk; the closer together the particles on the disk, the higher the disk capacity. Typically, 3½" floppy disks come in two densities: DD (double density)—720 Kb, and HD (high density)—1.44 Mb.

floppy disk drive
A hardware component of your computer system. A drive used to transfer information back and forth between the RAM and a floppy disk.

floppy disk size
The physical size of floppy disks; typically, they are 3½". In the past, 5¼" was a common size for floppy disks.

folder
A structure that holds files and/or subfolders that are stored on a disk. A folder can also contain other objects, such as printers and disk drives. (Folders have traditionally been called *directories*.)

Folder Options
The command that switches between Web-style and Classic-style browsing environments.

folder window
A window that displays the contents of a folder (or certain other objects, such as disk drives). Folder windows offer many of the same folder-managing features as Windows Explorer. Click a folder (if Web-style browsing is enabled) to open its window and see what is in it.

font design
A complete set of characters designed in a specific style, such as Arial or Times New Roman. Also called *font face*.

font styles
Font characteristics, such as bold, italic, and underline, that are used for text emphasis.

Forward button
Moves "ahead" to a previous view when navigating through folder windows or Web pages.

FTP (File Transfer Protocol)
A method of remotely transferring files from one computer to another over a network (or across the Internet) using special communication software.

Full Screen view
A View menu option in Internet Explorer in which only one bar is displayed (at the top), leaving the entire screen available for Internet content.

GIF (Graphics Interchange Format)
A standard format for image files on the Web. The filename extension for GIF images is *.gif*.

gigabyte (GB)
See *byte (b)*.

Gopher
A browsing system for Internet resources that predates the World Wide Web. Gopher works much like a directory, listing Internet sites in a hierarchical menu of files.

graphical user interface (GUI)
A phrase that is commonly used to describe Microsoft Windows 98 and other operating sytems that use pictures (i.e., graphics) to help you connect to the computer system's hardware and software in an easy-to-understand, intuitive way.

group folder
A folder within the Start Menu folder that holds groups of program shortcuts and other folders; they each represent menus within the Start menu.

hard disk
A hardware component of your computer system. A large capacity storage area on/from which information can be quickly stored and retrieved.

hard disk drive
A hardware component of your computer system. A built-in storage device that has a nonremovable disk (a fixed disk) with a large capacity.

hardware
The group of components that makes up the computer system, including: the CPU, modem, CD-ROM drive, floppy disk drive(s), monitor, keyboard, mouse, printer, and speakers. Hardware can be seen and touched.

Help
This feature is your main source of information on Windows 98. The Help feature is always readily accessible from the Start menu. The Contents, Index, and Search tabs in the Windows Help dialog box each provide help in different ways. Within a dialog box, you can click the question-mark button on the title bar to access context-sensitive help.

hidden files
Files and/or folders to which the Hidden attribute has been applied.

hierarchy
A system of things (or people) ranked one above the other. With regard to computers, the term *hierarchy* describes the multilevel structure of folders and subfolders on a disk. In the case of Windows 98, it further describes the multilevel structure of objects on the entire computer system. This structure is also referred to as a *tree*.

History
A list of previously visited Web sites that are stored by Internet Explorer automatically.

home page
1. The first page of a Web site. The home page usually outlines what the site has to offer, somewhat like a book's table of contents.
2. The first page you see when you open Internet Explorer (or another Web browser). In Internet Explorer, click the Home button to return to the home page.

Also called the *start page*.

HTML (Hypertext Markup Language)
The programming language used to create Web pages so that they can be viewed, read, and accessed by any computer running on any type of operating system.

HTML document
A document whose filename extension is *.htm* or *.html* and that can be viewed in a Web browser.

HTTP (Hypertext Transfer Protocol)
The protocol (standardized set of rules) that allows computers to communicate across the World Wide Web and connects Web pages to each other via hyperlinks.

hyperlink
Text or graphics that, when clicked, connect(s) to one of the following:
- another place on the same Web page.
- another Web page on the same Web site.
- another Web page on a different Web site.

In Windows 98, hyperlinks are also used to connect one location to another within your computer system. When you point to a hyperlink, the arrow pointer becomes a hand. Also called a *link*.

icon
A small picture (on the desktop or in folder windows) that represents one of the many objects that you use when working with the computer system.

icon titles
A name under large icons or to the right of small icons that identifies the icon, for example, My Computer and My Documents.

Internet
A global collection of computers that communicate with one another using common communication protocols (e.g., HTTP).

Internet Explorer
The Windows 98, Web-browsing program with a built-in interface to the Active Desktop and with many easy-to-use features that open the door to the world of information on the Internet.

Internet icon
The button at the right end of the menu bar, illustrated with a Windows flag, that accesses the Internet when clicked.

Internet service provider (ISP)
A company (often local) that provides you with a connection to the Internet for a fee. An example of dial-up access.

jump arrow
A small arrow that appears on the lower-left corner of shortcut icons, thereby distinguishing them from other icons.

justification
See *alignment*.

keyboard shortcuts
Key combinations that are used to activate certain commands as an alternative to using the mouse.

kilobyte (Kb)
See *byte (b)*.

landscape
A page orientation in which the paper is wider than it is tall when you print your document.

launch
To *start a program*. The terms *run* and *open* are also used frequently.

Links toolbar
The toolbar that provides quick access to commonly used Web sites.

list box
In a dialog box, a box that displays a list of options from which you can choose only one. Scroll to view additional options.

log off
Use the Log Off feature to do the following:
- Close all programs.
- Disconnect your computer from the network (if you are on one).
- Return Windows 98 to the Logon screen so you or someone else can log on again.

log on
To identify yourself with a user name and a password, to:
- Your computer. Opens the Windows 98 desktop.
- Your online service or Internet service provider. Opens your Internet connection.

Logon screen
The opening Windows 98 dialog box that appears when you first turn your computer on or connect to the Internet.

long filename
A filename that is up to 255 characters long and can contain spaces and most symbols. See also *short filename*.

Maximize button
The button in the middle of the three buttons located at the right end of the title bar on a restored window. This button enlarges a window to its greatest possible size. When you maximize a window, the Maximize button is replaced by the Restore button.

megabyte (Mb)
See *byte (b)*.

memory
See *RAM (random-access memory)* and/or *ROM (read-only memory)*.

menu
A drop-down or pop-up list of items from which you may choose only one at a time.

menu bar
The bar located under the title bar that lists the available menu items for the open document or folder.

menu item
One of the choices on a menu.

Minimize button
The button located on the right side of a menu bar and/or title bar that you can click to reduce a window to a taskbar button.

modem
A hardware component of your computer system. A device that converts data so that you can transmit it over telephone lines. Also called *fax/modem*.

mouse
A hardware component of your computer system. A small, hand-held device used to control the pointer on the screen and issue commands to the computer.

move pointer ✛
The four-headed arrow that appears when you point to (or click) some areas, for example, the small area to the immediate right of a sizing handle on the taskbar. Once the move pointer appears, the Move procedure is available.

MS-DOS (Microsoft Disk Operating System)
The main operating system used before Windows was developed.

MS-DOS–based application
A program that is designed to run under the MS-DOS operating system rather than the Windows operating system.

MS-DOS prompt
The signal that MS-DOS is ready for you to tell it what to do. The default MS-DOS prompt displays the path to the current folder followed by the greater than sign (>) and a blinking underline. For example, if you are in Windows, the MS-DOS prompt will look like this: C:\Windows>_

multimedia
The combination of various communication methods, including text, graphics, sound, animation, and video.

multitasking
The ability of an operating system to run more than one program at a time.

My Computer
A special folder (with an icon that appears on the desktop by default) that gives you a quick route to the disk drives, folders, files, and other objects on your computer system.

My Documents
A special folder (on the desktop by default) that is designed to store your personal documents. My Documents is the default folder that is displayed when you open the Save As or Open dialog box in Windows accessory programs.

network
Two or more computers that are linked together to share programs, data, and certain hardware components, for example, a printer.

network interface card
A specialized computer circuit board that allows a computer to communicate with other computers and devices on a network. A Network Interface Card is an optional hardware component of your computer system.

Network Neighborhood
An object that may appear on the desktop; it lets you browse through other computers on your network.

newsgroup
A collection of special-interest messages posted by individuals to a news server on the Internet. You need a special program to read and respond to newsgroups.

new taskbar toolbars
Toolbars that you can create on the taskbar to show the contents of any folder desired.

object
One of the many things that you use when working with the computer system—items such as: files, programs, folders, shortcuts, disk drives, Control Panel tools, My Computer, Network Neighborhood, the Recycle Bin, and My Briefcase.

offline
Not connected to the Internet.

online service
A business, such as AOL, CompuServe, or Microsoft Network (MSN), that offers access to the Internet (along with other services) for a fee. An example of dial-up access.

operating system
System software that acts as a link between the user, application software (i.e., programs), and hardware.

option button
In dialog boxes, the circles next to the items in a list from which you may select only one. Selected option buttons contain a dot.

password
A combination of characters that you type, when prompted, in order to access Windows (or another feature). Characters appear as small *x*'s when you type. The Password feature is a security measure that prevents access to a Windows network (or another feature) without the correct combination of characters.

paste
To copy information from the clipboard into a folder or document. Paste leaves the information on the clipboard so it can be pasted again (until you replace it with newly cut/copied data).

path
The route to an object; it consists of the disk drive, folder, subfolders (if any), and the filename (if the path is to a file).

phrase
A combination of letters and/or numbers with one or more space(s).

point
A mouse action in which you move the mouse until the tip of the arrow pointer is over the item you wish to select.

pointer
The arrow-shaped cursor on the screen that moves with the mouse as you slide it over a flat surface. The pointer's shape changes depending on the job it is doing (or can do) at the current time. Also called *arrow pointer* or *mouse pointer*. See Topic 8, *Common Pointer Shapes*, page 10, for more information.

portrait
A page orientation in which the paper is taller than it is wide when you print your document.

pressed
A 3-D effect in which a button (or other item) appears "sunken", indicating it is selected (or active). See also *unpressed*.

processor
See *CPU (central processing unit)*.

program
A set of instructions that your computer follows to perform a specific task, such as word processing or creating a graphic. While the term *application* is used a lot in Windows, this book uses the term *program* more often.

program file
A file containing a set of instructions that your computer follows to perform a task, such as word processing. Also called *application file*.

Programs menu
A submenu of the Start menu that holds programs and submenus which contain groups of related programs.

properties
Characteristics of an object; for example, the color scheme on the desktop is one of the desktop's properties. Changing the properties for an object lets you customize that object.

Properties dialog box
A special kind of dialog box that groups the settings for a specific object's properties.

protocol
See *communications protocol*.

push
A new technology that allows content providers to send information to you without your having to go to their Web sites. With push technology, you can schedule automatic downloads of updated channel content.

Quick Launch toolbar
A toolbar that appears next to the Start button on the taskbar (by default) and contains buttons for the following frequently used features: Internet Explorer, Outlook Express, desktop, and channels.

Quick View
A simple program that lets you look at the contents of a file quickly, without opening the program in which that file was created. Quick View appears on the menu only if there is a viewer available for the type of file you select and if it has been installed. (The Typical install option does not include Quick View.)

raised
A 3-D effect in which a toolbar icon that is normally flat is defined as a button when you point to it. If you rest the arrow pointer on a button, a ToolTip appears. See also *flat*.

RAM (random-access memory)
The workspace area of the computer that temporarily holds the instructions (software or programs) and information (data or commands) you give it. When you turn the computer off, everything in RAM disappears. Also called *memory* or *working memory*.

read-only memory (ROM)
See *ROM (read-only memory)*.

Recycle Bin
A special folder on the desktop whose icon looks like a wastebasket. The Recycle Bin temporarily holds "deleted" files so you can restore them if you change your mind. But, once you empty the Recycle Bin, you cannot restore (or Undo Delete for) any items that were in it.

Restore button
The button in the middle of the three buttons located at the right end of the menu bar and/or title bar on a maximized window. This button returns a maximized window to its previous size. When you restore a maximized window, the Restore button is replaced by the Maximize button.

right-click
A mouse action in which you press and quickly release the right mouse button.

right-drag
A mouse action in which you complete the following steps:
• Point to the item to move.
• Hold down the right mouse button.
• Slide the arrow pointer to desired location.
• Release the mouse button.

ROM (read-only memory)
A computer chip that holds information that cannot be changed.

sans serif
A font design that has no cross-strokes at the top and bottom of the characters; it is straight.

For example: T

Save
The command that saves changes to a previously named document or opens the Save As dialog box so you can save a new document.

Save As
The command that opens the Save As dialog box, which lets you save a new document or rename a previously saved one.

scanner
A digital input device which captures and converts optical information to data, so that it can then be displayed and manipulated. A scanner is an optional hardware component of your computer system.

scroll
To move through a document or list box using a scroll bar.

scroll arrows
The arrows at each end of a scroll bar. Used to scroll through the contents of a document or list box.

scroll bar
The bar that appears at the right and/or bottom edge of a window or list box when the document's or lists contents are not completely visible. Each scroll bar contains two scroll arrows and a proportional scroll box.

scroll box
The box in a scroll bar. It shows two things:
- The *position* of the information displayed in relation to the entire document or list. For example, if the scroll box is in the center of the scroll bar, you are looking at the center of the document or list.
- The *size* of the entire document in relation to the screen size. For example, if the scroll box takes up a large part of the scroll bar, you can see most of the entire document or list; but, if the scroll box takes up just a little part of the scroll bar, you can see only a small portion of the entire document or list.

search criteria
Guidelines you define that tell the Find program what file and folder characteristics to look for when searching. For example, you can search for all the files that contain the .doc filename extension or all the files that were created in the last month.

search engine
A program that searches Web pages for information you want to find (e.g., InfoSeek, Excite, Yahoo!, Lycos). Also called *search service*.

Search feature
A Windows 98 feature that uses the Explorer bar to present several popular Internet search engines so you can easily find information on the World Wide Web.

search results
The files or folders (or Web pages) that meet the search criteria you specify. In the Find program, the search results appear in a list box at the bottom of the Find program after you click the F̲ind Now command button.

search term
A word, phrase, or exact phrase that you type into a search term box to describe what you are looking for. Also called a *keyword*.

search term box
Within a search engine, the (usually) unnamed text box in which you enter your search term(s) when conducting an Internet search.

second-level domain name
See *domain name*.

serif
A font design that has small cross-strokes at the top and bottom of the characters.
For example: T

server
A computer that can be accessed by other computers (i.e., clients) on a network.

shortcut
An icon containing a direct route to a specific object and displaying a small jump arrow on its lower-left corner. Click the shortcut icon to quickly open the file or program it represents. You can customize your desktop by creating shortcuts to the documents and programs you use most often.

short filename
A filename that is no longer than eight characters, can contain a filename extension, but cannot contain spaces and certain symbols. See also *long filename*.

shut down
To use the Shut Down feature to quit Windows 98 properly so the computer can safely be turned off.

sizing handle
An area in the bottom-right corner of windows that can be sized. It is used to size windows. You can size a window using any of its corners. However, because the bottom-right corner has a sizing handle that covers a large sizing area, the arrow pointer changes to a sizing pointer more easily than it does in other window corners. Sizing handles are also available for taskbar toolbars (and taskbar "areas") on the left-hand side of toolbar titles.

sizing pointer
The arrow pointer becomes a double-headed arrow when you point to a sizing handle or certain borders. The sizing pointer is used to size a window or the taskbar. Sizing pointers can appear in any of the following forms:

↕ vertical
Appears on the top or bottom window border.

↔ horizontal
Appears on the right or left window border.

↘ diagonal
Appears on the top-left or bottom-right corner of a window.

↗ diagonal
Appears on the bottom-left or top-right corner of a window.

slider
In a dialog box, a text box that is used to set a value by clicking an up or down arrow to change the original, preset value. A new value can also be typed in.

software
Instructions that tell your computer how to perform a task. Software is stored on disks in program files. Unlike hardware, software cannot be seen or touched. There are two main kinds of software: system software and application software.

sort
When you arrange icons using the V̲iew menu or the shortcut menu, you can sort files only from A-Z or 0-9 (ascending). When you arrange icons using column headings, however, you can sort files from Z-A or 9-0 (descending) as well as in ascending order.

source disk
A floppy disk from which original files are copied. See also *destination disk*.

special folder
A folder designed to hold specific items, for example, My Computer, drive C:, and My Documents.

spin box
In a dialog box, a text box containing a preset value which can be adjusted incrementally by clicking its up or down arrow. Click the up button to increase the value; click the down button to decrease it. A new value can also be typed in. Also called *increment box*.

standard desktop
A place to put objects (such as icons for shortcuts, folders, and files) for quick and easy access. The standard desktop cannot, however, display HTML objects.

Standard toolbar
A bar of buttons that provides access to frequently used commands.

Start button
The button located at the left end of the taskbar that is labeled *Start*. Click the Start button to open the Start menu, from which you can open submenus and launch programs.

start page
See home page.

start-the-search button
The button in every search engine that starts your search when clicked. Different search engines have different terms on this button (e.g., Search, Go, Seek, Go Get It, Find!).

startup disk
A disk that contains certain system files that create a system disk. It is a good safeguard to have a startup disk for drive A:. If the hard disk should have a problem, you can boot the computer using this floppy system disk. This is also known as a *bootable disk*.

status bar
The bar at the bottom of a program or folder window. It displays information about the program or folder, and it can be turned on and off from the View menu.

subfolder
A folder contained within another folder.

submenu
A menu that cascades out from another menu. A right-pointing arrowhead on a menu item indicates that a submenu will appear when you point to it. See also *directional arrowhead*.

subscribe
To set up your Web browser to check a Web page for new content and then notify you that the site has been updated. You may also set up your browser to download any updates automatically. See also *channel*.

system software
Software that runs the computer system. This includes firmware and your operating system.

system tray
The area at the right end of the taskbar that displays system icons and offers easy access to (and information about) those system features.

tabs
In connection with dialog boxes, *tabs* refer to the "flaps" at the top of a series of separate groups of settings (sometimes called *pages*) that appear in some dialog boxes, particularly in Properties dialog boxes.

target
The path (including the name) to the object a shortcut is pointing to.

task
An open, but not necessarily active, program.

taskbar
The bar that appears by default at the bottom of the desktop and lets you quickly start programs, switch between tasks, and access the tools (and toolbars) of your choice. See also *Quick Launch toolbar*, *system tray*, and *Start button*.

taskbar button
A button located on the taskbar that represents an open program. Each taskbar button displays the program icon and name of each open program.

taskbar toolbars
Another tool that offers several ways to customize Windows 98 and make it easier for you to use. While you can create a toolbar of the items in any folder, four useful toolbars appear on the Toolbars submenu by default for easy access: Address, Links, Desktop, and Quick Launch.

Telnet
A program that lets one computer log onto a remote computer. Telnet is often used to search libraries and databases.

text box
In a dialog box, a box that provides space for typing information needed to carry out a command.

text labels
A feature that lets you hide or display Standard toolbar button names. Click View, point to Toolbars, then click Text Labels to select or deselect the feature. *Show Text* is a similar feature that lets you hide or display names for buttons on taskbar toolbars. Right-click an empty space on the taskbar toolbar (or its title), then click Show Text to select or deselect the feature.

ticker
Information that cycles through a heading that can be updated manually or automatically. Stocks, sports scores, and news headlines are common types of information to use in a ticker.

tile horizontally
To resize and arrange the windows on the desktop one on top of the other so that each window displays part of its workspace.

tile vertically
To resize and arrange the windows on the desktop side by side so that each window displays part of its workspace.

title bar
The horizontal bar at the top of a window that provides the name of the open document and/or program.

toolbar
A row of buttons, usually along the top or bottom of the screen by default, that provides access to frequently used commands, tasks, or other objects such as Internet addresses and hyperlinks. See also *bar*.

toolbar button
An icon on a toolbar that "illustrates" its function (e.g., the Print button is a picture of a printer, the Cut button is a picture of a pair of scissors). You can often display or hide text labels under toolbar buttons.

ToolTip
A pop-up box that displays the name of, and/or information about, a button or an icon.

top-level domain name
See *domain name*.

TrueType font
Scalable fonts that are shipped with Windows 98 Arial, Courier New, Lucida Console, Symbol, Times New Roman, and Wingdings.

unpressed
A 3-D effect in which a button (or other item) appears "raised," indicating it is deselected (or inactive). See also *pressed*.

Up button
When navigating through folder windows, moves to the folder that is up one level on the system hierarchy from the open folder.

upload
To copy data files (e-mail, software, documents, etc.) from one's own computer to a remote computer. See also *download*.

URL (Uniform Resource Locator)
The unique address assigned to each page on the Web. Your Web browser uses URLs to locate and retrieve Web pages. Also called *address* or *Web address*.

Usenet
A global system of discussion groups called *newsgroups*. Many Web browsers include a newsreader program to access the newsgroups—Internet Explorer uses Outlook Express to access Usenet.

user name
A name given to a Windows user. Using different identifiers and passwords for different people allows each operator's work to be kept secure.

View Channels button
A button on the taskbar's Quick Launch toolbar that opens Internet Explorer in Full Screen view and displays the Channel bar.

Web browser
A program that lets you access the Web and view Web pages. Also called *browser*.

Web page
A document created using HTML that can be posted on the World Wide Web by a Web server.

Web-page name
A descriptive title given to a Web page; not its URL. The name of the loaded Web page appears in the Internet Explorer title bar.

Web-page object
An object that appears in Web pages, such as text, a hyperlink, a graphic image, or an animated graphic image.

Web Page view
A Windows 98 feature in folder windows (and Windows Explorer) that displays: a picture of the selected item in the top-left corner of the workspace, the selected item's name, and information about the selected item along the left side of the workspace. While this feature is turned on automatically in Web-style mode, it can be used in Classic-style mode as well.

Web server
A server that uses HTTP server software to serve up HTML documents when requested by a Web client, such as a Web browser.

Web site
A group of related Web pages served up by a Web server on the World Wide Web. A typical Web site has a home page and includes hyperlinks to other Web pages on the site.

Web style
The Web-page approach to working with folders, icons, and the desktop. It includes:
- browsing windows using the same window
- point-to-select/click-to-open browsing
- underlined icon titles
- enabling Web-related content in folders and on the desktop

See also *Classic style*.

window
A rectangle that holds a dialog box, folder, program, or document.

window border
The boundary that marks the edges of a window and can be used to size that window.

Windows Explorer
The Windows 98 program that you can use to look at and manage objects in your computer system, including remote computers if your system is networked. The left pane displays *All Folders* (a hierarchy of folders); the right pane displays the contents of the folder that is selected in the left pane.

window title
The name of a window, located just to the right of the Control menu button. The document name, if any, is listed first followed by the program name.

wizard
A tool that walks you through a complex task step by step.

work offline mode
A condition in which you can view Web pages (and Web-page objects) that are stored on the computer without being connected to the Internet.

workspace
The inner part of a window where the work in a document or program is carried out.

World Wide Web
The graphical part of the Internet that uses hypertext to link Web pages on Web sites around the world. Also called *Web*, *W3*, or *www*.

INDEX

FREE CATALOG
AND
UPDATED LISTING

We don't just have books that find your answers faster; we also have books that teach you how to use your computer without the fairy tales and the gobbledygook.

We also have books to improve your typing, spelling and punctuation.

Return this card for a free catalog and mailing list update.

275 Madison Avenue,
New York, NY 10016

☐ Please send me your catalog and put me on your mailing list.

Name

Firm (if any)

Address

City, State, Zip

Phone (800) 528-3897   Fax (800) 528-3862

SEE OUR COMPLETE CATALOG ON THE INTERNET @: http://www.ddcpub.com

---

FREE CATALOG
AND
UPDATED LISTING

We don't just have books that find your answers faster; we also have books that teach you how to use your computer without the fairy tales and the gobbledygook.

We also have books to improve your typing, spelling and punctuation.

Return this card for a free catalog and mailing list update.

275 Madison Avenue,
New York, NY 10016

☐ Please send me your catalog and put me on your mailing list.

Name

Firm (if any)

Address

City, State, Zip

Phone (800) 528-3897   Fax (800) 528-3862

SEE OUR COMPLETE CATALOG ON THE INTERNET @: http://www.ddcpub.com

---

FREE CATALOG
AND
UPDATED LISTING

We don't just have books that find your answers faster; we also have books that teach you how to use your computer without the fairy tales and the gobbledygook.

We also have books to improve your typing, spelling and punctuation.

Return this card for a free catalog and mailing list update.

275 Madison Avenue,
New York, NY 10016

☐ Please send me your catalog and put me on your mailing list.

Name

Firm (if any)

Address

City, State, Zip

Phone (800) 528-3897   Fax (800) 528-3862

SEE OUR COMPLETE CATALOG ON THE INTERNET @: http://www.ddcpub.com

BUSINESS REPLY MAIL

FIRST CLASS MAIL   PERMIT NO. 7321   NEW YORK, N.Y.

POSTAGE WILL BE PAID BY ADDRESSEE

DDC *Publishing*

275 Madison Avenue
New York, NY 10157-0410

NO POSTAGE
NECESSARY
IF MAILED
IN THE
UNITED STATES

BUSINESS REPLY MAIL

FIRST CLASS MAIL   PERMIT NO. 7321   NEW YORK, N.Y.

POSTAGE WILL BE PAID BY ADDRESSEE

DDC *Publishing*

275 Madison Avenue
New York, NY 10157-0410

NO POSTAGE
NECESSARY
IF MAILED
IN THE
UNITED STATES

BUSINESS REPLY MAIL

FIRST CLASS MAIL   PERMIT NO. 7321   NEW YORK, N.Y.

POSTAGE WILL BE PAID BY ADDRESSEE

DDC *Publishing*

275 Madison Avenue
New York, NY 10157-0410

NO POSTAGE
NECESSARY
IF MAILED
IN THE
UNITED STATES